WHY
I AM A
LIBERAL

WHY I AM A LIBERAL

A Manifesto for Indians Who Believe in Individual Freedom

Sagarika Ghose

PENGUIN
VIKING

An imprint of Penguin Random House

VIKING

USA | Canada | UK | Ireland | Australia
New Zealand | India | South Africa | China

Viking is part of the Penguin Random House group of companies
whose addresses can be found at global.penguinrandomhouse.com

Published by Penguin Random House India Pvt. Ltd
7th Floor, Infinity Tower C, DLF Cyber City,
Gurgaon 122 002, Haryana, India

First published in Viking by Penguin Random House India 2018

10 9 8 7 6 5 4 3 2 1

ISBN 9780670088973

Typeset in Aldine401 BT by Manipal Digital Systems, Manipal
Printed at Replika Press Pvt. Ltd, India

www.penguin.co.in

For all Indians who believe in individual freedom

Contents

Introduction

Why this long essay on why I am a liberal? What is the need for it? What are the reasons for trying to create a manifesto or a charter for Indian liberals at a time when the word 'liberal' itself is considered discredited and is almost a term of abuse? These days it's fashionable to write on the Indian's religious or cultural identity. Perhaps it's less in tune with the prevailing zeitgeist to write on the Indian's modern liberal identity. Does the twenty-first century Indian even have a liberal identity which is both self-aware, self-critical and committed to modern liberal values?

The word 'liberal' is central to the political and public debate at this moment. For many, the liberal is the arch-enemy; the liberal is considered 'anti-national', 'anti-Hindu', 'anti-religious', even 'anti-India'. Liberal women, particularly, are perceived to be on a collision course with 'Indian values'. Women seen in a bar are liable to being dragged out by the hair and beaten. Women protesting against discrimination and harassment in a university hostel are liable to being accused of 'marketing their modesty'. Liberal women who dare to fall in love with men from a different religion are liable to being hauled up before the courts and described as helpless, unthinking, infantilized beings who have been either brainwashed, lured into infamy or led astray.

The mantra goes: the Indian who displays muscular nationalism is the authentic Indian! Rooted in Indian values! Rooted in Indian soil! The liberal? Hah! The liberal is cast as disconnected and anti-Bharatiya sanskriti. Millions of Indian citizens who define themselves as broadly 'liberal' or in Hindi 'pragatisheel', 'udaarvaadi', 'reformist' or 'secular' are puzzled by this enmity directed at them. They are taken aback by the hatred that self-proclaimed 'nationalists' direct against them. Who are they, these millions of Indian liberals? There are so many. There are the various followers of the dazzling procession throughout India's history of non-denominational prophets, philosophers and thinkers who were thought leaders on self-criticism and change. There are the progressive thinkers toiling to bring change at the grassroots. There are those who freely raise slogans at a university. There are those who participate in Dalit protests against injustice. There are those who interrogate Hinduism's rich traditions. There are those who question caste injustice, superstition and black magic. There are those who popularize the works of twelfth-century spiritual reformers like Basavanna. There are those citizens who work to bring welfare measures to areas where armed Maoism is dominant. There are those who support the right to eat the food of your choice, who support the right to worship according to choice, who love others of the same sex, who marry outside religious boundaries, who dare to fall in love and link hands in public.

Are all these millions of people against India and her traditions? When moral policemen and vigilante mobs enforce their idea of 'Indian values,' when police form 'Romeo squads' to target young lovers, when a jeans-clad young woman speaking on a mobile phone is seen by university authorities and khap panchayats as a she-devil whose dangerous inner energy must be curbed by patriarchal control, and when the government of the day lends them support, when religious minorities find themselves constantly in mortal danger, then indeed it does seem as if the light of our quiet, home-grown liberalism, so beloved of so many, is flickering, if not dying out altogether. But if that liberal light is dying, then this book throws its arms (however flimsy) around the liberal flame to protect it from the threatening gusts, and cries out, 'Do not go gentle into that good night . . . rage, rage against the dying of the light.'[1]

So perhaps this is precisely the right time to write this essay. Precisely because people perceived to be 'liberal' are under unprecedented attack. This book is a journalistic reportorial essay written in the spirit of advancing an argument to spark a debate among interested citizens. It makes no claim to have all the answers; instead, like a pilgrim, it's only the beginning of a quest for the answers, the start of a journey. The seeker seeks and invites others to join in the search. In the spirit of the Upanishads—the word, as India's philosopher–president S. Radhakrishnan so beautifully describes, means to 'sit near'[2]—this book is written to open a dialogue, to ask who is the Indian liberal, what does Indian liberalism mean and why is the liberal so misunderstood and so caricatured by those who are anti-liberal? Let's open the dialogue.

First, a definition of liberalism, a look at the way the word and the philosophy is generally understood. 'Liberalism is a move for freedom from monarchical and feudal control . . . for freedom of speech, freedom of membership of groups . . . for the independence of the ordinary man from the state or from organized labour . . . liberals are committed to the equality of the Left . . . and laissez faire economic theories, often seen as the "middle", although liberals see themselves as radicals, wishing to change society.'[3]

There is little agreement on what liberalism exactly means, although all liberals are united in their primary belief in limited government, autonomous institutions, individual freedom and the rule of law. Liberalism seeks, above all, to 'limit political power and enables individuals to experiment freely in various spheres of life'.[4] Daniel H. Cole and Aurelian Craiutu quote that liberalism is not a single ideology but a 'big tent' of theories advanced by many thinkers. They quote thirty types of liberalism, from Old Liberalism to New Liberalism, Progressive Liberalism, Classical Liberalism, Radical Liberalism, Economic Liberalism, Orthodox Liberalism and others. Liberals are divided on the exact role of the government or the Big State and how free markets and trade should be, although 'hardly anyone agrees that they should not be regulated at all or that they should be centrally planned by self-anointed experts'.[5] Liberalism is 'a supreme form of generosity',[6] accepting dissent, disagreement, minority rights and religious freedom; liberalism need not be an advocate for open borders but because liberals place great store in equality before the law, immigrants cannot be restricted on the basis of race or religion, they write.

Liberalism is a set of beliefs marked by its humility, which constantly seeks dialogue and is sceptical about utopian claims of human perfectability. Thus, 'liberalism has no ready made easy solutions . . . and is inseparable from the doubts we feel about it.' The authors point out that 'Modern liberal societies are the best political systems we fallible humans have managed to create.'[7] In an essay in *Aeon* magazine, Nabeela Jaffer[8] quotes political philosopher Hannah Arendt to say that it's the internal moral dialogue within oneself which is the highest form of thought and quotes Arendt's phrase that 'loneliness is the common ground of terror and extremism'. While liberals are comfortable with self-doubt and the inner moral dialogue, those non-liberals attracted to 'totalitarian ideologies and charismatic strongmen . . . experience a loss of trust in their own self and are cut off from human commonality'.[9]

In India, liberals may be Left liberals (that is, believers in social freedoms but in a more or less government-controlled economy, like many liberals in the Congress party) or they may be Right liberals (believers in laissez faire economics but uncaring about assaults on individual personal and civic freedoms such as attacks by gau rakshaks or the various moral policeman senas, like some liberals in the Bharatiya Janata Party [BJP]).[10]

For the purpose of this essay I have chosen to emphasize the Gandhian definition of the term 'liberal'. Mohandas Karamchand Gandhi was, in many ways, the most successful liberal politician of all time.

Why was Gandhi India's greatest liberal? First and foremost because of his steadfast commitment to non-violence. Second, his deep mistrust and scepticism about an all-powerful centralized big government or Big State. One of the thinkers Gandhi admired was the nineteenth-century American philosopher Henry David Thoreau, who believed: 'That government is best which governs the least.'[11] Third, an abiding belief in the capabilities and innate good sense of the individual, and the power of the individual conscience, both moral and spiritual—what Gandhi called the individual satyagrahi. Fourth, a commitment to India's constitutional values and rule of just laws and equality for all before the law. Fifth, and most importantly, a fundamental respect for dissent and disagreement. As Gandhi told Nehru: 'Resist me always when my suggestion does not appeal to your head or heart. I shall not love you less for that resistance.'[12] The idea that even without a 100 per cent agreement there can still be love, friendship and cooperation is a crucial Gandhian belief.

The Indian liberal, for this essay, is not just the legatee of Gandhi, but also a legatee of the spiritual liberal and questioning traditions embodied by the venerable Yajnavalkya, sage of the Brihadaranyaka Upanishad, of Lord Krishna in the Bhagavad Gita, of the great spiritual leaders and crusaders for individual dignity such as Gautama Buddha and Mahavira, of Bhakti reformers like Kabir in the fifteenth century and Mirabai in the sixteenth century, and later Narayana Guru or Jyotirao Phule, and even later, inheritors of Rammohan Roy, G.K. Gokhale, Rabindranath Tagore, Kamaladevi Chattopadhyay, C. Rajagopalachari and Jawaharlal Nehru, who was a liberal in his entire being, although he did reject the liberal economy, fearing the ravages of capitalism on the poor.

The argument of this essay is in favour of social and economic liberalism in the belief that the two cannot be segregated. It also recognizes, as liberals have done, the need for rational and reasonable government action in certain spheres in the form of the democratic welfare state. However, it advances that argument that unless what we are calling the 'Big State' is confined to a limited role, pushed out of overweening control of economic, cultural and social life, citizens will inevitably get caught up in the patronage systems of this big government and society will be polarized and politicized at every level. When every sector of society is yoked to different powerful politicians (who control this Big State) the scope of citizens' individual freedom becomes linked to the inclinations of politicians in power. Throughout India's post-Independence history, we have seen the Big State keep increasing its power.

The expansion of the state is linked to the rise of identity politics. This is because as the state expands into more and more areas of life, it keeps acquiring clients who it seeks to keep happy in order to increase its own power. These clients are invariably identity groups; caste and regional groups of various kinds. The rise of the Big State is thus one of the causes for the rise of identity politics. Also, because the state is so powerful, it becomes a necessary ally for a range of entities. These entities—media, corporates and social groups—seek the powers of the Big State to advance their own interests.

Big Government in India has only rarely worked for what is called the 'common good'; instead, it has worked to maximize its own partisan political power. A massive government driven by a political–ideological agenda with a strongman or strongwoman leader who prefers to scorn rather than maintain slow, arduous democratic processes, norms and institutional procedures spells disaster for the freedom of the Indian citizen. In important ways, this Big Government or the Big State was created by so-called political liberals or socialist-seculars. Nehru, as we have mentioned, believed in government control over the economy, and Indira Gandhi used the power of the Big State to create her own desired form of socioeconomic transformation.[13] Hindutva ideologues have inherited this Big Government from the seculars and are using it for their own ideological purpose, as the seculars did in the past.

This manifesto also tries to be introspective and cast a hopefully honest gaze at where liberals have gone wrong. If India's liberals are to reinvent themselves and invest their arguments with new energy, they need to squarely face up to their past failures and render a mea culpa, both to themselves and to those who find fault with them, often with good reason.

After rendering that mea culpa, it's necessary to reiterate the need for a robustly functioning liberal position at a time when Hindutva-based nationalism and supremacy of government power is the dominant public narrative. It seems as if today Indians may be born free, but everywhere they are in chains. Why are Indians imprisoned? Who imprisons them? The Indian citizen is imprisoned by the Big State, a kind of monster in our midst, a Godzilla prowling the streets, a mega government structure that controls citizens' lives, snoops, regulates,[14] seeks to regiment[15] and influence culture and society.[16] When the state is dominant, government (the controller of the state) is dominant, and when government is dominant the politician becomes the uncrowned king of the ring and the setter of the terms of debate.

Another definition is perhaps required here. What do we mean when we say 'state?' The state (as opposed to civil society, which implies citizens' groups, families, schools, clubs, temples, etc.) is not strictly the government because governments come and go but the state stays fixed. The government of the day, however, controls the state. The state is the 'whole fixed political system, the set-up of authoritative and legitimately powerful roles by which we are finally controlled, ordered and organized. Thus, police, army, civil service, parliament (government ministries) make up the state ... the state is the set of fixed roles and institutions that make up the generally legitimate political institutions within which partisan conflict is combined.'[17] The most visible manifestation of the state is the government of the day. When a government takes over all aspects of the state it becomes what we are calling the Big State.

In India today, everywhere you look: government, government, government. Everywhere you turn: government chains, government chains, government chains. It's a prison from which there has been little escape, whatever the colour of those governments, except for brief periods when state power was rolled back; for example, with the economic reforms of 1991 or during the government led by P.V. Narasimha Rao or during the Atal Bihari Vajpayee–led government of 1999–2004. An ascendant state means rising power for politicians and a politicized society. An expansive state also means a greater capacity for violence, because from encounter killings to human rights abuse to complicity in riots to use of force against dissenters to jailing opponents to imprisoning journalists to arresting rights campaigners to imposing its authority, the government has an almost unlimited right to use violence against citizens.[18]

The liberal stands against this massive, expansive, inherently violent Indian state. The liberal stands for the individual and argues for limited government. The liberal wants every Indian to be set free. 'The assertion by the individual of his own opinions and beliefs, his own independence and interest—over and against group standards—is the beginning of reform,' said the draftsman of India's Constitution, B.R. Ambedkar.[19]

Let me start with a personal example. As a journalist over the last three decades, I have seen up close and personal the havoc wreaked by government control on the media sector. The government's control over the media is immense, from TV licences, to government advertising to journalists' access to government decisions and policies; it also increasingly has the power to have troublesome journalists removed from their organizations. It is strange indeed that democratic governments, elected by the people, can in turn deny the people—for journalists are only agents of citizens—access to or knowledge about how their policies are made and deny access to decision-making processes.

Perceived instances of corruption in the media are thus no different from corruption in other spheres. When a sector is hugely controlled and regulated by the government, media bosses, like typical corporate bosses in India, will always tread very carefully and become trained to second guess what political leaders want. Fearful corporate bosses in India are very careful about what they publicly say, in contrast to the often open criticism that US or UK businesses direct towards their governments. In June 2018, prominent business leaders in the United States, from the Airbnb CEO to the Apple CEO, roundly condemned the Trump administration on its immigration policies.[20] In India, because the Big State or the government is so powerful and has so much power over business, such criticism is rare. Among the few top corporate voices to have voiced some criticism against the present government's meddling in the economy so far has been that of industrialist Adi Godrej, but only with a rather mild note of caution.[21] The predicament of a media owner in India is thus no different from a corporate proprietor— fearful of crossing the line. Thus, in my view, freedom of the press in India is largely dependent on government whim and inclination, and whether or not journalists can cultivate friendly politicians through personal associations. Institutionally, India's free press is dreadfully and shockingly weak.

Today in times of muscular 'nationalism', echoing the line of the ruling party has become the norm. But, to quote veteran American journalist Edward Murrow, 'We must not confuse dissent with disloyalty . . . we will not walk in fear into an age of unreason . . . we are not descended from fearful men, from men who feared to write, to associate, to speak or defend causes that were, for the moment, unpopular.'[22]

* * *

We are indeed not descended from fearful men or fearful women. The foundations of independent India as laid down by our forefathers and foremothers in 1947 are deeply liberal. Courageous Indian liberals—if 'liberal' is broadly defined as those who believed in individual freedoms and liberties, values of pluralism, a secular state, the rule of law, equality before the law and a free press—founded the Indian republic in 1947. Writes the great chronicler of India's society, M.N. Srinivas: 'A westernized intelligentsia had emerged among Indians by the 'sixties of the nineteenth century and leaders of this class became the torchbearers of a new and modern India. The leaders included such great names as the Tagores, Vivekananda, Ranade, Gokhale, Tilak, Patel, Gandhi, Jawaharlal Nehru and Radhakrishnan. The westernized intelligentsia increased in strength and numbers, and the dawn of independence in 1947 invested them with the power to plan a peaceful revolution of Indian life.'[23]

This intelligentsia was rooted as well as Westernized, globalized yet introspective, each engaged in a rediscovery of India in the light of Western values.[24] However, as we'll see in this essay, their legatees have served them badly. Liberals founded India, but liberalism has fallen into disrepute in some circles and been given a bad name because of the compromises and failings of those who inherited the founders' mantle. That's why in order to reassert her values the liberal needs to accept the sins of omission and commission of those who could not live up to the ideals of India's liberal founders and to realize that the need to stand up for liberal values has never been greater.

Mohandas Karamchand Gandhi placed his faith in the individual conscience and viewed Big Governments with deep suspicion. Gandhi was not just the father of the nation; he was also the father of Indian liberalism. Some argue that Gandhi was liberal to the point of being a libertarian, although others have called him a conservative because of his devout Hindu beliefs. Gandhi's piety is interesting. He was a believer who didn't believe in imposing his beliefs on the citizenry at large through state power. He chose an atheist/agnostic—Jawaharlal Nehru—as his successor. Gandhi was a Hindu who completely disassociated himself from the Hindu orthodoxy, and in fact was so hated by political Hindus that they assassinated him.

Gandhi was consistently wary of a big controlling government, or the Big State, which as we have been emphasizing is the enemy of the liberal because the Big State in India intrudes into too many sectors of life. The Mahatma's beliefs in the individual satyagrahi, the village republic and self-help and spiritual empowerment of the individual to change society reveal his very deep liberal impulses. It was because Gandhi was deeply apprehensive of state power that he did not believe in enforcing his personal ideology through government agencies. A devout Hindu, he never wanted a law banning cow slaughter and was firm in the belief that no individual should be harmed in the name of cow protection. Gandhi wrote, 'Hinduism's worship of the cow is its unique contribution to the evolution of humanitarianism.'[25] But for Gandhi, the individual rights of others were greater than his own beliefs, and thus in his lifetime he did not campaign to make cow protection enforceable by law.

For Gandhi, the atma, the quickening of the inner being, the battle within for truth, the distinct spirit of the individual was supreme. Gandhi had unlimited faith in the power and goodness of individuals, which is why he saw the freedom struggle as a personal struggle too, a lift-off into personal as well as political regeneration. 'My life consists of nothing but experiments with truth . . . [from] experiments in the spiritual field . . . I have derived such power as I possess for working in the political field.'[26]

To Gandhi, the means were always much more important than the ends. He called off the 1921–22 Non-cooperation campaign because it descended into violence in Chauri Chaura, where a mob burnt down a police station, killing many policemen. The movement thus failed to be the just means to a cause. For the liberal, means are always just as important as ends. Why? Because once the ends are achieved, the means shape the nature of the victory. Without the benchmark of moral and ethical means, the ends often degenerate into an anything-goes power lust. The anything-for-power syndrome could easily become a descent into dictatorship rather than a path to democracy. As the playwright Anton Chekhov put it, 'Despicable means used to achieve laudable goals render the goals themselves despicable.'[27]

Over the last seventy years, I think liberals have perhaps committed many errors of choosing the wrong means to their stated ends (see Chapter 2 on the tragedy of illiberal secularism). They have failed to uphold the distinction between means and ends, consequently ignoring or even endorsing a huge expansion of state power,[28] consequently ignoring or even endorsing a huge expansion in state power. This has set us on the road to a competition for ever greater political patronage as different groups have sought their own share of government patronage and there is intense competition for pieces of the sarkari pie.[29]

Instead of seeking to strengthen the power of the government or seeking patronage for themselves, should Indian liberals have strengthened civil society more than they did? Did they contribute towards the mega government by seeking too much government sponsorship and too many favours? Have liberal intellectuals gravitated too far towards governments and friendly politicians rather than keeping them at arm's length and refusing to be co-opted? Should liberals accept government awards or government grants? These questions must trouble the twenty-first-century liberal as she tries to find the balance between government power and the citizen.

India's first prime minister, Jawaharlal Nehru, differed with Gandhi on the role of the government. Yet, he was a quintessential social liberal and constitutional democrat. Nehru may not have been a believer in a free economy or 'the jungle of the market economy',[30] as the Marxist historian Eric Hobsbawm called it, or an economy based on individual freedom; he preferred the establishment of a socialist state which would control the country's commanding heights.

Yet it's not as if Nehru sought to control the 'leviathans of the economy' for personal benefit to himself or his party, as seen in the constant measures he used to share and disperse power. Nehru's belief was that to leapfrog from the deindustrialized agricultural primitiveness which the British left India to an industrialized economy, it was the government and not private capital which needed to guide the economy.[31] The public-sector-guided economy was the dominant belief in the world in Nehru's time. But even as he was no economic liberal, Nehru was a convinced social liberal for whom constitutional morality and individual freedoms guaranteed by the Constitution were uppermost.

India's first prime minister was the towering political figure of his era. Yet, he rejected absolute power and constantly sought to build a consensual style of leadership, writing fortnightly letters to state chief ministers, painstakingly trying to maintain the integrity of institutions like Parliament and the judiciary and welcoming into his cabinet those with whom he disagreed ideologically, such as the Hindu Mahasabha leader Shyama Prasad Mukherjee. He tried to nurture an Opposition and in 1937 even published a highly self-critical essay under the pen name 'Chanakya' in which he stressed the need to question all-powerful political leaders.[32]

B.R. Ambedkar, draftsman of the Constitution, was also a quintessential liberal. He espoused individual action, democratic debate and opposition to personality cults and called for social justice to be the basis of democracy.[33] 'For India,' Ambedkar said, 'Bhakti or what may be called the path of devotion or hero-worship plays a part in its politics unequalled in magnitude by the part it plays in the politics of any other country in the world. Bhakti in religion may be a road to the salvation of the soul. But in politics, Bhakti or hero-worship is a sure road to degradation and to eventual dictatorship.' Also, Ambedkar believed, as he said during a speech in the Constituent Assembly on 25 November 1949, 'We must make our political democracy a social democracy as well. Political democracy cannot last unless there lies at the base of it social democracy.'[34]

A diehard critic of Gandhi, Ambedkar supported constitutional means of protest and rejected satyagraha or civil disobedience.[35] 'The first thing in my judgement we must do is to hold fast to constitutional methods of achieving our social and economic objectives. It means we must abandon the bloody methods of revolution. It means that we must abandon the method of civil disobedience, non-cooperation and satyagraha. When there was no way left for constitutional methods for achieving economic and social objectives, there was a great deal of justification for unconstitutional methods. But where constitutional methods are open, there can be no justification for these unconstitutional methods. These methods are nothing but the Grammar of Anarchy and the sooner they are abandoned, the better for us.'[36]

Ambedkar's view of Hinduism differed sharply from Gandhi's. As Ambedkar famously wrote: 'The Hindu civilization . . . is a diabolical contrivance to suppress and enslave humanity. Its proper name would be infamy . . . What else can be said of a civilization which has produced a mass of people . . . whose mere touch (can) cause pollution'.[37]

While Gandhi was in favour of the village republic, Ambedkar placed individual over village. As he said: 'What is a village but a sink of localism, a den of ignorance, narrow-mindedness and communalism? I am glad that the Draft Constitution has discarded the village and adopted the individual as the unit.'[38]

These views, as well as Ambedkar's declarations that anyone who read Hindu books like the Vedas, shastras and Puranas should be penalized by law,[39] were the polar opposite of Gandhi's, who constantly praised Hinduism's freedom from dogma, non-violence and tolerance.[40] To Ambedkar's attack on Hinduism, Gandhi responded: 'Can a religion that was professed by Chaitanya, Jnandeva, Tukaram, Tiruvalluvar, Ramakrishna Paramahamsa, Raja Rammohan Roy, Maharshi Debendranath Tagore, Vivekananda and a host of others be so utterly devoid of merit as made out by Dr Ambedkar?'[41] There may not have been too much of a meeting of minds between Gandhi and Ambedkar, yet the crucial fact to note is that these two ideological adversaries together put their shoulders to the wheel for the cause of a liberal, individual-rights-based Constitution. This is an important lesson for us to learn. It shows that there was a time in India when 100 per cent agreement on political principles was not imperative or necessary for cooperation or for conversation. Such respect for disagreement is an extremely important liberal premise.

Rabindranath Tagore, another great liberal ancestor of independent India and the author of India's national anthem, was deeply fearful of nationalism located in race and community. Tagore identified liberal humanism as the goal of mankind. Tagore was a stubborn critic of race-based, community-based nationalism, instead calling for a multicultural India which would be welcoming of all, the home of many races, religions and creeds. As he said: 'Today, cannot India rise above her limitations and offer the great ideal to the world that will work towards harmony and co-operation between the different peoples of the earth?'[42]

Tagore stood for an east–west embrace, as did Gandhi. They both kept emphasizing that their opposition to the British raj was a protest at the injustice of colonial rule; they hated injustice, not the British people or the white race, who they exhorted to stay on in India and feel welcome, not as masters but as equals.

Raja Rammohan Roy is one of the greatest ancestors for Indian liberals. M.N. Srinivas calls Raja Rammohan Roy 'the prophet of modern India' and indeed Roy is the beacon of Indian liberalism, fighting orthodox Hindus yet appealing to the Upanishads and the Vedanta to argue the value of reason in Indian Hindu thought. Roy and the Brahmo Samaj (founded in 1828 as a reformist movement by Roy) laid down many of the intellectual foundational principles which later found their way into the Indian Constitution in the form of legally guaranteed fundamental rights, equality of women and, most important of all, universal adult franchise. Liberals believed that not only was secularism a universally desired ideal for multi-faith India but a principle that embodied essential Hindu traditions of tolerance. 'Hinduism is essentially tolerant and it would rather assimilate than rigidly exclude,' wrote S. Radhakrishnan, who like Roy attempted to discover modern values in Hinduism.[43] Roy, in a sense, was carrying forward the message of the Bhakti movement during the medieval period, a moment when the individual spirit of freedom revolted against caste inequalities and priestly dominance and led to the spread of a form of spiritual democracy and equality before the eyes of the divine.

Roy was also a strong champion of a free press: 'Every good ruler must be conscious of the great liability of error . . . [therefore] the unrestrained Liberty of Publication is the only means that can be employed.'

An important figure in the evolution of post-Independence Indian liberalism was Chakravarti Rajagopalachari or Rajaji, once called the 'wisest man in India', someone who Gandhi called 'my conscience keeper', whom historian Rajmohan Gandhi describes as a 'brainy Brahmin'.[44]

Learned visionary, brilliant intellectual, close associate and later a piercing critic of Nehru, Rajagopalachari believed in the individual over dominant state power and founded India's first liberal-conservative party, the Swatantra Party, along these lines. Rajaji's words inspire liberals to this day. In 1991 when government control over India's economy brought it to the edge of ruin and the then prime minister P.V. Narasimha Rao with his then finance minister Manmohan Singh were forced to dismantle government controls, Rajaji's words proved prescient. Rajaji differed with Nehru on the question of expanding government control on the commanding heights of the economy. But on Nehru's death, Rajaji wrote the most moving tribute to his beloved opponent: 'The old guardroom is completely empty now. I have been fighting Sri Nehru all these ten years for what I consider faults in public policies. But I knew all along that he alone could get them corrected. No one else would dare do it, and he is gone, leaving me weaker than before in my fight. But fighting apart, a beloved friend is gone, the most civilised person among us all.'[45]

Rajaji was a believer and Nehru was an agnostic-atheist; they differed on the role of the government in the economy, but respected each other's beliefs. As we have noted, this ability to respect dissent is the crucial hallmark of the liberal.

In creating a manifesto for the Indian liberal, here's a guiding principle from Rajaji's philosophy, today considered a statement of modern Indian liberalism: '[We stand for] minimum government and minimum State interference, for minimum expenditure in administration and for minimum taxation, for minimum interference in the private and professional affairs of citizens and for minimum regulation in industry and trade . . . regulation must be limited to requirement and not expanded to the point of killing individual incentive.'[46]

These words are important starting points to seriously debate the role of the State and government in the lives of citizens.

In 1959, Rajagopalachari founded the Swatantra Party, mainly as a reaction to Nehru's socialist ideology. The Swatantra Party, Rajaji declared, '. . . is founded on the conviction that social justice and welfare can be attained through the fostering of individual interest and individual enterprise in all fields better than through state ownership and government controls.'[47] In their plea for economic liberalization, the Swatantra liberals 'were three decades ahead of their times',[48] many of their ideas adopted by the Congress in 1991, when it liberalized the economy. The Swatantra liberals, I believe, are an extremely important brain bank for any Indian seeking prescriptions for social and economic liberalism, for anyone seeking a thoughtful combination of secularism and an economy that encourages individual enterprise. C. Rajagopalachari held to insightful liberal ideas on justice, economy, language, individual freedoms, religion and even Kashmir (for example, Rajaji was highly critical of the way Nehru created the merger of Kashmir with India). Any Indian who wants to call herself a liberal should delve into the thoughts and writings of Rajaji. The writings of Rajaji's companions and disciples like Minoo Masani[49] show how deeply many Indians down the generations have written and thought about how a massive state structure has the potential to stifle the freedoms of Indians. They have written in detail on just how unfree Indians can become unless they resist the mighty government that spills into everything, from controlling the economy, food choices, popular entertainment and the content of textbooks and school curriculum. A massive, interfering government leads to an irrevocable politicization and subordination of society as a whole.

C. Rajagopalachari and Minoo Masani were stalwarts of Indian liberalism but came from very different backgrounds. Rajaji was a devout Hindu, Masani an atheist. Rajaji's politics were deeply influenced by Gandhi. Masani was an urbane, Westernized metropolitan intellectual whose political journey began as a socialist before he evolved into a liberal. The key to note here is that differences in view were respected and there was no attempt to call anyone an 'anti-national' or 'traitor' simply because of differing viewpoints. Masani's son, Zareer Masani, writes evocatively about arguments between Nehru and Minoo Masani in Parliament and how amiable they were. 'After one such chivalrous exchange, Acharya Kripalani called out, "If you have such a high opinion of Masani, why don't you take him into your Cabinet?" Nehru cheerfully replied, "Because he would try to stop me doing what I wanted, and I would do the same to him. Now we're both free to do as we please.'[50]

Today, as we shall see through this book, a constantly expanding bureaucratic government and government takeover of almost every aspect of citizens' lives has in my view crushed the liberal dream of empowered citizens and the liberal ideal of a limited government restricted to maintaining law and order and facilitating individual enterprise. The liberal in India wants citizens' freedoms enhanced responsibly and lawfully. The liberal has always chafed at controls, both against economic controls like the licence permit quota raj as well as against overpowering social controls through morality cops and emerging theocratic tendencies.

A crucial caveat: this essay is emphatically not arguing the cause of or attacking any present-day political party. The ruling BJP in today's avatar is governed by a highly illiberal ideology known as

Hindutva nationalism, but this does not mean that the opposition Congress has not been guilty of rampant illiberalism in the past. Dynastic succession, surely an aberration in liberal democracy, is an example of the illiberalism of the Congress; so is the manner in which the Congress has dabbled in religious politics and has massively expanded the role of the government at the cost of individual rights at different points in the recent past.

The Modi-led BJP is a highly illiberal force, although the Vajpayee-led BJP did try to move slightly towards a liberal economic orientation when it embarked on freeing the economy in important sectors. The Vajpayee-led years, 1999–2004, were perhaps the BJP's most 'liberal' moment. However, even during Vajpayee's time, the influence of the Rashtriya Swayamsevak Sangh (RSS) led to copycat imitations of trying to control history-writing and textbook-writing, as Indira Gandhi's socialist dispensation had done in her time.

Interestingly, Shyama Prasad Mukherjee, Vajpayee's precursor in the Hindutva nationalist movement and the founder of the Jana Sangh, can be called a liberal in some respects as he had argued strongly against Nehru's first amendment of the Constitution, which restricted freedom of speech. It is tragic that Mukherjee's political descendants today in the twenty-first century are trying their utmost to stifle free speech and propagate only what they consider Officially Approved Nationalist Speech.

Before the Vajpayee interregnum, the liberalization of the economy in 1991 was the Congress's best liberal achievement, when it rolled back the government's predatory hold over the economy. In an interview, former prime minister Manmohan Singh's daughter, author Daman Singh, pointed out how her father had always upheld the cause of liberal economics,[51] and indeed 'Manmohan-economics' is the name given to liberal economics, Indian style. However in his tenure as prime minister, Manmohan Singh's liberal orientation was increasingly blocked by a populist-inclined Congress party, and Leftist opinion has attacked Manmohan Singh for his 'neo-liberal' outlook. As prime ministers go, however, the Oxbridge-educated scholar–economist Manmohan Singh was among the most liberal India has had.

As we shall see through this essay, in India, Leftist orthodoxies have sometimes been as intolerant as Rightist ones, even though when West Bengal's communist chief minister Buddhadeb Bhattacharjee broke with his party line and embarked on a liberal, business-friendly approach, he received a thundering three-fourths majority from the people.[52] Yet, party orthodoxies have often disregarded public sentiment.

India's regional parties, with their thrust on personality cults and populist economics, have hardly been liberal formations, even though individual politicians like former prime minister P.V. Narasimha Rao, Andhra Pradesh chief minister N. Chandrababu Naidu and former Karnataka chief minister S.M. Krishna— who could fit the definition of liberal in their encouragement to individual enterprise and not over-expanding state power—have occasionally emerged and tried to create a combination of social and economic liberal policies. Secularism, the so-called article of faith for India's liberal parties, has often been an illiberal ideology in the hands of politicians who have disregarded the liberal premise of equality before the law and justice for the individual. The secularism practised by Prime Minister Rajiv Gandhi, for example, was deeply illiberal in the manner in which justice was denied on religious grounds to the Muslim divorcee Shah Bano or the way Salman Rushdie's book *The Satanic Verses* was, in a stark moment of government-overreach, banned in 1988 (India was the first country to enforce the ban).[53]

The kind of official secularism currently being practised by West Bengal chief minister Mamata Banerjee could also be in danger of falling into the illiberal trap if religion is allowed to determine government policy. The essence of secularism is even-handed justice where all faiths receive the same treatment from the state and equality of all religions is guaranteed by law. When secular governments also use strongman squads for political gains, liberal secularism gets a bad name.[54] If secularism becomes as much about bullying tactics as Hindutva, if secular parties also become known by their violent streetfighters, it's only a matter of time before an old don is replaced by a newer one.

For example, the Trinamool Congress (TMC) is a strident opponent of the BJP. Yet, it operates at the grassroots through party bosses like local 'dada' Anubrata Mondal, the TMC's strongman in Birbhum, who, during the Panchayat polls, said, 'In my Birbhum there is no election.'[55] In the forty-two seats in the area, the TMC won by default as there was simply no opposition in sight; 34.2 per cent seats in the Bengal panchayat elections were uncontested. Such is the might and muscle power of the TMC in Bengal. In fact, across the board, 'secular' parties like the Rashtriya Janata Dal, Samajwadi Party (SP), Bahujan Samaj Party (BSP) and even the Congress have faced similar accusations of armed street thuggery, rule by dictatorial local commissars and 'Dabanggs', and also of graft. As Alex Traub writes, Bengal's 'high minded secularism' is becoming 'egalitarian dictatorship and authoritarianism'.[56] Thus, can parties professing 'liberal' secularism but operating through ruthless local toughies be accurately called 'liberal'?

This essay mounts an argument against Hindutva politics as much as it does on the politics of maximalist all-powerful governments, the kind created by Indira Gandhi, Rajiv Gandhi and Narendra Modi. Take, for example, the Ministry of Human Resource Development (HRD). This ministry, created by Rajiv Gandhi in 1985, is a monument to the fundamentally illiberal nature of the Indian state. The HRD ministry has several departments and is manned by legions of officers, pushing government controls into textbook-writing, the arts, museums and culture in general. It seems to operate by the principle that the human mind is a passive mass of brain cells to be shaped at will by the all-knowing state for the purpose of serving it.

A Ministry of Culture exists too. This ministry controls libraries, the arts Akademis and zonal cultural centres, thus pushing the writ of the ruling party into dance, music, theatre, et al. The HRD ministry, recently in the news for its attempts to interfere in academic institutions and prescribe curricula, and the equally outdated information and broadcasting ministry[57] remain examples of the illiberal impulses of so-called liberal parties.

Indira Gandhi created a huge, creaky socialist machine of a government, which tried to take over institutions and clamped the Emergency on individual freedoms. Rajiv Gandhi banned books like *The Satanic Verses* and made only partial attempts to roll back state power, increasingly ruling through a personality cult. The reason why the current Hindutva nationalist government has been able to create its own version of the Big State is precisely because this Big State was legitimized by the seculars.

In 1991, the so-called licence era raj did come to a partial end, and as the economy bounded forward so did individual freedoms. However, some pernicious cultural controls like the film 'censor' board, CBFC, remain, and violent mobs that attack writers and painters in the name of protecting 'culture' derive their sense of legitimacy from the many bans and restrictions that governments have regularly imposed.[58]

Liberal activists have made serious mistakes by seeking patronage from the same Big State instead of reawakening a sense of social self-help and social agency among citizens or working to create networks of citizen-based groups. It is the Big State which politicizes society and often willy-nilly outsources its ideological agenda to non-state actors, either seen in the form of violent communist cadres or Right-wing gau rakshaks or thuggish moral policemen. Often, liberal social platforms did not create mechanisms to deal with dissent and disagreement for meaningful negotiations, leading to a splintering of civic society movements. The manner in which the Aam Aadmi Party (AAP) roughly expelled its key founders, Yogendra Yadav and Prashant Bhushan, showed how this particular citizens' movement failed to develop internal systems to rise above disagreements.[59] The inability of liberals to transcend disagreements, indeed to respect and be tolerant of dissent, has been one of the reasons why liberals perhaps have painted themselves into an intolerant, sometimes snobbishly judgemental corner and lost sight of the larger battle.

In May 2017, the photograph of a blood-soaked father of three, Mohammad Naeem, a cattle trader, urgently negotiating for his life minutes before he was beaten to death by a mob in a Jharkhand town, sent waves of horror across the country. It revealed the impunity a mob enjoys when violence goes unpunished. There have been sporadic instances of mob violence down the decades, indicating the institutional decay of the police and the judiciary. But today, for the first time, this institutional decay is being politically leveraged. What was earlier occasional mob violence has now become routine mob violence, turning neighbour against neighbour.[60] Is the rule of law becoming only weak, liberal, wishful thinking in times of cow hooligans and enraged mobs enforcing street retribution?

It is the regular outbreaks of such violence that have led many to believe the liberal project is dead in India. This is supposed to be the era of macho patriotism, of an aggressive attitude towards minorities—sometimes euphemistically called 'cattle-smugglers'—a time when those arguing for a dialogue with Kashmiri stakeholders or talks with Pakistan and those who question religious nationalism are shouted down as 'anti-nationals', 'half-Maoists' and 'jihadists' (see Chapters 1 and 2). In a tweet on 8 June 2018, finance minister Arun Jaitley said, 'The "half-Maoist" is a serious threat to Indian democracy. Willingly or otherwise, they become the overground face of the underground.[61] Unfortunately, some political parties see the Maoist as their instrument in the anti-NDA cause. It's high time that people recognize this malaise.' Driven into silence by an anti-liberal, anti-minority 'nationalistic' fervour, the idealistic middle class, once the great bedrock of India's freedom movement, is missing in action, confused, powerfully drawn to Hindutva and 'muscular nationalism' and seemingly disenchanted with liberal values. In the CSDS-Lokniti opinion polls in 2018, satisfaction levels with the Modi government were still high—61 per cent among the upper middle class and 56 per cent among the middle class.[62]

The loss of liberal values among the educated middle class can become a tragedy of monumental proportions. But it's not too late to recover if liberals speak up strongly on why the liberal project is worth defending and why religious majoritarianism may look as if it's a 'strong government' but in fact is a fundamental assault on individual rights. Tomorrow, if your daughter's wedding was disrupted by a religious or 'nationalist' vigilante squad, enraged that you were playing 'anti-national' music or wearing 'anti-national' clothes, what would you do? To whom would you turn?

In many instances, Indian liberals are accused of belonging to a small 'Westernized elitist club'. The word 'Lutyens' elite is used by Right-wing Twitter handles to attack what is shorthand for the entrenched Indian elite liberal, generally those part of political dynasties living in the Lutyens' Bungalow Zone in New Delhi.[63] But it is simply not true that Indian 'liberals' have been an elitist and disconnected lobby with no roots in India. Not only have Hindu traditions always been deeply liberal, not only has the subcontinent been marked down the ages by liberal spiritual reformers, not only were the founders of independent India liberals, but numerous liberal protestors who down the decades have fought for progressive values have hardly been disconnected and elitist. Those who stood by Tamil author Perumal Murugan after he was slapped with criminal complaints, rationalists like M.M. Kalburgi, Govind Pansare, Gauri Lankesh and Narendra Dabholkar, those who fought for women's empowerment like Ela Bhatt, for farmers' rights like Sharad Joshi, to deepen democracy at the grassroots like Sandeep Pandey and Aruna Roy, none of them were or are 'Westernized elitists', and support for them crossed class boundaries.

In fact, it almost seems as if there is a bubbling invisible river of liberal humanism in India that surges just under the surface of daily life, only waiting to burst forth into refreshing fountains.

Yashpal Saxena, the Hindu father in Delhi whose son was killed by the Muslim family of the girl he loved, celebrated a multi-faith Iftaar in 2018. Maulana Imdadullah Rashidi in Asansol, Bengal, who lost his son in a riot, rushed towards his flock, counselling peace to his followers and stopping them from seeking revenge in his son's name.[64] The no-nonsense Shwetambari Sharma, the Hindu woman police officer in Jammu who was part of the team investigating the Kathua rape case, who said my uniform is my only religion, and the valiant Deepika Rajawat, who stood up to be the lawyer for the Kathua victim, are examples of the liberal Idea of India still alive at the grassroots. There are other examples too: Gagandeep Singh, the Sikh police officer in Uttarakhand, charged into a mob to protect a Muslim youth being attacked for so-called 'love-jihad'. Dr Kafeel Khan, the doctor in Gorakhpur, worked frantically into the late hours trying to save lives. Describing his efforts to procure oxygen for dying children, Dr Khan wrote in a letter: 'I frantically called everyone, I begged, I talked, I ran, I drove, I ordered, I yelled, I screamed, I consoled, I counselled, I spent, I borrowed, I cried. I did all that is humanly possible.'[65] The rooted, salt-of-the-earth liberal, marked by compassion for his fellow individual, above caste and creed, is found in every Indian small town and city.

The nationalist Right-wing (like the ideological Left) prioritizes government over individual. Both ideological orthodoxies of Left and Right believe in a gargantuan state machinery, in unbounded state power and in the state's superior rights over the individual. In 2017, in the case on whether PAN cards should be linked with Aadhaar cards, then attorney general Mukul Rohatgi's comment was telling. Arguing that citizens do not have absolute rights over their bodies, he said, 'Even if you want to be forgotten the State is not willing to forget you.' Here the former attorney general sounded a bit like a Soviet commissar! The erstwhile Soviet Union had no private property, citizens had no privacy, people were tools in the hands of the state, to be abused and dealt with as the state pleased.

Privacy, in essence, is a reflection of the quality of protection of private property, both of the mind and of the body. Thus, as analysts have said, saffron is the new red.

Indian liberals have always stood against rampaging state power and for individual rights. Those who protested against the Emergency, against the 1988 Anti-Defamation Bill,[66] against bans on books and movies and those who campaigned for citizens' rights have all held firm against government muscle-flexing.

Indian liberals, in fact, represent a mighty tradition because as we shall see later in the book, Hindu religious traditions are deeply liberal. The tradition of individual assertion is seen in the rise of protest movements against Brahminical dominance throughout history.

Liberal ways of thinking are found in the Upanishads, in the Bhakti movement, in the Sufi movements, in the numerous sects and reform movements across India which questioned idol worship and ritualism and pursued individual freedom and dignity. The Indian liberal tradition is neither confined to a small minority, nor elitist, nor Westernized nor simply restricted to any political party.

Yet, with such a strong tradition why then are liberals losing out to the votaries of majoritarianism? Perhaps because the liberal language has become mired, as French President Emmanuel Macron once pointed out, in negativity and fear.[67] It's become too focused on denigrating and demonizing opponents. Instead, liberals should propose something positive, open and persuasive, a language that stimulates goodness and a sense of justice in every citizen and encourages every citizen to be her best (not her worst) self. As Macron said, this language should encourage private enterprise, not crush or overprotect it and seek ways out of poverty for globalization's victims. Above all, it should recognize the freedom of every citizen to pursue his or her goals without harming others.

This is not the time for liberals to cower and be fearful. The liberal is watched over by the powerful spirit of the founders of the Republic of India in 1947. She is also protected by formidably ageless subcontinental spirits which have regularly risen from deep within the earth, through the centuries, to challenge those who insist on prescribed behaviour codes, caste codes, religious codes, bans on free speech and restrictions on religious beliefs and intellectual, dietary and sexual freedom. Confronted with a control-freak Big State, the liberal must speak up against those who seek to control thought, food, books, movies, culture and history textbooks in the name of so-called 'Hindu tradition' and 'nationalism'.

This is not the time to shy away or secede or retreat from the debate. This is the time to speak boldly and constantly on every current issue and emphasize the liberal version of patriotism, grounded in law and respect for all faiths. It is also a time to be inclusive, to listen to counterarguments and learn from them and recognize that the term 'liberal' has been distorted and corrupted by its own guardians.

The liberal manifesto for India ought to have been one that is headlined: India: Liberal, Just, Prosperous and Global, India for all.

There's another reason for trying to create this liberal manifesto. Today, there is not just economic and material poverty but moral, cultural and political poverty. Mind-numbing TV debates between screeching party apparatchiks have become the norm; PR campaigns are the only politics we recognize. Our vocabulary is coarse, our attitudes harsh and our minds closed, dulled by soap operas and reality TV. We need to once again emphasize that the way out of this degradation is not to seek solutions from governments and politicians who control the government, but from ourselves. And in seeking those solutions from ourselves we need to ask ourselves: how important are our individual freedoms in the social, personal, political and economic spheres? These freedoms must be linked to Gandhi's moral framework for individual and collective salvation, namely, moral means justifying the ends, taking charge of our own conscience and being our best selves. Only such enlightened individual action and thought can lead to the social and moral rejuvenation India so sorely needs.

The coming to power of the Narendra Modi government in 2014 has opened the floodgates of religious identity. A powerful centralizing government is arrogating greater powers to itself, and a Hindutva-based ruling party has launched an all-out drive for the Hinduization of India. In an earlier time, a socialist-based ruling party under Indira Gandhi had launched an all-out drive for making India more socialist with campaigns like the 20 Point Programme. The Indira government may not have intruded into personal freedoms as much the Hindutva state is doing, but it set the tone, in a way, for a controlling government. Hindutva, as pointed out earlier in many ways, is the child of the mega socialist state, inheriting the worst features of a bureaucratic machinery. Many elements in this illiberal state have traditionally dispensed patronage to favoured groups in the face of artificial scarcities created and instituted by short-sighted dogma. Indira's 20 Point Programme and Sanjay Gandhi's 5 Point Programme set the tone for Big State or Big Government schemes under the Modi-led government like Swachh Bharat, Digital India, Start-up India or Skill India. Sanjay Gandhi's slogan 'Talk Less, Work More' again set the tone for Big Government–style social engineering and an attempt to dictate a civic morality from on high on citizens whom it mistrusted and held in contempt. It is rather like the Modi government's 'Beti Bachao, Beti Padhao' cry, which attempts to impose a well-intentioned moral choice on citizens, but considering the rising crimes against women it has remained an empty slogan.

Perhaps for the first time in the history of independent India there is a serious attempt to transform the very idea of India. A patchy but enduring vaguely liberal consensus has endured since India became independent in 1947. Yes, there was the Emergency between 1975–77, but, generally, governments in India have not moved towards direct interference in personal and individual freedoms the way we have seen in the last four years.

Two recent letters—one of them a suicide note—should cause grave disquiet to every Indian citizen and warn them about the dangers that democratic institutions face today, and make us all introspect.

The first letter that should concern us is the suicide note of PhD scholar Rohith Vemula. On 17 January 2016, the twenty-eight-year-old Hyderabad University student committed suicide by hanging himself. Before he died Vemula had been suspended for taking part in an Ambedkar Students Association agitation. In his suicide note Rohith wrote about his birth (in a poor, backward caste family) being a 'fatal accident' and asked that his scholarship money be given to his family. Would Rohith still be alive today if he had not been suspended for only taking part in a democratic protest, is the question that must haunt every democratically minded citizen.

The second important letter that should agitate every citizen is the letter written on 12 January 2018 by none other than four senior judges of the Supreme Court. It's a letter that caused a mini-earthquake as it publicly pointed to irregularities in the functioning of India's highest court, saying that unless proper rules are followed, it 'would not only lead to unpleasant and undesirable consequences of creating doubt in the body politic about the integrity of the institution'.

A suicidal student and four senior judges have written letters that are serious indictments of democratic processes, casting the rule of law in doubt, warning citizens of what the clear and present dangers are. The letters show that every citizen needs to wake up and act to preserve rule-based liberal democracy and act against the prevailing atmosphere of illiberal censoriousness, before it is too late.

To paraphrase the motto of the *Washington Post* newspaper, 'democracy dies in darkness'—it also dies in apathy. Where is our collective morality? Can there even be a collective morality without an individual morality? Surely, personal morals or the awakening of personal morality is best achieved when such a choice is voluntary and made as a conscious selection. Morality cannot be imposed either by a government or priesthood; it must come from within, and it can only come from within when the individual is free. Individual freedom is valued by those who have the self-confidence to trust others as equals. This is why the liberal campaign of empowering the individual and rigorous rule of law have to be the cornerstones of the new liberal ideology. A moral renaissance is the crucial need of the hour because morality and ethics are being torn away in the flood of legislation designed to appeal to vote banks. Justice and the law are articles of faith for the liberal, and a focus on Gandhian means rather than ends of grabbing power any which way.

The Latin American author Mario Vargas Llosa has recently written a book called *La Llamada de la Tribu*[68] in which he says that the 'ignorance' of liberalism is the reason liberalism is so weak in Latin America. In India, citizens have never really been called upon to define any form of liberal beliefs; they've generally taken for granted that there's a mai-baap government structure which lays down all kinds of rules and regulations on business and trade but generally (with some exceptions), in return for law-abiding behaviour, leaves citizens alone to at least eat what they want, pray to whoever they want to and do whatever they want to with their cash. In any case, only a small percentage of the working population directly works under the shadow of the Big State. Most workers are in the informal sector where they get by by largely ignoring the government or buying peace by submitting to various extortion rackets run by the many agents of the Big State. Indians have by and large never felt unfree because the phrase 'chalta hai'—roughly translated as 'anything goes'—has been the umbrella platform of an 'anything goes' culture where everything is possible as long as you either bribe the authorities or hide things from them.

In a sense, the illusion of freedom also comes from the fact that the Hindu religion in essence is generally a highly freeing liberal body of philosophies with no single church, no single set of beliefs, no concept of heresy or blasphemy, no common deity or rituals— placing almost its entire focus on individual choice and practice. The Hindu guru and his ashram are globally renowned for free individual action. Those who enter 'Hindu' in the religion column access that long tradition of personal freedom in which they and their families or caste clan can choose their own belief systems.

But this age-old, vague, taken-for-granted freedom is now in serious danger. Today, Hindutva nationalist forces, while claiming to reverse and oppose the 'pseudo-secular' agenda, are imitating erstwhile socialists and infusing a massively interfering, freedom-suppressing state with their own saffron hue.

The last four years have given Indians a rude shock in majoritarian authoritarianism practised in the name of religious nationalism. The Modi government is a Big State, its members loyal to the Hindutva ideology, which prescribes to its citizens what to eat (by imposing beef bans), what to do with their money (by announcing demonetization), instructing people to do yoga and reading out lessons in how to be a good 'nationalist' (Sedition cases have been filed against those described as 'anti-national'). Each new scheme unveiled by Prime Minister Modi shows an expansion of the state and an increase in the power of the government.

That's why a liberal charter is so important. Citizens must understand that what the government is doing in the name of religious nationalism—as governments once did in the name of socialism, but perhaps not to this extent—is intruding fundamentally and irrevocably into the individual freedoms so carefully guaranteed in the Constitution.

These intrusions are not just by the government but also by newly empowered 'non-state actors' or a range of Right-wing Hindutva activists or morality cops hounding, harassing and browbeating anyone with a view different from the ruling party.[69] When Hindutva is outsourced to non-state actors, it allows the state to escape responsibility. Hindus and Muslims mustn't marry, Christmas is no longer quite acceptable, carol singers may be intercepted, beef- or even meat-eating is not acceptable, cattle traders can be lynched with impunity, young couples can't be seen romancing in public, journalists must be bullied into submission, as must Parliament, judiciary and the Opposition parties.

And all this is happening in the name of Hinduism, which in reality is the most freedom-imparting religion in the world. Hinduism's basic tenets of freedom and interrogation are being turned inside out by Hindutva, which permits no questioning or counterargument.

As a journalist and columnist, a liberal, an admirer and student of Tagore, Gandhi, Nehru and C. Rajagopalachari, and as a journalist whose job it is to follow the daily news, I can see fundamental incursions being made by the Hindutva-oriented Big Government into the idea of the Indian liberal republic so carefully built by our founders and by the millions who followed them in their struggle to get rid of the colonial yoke. India's Constitution is a blast of modern democratic freedoms in an illiberal society still wallowing in many parts in unquestioning traditions and blind beliefs.

That life-giving lamp of progressive liberal thought cannot be extinguished. It cannot. If it is, India as we know it will cease to exist. Without that guiding lamp, we will sink into a quagmire of regressive beliefs when sati is condoned (see Chapter 5 on Rajput women and jauhar), women are consigned to the home (see Chapter 5), children are violated on religious grounds (see Kathua rape case), Muslims are attacked (see list of cow-related lynchings in Chapter 3), intellectuals forced into exile (see attack on Amartya Sen), dissenters killed (Gauri Lankesh and rationalists Dabholkar, Kalburgi and Pansare), caste discrimination legitimized (Una attacks) and Bollywood transformed into a mindless, tradition-spewing dream factory (see Chapter 5 on *Padmaavat*) instead of being known for the boldly convention-challenging films that marked its beginnings. Free-spirited entrepreneurs will flee rather than submit to government diktats. Businessmen will turn into cronies living off political patronage rather than earning a just profit by satisfying paying customers.

Politics will cease to be deliberative and participative and will become the monopoly of tycoons and populist demagogues who will capture parties through money power and prevent the talented from entering. Courts and Parliament, crucial institutions designed to check political power, will instead bow before a super-powerful executive even as the media becomes a mere propaganda outlet for whoever occupies the highest political office.

Most dangerous of all, individual freedoms will cease to exist: the freedom to eat, worship, marry, love will all be taken over by the rampaging state on the pretext of nationalism and 'tradition'. The creativity of artists and intellectuals will be curtailed. Free thought and debate will be stamped out. Most tragic of all, Hinduism will be reduced to a caricature of its philosophical self.

That's why every Indian citizen needs to understand what liberalism is and why it is the only safeguard against a rampaging state and the terrifying power of religion-based nationalism. Liberals need to understand what Gandhi and Rajaji warned of decades ago. During the freedom struggle, millions participated in andolans and thousands died in the battle for freedom, both for the country and the individual. It took three years of debates in the Constituent Assembly, each Article tortuously debated, for us Indians to gain our liberal, individual-rights-centred Constitution. Now Indians have to rekindle once again that spirit of freedom, begin the second freedom movement—not from the British, but from an ideologically driven Big State determined to crush individual freedoms.

I have organized this book into five chapters: Chapter 1 is titled 'The Liberal Patriot'—as opposed to the muscular 'nationalist'—in which I contrast liberal patriotism based on inclusion and debate versus an aggressive nationalism based on hatred and demonizing the other. Chapter 2 focuses on 'The Liberal Hindu' versus political Hindus. In Chapter 3, 'The Liberal Thinker', I look at how massive government initiatives are seeking to police and regulate citizens in unprecedented ways. Chapter 4 looks at 'The Liberal Dissenter' where I show how the lives of those brave enough to voice dissent against religious majoritarian nationalism are in danger from various non-state actors loyal to the ruling ideology. In the last and final chapter, I look at 'The Liberal Woman' and her struggle against aggressive traditionalists, against those who see women's freedom as a 'femi-nazi' bid to destroy so-called 'family values.'

Through the book, I make the argument that liberals should not let their personal freedoms be destroyed in the name of a particular version of nationalism defined on ethnic or religious lines. Why do we have to keep taking the patriotism test? Instead, let's say 'I am a patriot because I am liberal, a true Hindu because I am liberal, a believer in individual freedom because I am a liberal and a warrior for gender justice because I am a liberal'. Liberal doesn't have to be a term of abuse. It can be a badge of honour, the mantra of the optimist and the proud marker of a believer in India's Constitution.

Maybe there will come a day when we can all—rural and urban, rich or poor, English-speaking hepcat or mofussil dweller—say:

'Garv se kaho hum liberal hain. Hindustan ko Hindutva ki ghulami manzoor nahin hain!'

India's liberals, don't let your personal freedoms be destroyed in the name of a particular version of 'nationalism'. Instead, say 'I am a patriot, because I am liberal. A believer in individual freedom because I am a liberal. A warrior for gender justice because I am a liberal. And as a liberal Hindu or liberal Muslim or liberal of any religion, I have no reason to go to war against any other religion.'

[1]

The Liberal Patriot

Why the liberal Indian is a greater patriot than the 'Hindutva nationalist'

Hey more chitto punno tirthe jagore dhire
Ai bharoter mahamanober sagortire . . .
Aso hey Arjo, aso Anarjo, aso Hindu Musalman
Aso aso aaj tumi Ingraj, aso Kristan
Aso Brahmin suchi karo mon, dharo haat sabar,
Aso hey patito, hoke apanito sob opomanbhar . . .
Ai bharoter mahamanober sagortire.

—*Gitabitan*, Rabindranath Tagore

[My heart wakes up to a pure pilgrimage
Come all to this India, this shoreline of great humanity . . .
Come Aryan, come non-Aryan, come Hindu, come Muslim
Come English, come Christian
Come Brahmin and hold everyone's hand
Come those who've been insulted and put down your insults in
     freedom . . .
Come all to this India, this shoreline of great humanity.]

1

Is it an act of 'nationalism' to label anyone holding different views 'anti-national' or un-Indian?

Does waving the national flag sanitize a crime and imbue the accused person with a sense of higher purpose? And is it an act of 'nationalism' to wave the national flag to defend those accused of crimes?[1]

Is it an act of 'nationalism' to assault a disabled person who is unable to stand up for the national anthem?

Is it an act of 'nationalism' to be abusive and hostile to religious minorities?

Is it an act of 'nationalism' to clamp down on any questioning of the government?

The Legacy of Liberal Patriotism

Citizens of India, it's a choice. Are you a liberal patriot? Or is your brand of nationalism one where your love of the country means hatred for someone else? The creed of the 'muscular Hindutva nationalists' is 'My country, right or wrong'—the nation as only a geographical entity defined by a particular religious and racial community. A blind 'nationalism' overwhelms any thoughtful and inclusive expression of patriotism. The desh-bhakti of Hindutva nationalists means rage against religious minorities, dissenters, communists and immigrants like the Rohingyas, liberal journalists, Christian missionaries, Western non-government organizations (NGOs), even those recently described as 'urban Naxals' and anyone who does not share their rigidly imposed view of the 'nation'. Their apparent devotion to country has degenerated into loyalty only to a single political party. Their view is, if you're not with us, you are against us. For these 'nationalists', the 'nation' is synonymous with the party, with the government to which they are blindly loyal, and with the political leaders whose 'bhakts' they are.

Can an entire nation ever be synonymous with a political party or with a single leader or a single political ideology? In a letter to Sardar Vallabhbhai Patel in 1946, B.R. Ambedkar wrote: 'You think Mr Gandhi is greater than the country. My view is different. I think the country is greater than the greatest man. You think to be Congressmen and to be nationalists are synonymous. I think a man can be a nationalist without being a Congressman.'[2] Ambedkar makes it clear here that you don't have to be a member of a certain party or loyal to a particular leader to be a patriot or a nationalist. In the first two decades after Independence, there was a recognition and respect for different perspectives—contrasting, clashing views were seen as a legitimate part of the national outlook. Disagreeing with someone did not automatically make anyone less of a patriot. For example, Netaji Subhas Chandra Bose made no secret of his anger when Mahatma Gandhi abruptly called off the 1921–22 Non-Cooperation Movement. 'It was nothing short of a calamity [calling off the movement] . . . Mahatma Gandhi was repeatedly bungling.'[3] Gandhi and Bose may have trenchantly disagreed on how to push forward the freedom struggle but they never cast doubt on each other's patriotism. C. Rajagopalachari (Rajaji), Congress stalwart and one of Gandhi's loyal lieutenants, opposed the Gandhi-led Quit India movement in 1942 on the grounds that it was harmful to India at a time there was a threat of invasion.[4] Yet, no aspersions were cast on the patriotism of Rajaji. The pledge of the liberal patriot therefore is: India belongs to me as much as to anyone else and I will not allow anyone the right to label anyone else as anti-national or un-Indian simply because their views are different from mine.

Who is the liberal patriot? To quote the liberal Minoo Masani, one of the founders of the liberal Swatantra Party,[5] 'I have been an ardent nationalist in my time . . . nationalism is like the measles. When you grow up you don't have children's diseases like chicken pox and measles . . . nationalism is a disease of foreign rule . . . of course love of the country must be there . . . but we don't want to be chauvinists . . . when you are free you don't have to go on talking about nationalism . . . nationalism has had its day . . . we can afford to relax on nationalism.'[6] Masani also says, 'The liberal is of necessity a pluralist, that is, he does not accept the predominance of any one line of thought or dogma.'[7]

To define the liberal patriot: The liberal patriot loves her country, but believes that it is precisely because she loves her country that her patriotism should not stop her from questioning her country's leaders, armed forces or other institutions that wield power over the citizen. The liberal patriot believes in equality before the law and rule of law and bringing the due process of law to every citizen. The liberal patriot is a lover of liberty and believes every citizen is innocent until proven guilty by a rigorous, impartial legal system. The liberal patriot believes in challenging the Big State or Big Government that intrudes too far into citizens' lives, stunting and even destroying the intellectual and moral integrity of citizens. Thus, the liberal patriot should always stand for limited government.

The so-called muscular Hindutva nationalists believe that 'nationalism' implies an end to all questioning, a blind worship of the armed forces and of Hindutva politicians. 'Muscular' nationalism often holds any questioning of the government or 'nation' as seditious and as acts of treason.

The liberal patriot stands for positive aspirations towards her country. The liberal patriot claims as her comrades members of diverse parties, from the BJP, Congress or regional parties, who are willing to define their patriotism on principles other than hatred and violence towards others.

Today, the word 'anti-national' is raining down on citizens' heads like a monsoon downpour. Asking questions about the government? You're 'anti-national'. An investigative journalist probing how the business interests of a VIP's son are suddenly prospering? 'Anti-national' journalist! An author returning a Sahitya Akademi award in protest against the murder of another Sahitya Akademi awardee?[8] 'Anti-national' writer! Failing to stand up for the national anthem in time or asking why the national anthem should be played in cinema halls? 'Anti-national!' Supporting the right to eat beef? 'Anti-national beef-eater!' Sceptical of army actions in Kashmir? 'Anti-national terrorist sympathizer.' Speaking in support of Adivasi communities in Chhattisgarh? 'Anti-national urban Naxal!' Students organizing protest meetings against capital punishment? Environmental activists protesting against certain development projects? 'Anti-national!' 'Anti-national!'

Charges of sedition, dating from the colonial era, enacted as Section 124-A of the Indian Penal Code (IPC) in 1898,[9] designed to repress freedom fighters from Mahatma Gandhi to Jawaharlal Nehru, are being clamped by a democratically elected government on its own citizens in the name of 'nationalism'. The act of slamming sedition charges on enemies of the Big State and the normalization of the abuse of state power cuts across party lines. In the 1970s, Indira Gandhi invoked the 'foreign hand'[10] or 'CIA agent' to brand those who opposed her. In 2011, the Tamil Nadu government headed by the then chief minister, the late Jayalalithaa, accused 3500 protestors in Kudankulam village of sedition for protesting against a nuclear power plant.[11] In 2010, when the Congress-led United Progressive Alliance (UPA) ruled in Delhi, doctor and rights activist Binayak Sen was charged with sedition. In 2016, Jawaharlal Nehru University (JNU) Students' Union president Kanhaiya Kumar was charged with sedition. In 2016, Amnesty International was also charged with sedition for organizing a campaign against victims of human rights violations in Jammu and Kashmir. Accusations of sedition by Hindutva nationalists were never as much in vogue as they are now.

This 'muscular nationalism' is manufactured. It is communal Hindutva rage; in fact, the word 'communalism' itself is India's contribution to the English language.[12] It is a demonization of Muslims and other religious minorities. It's a nationalism centred on the persona of Prime Minister Narendra Modi as the Hindu *hriday samrat*, the nationalist hero, posited as representing authentic

Bharat against foreign educated Macaulayputras, or English-speaking, foreign oriented Indians who are cut off from the grit of the Indian soil, the so-called mythical 'Lutyens elite' or 'Delhi sultanate' or 'dynastic rulers'. These words are a clever amalgam of all things foreign, privileged and somehow illegitimate. The attack on Sonia and Rahul Gandhi's 'foreign origins', the prime minister's comment that he preferred 'hard work to Harvard', the comment of the RSS affiliate, the Swadeshi Jagaran Manch, on the resignation of the chief economic adviser, Arvind Subramanian, that the next economic adviser should be one 'who believes in Indian ethos and values'[13] signals that to the 'nationalists' liberals are somehow all elite and alien, disconnected from 'Bharat', and basically un-Indian.

This is a furious nationalism. As the lustre of multiculturalism and globalization ebbs, there are big, political rewards for those who wield the power of this angry nationalism for votes—seen in the victories of Donald Trump in America, Viktor Orban in Hungary, Recep Tayyip Erdogan in Turkey, Vladimir Putin in Russia, and Modi's victory in India and his 'Bharat Mata ki jai' war cry. This virulent nationalism spills onto the Internet as diatribes against an imagined class—those called 'libtard', 'Macaulayputra' or 'Lutyens elite' on social media by Right-wing trolls—a war cry against the 'Western-educated' privileged class, against Nehru, seen as the fountainhead of this alien atheist force, grafted by the accident of birth on innocent, authentic 'real Indians', who have been deprived of their true voice by liberal Western-oriented elitists.

It's almost as if 'nationalists' believe they are fighting a culture war as well as a class war against decades of apparent dominance by a 'Left liberal' line of thinking, in which Westernized, well-heeled, well-born Nehruvians uphold faddish secularism against the 'nationalist' urges of the majority.[14]

But modern India's founders, those who laid down the founding principles of Indian patriotism, were neither angry, nor hate-filled, nor loaded with injured pride, nor did they demonize imagined enemies. They did not visualize a binary opposition between Indian and British or between East and West. Rabindranath Tagore, Mahatma Gandhi and Jawaharlal Nehru opposed British imperialism with all their heart but also spoke of learning from and appreciating the British people. Rammohan Roy, the father of Indian liberal patriotism, wrote how Indian minds may benefit from contact with Englishmen: '. . . the greater our intercourse with European gentlemen, the greater will be our improvement in literary, social and political affairs, a fact which can be easily proved by comparing the condition of my countrymen who have enjoyed it.'[15] Gopal Krishna Gokhale, whom Gandhi called his guru, wrote about how the majority of Indians remained sunk in ignorance, barbarism and degradation and needed to be exposed to modern Western civilization and thought. As B.R. Nanda writes, Gokhale 'hated foreign rule, but he did not blame all the ills from which India suffered on the British. He wanted her to shake off the shackles of social and economic backwardness as well as political subjugation. He wanted to turn the encounter with the Raj into an opportunity for building a secular, modern and democratic society.'[16]

For Gandhi, love of one's own country did not mean defining this love through the hatred of the other, whether within the country or outside. 'I am not anti-English, I am not anti-British . . . I am not anti any government . . . I am anti-untruth, anti-humbug and anti-injustice. So long as the government spells injustice it may regard me as the enemy, implacable enemy,' said Gandhi.[17] He also said, 'My personal religion . . . enables me to serve my countrymen without hurting Englishmen or for that matter, anybody else. What I would not be prepared to do to my blood brother, I would not do to an Englishman.'[18] Gandhi wrote in 1918, 'India would be nowhere without Englishmen. If the British do not win, to whom shall we go claiming equal partnership? Shall we go to the victorious German or Turk or Afghan for it? The liberty loving English will surely yield after seeing we have laid down our lives for them.'[19] In Tagore's words, 'East and West are complementary to each other . . . West is necessary to the East . . . I have a deep love and a great respect for the British race as human beings.'

India's freedom movement was a highly liberal force, based on the search for liberal progressive humanism. Our founding patriotism—the patriotism of Rammohan Roy, Tagore, Gandhi, Nehru, Ambedkar and Gokhale—in its commitment to pluralism and inclusiveness has been overwhelmingly liberal.[20] It defined patriotism as a call of duty to serve the nation through talent, education and moral courage, not patriotism as a weapon of destruction. The Hindutva nationalist government born in 2014 has shattered the fragile yet prevailing liberal consensus that had existed since 1947.

In February 2016, at a meeting of vice chancellors, then Human Resources Development (HRD) minister Smriti Irani decreed that all central universities were required to fly the national flag on a 207 feet tall flag mast. In November that year, the Supreme Court, in a judgement in tune with the Modi-era zeitgeist, laid down that the national anthem was to be played at cinema halls in order to 'instill a feeling of committed patriotism and nationalism'. That order has now been amended[21] but at the time 'nationalists' went on the rampage, wreaking nationalist rage on even disabled persons who were unable to stand up during 'Jana Gana Mana'.[22] Ironically, Tagore, author of the anthem, argued all his life against the dangers of a nationalism which worshipped the state or a race or even the sanctity of geographical boundaries. As he said, 'I love India not because I cultivate the idolatry of geography, not because I have had the chance to be born in her soil but because she has saved through tumultuous ages the living words that have issued from the illuminated consciousness of her great ones.'[23] The liberal patriot believes in the ideals India represents, not in an exclusive, isolated geographical enclave of cultural paranoia.

On social media, anyone seen as opposing the 'nationalist' government is hounded and harassed. Certain journalists are 'anti-national', authors like Arundhati Roy are 'anti-national', actors like Prakash Raj are 'anti-national', Muslims are by definition 'anti-national', NGOs are 'anti-national', and students of JNU are 'anti-national'. 'Anti-national' is the blanket term to delegitimize and marginalize all those who raise questions, those the Hindutva nationalist government sees as its enemy. 'Anti-national' is the sweeping indictment that renders dissenters and critics voiceless. Any critic of the government is not only a 'traitor', a 'communist' or a 'dynasty worshipper' but someone who must go to the national enemy or Pakistan. During the Bihar election campaign in 2015, BJP president Amit Shah declared that there would be fireworks in Pakistan if the BJP was defeated.[24] During the 2014 general election campaign, BJP leader Giriraj Singh said those 'opposing Narendra Modi are looking at Pakistan, and such people will have a place in Pakistan and not in India'.[25] In Gujarat 2017, the prime minister accused his predecessor, Manmohan Singh, of treason and accused the Congress of plotting with Pakistan to install Ahmed Patel, a Muslim, as Gujarat chief minister.[26]

Another phrase has recently been added to the 'nationalist' vocabulary to describe a critic or dissenter: the 'urban Naxal' or 'half Maoist'. In late 2017, an Elgaar Parishad was held in Pune to commemorate 200 years of the battle of Bhima Koregaon, organized by eminent judges and academics. As the event was in progress, violence erupted during Dalit protests. On 6 June 2018, five academics and activists were arrested and charged with having 'Maoist' links, for instigating violence during the protests of 1 January 2018 and charged under harsh sections of IPC. One of the arrested academics was Shoma Sen, a Nagpur-based professor of English. 'I no longer understand what is the definition of "anti-national". Possessing books on Marx, Lenin and Mao does not make anyone anti-national. Activism is suddenly a derided term,' Shoma Sen's daughter wrote for a website.[27] The news channel Republic TV claimed in a broadcast on 4 July 2018 that human rights lawyer Sudha Bharadwaj had allegedly identified herself in a letter as 'Comrade Advocate Sudha Bharadwaj' and written to a 'Comrade Prakash' saying 'a Kashmir-like situation has to be created in India'. In a public statement, Bharadwaj denied this and called Republic TV's allegations 'ridiculous, scurrilous, false and completely unsubstantiated'.[28] On 28 August 2018 Sudha Bharadwaj, along with other rights campaigners, Gautam Navlakha, Varavara Rao, Arun Ferreira and Vernon Gonsalves, were arrested by the Pune police in connection with the events around the Bhima-Koregaon protests and Elgaar Parishad. The police said they had recovered a letter allegedly linking them to a plot to assassinate the prime minister.[29] Voicing a grave note of concern at the arrest of the activists, the Supreme Court held on 29 August 2018, 'Dissent is the safety valve of democracy. If dissent is not allowed, then the pressure cooker may burst.'[30] For the liberal, dissent is not just the safety valve but the very essence of democracy, the most fundamental aspect of freedom of expression and an extension of the fundamental right to think. It is an integral part also of the equality of citizens who in a democracy are empowered to hold the powerful to account through questioning and criticism.

* * *

On 30 July 2015, Mumbai-based chartered accountant Yakub Memon, convicted in the 1993 Mumbai bomb blast case, was hanged in Nagpur Central Jail. The death sentence on Memon was challenged by a range of personalities, from Supreme Court judges to former intelligence chiefs.[31] Before the hanging, a group of citizens petitioned the President of India to consider Memon's mercy petition.[32] Nationalists flew into a blustering rage. BJP member of Parliament Sakshi Maharaj declared that all those asking for mercy for Memon were 'anti-national' and should be charged with sedition.[33] Any reasonable debate over the death penalty or opposing views on capital punishment were swept aside in the thundering accusation: 'anti national!'

Rule of the mob, on the street and in cyberspace, takes the place of rule of law when 'nationalist' sentiments are whipped up sky high.

Yet, as Masani reminds us, for the liberal the essential prerequisite of democracy is rule of law or due process of law. Individual freedom is only possible when there is rule of law. 'It is the rule of law [which] protects the citizen from arbitrary action on part of the government and gives him the protection of the Court in case the law is violated. Obviously when Courts are not independent and there is no rule of law, rule by parliamentary majority can be highly tyrannical and undemocratic.'[34]

The increase in instances of bloody lynching on the streets[35] is only a more extreme manifestation of the desire to do away with due process of law and opt for street retribution. High-decibel trials by media, knee-jerk reactions of the government and the emotional tone of some judgements[36] indicate a climate where 'majority sentiment' rules supreme.[37]

Politicians often use strong legal provisions (for example, the sedition charges slapped on the JNU students) as a quick way to win votes. In the absence of any systematic attempt to reform the police,[38] with news TV often seeking and creating an 'anti-national enemy' in prime-time broadcasts, the syndrome of the witch hunt, or the 'guilty-until-proven-innocent' premise (the opposite of the democratic principle of innocent until proven guilty) begins to gain public legitimacy, further perpetuating the repeated flouting of due legal process.

For the liberal who seeks to invigorate the liberal position for twenty-first-century India, the law and equality before the law must be the cornerstones of the new liberal ideology, replacing the old discredited political symbolism that some so-called earlier 'secular' governments have practised, a secularism which has often only masqueraded as liberal ideology. Secular governments too have often been motivated by the hunger for power over other considerations, which has on occasion resulted in a repudiation of the rule of law and the idea of equality before the law.[39] This drive for power by successive Indian governments, to try and cultivate vote banks through law-making, has led to a divorce of moral values and ethical principles from the flood of legislation and regulations that only pretend to reflect the law. In reality, because of the lust for power and vote banks, the moral basis of the law is in danger of being bled to death by a thousand cuts.[40] The majority sentiment, or voter sentiment, cannot be the basis for the law because, as Masani writes, for the liberal 'the concept of majority rule in countries which are not homogenous is a particularly pernicious one . . . in India it would mean domination of Hindus over the Muslims, Sikhs, Christians and other minorities. Majority rule is not democracy and can often be undemocratic.'

It may be interesting to add another of Masani's thoughts here: 'It is quite clear that a government which is not limited to essential purposes, but dominates economic, educational, literary and artistic life of a country cannot be a democratic one.'[41]

A year after Memon's hanging, on 9 February 2016, the JNU Students' Union held a protest meeting against the execution of alleged Kashmiri militant Afzal Guru, who was hanged in Delhi's Tihar Jail on 9 February 2013. Later, there were reports and allegations that the slogan 'Bharat tere tukde honge inshallah inshallah' was apparently heard at the protest. It was also alleged that the JNU Students' Union president Kanhaiya Kumar and his companions had raised them, even though these accusations have still not been proven. On 12 February 2016, Kanhaiya Kumar and two other JNU students, Umar Khalid and Anirban Bhattacharyya, were arrested and charged with sedition. The same government, comprising many student leaders like information technology minister Ravi Shankar Prasad and finance minister Arun Jaitley who as students had marched against Indira Gandhi's Emergency, revealed a ferocious antipathy towards students who dared to believe in free speech. What would the 'nationalists' have made of the Oxford Union debate in 1933, which argued on the motion, 'This House will under no circumstances fight for its King and Country'? What would they have made of the University of California, Berkeley's student protests of the 1960s, which fired up youth all over the world and became beacons of free speech and academic freedom? When students may raise anti-establishment slogans but surely it is not the content of these slogans but the spirit of their rebellious independence that a democratic government should consider.

What kind of 'nationalism' is this that targets the free thinker? This 'nationalism' is only a euphemism for targeting Muslims, liberals, dissenters and any critic of Hindutva nationalism, where the word 'Pakistan' is a metaphor for protestor or 'Muslim', a not-so-subtle painting of every Muslim citizen of India as loyal to the enemy country. This kind of nationalism becomes a licence to pursue witch-hunts and ostracism, leaving little space for any diversity, pluralism or contrarian views.

Liberal citizens of India, you are not nationalists of this aggressive violent kind. Instead, you are liberal patriots who salute every citizen as equal, and refuse any salutation if the only objective of that ritual is to use the flag as a stick to beat other citizens. The liberal patriot seeks to heal every instance of mistreatment meted out to fellow citizens and refuses to join the chorus for the national anthem if the only objective is to drown out calls for justice for other citizens.

To stain the idealistic Indian flag with hatred is the greatest disrespect to the basic values symbolized in both flag and anthem. Liberals who have fought for justice, who have struggled for equal rights and access to laws for all, who believe student protests are an important component of campus life where intellectual freedom offered by a university provides young minds the capacity to choose, argue and find their own way of thinking, are surely better servants of flag and anthem.

Nobel laureate Amartya Sen writes in his book, *Argumentative Indian*, that any defence of an 'Indian' tradition is to defend a tradition of argument and counter-argument, any defence of an 'Indian' identity is also to defend an identity that is open to being contested, any defence of 'Indian' values is to defend the values of doubt, uncertainty and acceptance of difference. The stamping out of difference, the quelling of argument and the burial of argument is the most un-Indian thing of all. Anyone who seeks to end that dialogue process or stamp out the subcontinental identity-in-dialogue is turning his back on Indian patriotism.[42]

Tagore was a die-hard critic of this furious xenophobic nationalism, even though he was one of India's greatest patriots. Tagore stood for humanism above nationalism, for a union of East and West above the narrow confines of racial pride or religious exclusiveness. In Tagore's vision, the new India born after Independence would not be one based on exclusion or hatred, instead it would be an India which would belong to all of humanity. Tagore said, '. . . the Nation which is the organized self-interest of a whole people, where it is *least* [emphasis added] human and *least* [emphasis added] spiritual . . . the Nation [is] a thick mist of a shifting nature covering the sun itself.'[43] For Tagore, those in blind thrall to the geographical and racial nation were always in danger of forsaking the values of humanism and spirituality, the nation being the least spiritually enriching and humanist of all entities.

Gandhi's patriotism wasn't narrowly nationalistic either. He opposed the British Raj with all his powers but constantly emphasized that the British people were welcome to stay on in India as equals. Indian patriotism is not about making enemies of other human beings, it's about making enemies of injustice, oppression and prejudice. To reduce the love of a country and nation-building to the service of a political party, is to tragically undermine those who have striven and continue to strive to keep alive the liberal dream of 1947.

* * *

We have seen that the very definition of modern Indian patriotism as articulated by Gandhi, Nehru, Tagore, Gokhale and Ambedkar is in fact a highly liberal one. Therefore, it is the liberal Indian who is the heir and legatee of the liberal patriotism of India's founders. As far as the 'Hindutva nationalists' are concerned, the Hindu Mahasabha and the RSS stayed away from the Gandhi-led freedom movement, the RSS kept 'strictly' aloof from the 1942 Quit India movement. Vinayak Damodar Savarkar, president of the Hindu Mahasabha, urged Mahasabha members to 'stick to their posts and continue to perform their regular duties', and Shyama Prasad Mukherjee who would found the Hindu Right-wing Bharatiya Jana Sangh in 1951, was actually a Bengal minister when freedom protests in Midnapur were being ruthlessly suppressed by the British. In 1930, during the salt satyagraha that began with the Dandi march, RSS founder K.B. Hedgewar sent out the directive that the Sangh would not participate; however, also stating that those wishing to take part individually were not prohibited. Hedgewar himself participated as an individual.[44] In the past, Hindutva outfits have never accepted India's national flag. The RSS mouthpiece, the *Organiser*, wrote in an editorial dated 17 July 1947, 'the word three is in itself evil and a flag having three colours will certainly produce a very bad psychological effect and is injurious to the country.'[45]

Hindutva nationalists today claim a monopoly on patriotism, but it was the Hindutva nationalist ideology that took the life of Mahatma Gandhi, India's greatest patriot. Hindutva nationalists have generally been opposed to the Gandhian world view, which emphatically rejected the Hindu Rashtra. Nathuram Godse, who shot Gandhi on 30 January 1948 (he disingenuously claimed to have quit the RSS before he pulled the trigger), had once been a member of both the RSS and the Hindu Mahasabha. According to a letter written by then home minister Sardar Vallabhbhai Patel to Golwalkar dated 11 September 1948 after the news of Gandhi's slaying, 'RSS men expressed joy and distributed sweets after Gandhiji's death'.[46] Do the descendants of those who had a tenuous connection with India's freedom struggle now have monopoly rights on India's patriotism?

Nationalism cannot be used as a weapon to clamp down on freedom of thought. Nationalism cannot become a piece of ticker-tape pasted across citizens' mouths to stop them from speaking. To conclude this section, let's hear once again from Rajaji: 'No theory of civil life, no ism will work satisfactorily unless the citizens in a democracy are willing to undertake responsibility of thinking and judging for themselves . . . instead of independent thinking and free judgement, the manners of parrots have been growing . . . a parrot culture has seized the country . . . what I plead for is a climate of independent thinking among citizens . . . without this essential accompaniment, self-government through democracy will prove itself to be a house of cards.'[47]

Islamophobia against Whom?

Pervez Hoodbhoy, veteran campaigner for civil liberties in Pakistan, writes, 'Liberals in Pakistan have been an endangered species for a while . . . liberals everywhere are winning only rarely. It's so much easier to be sectarian and nationalist than accommodative and universal.'[48] Substitute 'Pakistan' for India and he could well be describing the way liberals in our country are cast as unpatriotic, treasonous, anti-Indian and losers in the argument.

Hindutva 'nationalists' believe there is no place for the liberal in a world being pummelled by Islamic terrorism. They believe when innocents are repeatedly being slaughtered by violent Islamism, it's unacceptable to talk of avoiding the language of hatred or upholding the rule of law or even avoiding religious prejudice. A liberal who doesn't chant the mantra of aggressive counterterrorism is branded as 'appeaser of Muslims', 'apologist of terrorism,' 'mullah-lover', et al. Hindutva nationalists thus have a Muslim-centric world view, their 'nationalism' defined almost entirely by their Islamophobia. Are you willing to condemn Islam? Are you willing to hold Muslims perpetually guilty? Are you willing to unleash hatred against all Muslims, discriminate against them, deny them housing, abuse them on social media, obliterate India's proud Mughal history, see every Hindu–Muslim romance as an evil plot by Muslim men to start a 'love jihad'? If not, you're not a 'nationalist'. In fact, the Islamophobia of Hindutva nationalists is a mirror image of the Hindu phobia among Islamist hardliners and their strategic allies in the Pakistani establishment. Despite their flamboyant hatred towards Muslims and Pakistan, Hindutva nationalists' ultimate desire seems to be to reshape the idea of India along the lines of a theocratic Iran or Saudi Arabia; they often behave like imitators of Islamic zealots in Pakistan.[49] Of course, Hindutva nationalism is not just Islamophobia. It is also Dalit phobia, feminist phobia, beef-eater phobia, JNU phobia, liberal phobia, NGO phobia and the phobia of any 'other'.

Do Hindutva nationalists understand that for every Islamist terrorist there are Muslims who are daily confronting the militants within their own religion? As many as a staggering 50,000 have died in the Kashmir violence between 1947 and 2009,[50] the overwhelming number of them local Kashmiri Muslims.[51] It was the courageous late Asma Jahangir who risked her life daily against fundamentalists. (She died after a period of illness on 11 February 2018.) Muslim liberals are in the vanguard of the fight against Islamic terror.

On the night of 1 July 2016, in the worst terrorist attack in the history of Bangladesh, terrorists struck a cafe called the Holey Artisan Bakery in a posh locality in Dhaka. It was a brutal attack in which twenty-nine were killed. Three names stand out from among the victims: twenty-year-old Faraaz Ayaaz Hossain, undergraduate student at Emory University in the US, his friend, nineteen-year-old Abinta Kabir, also studying at the same university, and forty-five-year-old Dhaka-based management professional Ishrat Akhond. During that attack, educated and chillingly polite terrorists[52] asked if anyone present could recite the Koran and offered to release those who could. Faraaz was indeed able to recite the Koran and was allowed to leave the cafe. But the braveheart youth chose to stay on and die with his friends, one of them nineteen-year-old Tarishi Jain from India, a student at the University of California, Berkeley. Abinta Kabir too chose to stay on and die.

The fiery, independent-minded Ishrat Akhond had always refused to wear the hijab. When terrorists asked her to recite from the Koran, she too refused, choosing death over a sacrifice of her principles. With raw courage as their shield, Hossain, Kabir and Akhond, unarmed liberal Muslims, faced down hate-driven religious fanatics and died as the heroes they were. In May 2016, the Sheikh Hasina government of Bangladesh imposed the death sentence on Jamaat-e-Islami chief Motiur Rahman Nizami, the head of an armed militia charged with rape, genocide and torture well as colluding with the Pakistan army in the 1971 Bangladesh war. A Muslim politician put to death an orthodox Muslim religious leader.

On 4 January 2011, the liberal Pakistani politician Salman Taseer was assassinated by one of his own bodyguards, Malik Mumtaz Qadri, who, in an open marketplace, emptied his AK-47 into the body of the man he was supposed to protect. Taseer was killed because religious zealots loathed and feared his campaign against Pakistan's fearsome blasphemy laws. Almost sixty persons have been killed in Pakistan since 1990 for alleged blasphemy. From 1987 to 2014, over 1300 persons were accused of blasphemy, many of them liberal Muslims.[53] The savage torture and killing of twenty-five-year-old liberal student Mashal Khan in April 2017 at Abdul Wali Khan University in Mardan only because he apparently held socialist and Sufi views reveals the grave dangers liberal Pakistani Muslims face. Liberal Muslims are fighting terrorists and zealots with their lives, and carrying on the fight in the face of looming death, yet Hindutva 'nationalists' want to taint every Muslim with the same brush of 'terrorist'.

Is the Islamic terrorist the only entity to use religious identity to perpetuate violence? Surely many political and social movements have similarly used identity for violent campaigns. Should we therefore say that *all* Tamils are Liberation Tigers of Tamil Eelam (LTTE) supporters, *all* tribals are Maoists, *all* north-easterners are insurgents and *all* Sikhs are supporters of Khalistan? To hold Islam itself guilty of terror would mean saying that the Tamil sentiment is responsible for the LTTE or a belief in Marxism is directly responsible for Maoist killings. If Islamic terrorism forces hatred and prejudice against Muslims, don't we begin to speak the language of the terrorist? This is the language that the 'muscular nationalists' would like to speak and use to legitimize their war on minorities.

The liberal is not against religious traditions. Gandhi, who in this essay, we are hailing as India's greatest liberal, deeply respected traditions and sought to build change on the basis of tradition. Yet the liberal stands against militant traditionalists who want to hark back to a mythical golden age to silence those who uphold the cause of modern civil liberties and individual freedoms and rule of law.[54] Those who argue today for rule of law, for justice, for individual liberties and a patriotic commitment to constitutional values are vilified because the only law in place seems to be the law of the mob and of force. Liberals are cast as 'anti-tradition' if they argue for the rule of law. For instance, on TV, anyone arguing for a law-based approach to allegations of human rights abuse in Jammu and Kashmir is immediately shouted down as a so-called 'terrorist sympathizer' and as an 'anti-Hindu' voice. Why is arguing for an impartial legal process, in certain instances like the Kathua rape and murder case, seen as an assault on 'Hindutva' sensibilities? Without laws there can be no legally guaranteed freedoms; without individual freedom, the greatest catalyst for change is lost.

The voice of the liberal strongly counters the voice of the militant and the terrorist, which is why liberals need to speak up and refuse to be silenced by 'nationalist' war cries. Liberals need to demand that society and state uphold the essence of the law, which is justice and fairness. If state institutions are not seen to provide justice, if law courts and the police are seen by the public to be on the same side of the powers that be,[55] if the state begins to resemble a partisan militia which imposes its force on those who do not accept its authority, militant ideas will only grow. Unless there is an attempt to reach out and engage in the crucial battle of ideas, terrorists will only gain more supporters. Can a killing-machine Big State or Big Government 'encounter' them all?

Kashmir: Patriot Games

Let's examine a recent reflexive moment in 'muscular Hindutva nationalism': the 'encounter killing' of Kashmiri militant Burhan Wani. On 8 July 2016, in the small village of Bamdoora in the Kokernag region of Kashmir, twenty-one-year-old Burhan Wani and two others were killed in an 'encounter'. Wani, the self-proclaimed commander of the Kashmiri militant group Hizbul Mujahideen, prided himself on his social media profile; in fact he was something of a social media phenomenon. Repeatedly uploading photos of himself in full militant regalia, his mission was murderous. Yet, Wani had achieved folk hero status among Kashmiri youth as a sort of romantic Che Guevara figure whose machine gun was (for them) an avenging sword, his defiance seen by his fans as an act of manhood against the Indian army.

After the 'encounter', photos of a dead T-shirt-clad Wani circulated fast. A spontaneous mass uprising flared up across the Kashmir Valley. By the end of the revolt, ninety-six had died and 15,000 civilians and 4000 security forces were injured.[56] Today, protests still simmer.

Hindutva nationalists tout the killing of Burhan as an act of muscular nationalist assertion by a powerful government. But, surely, any so-called 'encounter killing', or killing that takes place outside the judicial system, should be abhorrent and repugnant in a democracy? Liberals must thus roundly condemn the 'encounter killing'. Encounter killings in India illustrate the breakdown of the rule of the law and a terrifying lawless mentality among law enforcers. The argument is made that given the slow and tortuous justice system, 'Dirty Harry' cops who simply pull the trigger on criminals are making society safer. But are they? In Mumbai, policemen known as 'encounter specialists' gunned down members of the criminal underworld between 1999 and 2001 and were unthinkingly glorified by Bollywood. The Yogi Adityanath government in Uttar Pradesh has also initiated an 'encounter raj' in which fifty 'criminals' have been killed in 'encounters' since 2017.[57]

As we have seen, Gandhi opposed the Big State precisely because it is capable of massive use of force and legitimizes and permits the use of violence. On the one hand governments abdicate responsibility in maintaining law and order and on the other tacitly endorse violence. If governments are accused of staging 'fake encounters', why shouldn't vigilantes do the same? If governments are accused of being complicit in riots, such as in Uttar Pradesh and human rights abuse in Kashmir or they stand by and do nothing in the face of the depredations of violence-inclined cultural outfits like the Karni Sena, they signal that non-government actors for violence have been given permission to do what they want.

Sometimes governments simply outsource violence to non-state actors, thereby escaping accountability. A Congress government once created a terror-spreading Jarnail Singh Bhindranwale in Punjab in the 1980s; today's BJP-led government rarely condemns terror-spreading cattle-protectors or gau rakshaks. Gandhi regarded big governments or the mega state with such deep suspicion precisely because of the violence they are capable of. That's why the Big State or the big government has to be rolled back from enforcing its writ on citizens through various forms of violence. The Big State normalizes violence in society, since it imposes its writ by violence.

So-called 'encounter killings' or killings outside the justice system substitute the law with violent vigilantism, due process with criminality, justice with bloody retribution. Every encounter begets more criminals both within and outside security agencies.[58] The government cannot mimic a terrorist. The dignity of the Indian republic, based on the will of the people, cannot be reduced to the level of a street gangster who murders his enemies in cold blood. If the Indian state was committed to the rule of law, shouldn't Wani have been brought to trial and sentenced if convicted? Should the circumstances of his death not be probed? By demanding a thorough probe into the circumstances that led to Wani's sudden killing, accountability on the part of the security forces and proof that they opened fire only as a last resort, by insisting that the Big State does not get away with 'extrajudicial killings', the liberal patriot—perhaps caricatured as 'human rights wallahs'—protects the rule of law. By contrast, 'muscular nationalists' champion the cause of a so-called tough state that hands out retributive justice bypassing the rule of law.

The demand for justice means holding state agencies accountable. The liberal patriot is not being a 'terrorist sympathizer', as many will say she is, when she asks: What were the circumstances of Wani's death? Why did he have to be killed? Could he not have been captured, arrested and brought to justice? The UK battled Irish Republican Army (IRA) terrorism for decades but still upheld the cause of justice. The Birmingham Six who were convicted of terrorism but later found to have been wrongfully prosecuted were not only let off but even awarded compensation.[59]

Liberal patriots demand that the state act against perpetrators of terror and violence but act lawfully. It is the commitment to rule of law which alone can distinguish between terrorist violence and lawful use of force by the government. Only when the legitimacy and credibility of government authority is restored does the terrorist lose his raison d'etre.

Today, militants like Wani, young, fiercely and ideologically motivated and addicted to violence no longer hide their identities; instead, they display their aims and ideology on social media. Thousands of youth flocked to Wani's funeral as they did even to the funerals of Lashkar militants killed post 2016. Why are so many young Kashmiri men thronging to militants' funerals? Why is the gun increasingly attractive, glamorous and seductive for them?[60] Because successive governments in Jammu and Kashmir have failed to deliver and been seen to have failed to deliver justice, welfare and individual freedoms. The counter-narrative of a dignified existence with the rest of India is simply not strong enough. When extreme force is used to hold down a populace, they too will hit back with extreme violence. Violence is the mother of more violence.

Bad ideas flourish when there are fertile conditions for them; they can only be fought with better ideas, not by just wiping out the practitioners of those bad ideas. In 2005, when then prime minister Manmohan Singh apologized to the Sikhs for the 1984 riots, an act described as a 'Gandhian moment of moral clarity' and 'a singular act of political courage', it became a powerful idea against the Sikh sense of injustice. In 2002, when the late Mufti Mohammed Sayeed, Peoples Democratic Party (PDP) leader and the former chief minister of Jammu and Kashmir, initiated the 'healing touch' of a public reach-out to Kashmiris at large, trying to minimize the interference of the army in daily life and creating a people-friendly welfarist government, he brought forward an idea that frontally challenged zealots. Wrote Rajaji when Sheikh Abdullah was arrested in 1953: 'A statement has been made by a Pakistan minister that "any one lacking in love for Islam and the Holy Quran cannot be a true Pakistani". We too have politicians who talk increasingly of being pro-Pakistani and (not) loyal citizens. We cannot apply this loyalty test to Sheikh. It is a breach of liberty. To impose a loyalty test and intern a man is to follow the statecraft of a bygone era. The essential principle is forgotten that punishment can be awarded only for acts and not opinions held, disclosed or undisclosed.'[61]

Patriotism tests and loyalty tests have no place in the twenty-first century when liberty and justice should mark how a state views its citizens. There should be zero tolerance of terror, as well as zero tolerance of hate and manifestations of hate. Where the 'nationalist' argues for summary killings, the liberal argues for justice. State and society institutions need to go the extra mile and demonstrate their moral superiority and capacity for rule of law and fair play. In this constant demand, Indian liberals have a proud inheritance; it is they who stood by the rights of victims of state violence and campaigned for democratic liberties. It is they who have constantly pulled every

government towards constitutional principles, be it during the
Emergency or the communal riots of 1984 and 2002.

The liberal impulses of many citizens came to the fore when
many, following in the footsteps of Gandhi, Nehru and Jayaprakash
Narayan, fought for democracy after it was snatched away in 1975.
Civil liberty groups like the People's Union for Civil Liberties
(PUCL) and the People's Union for Democratic Rights (PUDR)
intervened on behalf of the victims of the 1984 riots, while in the
aftermath of the 2002 Gujarat riots, liberal Indians and rights groups
acted as bridge-builders between Muslims and an Indian state they
had ceased to trust.

The liberal Indian is accused of not supporting the cause of
the Indian army, of not supporting men at arms in the fight against
secessionists who question India's existence and integrity.[62] Liberals
are apparently ranged on the side of Kashmir's stone-pelters,
turning a blind eye to the machinations of Pakistan in the Kashmir
Valley. Liberal Indians are accused on social media of being part
of the 'Bharat ke tukde tukde gang', so named after the supposed
'Bharat tere tukde honge' slogans raised at JNU on 9 February 2016.

Liberal Indians are painted into a sinister corner of fifth
columnists who refuse to see Afzal Guru—accused in the terrorist
plot to attack Parliament in 2001—who was hanged in 2013, as
the 'terrorist' the 'nationalists' insist he apparently was. Yet, Afzal
Guru's guilt was cast in serious doubt and questioned by many
distinguished lawyers as well as by human rights groups,[63] as was
his secretive grim hanging. Afzal was executed by the Congress-
led UPA which loudly and vociferously proclaims its secularism
but whose illiberal impulses have been glaringly exposed over the
years. In the quest for popularity, to bolster its own 'nationalist'
credentials, the government did not initiate a debate or consultation
on a highly contested death sentence; instead it surrendered to the
ghoulish death calls of so-called 'muscular' nationalism. Upholding
the death sentence on 4 August 2005, the Supreme Court held: 'The
collective conscience of the society will only be satisfied if the capital

punishment is awarded to the offender.' But the question may be asked here, what is the 'collective conscience'? Can the awarding of the death penalty itself not be a cause of debate, be a response to what is defined as the 'collective conscience' and can the citizen not ask these questions?

Why can't a citizen of India question a verdict of capital punishment without being called a 'traitor' by politicians? Why could the political executive not have risen above the 'collective conscience' in the Afzal Guru case, and in the light of the powerful arguments made on the lack of proper legal representation re-examine whether there was grounds for mercy for Afzal Guru? I believe it ought to have been done. Sometimes, insidiously and tragically, too much attention seems to be paid to public sentiments and mood even as governments succumb to the temptation to please and not lead. Today, Afzal Guru's execution continues to be a festering sore in Kashmir. In some quarters, he has even acquired the status of a martyr.

As dawn broke on 10 February 2018, the Sunjuwan military camp in Kashmir was attacked. It is believed to have been carried out by a group called the Afzal Guru Squad, fast becoming a serious challenge for security forces in the Valley. Coming as it did in early February, the attack was seen as timed to coincide with the death of Guru. But then, where there is death there is also life, and darkness falls with the promise of daybreak. In a small house in Sopore, a lamp still burns the midnight oil, and with it burns almost unnoticed a small triumph of the idea of India, one that would bring a smile to the faces of Gandhi and Nehru. There, in that house sits a bright-eyed boy called Ghalib Guru, bent over his books—Afzal's son, a school topper who dreams of becoming a doctor. He's a fan of the actor Hrithik Roshan and the cricketer A.B. de Villiers, and says with a grin, 'I hope to be able to study in AIIMS one day.'[64]

By campaigning to make the state more humane, the liberal Indian, lover of liberty and individual rights, campaigner for the limited government, passionate advocate of equality before the law, is more of a nation-builder than those arguing for a blood and iron state policy. Those who believe that pouring in more troops is the only way to subdue and bring to heel the recalcitrant Kashmir are ignorant of the long-term effects of militarism. For the liberal, terrorism can't be fought by adopting the same disrespect for values as the 'enemy', because terror can't be conquered by counterterror. Gandhi's courageous ideal of satyagraha was not passive resistance. Instead, it was a constant struggle for higher values, values that are morally superior to the enemy's, means that are far nobler, far more decent than the terrorist would ever adopt.

When former prime minister Manmohan Singh reached out to all aggrieved parties[65] in Kashmir, was the government letting down Indian interests and showing weakness in the face of bare-fanged militancy? No, in fact it was a sign that the government recognized that at the bottom of the azaadi demand, on the fringes of the anti-India slogans, was a cry for justice for Kashmiris, a cry for equal citizenship in India, as well as a cry for liberty from suspicion from the Indian Big State.

Manmohan Singh was able to successfully 'soften' the India–Pakistan border by encouraging cross-border trade and people-to-people contacts. But paradoxically, a muscular 'nationalist' government has created an unprecedented atmosphere of violence in Kashmir that is singeing the country every day. A total of 263 soldiers were killed over 2014–17 in contrast to 177 in the previous four years; the number of civilians killed in 2017 was the highest in the last four years, at fifty-seven.[66] In the Manmohan Singh years, even the 2008 Mumbai terror attack did not see the kind of escalation in violence in Kashmir as we are seeing now.[67] The BJP–PDP government has fallen in Jammu and Kashmir, the successive breaking points of the BJP–PDP alliance being the Kathua rape and murder, the failure of the Ramzan ceasefire and the high-profile killing of journalist Shujaat Bukhari on 14 June 2018. So, which approach works better in Kashmir? The muscular approach or the liberal one?

* * *

On 9 April 2017, during the Srinagar bypolls, stone-pelting mobs took on the army. Amid riotous youth, in a bizarre attempt at crowd control, Indian army major Leetul Gogoi strapped a local artisan and resident of Budgam, twenty-seven-year-old Farooq Dar, to the bonnet of an army jeep. Gogoi then drove through half a dozen villages using Dar, bound by his chest to the front of the jeep, as a human shield.

By the time the jeep finally stopped at a CRPF camp, an innocent Kashmiri had been publicly humiliated and forced into helpless indignity, even as 'muscular nationalists' hailed[68] Gogoi, who was later even awarded a commendation by the army. 'Was I an animal to be tied and exhibited in that way?' Dar later asked. As the Internet nationalists crowed, actor, BJP leader and social media nationalist Paresh Rawal even suggested that author Arundhati Roy, known for her pro-Azaadi views on Kashmir, be similarly strapped to a jeep. Rawal later deleted this tweet in May 2017.[69]

The image of Dar tied to the bonnet of a jeep went viral. It became a textbook symbol of individual powerlessness against a military machine. 'Muscular' nationalists were thrilled at this assertion of machismo by the army, apparently unaware of the Geneva Convention in which human shields are regarded as war crimes.[70]

That image of Dar should repel every liberal Indian. It showed a helpless Kashmiri reduced to grinding dishonour by an army whose presence is already the focus of overwhelming resentment. In fact, such an image does a disservice to the army, to the many officers and soldiers who have gained the confidence of Kashmir's villagers through strenuous flood relief and educational and other welfare schemes, often winning hearts for troops in the Valley. This was not crowd control and effective soldiering; it was an act of muscle-flexing dominance, of demonstrating power and of ignoring the context in which the army operates in Kashmir.

When you occupy almost every backyard, town park and country lane, your overwhelming presence cannot underline hostile aggression but must attempt to uphold 'people-friendly' methods. Even if the act was unavoidable and a way had to be cleared for the convoy, extreme tact and sensitivity goes a long way in sending out reassuring optics. A lone stout-hearted citizen–soldier spoke out on Gogoi's folly. 'The image of a stone pelter tied in front of a jeep as a human shield will forever haunt the Indian army and the nation,' tweeted Lt Gen. H.S. Panag on 14 April 2017. The liberal patriot is a better well-wisher of the army when she reminds the forces to retain their integrity and professionalism by upholding the norms and conventions of battle that have long distinguished India's armed forces. The liberal patriot is not being 'anti-India' when she argues for a softening of laws such as the Armed Forces Special Powers Act (AFSPA)[71] which give overweening powers to the army. A partial calibrated roll-back of this law on a trial basis in parts of Jammu and Kashmir would win for India a far tougher shield of popular goodwill and civilian support than any shield made of guns and iron.[72] When the liberal patriot asks for a partial lifting of AFSPA, she is not attempting to weaken the capacity and morale of the security forces, but striving to win the war for values and decency, that ultimate war that was so crucial to Gandhi. Is India fighting to kill? Or is India fighting terrorism for the sake of her civilizational ideals?

The liberal recognizes that in Kashmir the outstretched adolescent arm that throws a stone at the advancing army tank is not necessarily an arm that is repudiating India.

Instead it is a stone held in the arm of rebellious youth enraged at being denied justice and opportunities, at being viewed through the barbed wire and sandbags of army occupation, frustration at being caged in the 'national security' mentality. 'Azaadi' may imply a political lever used by separatist Hurriyat leaders but there are scores of Kashmiri youth who want to belong to the India story and instead have been insulted, humiliated and violently rebuffed in the rest of India.[73] Many youths are bristling to belong, not straining to leave, they are screaming for respect and equal treatment, not declaring war with a feeble arsenal of bricks and pebbles.

In militant-affected Kupwara, phiran-clad ruddy-complexioned youth were hopeful of a future in India. 'When you have an MA, your parents keep yelling at you to get a job, something happens to your brain. Dimaag kharab ho jaata hai. Sometimes you want to pick up the gun. But those who have opportunities don't go down that road. We want jobs, we don't want Pakistan here.'

The liberal patriot does not see every teenage Kashmiri child with a stone as a potential terrorist to be targeted by a pellet gun. The liberal Indian sheds tears at the death of seventeen-year-old Tufail Mattoo, who was killed in 2010 after being hit in the chest by the army's pellets as he made his way to tuitions amidst street protests against the Machil encounter killings. The use of the pellet gun by the army has become a symbol of 'Indian occupation'. So far, 14 per cent of pellet-gun victims in Kashmir are below the age of fifteen.[74]

* * *

The liberal patriot is able to see that tragedy of fourteen-year-old Insha Mushtaq from Shopian, who once wanted to be a doctor and today is blinded in both eyes.[75] The liberal sees the tragedy of Kashmiri student Mohammad Rafiq Shah, who was arrested in 2005 in Srinagar, spent twelve years in jail, wrongly accused of perpetrating bomb blasts in Delhi in 2005 before a court finally acquitted him, clearing him of all charges and declaring them to be ridiculously baseless and flimsy.[76] This is only another chilling example of how the Indian state looks on the Kashmiri Muslim: guilty even after being proved innocent. Delivering governance and justice on the ground in Kashmir has always been the ultimate litmus test for India's credentials as a secular society. It's a test that India has failed.

In the decades following Independence, through blunders and missteps, through violence and political short-sightedness, in its own chaotic way, the liberal Indian state forged a rough alternative universe. Behind the tanks and soldiers, many Kashmiris slowly became aware

of another possible reality, an alternative destiny. Kashmiri cricketer
Parvez Rasool was wrongfully detained by the Bengaluru police in a
cricket tournament and went on to score 50 runs in 47 balls. He later
said, 'I had to prove I'm a cricketer, not a terrorist.'

Twenty-seven-year-old Shah Faesal topped the civil services
examination in 2009 and chose to become an Indian Administrative
Services (IAS) officer. Novelist Basharat Peer's book *Curfewed
Night* became a bestseller across India. Kashmiri women Dr Ruveda
Salam and Dr Syed Sehrish Asgar also cleared the civil services
examinations. Mehrajuddin Wadoo and Ishfaq Ahmed have become
successful footballers across India. Thousands of Indians crowded
into movie halls to see the film *Haider*, Vishal Bhardwaj's rendition
of *Hamlet* set in 1990s Kashmir when militancy was at its height.
Bollywood generally steers clear of Kashmir stories but mainstream
middle-class audiences responded with real sympathy about India's
first commercial film about militancy.

In the 1992 film *Roja*, the hero was a Hindu Research and
Analysis Wing (R&AW) agent and the heroine a girl from Tamil
Nadu, trapped in the cross-fire of Kashmiri violence, but in the
2014 film *Haider*, the hero is a Kashmiri Muslim drawn to violence,
a Kashmiri Prince of Denmark, a militant sympathizer with an
Oedipus complex and a machine gun, an unlikely protagonist to hold
middle-class metropolitan audiences transfixed. Hopes of a liberal
contract between Kashmiris and the rest of India are not entirely
lost. In September 2013, when Zubin Mehta's orchestra struck up
Beethoven and Tchaikovsky in Shalimar Bagh, it was a reminder of
the beauty that was once synonymous with Kashmir, a reminder of
1960s and 1970s films like *Kashmir Ki Kali* and *Aan Milo Sajna* when
lovers romanced on Gulmarg's scenic slopes or along chinar-lined
avenues, of a time when there was an alternative reality in Kashmir,
away from death and violence, when the presence of the Indian Big
State was not such a harsh reality.

Down the years, liberal patriots have reached out and been
able to create the politics of generosity in Kashmir. Morarji Desai

held what are regarded as Kashmir's first free and fair elections in 1977. Atal Bihar Vajpayee declared 'insaniyat' was to be his guiding star in Kashmir and held elections in 2002. Then chief election commissioner J.M. Lyngdoh delivered a fair vote. In some rough way, these memories coexist with harsher recollections of the humiliating toppling of Farooq Abdullah in 1983 by Indira Gandhi and the shamefully rigged election of 1987 that led to the igniting of militancy in 1989.[77]

Yet, 'muscular nationalists' now want to undo the partial good that the patchy liberal consensus up to 2014 was able to achieve. For them, the Kashmiri is the perpetual anti-national for whom there can be no sympathy. 'Muscular nationalists' uphold the RSS world view that Kashmir is just a piece of land to be conquered and subdued through a revocation of Article 370 and other laws that give it special status in India. Kashmir is ours, but Kashmiris are jihadis, they thunder, signalling that they prefer the real estate over the inhabitants. They are reassured by the fact that Kashmir is a cantonment, patrolled by lakhs of security forces, its residents policed 24x7. The Hindutva nationalist is thus an ideological ally of Mohammed Ali Jinnah, who believed that Hindus and Muslims could not live together; the Hindutva nationalist is determined to prove Jinnah's Two-Nation Theory right and Jawaharlal Nehru wrong.

What about the Hindu Kashmiri Pandits, nationalists ask, who were forced out of their homes, does the liberal not bother about them because they are Hindus? Through the 1990s, the Valley was plunged into bloody militancy. Threatened and persecuted, Pandit families left their ancestral homes[78] and were forced to take up residences away from their beloved places of birth. The wrongs inflicted on the Kashmiri Pandits are tragic, horrendous, unforgettable. Elderly Kashmiris were consigned to drab existences in poky apartments and many died in sorrow, their homes lost forever. How can there be any reconciliation and reach-out to Kashmir, from which the Hindu community was forced out in such a terrible way? How can we forgive? Why should we forget? The charge of ignoring the uprooting and suffering of the Pandits is laid at the door of the liberal.

Yes, it could be argued that while Kashmiri politicians like the Abdullahs and Muftis had and have liberal inclinations, their brand of personalized politics and failure to provide a basic common vision for Kashmir has perhaps led to the declining legitimacy of the elected Kashmiri politician. This has contributed to the ceding of political space to militants who are now preventing the expansion of democracy. But both the Abdullahs and Muftis have spoken about the need for the Kashmiri Pandits to return to their homes. In fact, when Mufti Mohammad Sayeed was chief minister, he held out an open offer for Pandits to return.[79]

Another failure on the part of New Delhi to recognize and accept Kashmiri regional sentiment. Hindutva nationalists can accept 'Hindutva pride' but they recoil at the mention of Kashmiri pride. But the liberal Indian patriot rejoices in the notion of Kashmiri pride, recognizing that Indian patriotism was always meant to be inclusive and varied, an amalgam of proud regional identities and aspirations. What can be the building blocks of a new mentality towards Kashmir? These building blocks can be raised if the Indian security establishment becomes comfortable with the assertion of Kashmiri identity and Kashmiri pride. To allow Kashmir its regionalism, its regional pride and its regional assertiveness (while making sure that separatist tendencies are blunted by a political reach-out) is surely to make a break from the security-dominated mindset that reigns over the valley. Today, chief ministers across India evoke regional pride and regional sentiments. Nitish Kumar once gave the rousing cry of 'Jai Bihari', Narendra Modi as Gujarat chief minister and even as prime minister repeatedly lays claim to 'Gujarati asmita', Mamata Banerjee is the upholder of Bengali pride and sub-nationalism. Capital cities have been renamed to answer to regional legacies of states.

When every Indian state is entitled to its own flamboyant regional pride, why can't the Indian state accept the concept of

Kashmiri pride, when today every chief minister increasingly stands forth as the champion of their region? So if we can have Gujarati pride and Tamil pride and Bihari pride, why can we not have Kashmiri pride, rooted in the state's syncretic Sufi traditions? Why does championing any version of Kashmiri regionalism immediately become a threat to India and an invitation to Pakistan?

The patriotism of the liberal Indian lies in accepting federal aspirations, regional sentiments, in confidence and generosity, and without fear. The liberal must never baulk at greater autonomy for India's states. India's Constitution at its core is a federal one, with Article 1 declaring, 'India, that is Bharat, shall be a Union of States.' It would be anathema for a nationalist government to accept Pervez Musharraf's Four Point Formula for a Kashmir solution[80] but there is an urgent need to roll back the machinery of the overwhelmingly dominant Big State from Kashmir. All 'nationalist' bluster on the removal of Article 370 and 35 A should be set aside until an enormous amount of goodwill has first been created by free-flowing people-to-people exchanges between Kashmir and the rest of India. Let the people go where state machinery rules, let citizens meet each other instead of deliberations between politicians and babus taking place in seminar rooms. As A.G. Noorani wrote in 2002, 'The solution [of Kashmir] should be such that a Kashmiri leader could announce it in Lal Chowk.'[81]

Why should Kashmir's special status or unique identity be seen as an assault on Indian nationhood? Why should it be such, when it is simply a regional peculiarity that governs the state's relationship with India? The historical circumstances of Kashmir's decision to join India can hardly be saffron-washed away and must be accepted by liberals.[82] In 1947, when the Muslim-majority state acceded to India, it joined a brave homeland for all. India was not going to be a mirror image of Pakistan, a land created for a single religion. Instead, pluralism was to be India's creed, and a secular India laid claim to Kashmir by promising justice for all faiths. If secular India is replaced by a de facto Hindu Rashtra, the very premise of Kashmir's accession begins to look flawed.

A Muslim-majority province acceded to the Union of India because of the promise of equal treatment and justice from a multi-religious federation rather than a single-faith religious state like Pakistan. If that multi-faith, justice-delivering equal-rights-giving system begins to fade, a sense of exclusion will set in in many areas. The liberal patriot is loyal to this rainbow-hued Indian federation, loyal to the founding ideals of this federation, thus a greater champion of a united India than nationalists who want to snap the ties of federal multiculturalism that make India a whole.[83]

In 1991, India started the liberalization of its economy. The Indian government now needs to liberalize its mindset on Kashmir and place the individual Kashmiri, the human being made of flesh and blood, just like anyone in the rest of India, at the centre of its vision and accept the Kashmiri as an equal citizen of India like the Bengali or the Malayali. Words like 'separatist' and 'secessionist' should be used only when there is good reason to do so. The Indian Big State should recognize that Kashmiris—like Indians across the country—have the democratic right to protest. In fact, the freedom to protest is a reflection of the faith in the institutions of the Indian republic, even if the protestors repudiate those entrusted with office for the moment. Liberals see the right to protest as India's strength, 'nationalists' see it as India's weakness. If the BJP can hold Bharat bandhs, if the Left can hold mass rallies, if Patels and Jats can stage huge protests, why don't Kashmiris have the right to protest without the looming spectre of the pellet gun?

The liberalization of the mentality about Kashmir means not branding every Kashmiri stone-pelter as a Lashkar operative and trying to subdue him with overwhelming force. Kashmir cries for azaadi, not from India but from an old Indian 'national security' militarist mindset. Only the liberal patriot can reach out towards Kashmir and create a new social, cultural and political union, a union reinvented for the twenty-first century.

The Kathua rape and murder[84] has brought into glaring focus the terrifying communal divide that is deepening by the day between a 'Hindu' Jammu and a 'Muslim' Valley, a divide being made bloodier and wider by the politics of Hindutva nationalism. A sense of statewide unity can only be built by a civic-minded, liberal, large-hearted leader, able to foster a sense of pride in diverse, multi-religious Jammu and Kashmir as a possible inspiration of Hindu–Muslim coexistence in the world, a jewel in India's secular crown.

Yes, for Pakistan, Kashmir remains Partition's unfinished agenda. A hatred of 'Hindu rule' among elements in Pakistan has spawned a terror machine. But can Pakistan's 'proxy war' be countered only by pouring in more Indian troops and guns, an arms build-up in which Kashmiris cease to be human beings and only become 'modules' or 'sleeper cells' or 'operatives'? Spook-speak dominates India's narrative on Kashmir. Just as the security establishment in Pakistan profits by keeping the relationship with India on edge, the Indian security establishment too, police and bureaucracy, or the Indian Big State, retain an important role if the conflict in Kashmir is kept alive.

The liberal solution for Jammu and Kashmir is to liberate it from excessive government control, just as the economy was liberated in 1991. Even as the state recedes, citizens must take the lead in forging a new reinvented bond based on Kashmiris as individuals and not as just a piece of land. The liberal agenda on Jammu and Kashmir must be centred on a renewed emphasis on the federal principle of the Constitution and locate Indian unity in a federal union. To quote C. Rajagopalachari, India's first and last Indian governor-general and home minister in 1951–52, '[T]he solution is to concede greater autonomy to States, so as to minimize regional thinking at the Centre . . . federal powers on issues other than foreign affairs and defence should shrink to the barest minimum, while the powers exercised by the States should expand very greatly.'[85] Jammu and Kashmir as an autonomous region in a federal India where every state is now demanding greater autonomy within the overarching

Indian Union may be an idea whose time has come. An artificial calm, clamped through force, is meaningless.

Gandhi argued that peace is only meaningful when it is achieved on the basis of values. When riots raged in Bengal and Bihar in 1946–47, Gandhi rushed to those areas, to walk the blood-stained path, bringing peace where government and police could not. True courage lies in walking the tense streets, calling for calm as Gandhi did in Noakhali. Rajiv Gandhi did not venture into Delhi's streets in 1984, nor did then Gujarat chief minister Modi in riot-torn Gujarat in 2002; just the promotion of khadi does not make one an upholder of the Gandhian legacy unless his real values are upheld. Once again, the liberal Gandhian mantra of the means justifying the ends holds true. When the ends justify the means, it's a return to the law of the jungle, where might is right—either the might of the Supreme Leader or of the Big State.

But at the mention of decentralization for Jammu and Kashmir, nationalists are likely to shout, 'Over my dead body!' The 'nationalist's' desire to centralize is what Rajaji once called ridiculous and alarming. Today in a Big State based on a nationalism seeking to draw all identities into a Hindutva fold, the beef-eater, the rationalist, the liberal, the slogan-shouting student, the questioning journalist are all unacceptable. Most unacceptable of all is the Kashmiri Muslim and her longing for individual freedom.

Making Peace with Pakistan

Liberals are supposed to be overly sentimental and 'soft' towards the mortal nationalist enemy: Pakistan. Those who light candles at the Wagah border[86] are jeered at as the 'mombati mafia', hopeless woolly-headed romantics who are in denial about Pakistan's deadly intent. The liberal is seen as a misfit in the warlike hyper-nationalist spirit of the moment. Primetime warriors on television evoke a fantasy cartoon-strip machismo and call for India to 'finish off' Pakistan. Glamorous, well-heeled 'nationalists', their jingoism as much a fashion accessory as their furs and diamonds, yell nuke 'em, bomb them, flatten them. After the Indian army's surgical strikes of September 2016, Bollywood's leading lights took to social media to cheer on the army. Actor Arjun Rampal tweeted: 'Super proud that terrorism is spoken to in the language they understand. Let's unite borders by uniting against terrorism. #IndianArmy ki Jai.' Actor Riteish Deshmukh had this to say: 'Proud of our Indian Army & many Congratulations to our Indian Government for their effective steps against terrorism. #IndiaFirst #JaiHind.' In 2008, Simi Garewal on NDTV, made the comment, 'Go to the Four Seasons and look down from the top floor at the slums around you. Do you know what flags you will see? Not the Congress's, not the BJP's, not the Shiv Sena. Pakistan! Pakistan flags fly high.'[87] She also said, 'My suggestion is that the Indian army should go into PoK, do the job and come back without harming the country or its people.' Simi later apologized for her remarks, yet today a reverential cult of the army means no questions can ever be asked about well-publicized videos, the much-trumped surgical strikes that the Indian army launched on 28–29 September 2016 and cross–Line of Control (LoC) firing.

The question that the liberal patriot must ask about the surgical strikes is, is the government using them to drum up 'muscular nationalism' for votes, and thus politicizing army actions? The surgical strikes were launched six months before the Uttar Pradesh polls, apparently to take 'revenge' on Pakistan for the attack on the army camp in Uri. Less than a month after the strikes, Prime Minister Modi was seen on stage on 11 October 2016 at the Aishbagh Ramleela ground in Lucknow posing, Lord Krishna style, with a fake Sudarshan Chakra and being hailed as the 'avenger of Uri'. Once again, in 2018, in the run-up to the general elections of 2019, videos of the surgical strikes were made available to news channels. Should the political executive harness the valour and sacrifice of the army into an election campaign? Isn't this form of 'muscular nationalism' only a tactical ploy to use nationalism for the cause of a

particular political party? As it turned out, the BJP won a landslide
victory in the Uttar Pradesh polls of 2017, scoring 325 out of 403
seats.[88] The army's achievements belong to the nation and not to
any political outfit and to trumpet the surgical strikes is to mislead
and misinform citizens that they have made the border or country
significantly safer.[89]

War is always spectacular television. The gory, nasty reality
on the ground can so easily be ignored or denied. Naked displays
of power are mesmerizing for viewers accustomed to watching
larger-than-life Dabanggs and Baahubalis on the big screen. When
governments display power to impress not only their own fan base
but citizens at large, these displays become easy diversions from the
lack of substantive action to deal with the deteriorating situation on
the border. The greater the war rhetoric, an illusion is fostered of a
'strong government' even though there may be a decline in its real
accountability in dealing with genuine crises on the border.

The nationalist warmonger claims the patriotic space against
Pakistan. But it is the liberal on both sides of the border who is
the greater patriot. Why is this so? Because often, the well-heeled
aggressive warmongers who espouse war, know that they or their
Ivy League–bound children will never have to face a hail of bullets.
In air-conditioned comfort, they want the sons of the poor to
stand against their imagined enemy, the blood of jawans an elixir
of their cocktail party rage. When young soldiers die, they shrug
off responsibility. They demand war in TV studios, yet refuse any
accountability for the blood of young jawans, officers and Kashmiri
civilians.

On 4 February 2018, Captain Kapil Kundu, four months
short of his twenty-third birthday, was killed on the border, hit by
Pakistani shelling. Three other Indian soldiers died. The death of
captain Kundu became a television event, social media drummed
up a martyrs' cult and soldier-obsessed anchors' voices pulsated as
they ran emotionally charged programmes on how glorious death is
when a young man dies for the motherland.

But the death cult of the soldier in a democracy is neither liberal nor progressive, modern or even remotely patriotic. To celebrate the gory death of young men whose precious lives ebb away in a puddle of blood and slush with ritualized bloodthirsty fervour evokes feudal warrior cults and ideological holy wars. When TV glamorizes war it becomes part of a militarist syndrome obscuring the blood, grime, the waste of lives, the tawdry, grinding tragedy of a real war. War does not happen with an orchestra playing in the background. War does not take place in technicolour visuals edited to heart-pumping excitement.

Yes, India's 1971 Bangladesh war was seen as a pinnacle of national achievement, but a military victory as a country's moral purpose is only of limited value and shelf life. Only three years after becoming the supreme heroine of Bangladesh, Indira Gandhi plummeted to the nadir of her popularity. India was defeated in the 1962 war with China, but nevertheless, Nehru died a hero. India's democracy posits civilian institutions over army and citizen over soldier. The repeated loud orchestra of nationalist chest-thumping at the tragic death of a soldier on the India–Pakistan border reveals a gory medievalist war dance over the prone corpse of modern patriotic peacemaking and makes death one of India's national achievements.

The Kargil war of 1999 was India's first Primetime War. War at 9 p.m. War between the advertisements. War with an orchestral lead-in, its visual impact enhanced by glitzy computer graphics. In 1999, this TV war, bigger and better than ever, created a permanent appetite for the battle on TV channels.[90] War correspondents gushed about soldiers and strategic moves, breathlessly cheering from the sidelines as greater numbers went to their deaths.

Yet, the hallowed 'war correspondent' tradition in the West was not made by hanging on to the coat-tails of the men in uniform. It was made by documenting evidence that scrutinized the role of the military from the citizen's point of view. The question arises, should TV anchors become drumbeaters for the military? Or is this a carefully tailored packaging of war as entertainment designed to create more 'nationalist' voters?

TV reports on the Kargil war showed handsome soldiers sporting smiles, with transistors in their bunkers, ready for a challenge. There were no glimpses of the daily labours and the brutal hardships they must have to endure. TV provided cardboard cut-outs of a collective macho fantasy. TV prevented viewers from seeing the misery of human beings, of men pushed into the army for reasons of unemployment, rural impoverishment or debt. TV does not show the grief of war. The quiet grief which is grey, unglamorous and unending, spending itself in the day-to-day emptiness of ruined lives.

Warmongers fantasize, in a rather exhibitionist way, about war without responsibility. Yet, war isn't about ceremonial funerals, grave families and smiling, relentlessly brave soldiers. The constitutional morality of the democratic republic of India does not elevate the soldier to superman. This elevation serves two purposes. One, it is intended to be opium for the soldier, who is then expected to forget the grime and pain, to go unquestioningly and blindly into battle, without a clue about why it should be done. Two, the soldier cult is an intoxicant for citizens, just as the citizens of Rome cheered gruesome fights between gladiators centuries ago.

For the liberal, there is only one superman or superwoman in our system and that is the citizen of India. Creating temples to the soldier dislodges the deity that should sit in every Indian temple, which is the Constitution of India, where civilian patriotism takes a far higher place than militarist braggadocio. Illiberal nationalists, sunk in martial fantasies, as evident from the RSS sarsanghchalak's recent statement that the RSS can muster an army faster than the armed forces,[91] cannot make the crucial distinction our Constitution makes between political executive and the army. Calls for war tend to become a self-fulfilling prophecy. They fuel more violence, leading to even more demands for armed action. In the process, the government escapes all accountability and responsibility, and attention is diverted from the substantive reasons for conflict. India's biggest victory against Pakistan came in 1971 when a canny prime minister did not, in fact, listen to irresponsible cries for war and instead, on the advice of then army chief Sam Manekshaw, waited patiently for the right moment to actually go into battle.

Yet, calling for peace does not mean asking the military to meekly lay down weapons if the enemy is intent on conflict. Gandhi's satyagraha was not simply passive resistance, but a reaching for the highest possible values. Gandhi supported the war effort of the Allies provided they gave Indians the same values of freedom and dignity that they claimed to be fighting for. Instead, calling for peace means reaching out to higher values that go beyond treating war as a bloodstained scoreboard of who killed how many. The liberal patriot believes that peace is not just about the cessation of physical conflict but a hearkening to the underlying values on which India is based. India's foundation is the courage of satyagraha; not a simplistic laying down of arms in the face of terrorism. Gandhi was hardly a 'peacemonger' in the pejorative sense—he supported the Allies in the two World Wars provided they upheld the values of human dignity and individual freedom.

An imagined war with Pakistan may appease the 'muscular nationalists', but the need for soft borders, for people-to-people contact between cricketers, artists and actors was never greater. The most important component of this contact is trade. When goods are free to cross borders, armies don't need to. When trade is voluntary, both parties gain, giving rise to real peace constituencies on both sides. Yet, this is precisely what is lacking. This is why those in power profit politically as long as the people on both sides keep fighting. In a situation of perpetual conflict, only politicians gain and the people lose, the Big State gains, the individual is the loser.

That's why the liberal patriot argues constantly for dialogue. Even if there are strains of radical Islamism within the Kashmir insurgency, the Indian state cannot be seen to disengage from talking and reaching out. Liberal peacemongers have a crucial patriotic role here: they stand by as bridge-builders between the government and people. What would the Mahatma have done today? He would have sat on a fast at Lal Chowk in Srinagar until the stone-pelters and army stopped their endless confrontations. He knew that the barrel of the AK-47 would never provide a solution, because peace-at-any-cost is never a solution. The liberal peacemaker seeks peace on the basis of a set of values, else the peace will not attain the moral high ground.

Who is India at war with? Is India at war with terrorists or is India at war with Pakistani actors, singers, academics, cricketers and journalists, many of whom on pain of death are trying to lead normal lives, raising ever-weakening voices against the religio-terror virus raging through their land?

The dwindling liberal, soft-liner, dialogue-seeking Pakistani constituency is in dire need of empowerment. The more Indian political leaders pour abuse on Pakistani people, the more India strengthens precisely those forces which it is supposedly trying to fight and undermine.

The liberal argument is that as India ups the military ante, it must also up the civilian ante and emphasize that it recognizes the gap between common people and the terror machine. Sane, liberal India must be as determined to welcome Pakistani actors as it is to defend itself against Pakistan-based terror. Providing the blistering soundbites that ISI and militant voices like Hafiz Saeed want to hear only strengthens the suicide bomber's resolve.

Attempts at peace with Pakistan have brought reprisals. Vajpayee's Lahore bus journey in February 1999 led to the Kargil war. Modi's birthday diplomacy, when he made a surprise visit to Lahore on 25 December 2015, was followed by attacks on the Air Force base at Pathankot on 2 January 2016 and on an army camp in Uri on 18 September the same year. India's hardest targets have been hit, namely, well-fortified military camps, to nudge the subcontinental neighbours towards battle. Should Indian politicians then echo the words of Pakistani military dictator Zia-ul Haq and rage about bleeding each other by inflicting a thousand cuts?

Today, Pakistan has virtually no Hindu population, while India has the second largest Muslim population in the world. What does this say about India's success as a modern, open democracy, compared to Pakistan?

This statistic should be seen as India's strength. The desire of many Muslims from our eastern neighbouring countries to come to India to work or migrate should be seen as an indication of the appeal of the idea of India, with her pluralism and diversity. That people are willing to take great risks and vote with their feet is the best argument against the Two–Nation theory. India's Constitution-framers did not imagine Indian nationalism as Hindu hegemony over all Muslims in the subcontinent. Liberal Indian nationalism was always imagined as the hegemony of constitutional principles.

Does the Liberal Romanticize the Maoist?

Is armed Maoism a condemnable atrocious war against Indian democracy or an act of last resort by Adivasi communities, fighting to survive the onslaught of rapacious mining companies and brutal police? Liberal intellectuals in India are often dubbed 'urban Naxals' or 'half-Maoist' or apologists for Maoists and accused of not supporting India's security forces as they combat Maoist cadres in Chhattisgarh and Jharkhand. 'There is a tendency to romanticise Maoists and demonise security forces. Maoists are terrorists,' Jairam Ramesh said in 2013[92] when he was the minister for rural development, at a time when the so-called Operation Green Hunt (which the government at the time described as a media myth, and activists called a no-holds-barred operation against Maoists) was in progress.[93]

Then home minister P. Chidambaram said in a speech in 2011, 'The CPI [Communist Party of India] (Maoist) . . . have made it clear that elections are a "meaningless irrelevant pseudo democratic exercise" . . . how can a country that is democratic and a republic accept these pronouncements? If the Naxalites accuse the elected government of capitalism, land-grabbing, exploiting and displacing tribal people, denying rights of forest-dwellers, what prevents them from winning power through elections and reversing current trends?'[94]

Yet, the then home minister did not address the issue that just as the Naxalites have no qualms about using Adivasis and the poor as cannon fodder, so too the Indian Big State has had little hesitation about depriving traditional forest-dwellers of their rights and resources in the name of promoting development. Marginalized communities have not experienced the fulfilment of promised development. Yet, they are continually being asked to sacrifice even more.

Liberals must not sentimentalize those who use detestable violence but isn't there a need to recognize why violence has arisen in the first place? In 2007, Dr Binayak Sen was arrested, accused of having links with Naxals and charged under draconian laws.[95] Those who campaigned for his release and highlighted his pioneering work in bringing healthcare to the most desolate parts of Chhattisgarh were once again caricatured as lacking in adequate amounts of patriotism.

What were Binayak Sen's crimes? As general secretary of the Chhattisgarh PUCL, the idealistic doctor was involved in setting up a Shaheed Hospital for workers and peasants in Dallirajhara. When malnourishment or starvation bring slow and sudden death, Binayak Sen had asked, 'if it is not genocide what is it?' 'Ignoring hunger is nothing short of genocide.'[96] Sen was charged under draconian laws only because he met a detained Maoist leader in pursuit of his civil liberties campaigns. In striving to bring healthcare where it is needed most, working peacefully among those denied space in development or political representation, is Binayak Sen not a role model of public spirited citizenship? Granting bail to Sen in 2011, the Supreme Court held, 'We are a democratic country. He may be a sympathiser, that does not make him guilty. If Mahatma Gandhi's autobiography is found in somebody's place, is he a Gandhian?' Added Justice C.K. Prasad, 'If Gandhi's book was found in my house would that make me a Gandhian?' The apex court held that owning Marx's books didn't make you a Marxist, just as possessing Gandhi's writings did not make you a Gandhian. To follow from the court's observations, owning a copy of the Bhagavad Gita and proudly displaying it on your bookshelf makes you neither a good nor a true Hindu if you do not maintain its values.

* * *

On 6 April 2010, seventy-six Central Reserve Police Force (CRPF) personnel were killed by Maoists in Dantewada in the deadliest ever attack on security forces. Eight Maoists also died in this carnage. The cry went up in the mainstream media that human rights activists or liberals were selectively blind to the sufferings of Indian police 'martyrs'. 'The nation outraged', 'War between India and the Maoists', 'Country bids farewell to Dantewada martyrs', so ran the headlines and Breaking News flashes. The death of CRPF personnel is tragic. So are the deaths of innocent tribals at the hands of the forces. There can be no moral hierarchy among corpses. Declaring war on fellow citizens means you have no one else to blame but yourself if rival combatants die.

Today, violence on both sides, Maoists or security forces, is condemned equally by liberals and activists, however much rights activists in the past may have justified Naxal violence on grounds of the struggle for rights of locals. But having condemned all violence, the liberal patriot still stands in the way of the all-powerful Big State waging war on its own citizens. The liberal tries to humanize the Big State and attempts to ensure that a durable peace is secured by delivery of justice and welfare. The liberal patriot works for peace while the 'nationalist' pushes for war by the Big State.

The liberal argues that an enduring peace, whether in Kashmir or in Dantewada, can never emanate from the barrel of the gun or by the use of overwhelming force. By insisting on the dignity, humanity and rights of Adivasi communities, drawing attention to their loss of land, seeking to make them partners in progress and protecting them from rapacious mining companies operating in the area, the liberal Indian is not betraying India, rather strengthening it. Today, academics like Nandini Sundar[97] may have cases against them, but without their voices to oppose the dominant bludgeoning official narrative, can the lamp of Indian patriotism, the patriotism that stands up for the weak and defenceless, be kept burning? 'As long as there is inequality there will be Naxalism, and as long there is injustice there will be Naxalism,' said Badranna, a former Naxal in the Basuguda region who has now surrendered. 'The capitalists are opening factories and looting away our property, why should we not protest. Jab tak ganda phenkenge, machar ayenge. Agar hame machar nahin chahiye toh hame ganda phenkna band karna hoga. You can't deprive the locals in any area of their dignity or resources.'[98]

Today, several reports have surfaced of how certain wings of Maoists have simply transmogrified into mercenary operations well-funded by corporate interests simply to create disruptions. An ideology that rejects Indian parliamentary democracy cannot be part of a liberal's vocabulary even if such language fits into revolutionary or Maoist thoughts. Yet, within the definition of patriotism there must surely be space for those who speak up for the orphans of development, who want a better share of the resources that they believe belong to them.

'We have to get the right to our property and the right to dignity of our tribal leaders. Bring as much security force as you want but unless you finish hierarchy and bhed bhav, Naxalism will continue,' said Badranna.[99]

When anger at injustice and inequality runs so deep, who better serves the cause of the Indian nation in the fight against violent Maoism? Those who take the trouble to work with them, and bring their stories to the mainstream or those who insist that only a military solution can tackle the so-called 'vermin scum'? If the only long-term practical solution in dealing with Naxalism is peace talks and for peace to be delivered with justice, then it is liberal patriots who are putting their shoulders to the wheel for this process to gather steam.

The need, as always, is to limit the use of force by the Big State and allow greater local freedom and autonomy. To oppose the centralizing, authoritarian 'muscular nationalist' discourse of the Big State. But a police force bent on terrorizing the public and clamping down on dissent seeks to, as Praful Bidwai wrote, 'outlaw and discredit all dissent and obliterate the vital distinctions between hardcore Maoists, their sympathisers, members of parliamentary communist parties, Gandhians, civil liberties activists, progressive intellectuals and even health workers . . . the law cannot criminalise even non-violent protests.'

Over the years, hundreds of activists and rights workers have been rounded up, illegally detained and even tortured, as happened with the activist Soni Sori.[100] Others are made victims of police intimidation, like legal researchers and journalists Shalini Gera, Isha Khandelwal and Malini Subramaniam, who were forced to leave Jagdalpur.[101] The liberal Indian must be clear-eyed about the fact that violent Maoism is a threat to civil society. Yet, the liberal insists that the freedom to defend Adivasi rights in the face of the menacing Big State is an important democratic freedom. Much more ominous for India in the long run than immediate Maoist violence is injustice, extortion, expropriation of forest resources and locals deprived of their land. We mourn the forces who lose their lives in Naxal encounters, but should we not also mourn Adivasi girls and boys who are killed, tortured and maimed sometimes for simply being Adivasi? Does our heart not break for them too?

What does liberalization of the economy really mean in the public eye? Can the liberalization process or economic reforms process remain centred on fashionable words like 'capital markets', 'FDIs', et al? Does liberalization mean only shopping malls and MNCs for the rich? Or does liberalization also mean, as Amartya Sen and Jean Drèze have argued, the obligation to provide low-cost decent hospitals to all Indians, cheap and good primary schools in areas like Bastar, where so many young tribals are thirsting to study and make a life for themselves outside the endless cycle of violence? The government would claim that it is precisely to enable development that businesses must be allowed to access resources so that the state can then provide services. But when visible immediate services are not provided and only resources are extracted without accompanying welfare, the result is the legitimization of violence, directly or indirectly, by the Big State.

The economic reforms process should not be just about building smart cities and smooth roads for cars but ensuring roads and healthcare reach Bastar and that, crucially, the police is made more humane and more accountable. So far, because the police enjoy immunity and unlimited authority in the name of fighting Naxals, they have little incentive to really defeat them. The larger the police paint the Naxal problem to be, the greater is the opportunity for them to build their empire of impunity in so-called 'Naxal-infested' zones.

The fundamental tenet of the rule of law and due process of law, if demonstrated often enough, can dim the lure of the gun, as can greater decentralization over disbursement of resources in the area. Thoughts, ideas, books and reading materials are not criminal activities, only violence is. Permitting a free babble of speech and debate in Naxal-affected areas, slowly mounting the counter-narrative to the Maoist one, organizing visible and strategic troop withdrawals and showing clear intention of providing jobs and incomes is a possible basket of solutions that can be held out, instead of the Big State machine guns aimed from every tree-top. Former home secretary G.K. Pillai once said that Maoists are 'nothing but cold-blooded murderers . . . and we will give them a firm and fitting response.' Yet, the late E.N. Rammohan, former director general of the Border Security Force, had a more nuanced set of solutions. After long years fighting Naxalism, he proposed instead a permanent end to injustice. This meant giving back land to the tillers and forest land to the tribals and taking steps to bring down income inequalities in the region. Violence, he used to say, only begets more violence, and in the name of a counter-offensive if security-men begin to torture innocent tribals, the situation may be irretrievably lost. The liberal patriot, constantly campaigning for the freedom of the individual and free individual enterprise, believes that development and aspiration must be as available on the dirt tracks of Dantewada, Gadchiroli and Bastar as they are on the streets of Mumbai.

A 'Nationalist' Government and 'Anti-national' Journalists

When 'muscular nationalist' ideology is uppermost, the citizen must be forced to fall in with the accepted form of government-inspired nationalism, the kind of nationalism sanctioned by the Big State. While liberal democracy creates space for discourse, recognizes debates and respects dissent, a government or Big State driven by ideology seeks to discourage discourse, stifle debates and delegitimize dissent and brooks no reach out to citizens. Instead, citizens must be forced to demonstrate their commitment to the 'nation' at all times, an illustration perhaps of the 'nationalists' own lack of conviction in the idea of India.

Constant confrontation between citizens and the Big State thus becomes inevitable. On 28 September 2015, a farmer in western Uttar Pradesh, Mohammad Akhlaq, was killed by cow vigilantes in Dadri on the suspicion that he was storing beef in his home. The dead Akhlaq's son serves in the Indian Air Force. But rather than being treated with respect as the father of a soldier, Akhlaq was lynched on the suspicion that he was storing beef. The same year, the writer Nayantara Sahgal returned her Sahitya Akademi award in protest against growing hate crimes. In December 2017, Mohammad Afrazul was hacked to death in Rajsamand. But not a remorseful or consoling word was heard from the top echelons of the political leadership, no regret about the brutal murders.

Not one top leader uttered a word of sorrow after the suicide of Hyderabad University student Rohith Vemula, who ended his life on 17 January 2016 after his scholarship was stopped as a result of his participation in protests.

Rather than sound a note of reconciliation and conflict resolution, belligerent ministers and aggressive ruling party members revel in making provocative and bellicose statements rather than trying, as pragmatic governments generally do, to resolve matters, lessen tensions and push for a middle ground. This is because ideologues are in constant search of an enemy, in order that ideologically motivated cadres may be mobilized and energized to launch an assault on these perceived enemies. These enemies keep changing. Sometimes these enemies are Bangladeshis in Assam or the Muslim "ghuspetiye" (infiltrators),[102] or they are the "Babur ki aulad" of the Ram Janmabhoomi movement,[103] or they are the Kashmiri stone-pelters. The enemies almost always are Muslims or those seen to be sympathetic to Muslims.

'Dadri was an accident,' snapped culture minister Mahesh Sharma; students at Hyderabad University are anti-national, blustered labour minister Bandaru Dattatreya; Rohith Vemula was not a Dalit, fulminated foreign minister Sushma Swaraj;[104] writers' protests are 'a manufactured paper rebellion', scoffed finance minister Arun Jaitley; and JNU students are supported by enemies of India, proclaimed home minister Rajnath Singh on the basis of an apparently false tweet.[105]

In his public rallies and communications with party workers, BJP president Amit Shah is always at pains to emphasize that the BJP is not simply on a political journey but on a journey of ideology, or 'vichardhaara'. Hyperactive ideology, whether of the extreme Left or extreme Right, which wants to impose a monolithic identity, seeking to delegitimize any contending ideology, is a complete antithesis of the democratic republic. Creating political divides is the essence of extremist ideology. The far greater challenge for 'nationalists' is to confront the external issues of the Pakistani deep state or the China 'threat'. But, shying away from these fundamental policy challenges, it's so much easier to simply focus on the 'enemy within' who can be targeted at will—religious minorities, Dalits, Adivasis, liberal intellectuals, activists and students—in an attempt to show off the power of the ideology to its own supporters and cadres. When the pursuit of ideology is uppermost, it results in continuous brawls with citizens. In early 2016, during the arrest and court hearings of JNU Students Union leader Kanhaiya Kumar, when so-called 'nationalist' lawyers went on the rampage threatening women reporters that 'we will break your phones and your bones', they were only mildly censured by ruling party politicians.

A confrontational, ideologically driven government cannot then be a government that seeks accommodation or a give-and-take with detractors. A genuine reach-out to all stakeholders to defuse tension points becomes difficult when the 'us' versus 'them' mentality dominates. Ideologues cannot compromise on ideological purity. Ideologues (of Left and Right) divide the world into angels and devils, a moral binary which is once again the antithesis of liberal democracy.

In this scenario, the liberal journalist—particularly those who question the government—is a prime enemy of the 'muscular nationalist'. When battle lines are sharply drawn between Hindutva nationalists and anti-nationals, is nationalism the main responsibility of journalists? Or does the patriotism of the liberal journalist lie in first telling the truth?

Veteran broadcaster Karan Thapar writes that celebrated anchors now see themselves as guard dogs of the government, not watch dogs of power. In fact, every liberal patriot must resoundingly condemn the transmogrification of much of the Indian media into a 24x7 nationalist propaganda tool. It is the reason why the credibility of journalists today is probably at an all-time low. 'The grotesquely nationalist hashtags TV channels concoct to push a story or gather a response reek of ersatz patriotism. They're like drum beats designed to marshal or dragoon a response. They're artless and crude.[106]

Hashtags like #FightForIndia or #LoveMyFlag or #ProudIndian or #TerrorStatePak or #AntiNationJNU play with our emotions and infantalize us,' writes Thapar.

The journalist is the citizen's witness. She sees so she may relay the information to citizens. She asks because she believes citizens want answers. She interrogates the powerful not on her own behalf but on the behalf of those who trust her to ask their questions. She investigates a story because it's her duty to unearth the truth for the benefit of citizens, because of the citizens' right to know. She writes so that aspects of contemporary social and political behaviour may be illuminated for her readers. She reports so that she may truthfully and factually describe the reality of places her readers may not ordinarily visit. She, the journalist, exists because democracy exists. She is democracy's agent, democracy's ambassador because she must tell the truth for the citizen who hungers for it. The true journalist is a patriot when she tells the truth, a blind 'nationalist' when she falsifies it for political ends. Telling the truth is not just the responsibility of the journalist as a professional commitment, but as a citizen committed to upholding the motto of the Indian republic, 'Satyameva Jayate'. For all liberal patriots, in fact, this motto has to be primary commitment. But how many even remember India's founding motto? How many care to recall those two words, 'Satyameva Jayate'? Today, the journalist must also ask the question asked by Helen Boaden, former director of BBC News: is the cutting-edge media technology that is today making us a global village really turning us into people of the village, with closed minds, prejudices and the narrow-mindedness of the village? Is all this new technology opening our minds or closing them?

Journalists who expose farmer suicides, who expose stock market scams, who expose the trafficking of girls, who expose female infanticide, are they expected to first answer the needs of 'nationalism'? Does a journalist reporting on a communal riot not have the duty to raise questions about its occurrence, instead of seeking answers to please those indirectly implicated in the crime?

Truth-telling does not imply amorality or partisanship. The journalist is not a mere technological communication system with neither conscience nor morality, simply a robot that broadcasts truth or falsehood with equal ease. Precisely because the power of media technology today is so suited for propaganda, values become key. Journalists cannot be amoral beings. They are instead moral beings and their morality lies in being true to the facts, rigorously verified and conforming to the standards needed for publication. Journalism that tries to be 'muscular nationalist' is only fake news.

Should courageous journalists who stood up to the Emergency of 1975 have given the government of the day the benefit of doubt because of 'nationalist' love for the motherland? In reporting on Islamist terror or saffron terror, is the journalist to be guided by what the political powers that be want her to say in the quest to be a 'nationalist'?

To quote John Tusa, the former managing director of the BBC World Service, 'The government has a right to be heard, but it's the duty of the journalist to subject the government's claim to the kind of scrutiny the average citizen would want to give if they had the time or the expertise. The journalist as critic is an agent of the audience. The freedom a journalist exercises is the freedom to be responsible, but beyond that calls for neutrality are only code words for censorship and accommodating the government of the day or acceptance of the prevailing government culture. Journalists must not be the outriders of authority.'

Prime Minister Narendra Modi and his followers are harsh critics of what they call 'biased journalists' or 'anti-national journalists'. Journalists have been called various names like 'presstitutes' and 'news traders' in a deliberate strategy to discredit the press. Journalists who have covered the 2002 Gujarat riots are seen to have unfairly placed the then Gujarat chief minister Modi in the dock. Journalists are expected to ask questions of the Congress for the 1984 anti-Sikh riots (as they have strongly done) but not ask any questions of the BJP for the 2002 riots in Gujarat. Journalists asking questions of the Modi government or about Hindutva mobilization or the circumstances of the death of Judge B.H. Loya in a Nagpur hospital or the encounter killing of Ishrat Jehan on the streets of Ahmedabad, any journalist not blindly loyal to the government's version of truth are all 'presstitutes' or 'news dalals', weaponized words designed to delegitimize and discredit the press. But as has been said, 'adversarial journalism, far from being treasonous, is the work of a patriot'.

Credible journalists are not 'muscular nationalists', instead they are liberal patriots because they interrogate the government or Big State, hold it to account, expose its failures and question its motives. How does the journalist keep alive the hopes of the democratic citizen? By never becoming an agent of any political party even as she upholds the principles of liberal democracy. The charge is made that journalists are biased, partisan, flagbearers of a particular political party and thus not 'neutral' or 'objective'. Neutrality is the wrong word. The journalist must never be overtly loyal to any political party but she is always loyal to a set of values. If Hindutva mobs enjoy immunity under a Hindutva nationalist government, the journalist is duty bound to report it. If dynastic succession within the main Opposition party, the Congress, is creating a persisting feudal culture, the journalist is duty bound to report that too. If the AAP government in Delhi or the TMC government in Bengal are engaging in lawless behaviour or stamping out dissent, the journalist reports those events too.

Those liberal patriots who campaigned to end sati in the nineteenth century, who until today seek the end of caste crimes, crimes against women and rights abuse in every part of India, from Jammu and Kashmir to the north-east, those who, as the great philosopher Isaiah Berlin said, listen to the cry of the toad under the hole, those who fight for the rights of Dalits, are they all as 'neutral' as the 'nationalists' want them to be? Journalists must be true to the facts, even if they advance an honest opinion—Leftist or Rightist or liberal—based on the facts. Opinions are, of course, a journalists' prerogative but facts are not. In reporting caste crimes or crimes against women, are journalists only neutral observers? There's no scope for neutrality with facts. When the commitment is to pursue the truth, there is the conviction that it is the truth which will illuminate the right path. For the 'nationalist', the commitment is not to the truth, but the desire to always be right. That's because the pursuit of truth necessarily requires one to accept the possibility of mistakes and the capacity to acknowledge or rectify them. But if the desire is to be always right, it is necessary to paint someone else as always on the wrong side, and an 'enemy' fits that purpose. The 'nationalist' needs an enemy like he needs oxygen. The 'nationalist' is motivated by a blind faith in a final solution, the liberal accepts uncertainty, seeks answers. The blind believer believes he has seen the light and therefore has no qualms about eliminating non-believers.

The journalist who pursues the truth cannot manipulate or 'fix' the truth for the benefit of any interest because she is always the partisan of the citizens' right to know. The journalist Jorge Ramos, who in 2015 was famously thrown out of a Donald Trump press conference, has this to say about journalists and neutrality:

> Neutrality is often an excuse journalists use to hide from their own true responsibility. Our responsibility is to challenge those in power . . . I didn't become a journalist to be a tape recorder . . . what happens if you're called to cover a dictatorship? Are you going to report what the dictator wants or will you confront them? Will you report only the official version? Spanish has a great word to describe the stance journalists should take: 'contrapoder' (anti-Establishment) . . . we journalists have to be on the opposite side of power.

Journalists are free to hold whatever opinion they choose, but they are not free to present facts according to their opinions.

The philosopher Isaiah Berlin was a critic of moral relativism of values. Political action is needed along humanist liberal lines to alleviate suffering, indignity and hardship; negotiations and compromises are part of the values for which the human being strives. The struggle for progress is based on values. Journalism too can hardly afford a moral relativism of values. While reporting on a Nazi concentration camp, if there is a 'balancing' of the Hitlerian need to kill Jews with the Jewish point of view on camp life, then this is only state propaganda and not journalism. A balanced journalist is therefore always standing by the citizen, a rugged, moral, partisan of the truth, far away from any antiseptic, amoral definition of 'neutrality'.

From the Kashmir issue to relations with Pakistan to the struggle against Maoism to the journalistic obligation to not echo the 'muscular nationalist sentiment', to a defence of personal freedoms, the liberal is a greater patriot than the Hindutva 'nationalist'. The liberal upholds the patriotism of Gandhi, Tagore, Gokhale and Ambedkar; it is the liberal who keeps alive the flame of 1947. Not because all the positions or actions liberals take are necessarily correct but because true liberals recognize that they are flawed and fallible beings and continuously struggle to grasp the truth. They are eternal seekers, not peddlers of certainties. The liberal patriotism of Gandhi, Tagore, Gokhale, Ambedkar and many others lay not in the fact that they agreed to a common ideology or an action plan. Rather, their patriotism and commitment to the pursuit of truth made them disagree with some of their peers, at times very strongly, but mostly without being disagreeable. Debate and dissent was therefore not seen as a threat to the other, but a recognition by the other that the dissenter may have his own merit. To use Gandhi's words to Nehru and his other critics, 'Resist me always when my suggestion does not appeal to your head or heart. I shall not love you the less for that resistance.'

The liberal may be called 'desh drohi', 'anti-national' or 'traitor' but when it comes to who is a greater patriot and a greater servant of India, it is the liberal patriot who wins and the angry 'muscular nationalist' who loses. To the slogan 'Jai jawan, jai kisan', the liberal adds, 'jai insaan'. At a time when articulations of nationalism are becoming virulently aggressive, we need to return to Tagore, the author of our national anthem, to remind ourselves of the inclusive welcoming generous spirit that has always marked our land: 'Come all, come to this India, this shoreline of great humanity.'

[2]

The Liberal Hindu

Why the true Hindu is always a liberal and why the liberal Hindu is a better Hindu than the political Hindu

Theeyinul theral nee,
poovinul naattram nee,
Kallinul maniyum nee,
sollinul vaaymai nee,
Aratthinul anbu nee,
marathinul maindu nee,
Vedatthu marai nee,
boodatthu mudalam nee,
Venchudar oliyum nee,
thingalul aliyum nee,
Anitthum nee, anaitthin
utporulum nee.

—*Paripaadal* 111 (62–68), Kaduvan Ilaveyinanaar

[In fire, you are the heat,
In flowers, you are the scent.
Among stones, you are the diamond.

58

In words, you are the truth.
Among virtues, you are love
In a warrior's wrath, you are the strength
In the Vedas, you are the secret,
Of the elements, you are the first,
In the scorching sun, you are the light,
In the moonlight you are the softness
Everything, you are
Everything,
The sense, the substance of everything].

—Translation by A.K. Ramanujan

Must a Hindu define herself according to who her enemies are?

Does Hinduism teach violence, lynchings, foul language and anger?

Is Hinduism about the ruthless pursuit of political power and state patronage?

Is Hinduism about rigid rules, regulations and enforced obedience to a single deity, such as Lord Ram, and a single temple?[1]

Does Hinduism stand for an end to all questioning?

The True Hindu Is Always a Liberal Who Is Open to Change

'A freedom movement needs to be inaugurated,' wrote C. Rajagopalachari. '[There is] suppression of individual liberty and the state [is] a leviathan . . . a giant entity menacingly poised against the citizen, interfering with his life, mistrusting the people, imposing restrictions, controlling agriculture, industry, creating an army of officials, hypnotizing the people with slogans, a scheme in which the government is taken for granted and citizens are ignorant of their interests. Gandhiji emphasized maximum freedom for the individual, minimum interference by the state . . . fear is growing and because of fear people are getting corrupted, immoral and fraudulent.'[2]

Personal liberty is what the liberal seeks and personal liberty is what the Hindu has always sought. To quote Vivekananda: 'Freedom for the soul is the ultimate goal of Hinduism . . . we have got in our religion the provision for a Personal God . . . the Hindu religion consists not in believing certain doctrines and dogmas . . . but in spiritual verities like Atman, the soul and Brahman [God] . . . the soul is the repository of all power and virtue . . . the greatest of all Atmans [or God] . . . the Upanishads describe His realization to the Atman of man and man's duty to him in the most sublime poetry.'[3] For the Upanishadic sage Yajnavalkya, God 'is the inner controller immortal' of the individual and the world.[4] Yajnavalkya has been described as a 'monist', once again placing primacy on the oneness of the individual soul and the world.[5]

What is the soul or the Atman but the individual? And if God is the greatest Atman, then is not the soul of Man (or Woman) of primary significance in his relation to any authority, divine or temporal? Hinduism, in almost all its philosophical traditions, thus stands for individual liberty, whereas the current political avatar of Hindutva is a statist dogma, a government takeover of personal religion, something Vivekananda would have opposed with all his might. Citizens, are you going to let the government nationalize your atman? Make Hinduism into a public sector undertaking?

Citizens of India who enter 'Hindu' in the religion column while filling up a form, what kind of Hindu do you want to be? Do you want to be a Hindu who supports the destruction and defacement of mosques and churches, who discriminates against other religions, simply because others believe in a different God?

Or do you want to be a Hindu who can recognize differences and hold each other in respect to cooperate in a diverse society? Liberal Hindus are true to Hinduism's deep, varied and liberal traditions. Political Hindus are using Hinduism or Hindutva to grab political power.

Rabindranath Tagore and Mahatma Gandhi were deeply spiritual, yet their understanding of religion and spirituality was completely different. Even so, they held each other in high esteem. Tagore was a humanist, Gandhi a believer in the Hindu shastras. 'India has ever nourished faith in the truth of the Spiritual Man,' wrote Tagore, 'for whose realization she has in the past made innumerable experiments . . . India will be victorious when this idea wins the victory.'[6] Jawaharlal Nehru and Gandhi too had very different perspectives of religion, yet they all collaborated for decades for the cause of India's freedom.

In Gandhi's words, 'The essence of Hinduism is contained in the enunciation of one and only God as Truth and its bold acceptance of ahimsa, as the law of the human family.'[7] After Partition, Gandhi said, 'In the three quarters of the country that has fallen to our share Hinduism is going to be tested. If you show the generosity of true Hinduism, you will pass in the eyes of the world. If not, you will have proved Mr Jinnah's thesis that Muslims and Hindus are two separate nations.'[8]

Do you want to be a Hindu like Gandhi? Are you a Hindu who stands for Hinduism's values of acceptance and tolerance, for whom the oneness of God means any building sanctified by prayer is holy? Or are you a political Hindu for whom only certain kinds of rituals, superstitions and blind enmities confer religiosity, and for whom a small brick-and-mortar structure can become an object of loathing?

Hinduism is so rich precisely because it is so diverse. Those who discriminate against other Hindus by prescribing a long list of dos and don'ts, who lay down the law on vegetarianism, cow worship, rituals and set practices, refuse to recognize the long Hindu tradition of atheism and materialism running parallel with monotheism and a multitude of divinities. To quote Gandhi: 'I believe myself to be an orthodox Hindu and it is my conviction that no one who scrupulously practices the Hindu philosophy may kill a cow killer to protect a cow.'[9]

The liberal opposes the politicization of all religions and the misuse of religion for political ends. The liberal opposes the politicization of Islam, Sikhism, Hinduism and Buddhism in Sri Lanka or Myanmar. Religious extremism—both jihad and Hindutva—is an extension of politicization and leads to a degeneration of religion because of the coercion and violence that is needed to push the cause.

The liberal Hindu has no reason to invoke religion for social or political affairs since she has no reason to feel threatened by any other beliefs or non-beliefs. The easy acceptance of diversity is the best illustration of the liberal spirit of Hinduism. On a whimsical note, Hindus were liberals long before the idea of liberalism emerged as a civil and political ideal in the world!

The liberal Hindu has no problem with conservative Hindus or any other religious conservatives as long as they don't seek to impose their version of religion, through force, on those who don't accept their views on beef-eating, love jihad, caste discrimination, gender discrimination and other features that characterize today's Hindutva nationalists. According to liberal views, the orthodox Hindu is quite free to be vegetarian, egg-etarian or vegan, but not free to impose prohibition of meat or any non-vegetarian food on others, in the name of religion. To quote Vivekananda: 'Manu says that those who do not take meat at Sraddha and certain other ceremonies will be born as animals for such refusal . . . The modern Vaishnavas will find it difficult to reconcile themselves to the idea of Ram and Sita taking meat as stated in Valmiki's Ramayana . . . he who can afford it should take meat.'[10] Likewise, individuals are free to cover their heads or wear the tilak as a personal choice, but not impose those choices on others.

The principle of freedom in a democracy is that we all enjoy its privileges as long as we respect others' freedom too. Hindu conservatives enjoy their own freedom only so long as they don't force their views and methods on anyone else. So the argument here is not that conservative Hindus don't have a right to their beliefs, but that conservative/political Hindus don't have the right to impose their beliefs on others through state power, the power of the Big State, mob power or violence. If they expect to enjoy their own freedoms, they must accept others' freedoms too because religions can only coexist if a liberal framework for coexistence is accepted by all. To quote Hamid Dalwai: 'The real conflict in India today is between all types of obscurantism, dogmatism, revivalism and traditionalism on the one side and modern liberalism on the other.'[11]

Liberals Are Not Anti-religion but Believe in the Underlying Values of Religion

Liberals, unlike Marxists, don't oppose religion or spiritual pursuits.

'A good Liberal would tolerate and accept all religions equally,' says liberal stalwart Masani. Liberals point to the moral basis of religious philosophies, which are and have been movements for justice against oppression, such as Buddhism, Jainism and Christianity. Buddhism and Jainism were strong revolts against the 'hyper-developed sacrificialism of the Brahmanas'.[12] M.N. Srinivas points out that the Bhakti movement of medieval India embodied a strong rebellion and the pursuit of individual freedom against the idea of inequality inherent in caste as well as against the intellectualism of the traditional paths to salvation. Bhakti reformers attacked the idea of inequality and caste exclusiveness on food. They stood forth for individual rights and the right to seek a union with God without priests.

Liberals believe sustained inequality, injustices and perpetual oppression occur when there is an arbitrary and immoral use of authoritarian power, either by a clergy or a government. Religious and political philosophies become problematic when they seek to invoke state power to oppress others and suppress choices and freedoms. Liberals of all religions stand against injustice and inequality. Christianity was a revolt against the established clergy and the Roman emperor; the Bhakti movements were cries of protest against the priestly class. Importantly, the liberal believes that the power of morality lies in the freedom individuals have to exercise the choice to be moral, but not when such a choice is enforced by the might of the Big State. As Rajaji believed, citizens' liberty, a limited government and free enterprise are better ways to stimulate a moral sense than repressive control by the Big State and a cult of fear. 'If free institutions are to work effectively, every citizen must have a sense of moral responsibility.'[13] He also noted, 'Freedom should be the rule and control the exception, [today] the position is reversed.'[14]

Burka vs Trishul

A debate was recently initiated in the *Indian Express* between social activist Harsh Mander and historian Ramachandra Guha on the need for all Indian communities, Hindu and Muslim, to accept liberal values. One of Guha's ideas that attracted some outrage was that liberal Muslims should forsake the burka, just as liberal Hindus should reject antediluvian symbols like the trishul. Here, it is important to distinguish between symbols and the ideas they represent. Symbols are only meaningful when they are associated with particular ideas. The power of a symbol is drawn from the appeal of its underlying idea.

If attacking the burka is an attack on the Muslim community then such an attack is obviously reprehensible. Similarly, if Muslim men force Muslim women to wear the burka then it does become a symbol of injustice. But if the burka is worn as a free choice then the same burka becomes a symbol of that individual choice. Many young women in cities cover their faces while walking on the roads (which says a great deal about the visible lack of gender justice in the public domain in India), empowered by anonymity or simply to shade themselves from the sun or from the increasing air pollution. Is this not individual choice? In response to Guha, academic Syeda Hameed wrote, 'Guha . . . compares the word burka to the trishul. The burka, a humble piece of cloth, worn out from constant wear is hardly a weapon.'[15] The burka can be liberating for women who may feel empowered by the anonymity it provides to pursue their own goals. Liberals must constantly emphasize the underlying ideas of oppression and injustice instead of becoming trapped in the war of symbols: tilak vs burka, trishul vs sword, which is exactly what fundamentalists of all hues would like. If the law prohibits the open flaunting of dangerous weapons then that law must be followed by all. If the law permits wearing religious symbols, that law too applies to all.[16]

Liberal democracies generally embrace religious diversities. Western democracies, including the US, which ranks high among the most religious societies in the world, accept the personal freedoms of the Amish people, Mormons, beliefs in Scientology and various versions of Christianity. But they all enjoy this freedom only as long as they don't force them on others, including on their own followers.

Although in the US, with its constitutional separation of state and church, many presidents and leaders usually sign off their speeches with the wish 'God bless America', there is also a secularization of society seen in the fact that Christmas has almost become a non-denominational festival of goodwill similar to Thanksgiving. In earlier decades in India, Holi, Diwali and even Eid were on their way to becoming secular festivals of general public enjoyment before political activists intervened and began to give them an aggressively denominational colour. For instance, the Supreme Court's ban on Diwali crackers on grounds of air pollution was rejected as 'anti-Hindu' by some Hindu organizations.[17]

* * *

Today, there is large-scale Hinduization of popular culture. Many bestselling novels are written with themes from Hindu mythology.

The mass media has democratized sacred traditional culture, TV, radio and films use devotional themes or stories from the epics, and as Srinivas puts it, 'particularist loyalties of region, language, sect and caste are spread through sex, dance and song'. Temples are thronging with crowds. Yoga is fashionable across communities. Hinduness expresses itself in myriad ways. But, the question can be asked, what is the nature of this Hinduness? Is it a Hinduness that permits any complex interrogation of traditions?[18] Books, articles and paintings which interrogate or attempt to reinterpret Hinduism are met with violent protests from the culture police even though traditional Hindu texts like the Upanishads themselves are systems of continuous interrogation.

In the words of Nehru: 'The greatness of the basic Hindu approach of life was that it was not rigid . . . there is a spirit of tolerance; a man may be an atheist and still not cease to be a Hindu . . . it is not a religion in the ordinary sense . . . but when rigidity comes in it has brought many disasters to Hindu society . . . we have to break that rigidity.'[19]

Political Hindus Are Turning Their Backs on Modernity

Political Hindus are making us turn our backs on modernity and progressive thinking. In November 2014, photos appeared of then HRD minister Smriti Irani visiting an astrologer, Pandit Nathulal Vyas. Opposition members of Parliament (MPs) questioned a public figure displaying her superstitions. Reacting to this, BJP MP from Haridwar and former Uttarakhand chief minister Ramesh Pokhriyal 'Nishank' said, 'Astrology is the biggest science. It is in fact above science. We should promote it. We speak of nuclear science today. But Sage Kanad conducted nuclear test one hundred thousand years ago. And if Ganesh's head transplant was not plastic surgery, what was it? Astrology which can predict the future is far ahead of science. Science in fact is a pigmy compared to astrology.'

Now there's nothing wrong with a private belief in astrology, but when a government minister is seen openly consulting an astrologer, such a photo does a disservice to the ideals of India's rational secular state. In October 2014, at the inauguration of a hospital in Mumbai, Prime Minister Modi stated that Ganesh's elephant head and the birth of Karna were the result of advanced plastic surgery and genetic engineering, respectively. Here, we must ask, should this be accepted as Hindu belief?[20] Is it even within the realm of imagination that an elephant's head could be fixed on to a human's neck through plastic surgery?

The historian Mukul Kesavan writes, 'The average elephant's neck is more than two feet in diameter; the human neck, even if we choose a very large human is unlikely to exceed eight inches. How would you fix one on the other? . . . These claims are an inversion of the logic of faith . . . [and implies] Ganesha is not an instance of divine magic but the consequence of human technology . . . If Modi wanted to trumpet plastic surgery, he could have quoted the Sushruta Samhita's astonishingly detailed account of reconstructive plastic surgery.' Plastic surgery in ancient times! What next?

In 2014, Haryana chief minister Manohar Lal Khattar said that khap panchayats protect us against social evils.[21] In the same year, the external affairs minister, Sushma Swaraj, also said that the Bhagavad Gita must be recognized as the 'rashtriya granth' or national scripture.[22] Former Indian Council for Historical Research (ICHR) chairperson Yellapragada Sudershan Rao held that we need to accept the epics as 'true': 'Ramayana and Mahabharata are true accounts of the period, not myths. We can't say Ramayana and Mahabharata are myths.' To transform the Gita into an official government textbook when its mysteries or 'rahasyas' have enthralled every individual in richly varied ways is a grave injustice to its philosophy of argumentative individualism. The Gita is a 'popular poem for those who wander in the region of the many and the variable', wrote India's great philosopher–president, S. Radhakrishnan. 'It sees the many-sidedness of truth.'[23] In fact, Radhakrishnan pointed to five different interpretations and commentaries of the Gita—by Samkara (788–820 AD), Ramanuja (eleventh century AD), Madhva (1199–1276), Nimbarka (AD 1162), Vallabha (1479 AD)—saying that the continuing emphasis in the Gita is on the personal God, the personal Isvara. In the Gita, the Divine dwells in the innermost being of man and cannot be extinguished; the individual himself is a part of God. 'Arjuna typifies the representative human soul seeking to reach perfection and peace . . . bhakti leads to jnana or wisdom.' The Gita is thus an individual's search, an individual's varying experiences of the Brahman, it cannot possibly be reduced to an officially approved government-sanctioned text of the Big State.

Any move to make the Gita a government book would transform a text that is full of spiritual and moral questioning into an official diktat. If the government indeed needs a national book, why shouldn't the Constitution of India with its progressive ideals be the blueprint for a modern India? Furthermore, a khap panchayat should not be defended by a constitutional functionary whose aim should be to uphold the rule of law as defined by the Constitution. And an exhortation to accept the epics as 'true' runs counter to the sophisticated place allegory, legends and myths have traditionally held in the Hindu tradition.

An investigation by Reuters news agency revealed that there was a secret meeting in January 2017, of a committee which had been set up by the Modi government to 'prove' through archaeology and DNA that Hindu myths from the Ramayana and the Mahabharata are 'facts'. The chairman of the committee, K.N. Dikshit, told Reuters that he had been tasked 'to prepare a report that will help the government rewrite certain aspects of Indian history'. Culture minister Mahesh Sharma also told Reuters that those who think the Ramayana was a work of fiction are 'absolutely wrong'.

The government's aggressive defence of Sanskrit, Vedic science, palmistry, astrology and the factual basis of the epics has set it on a collision course with modernity itself.[24] As Hindutva nationalists campaign to rewrite textbooks along Hindutva lines, an Annual Status of Education Report (ASER) shockingly revealed that 9 per cent children in Class V cannot identify numbers, 44 per cent cannot read paragraphs and 29 per cent are unable to divide and subtract. Despite spending years in school, millions are growing up 'functionally illiterate'.[25] Even as Indian primary education recedes from global standards, political Hindus want to pull Indian students back into an illusory 'Vedic' Age.

Political Hindus make constant and skilful use of modern technological innovations like the Internet and mobile phones. But apparently they cannot tolerate modern values. While the prime minister promises a globalized future, the former HRD minister Smriti Irani in November 2014 attempted to banish the teaching of German in favour of Sanskrit as a third language in Kendriya Vidyalayas.[26] Listen to the words of Raja Rammohan Roy, liberal reformer and himself a Sanskrit scholar and a linguist: 'The Sangscrit [sic] language is so difficult that almost a lifetime is necessary for its perfect acquisition . . . it is well known that it has been for ages a lamentable check on the diffusion of knowledge . . . nor will youths be fitted to be better members of society by Vedantic doctrines which teach them to believe that all visible things have no real existence . . . no essential benefit can be derived by the student.'[27]

Roy also says, 'The Sangscrit system of education would be best calculated to keep this country in darkness . . . [government should] promote a more liberal and enlightened system of instruction embracing mathematics, natural philosophy, chemistry and anatomy.' Roy in fact opposed the establishment of the Sanskrit College in Calcutta in 1824 and campaigned for schools to impart modern education in English. It is no wonder that his harshest critics were orthodox Hindus, predecessors of today's Hindutva brigade.

The Sanskrit-imposing, khap-panchayat-and-astrology-publicizing orthodox Hindutva mindset runs counter to India's forward-looking progressive founding ideals. India is the land of the polemical

Bhagavad Gita and of the Bhakti saint-rebels. India is also the land of radical reformers like E.V. Ramasamy, widely known as 'Periyar', whose words in the essay 'The Radical Reformer' in *Makers of Modern India* are worth pondering over:

> What does it mean to be Hindu? Ninety out of hundred would have no answer. Yet their love for religion based on superstition is beyond description . . . our religion said to be millions and millions of years old says a majority of people should not read its scriptures; and if one violates it there are punishments such as cutting off the tongue that studies, pouring molten lead into ears that hear and gouging out the heart that learns. As a result only with the advent of the white government, 5 per cent are now literate. Of them 90 per cent are Brahmins . . . how much do we spend on rituals?
>
> Even if a child develops a fever a ritual is needed . . . money has to be coughed up...there are many Sankaracharyas, and Shaiva and Vaishnava pontiffs. They go about with their retinue in processions on elephants and camels . . . with our money . . . people are milked dry . . . people gain nothing from these.

Should twenty-first-century scholars try to prove the Mahabharata really happened? Or should they instead dignify the Ramayana and the Mahabharata by modern interpretation, which perhaps 1970s' Leftist historians failed to do? Instead of trying to impose Sanskrit, as a tribute to the spirit of the language, why not encourage linguistic brilliance in modern global languages as Rammohan Roy (himself a master of five languages and a scholar of Arabic and Persian apart from Sanskrit) exhorted youth to do? Imposing Sanskrit on the one hand and attempting to win elections through verbal violence, for instance, when Sadhvi Niranjan Jyoti demanded during the election campaign in 2014–15 that the people of Delhi vote for 'Ramzadon' rather than 'haramzadon' (those who are sons of Ram rather than those who are illegitimate), on the other hardly bolsters the cause of linguistic excellence.[28]

Political Hindus have a needlessly jaundiced view of modernity and deluded fantasies about the ancient Hindu past. Modernity need not mean only half-naked licentious decadence, Leftist history and an MNC-dominated economy. Those women members of the ruling BJP who are not sadhvis sport sindoor and mangalsutra as if battle-ready to constantly fight globalization. Yet, the T-shirt clad wrestling champions, the Phogat sisters from rural Haryana, probably keep alive the bold, independent spirit of the Upanishadic Gargi more than their outwardly docile Hindu sisters who follow orthodox prescriptions to the letter. Gargi was a woman philosopher in the Upanishads who in the Brihadaranyaka Upanishad dares to ask so many spirited and undaunted questions to Yajnavalkya that in the end Yajnavalkya says, 'Gargi, do not question too much lest your head fall off. Verily, you are questioning too much about a divinity about which we are not to ask too much. Do not, O Gargi, question too much.'[29]

When even the Vatican is re-examining its teachings on gay marriage, why do political Hindus see tradition as fixed in stone? Hindutvavadis must do a comprehensive social and intellectual rethink. Vatican II[30] was the Catholic Church's collective introspection on how to deal with the modern age. Perhaps we need a Hindu version of Vatican II so that many contested aspects of the Hindu tradition can be re-examined and questioned in the light of modern society, economics and even politics.

In politics, there is a need for Hindutva forces to embrace genuine modernity. The BJP as a Right-wing party urgently needs to become inclusive and modern and create a modern conservatism based on well-thought-out positions on the economy, modern education, gender justice, inter-religious marriage, youth morality and Hindu–Muslim relations. A conservative, liberal-Right social agenda is possible without becoming a party of religious extremists who attack lovers, modern women and Muslims as part of a so-called 'traditional' mission. Of course, the coexistence of social conservatism with fiscal prudence has had a short life across the world. This is because by legitimizing state intervention in social spheres, the Right wing paves the ground for state intervention in the economy as well. Once the BJP-led government began to intervene in social choices such as meat-eating or enhancing the scope of the Aadhaar identification process (see Chapter 3), the tone was set for a government-controlled economy as well.[31] If you want to control society, you will want to control the economy too.

How can the BJP evolve and become a normal Right-wing party, as it must? So far with its obvious inclination to create a muscular Big State, the BJP is the inheritor of statist ideologies of the Left as well as of the Congress. It must strive to become a secular rather than Hindu conservative movement. This means locating Right-wing ideology not in religion but in ideas that favour fiscal consolidation, encouraging individual responsibility, supporting private investment and generally believing that there should be less government in all walks of life. Rising above identity politics, this movement should differentiate itself from the left-of-centre Congress through its economic orientation and forever bury its militant Hindu identity.

The Vajpayee-led BJP perhaps came the closest in terms of the BJP attempting to distance itself from the communal undertow, in part due to Vajpayee's own liberal-conservative consensual persona. Yet, even in the Vajpayee years, the BJP was never able to free itself— perhaps it was never inclined to do so—from the backward tug of Hindutva cadres. Even in those years, the RSS moved to interfere in education and culture.

Conquering the communal demon is central to the BJP achieving modernity. As long as extremist figures remain vote-catchers, it will largely remain a party of religious fundamentalists, unable to achieve a modernist image. Indeed, the Indian Right's dilemma at the moment is where to draw the line between the Sangh world view and a modern political BJP. A modern BJP should ideally locate its right-wing identity in economics, not religion.

The modernity of jeans-clad, tech-savvy Sangh cadres is only skin deep. The BJP–Sangh combine needs to embrace a more substantive inclusive modernity beyond the shallow combination of smartphones and Vedic science. Instead of seeing Sanskrit as frozen in Vedic glory, it must imbibe its spirit of excellence. Instead of getting lost in proving the 'trueness' of the Mahabharata, it must pay tribute to it by throwing open the world of books and abandoning thought-policing and book-burning on campus. Instead of defending astrology as the best science, it should ensure every child has access to quality teaching so that modern India can replicate the golden era of mathematics and become a society that can give birth to Aryabhatas of the twenty-first century.[32]

A true commitment to India's traditions would be to imbibe their readiness to change and innovate and not destroy them by making India's centuries old open-mindedness an enemy of progress.

Why Do Hindutva Folks Hate Some Journalists?

Political Hindus generally detest some sections of the modern media. They only approve of those completely in agreement with them. Yet independent journalists are duty-bound to ask questions and report on communal conflicts. The BJP and Sangh Parivar view is that the media reflects an obsession with minority rights, leading to a neglect of vital debates on the grim realities of Islamist terrorism. The English language media particularly is often caricatured as a disconnected, elitist 'Macaulayputra' mouthpiece reluctant to focus on Hindutva issues. Yet, charges that the media is 'anti-Hindu' are only a means to browbeat and intimidate journalists and further shrink the space for raising questions. It is also a disingenuous charge. In order to play the victim card, Hindutvavadis need to loudly cry injustice, even when often it is they who are the perpetrators of injustice.

Today, a majority of mainstream media outlets and shrieking Right-wing anchors are feverishly upholding the political Hindu

line.[33] In this scenario, how can political Hindus claim the media is
against them?

In March 2016, a dentist in Delhi's Vikaspuri locality was
beaten to death by a mob. This immediately gave rise to a social
media campaign that declared that mainstream media was failing
to cover the incident with the same energy as it had the lynching of
Mohammad Akhlaq in Dadri in 2015, only because the Vikaspuri
victim was a Hindu. But journalists proceed on the basis of facts,
not ideology. No evidence emerged that the Vikaspuri murder was
motivated by religion. Instead, given the area's demographic profile
of upper-class enclaves cheek by jowl with slums, the killing seemed
to have been the result of street criminality.

By contrast, in Dadri, although there may have been some
reports that the killing was motivated by a property dispute, there was
ample evidence of rumours being circulated about Akhlaq's family
storing beef and of a public announcement being made on beef-
eating by Akhlaq. After the Dadri lynching, when BJP politicians
like Sakshi Maharaj said 'if somebody kills our mother, we won't
remain silent',[34] or Sangh leaders like Sadhvi Prachi asserted, 'those
who consume beef deserve such actions',[35] the media was surely
duty-bound to report the murder as a shocking, heinous assault on
minority rights. Equating Dadri with Vikaspuri is only an instance
of political point-scoring and a ploy by the political Hindutva lobby
to stop journalistic truth-telling.

In October 2015, a Bajrang Dal activist and flower merchant,
Prashanth Poojary, was brutally killed in Moodbidri in coastal
Karnataka, allegedly by a group of Muslim beef traders. Once
again, political Hindus took to social media to argue that not
enough media attention was paid to the Moodbidri killing.[36] It was
argued that in 2007 when author Taslima Nasrin[37] was assaulted
by All India Majlis-e-Ittehad-ul Muslimeen (AIMIM) activists in
Hyderabad, the event did not spur primetime TV debates, but when
in October 2015 columnist and author Sudheendra Kulkarni was
doused in black ink for inviting former Pakistan foreign minister

Khurshid Mahmud Kasuri for a book launch there was an outcry. The accusation is repeatedly made that the liberal media (and liberal Indians in general) are 'pro-Muslim' and 'anti-Hindu'.[38]

Whether in the Vikaspuri case, the Moodbidri murder, the killing of RSS workers in Kerala[39] or communal clashes in Malda in 2016,[40] when a Muslim organization held a protest against comments by a Hindu Mahasabha leader, it's argued that the media simply does not report on crimes committed by Muslims or by the Left as vigorously as it does on crimes committed by alleged Hindutva activists.

Does this sweeping accusation really hold? Can the Moodbidri killing really be compared to the Dadri lynching? A Bajrang Dal activist's conflict with a local 'beef mafia' appears more like an ongoing vicious political gang war compared to the dastardly killing of an innocent elderly man in Dadri purely because of his religion. Killings by competing political militias have long been part of India's bloody political landscape; the deaths of rival combatants can hardly be compared to innocents specifically targeted for religion or caste. It is certainly true that any murder is unacceptable, but is there really a 'secular liberal silence' when the victim is a Hindu, even if he is a Hindutva political activist?

National newspapers like the *Times of India* covered the Vikaspuri murder as a front-page headline.[41] Local news outlets in Kerala covered the Kerala killings in detail,[42] as did Bengali media with Malda.[43] If media is defined exclusively as English-language TV then we are inaccurately judging what a major chunk of audiences consume and the cries of media neglect are unfounded.[44] Trying to create moral equivalences between crimes is rhetorical politicking and an attempt to spread a polarizing agenda.

Perhaps the media was guilty of naming certain groups when reporting on the series of attacks on churches in 2015,[45] yet, equally hasty was the tirade on social media that Vikaspuri was a crime committed by 'Bangladeshi Muslims', a false perception corrected by a police officer who tweeted that even Hindus were among the accused in the Vikaspuri case.[46] In the Gauri Lankesh murder case, journalists who reported on the activities of Hindutva militant outfits at Lankesh's home were shouted down by Hindutva activists, yet, months later, investigations are clearly leading to the doors of various extremist Hindutva outfits.[47]

Violent language against journalists often spills into actual physical violence, as we saw in the attacks on women journalists at Delhi's Patiala House court during the Kanhaiya Kumar trial in February 2016[48] and in the murder of Gauri Lankesh in September 2017. To brand journalists as 'pseudo secular' enemies when they speak up against Hindutva majoritarianism is to target the media's role as truth-telling watchdog.

The Indian media has in the past generally steered a middle ground, but that legacy is today in serious jeopardy. In the past, the media has consistently spoken out against fatwa politics, with Taslima Nasrin being interviewed often.[49] Media outrage at the Shah Bano case in 1985 or on the banning of *The Satanic Verses* in 1988 was as vociferous as on Sangh Parivar campaigns like 'ghar wapsi' (Hindutva reconversion campaigns) and 'love jihad' (see Chapter 5 on the Hadiya case).

Liberal journalists who have challenged Hindutva politics have equally challenged the politics of dynasty and social injustice.[50] The media is a chaotic, multifarious and diverse platform where voices like the AIMIM leader Asaduddin Owaisi and Hindutva firebrand Sakshi Maharaj are heard equally. This plurality of almost 400 TV channels, where 'beef-eating Brahmins'[51] coexist with primetime nationalists, militates against any one ideology being consistently pushed, although very few media organizations today remain true to liberal values or are inclined to challenge Hindu nationalism frontally. How many media outlets are relentlessly pursuing the Gauri Lankesh murder investigations now that suspicions have turned on Hindutva outfits? Has the mainstream media seriously tracked and followed up the blood soaked saga of the innumerable lynchings by 'gau-rakshaks', from

Assam to Rajasthan to Kashmir to Haryana?[52] No, it has not. How many mainstream media outlets covered the Judge Loya case hearings in the Supreme Court?[53] Far from being 'anti-Hindu', much of the media today leans disproportionately towards the Hindutva brand of politics.[54]

Perhaps at one time the press was dominated by Left-leaning journalists and may have failed to report on the grievances of Hindu upper castes.[55] Today, the pendulum has swung almost to the opposite side with the viewpoints of Muslims, Dalits and other marginalized sections falling off the media map and the Hindu zeitgeist aggressively taking centre stage.

Hindutva forces are relentless in their efforts to constantly discredit independent journalists but in the process they are de-legitimizing a precious institutional pillar of democracy, namely, the free press (see Chapter 4 on targeting journalists). In fact, both the ideologically driven Hindutva Right and the ideological Left care little about free press or freedom of expression. Both invoke the power of the state to curb freedom of expression whenever it suits them. When invoking state power becomes futile, they play the victim card to pressurize the media.

In spite of campaigns by political Hindus through mainstream and social media if the question is asked: does what many call the Nehruvian Idea of India still endure at the grassroots and can we find examples of this? Yes, there are examples of the Idea of India that the media has perhaps not highlighted as well as it should have. One is the imam of Asansol, Maulana Imdadullah Rashidi, whose sixteen-year-old son, Sibghatullah, was killed in March 2018 as a result of violence on Ram Navami. In spite of his son's tragic death, the imam firmly declared that if anybody from his community retaliated or sought revenge for the killing, he would leave the town. 'I want peace. My boy has been taken away. I don't want any more families to lose their loved ones,' he said.

The other example is Yashpal Saxena, the father of Ankit Saxena, who also cried out for peace among communities after his twenty-three-year-old son was allegedly killed in February 2018 by the family of Ankit's Muslim fiancée. 'I don't want any inflammatory statements. I feel very saddened by what happened but I don't want anyone to create a hostile environment against Muslims. I have nothing against any religion,' said Saxena. In June 2018, he organized a multi-faith iftar in his area to spread love, tolerance and brotherhood. There are other examples. Damayanti Sen, Kolkata's first woman joint commissioner of police, who investigated and cracked the Park Street rape case and was transferred by chief minister Mamata Banerjee for her pains.[56] There is Shwetambari Sharma, the only female member of the Jammu and Kashmir Police special investigation team (SIT) which investigated the 2018 Kathua rape and murder, who said, 'As a police officer, I have no religion but my uniform.'[57]

These are inspiring examples of the Idea of India. They show that liberal ideas are often born at the grassroots and articulated by those who do not necessarily come from metropolitan backgrounds. They show how strongly and bravely the liberal flame burns, far away from big cities.

Political Hindutva vs Modern Governance

Since 1947, a broad though flawed liberal consensus (except the overt snatching away of democratic rights between 1975–77 during the Emergency) has existed. But this project is now in grave danger. It can only be rescued if the liberal project expands and if the fruits of development flow equally to all Indian citizens. It is only a liberal state and not a Hindutva nationalist one which can make true inclusive development possible.

Just as political Hindus have failed to evolve a modern identity on women's empowerment, Dalit rights or even marriage contracts, they remain at odds with inclusive, modern, decentralized governance. It is difficult to see how the promise of development can be realized in a highly statist Hindutva nationalist regime when the ideology calls for state intervention in society in a range of social and political matters. Like the ideological Left, Hindutvavadis invoke the Big State for constant intervention in the economy in the form of government schemes like demonetization or cattle trade rules. Often, these controls are sought to be enforced through violence by non-state ideological actors, such as the depredations of gau rakshaks on the cattle trade, or mob lynchings, thus affecting business confidence in stability and law and order, which in the long run could end up stalling growth.[58]

Gujarat chief minister Narendra Modi apparently ran a 'Hindutva plus development' model in Gujarat for twelve years. But it is now revealed as deeply flawed and relatively lacking in social welfare or employment opportunities. Academic Pranab Bardhan says the Gujarat model was one of growth but not job creation, because the state welcomed the highly capital-intensive petrochemical and pharma sectors, which did not provide jobs for the uneducated and semi-skilled majority in the workforce.[59] The Gujarat model of development was not particularly successful in creating an inclusive society. Not only have Muslims been largely ghettoized and members of the Dalit community attacked, but an official UGC report for 2015–16 shows that Gujarat University has the second highest number of cases of discrimination[60] against Dalits among central universities.[61]

The Hindutva nationalist economic model is about a massively controlling, citizen-distrusting state. In fact, Narendra Modi himself is a statist with no past record of rolling back government power. Schemes such as Swachh Bharat, Skill India and Startup India show a big controlling government imposing plans dreamed up by the high command rather like the socialist 20-Point Programme which was imposed by Indira Gandhi in the 1970s.

This Big State plays a crucial role in the propagation of Hindutva values, just as socialism was implemented through state power by Left-inclined regimes. In Yogi Adityanath–led Uttar Pradesh, the crackdown on 'illegal' slaughterhouses, setting up 'anti-Romeo squads', imposing a ban on government employees wearing jeans and T-shirts and making saris mandatory for women teachers, shows little tolerance for individual freedoms.[62] The ideological Big State—both of the Right and the Left—inevitably begins to encroach on individual freedom once it starts to use state power to push its ideology, ignoring the democratic principle of 'common good' and favouring only the state's own partisan ideological interest.

Yet, the liberalization of the Indian economy in 1991 showed that achieving high growth in the Indian context was not about asserting state power but rather about rolling back the powers of the state.[63] Given that the key challenge in India is job creation, an exclusionary ideology like Hindutva tends to block rather than create jobs. Cattle slaughterhouses, after all, provided livelihoods to both Hindus and Muslims, as did the cattle trade.

The core question is: can an openly illiberal ideology deliver development in a highly variegated country like India?

A liberal economy generally doesn't bear down on the individual with a plethora of rules. Instead, it aims to back off from areas where it ideally should not meddle. The summary closure of slaughterhouses in Uttar Pradesh is a powerful example of brute state power and a strongman chief minister, but does such flaunting of executive authority create business confidence?[64]

When arbitrary state action becomes policy, newer ideological enemies are needed every few months to demonstrate power. In Rajasthan, repeated instances of communal crimes are taking a toll on the state's development-friendly, tourist-friendly image.[65] The attack on a Jaipur restaurant last year by cow vigilantes,[66] the capitulation to the Karni Sena culture police on protests around the film *Padmaavat* (see Chapter 5) does not send out positive signals about a state which advertises itself as a mecca for tourists and literary festivals.

The Hindutva model of governance relies on increasing doses of state control which can even lead to citizen surveillance (See Chapter 4 on Aadhaar). It doesn't believe in genuine freedom for the citizen and instead considers regimentation and regulation as its ideal. The nationalist Hindutva state is not a Right-wing state at all in terms of economics. It is in fact similar to a massive socialist state with a religious hue. Can this Hindutva state adopt free market economic policies? Muscular nationalism that paints all dissent as anti-national cannot by definition free the economy. In Indian conditions, how can diversity bloom in the marketplace if diversity is stifled in society at large?

The Vajpayee-led National Democratic Alliance (NDA) (1999– 2004) and the Manmohan Singh–led UPA (2004–14), both by and large liberal dispensations, had realized that the state as 'mai baap' had to recede if genuine development is to take off. But today's political Hindutva forces are creating a model of triumphalist Big State power. When the state or government intrudes into every aspect of a citizen's life, when the ideology of the party in power becomes the dominant culture, there is no space for the citizen to remain a citizen—she is then either a loyalist insider or an ostracized outsider.

'A free economy,' said Masani, 'means government playing a limited part . . . controls should be to stop a man from doing what he should not . . . Communists ask: "Bread or Freedom?" Actually you can't get bread without freedom.' The Left opposed the liberalization of the domestic aviation industry. Post 1990–91, private players re-entered the aviation sector as the government repealed the Air Corporations Act in 1994. Today the Indian aviation sector is one of the fastest growing markets in the world, ferrying 117 million passengers in 2017.[67]

The Attempts to Semitize Hinduism, Create a Hindu Pakistan and Mimic Extremist Islamism

Who's a Hindu? Who's not a Hindu? Who is pro-Hindu and who is anti-Hindu? A political and cultural identity, an instrument of politics and electoral mobilization, the word 'Hindu' today dominates the discourse and means many things. Whether angry grievance or badge of pride, the word 'Hindu' is headline news almost every day. RSS chief Mohan Bhagwat believes all those who live in Hindustan are Hindus.[68] For certain kinds of book policemen, like moral policemen, who like to physically attack books they don't like (such as those who led the attack on some of the most scholarly works on Hinduism, such as A.K. Ramanujan's essay, 'Three Hundred Ramayanas') 'Hindu' is a crusading word, evoking a campaign against Macaulayite secularists who, they believe, have monopolized Indian post-Independence thought and education. 'Hindu' is posited as the opposite of the rootless and the Westernized.[69] India's Hindu past is wielded as an 'authentic Indian' riposte to centuries of Muslim and then imperialist Christian rule in India.

The fear of Westernization grips the political Hindu even as so many of them live highly globalized lives in Western capitals and pursue academic degrees from Western universities. Political Hindus believe that India's post-Independence ruling elite created a Left-dominated knowledge system that suppressed and ignored Hindu traditions, ignoring the fact that India's founders were by and large comprehensively bilingual and Indo-Western.

Nehru himself spoke fluent Hindustani and was an expert yoga exponent and despite being a lifelong agnostic he desired that his ashes be thrown into the Ganga. India's second President, S. Radhakrishnan, the great philosopher of Hinduism, steeped in advaita vedanta, was also Spalding Professor of Eastern Religions and Ethics at Oxford University. P.C. Mahalanobis, one of the first economist statesmen of India and one of the first members of the Planning Commission, was also a Bengali literary critic, Bengali litterateur and close friend of Rabindranath Tagore. Nobel Laureate economist Amartya Sen, a favourite target for Hindutvavadis, is also well-versed in Sanskrit, and once described the language as not only the language of the priesthood, but a medium which also questioned class; he has also said that his own notions of justice and the legitimacy of power were profoundly influenced by Shudraka's play *Mrcchakatika*.[70]

To quote Hamid Dalwai: 'Today Hindus have an influential liberal elite only because Hinduism is historically heterodox and can accommodate dissent. The modern Indian liberal tradition starts from Raja Rammohan Roy who was a product of Hindu society. It leads through such secular (as against Hindu) liberals as Nehru to the present time...The target of the Hindu liberal has been Hindu orthodoxy.'[71]

What's 'Indian' and what's 'Western' in our thousands of years of globalization? To quote Amartya Sen again, does the use of penicillin amount to Westernization? Is paneer 'anti-national' because cottage cheese was first brought to India by European settlers in east India? Are chillies non-Hindu or 'anti-national' because they were brought to India by the Portuguese?[72] In centuries of concourse with the world, to try to locate authentic Indianness and Hinduness is akin to chasing a mirage. The RSS's khaki shorts, now replaced with khaki trousers, are both Western imports.

In so much of Hindu tradition, education is not just knowledge. It's also about how we acquire knowledge, how we learn to ask questions. The pursuit of knowledge is as intellectually crucial as knowledge. 'Delivered from passion, fear and anger, absorbed in Me, taking refuge in Me, many purified by the austerity of wisdom have attained to My state of being.'[73] A Hindu sage spends his life seeking answers and exploring the new questions that each answer brings. A Hindu ascetic is in perpetual pursuit of perfection and better ways to become one with the universal spirit.[74]

Pride of place is given to the questioner, the free-thinker, the reformer, the iconoclast. Did Arjuna blindly accept his guru's command to go into battle? No, he did not. He asked questions and demanded answers. Did Gargi, the brilliant woman interlocutor of the Upanishads, fear her guru's wrath when she challenged Yajnavalkya to a debate? No, she did not, she dared to ask questions.[75]

The questioner, the atheist, the doubter and the agnostic can all exist under the Hindu umbrella. Many have traced the roots of atheist or agnostic ideas in Hinduism to traditions of scepticism in the Rig Veda. The Rig Veda contains a hymn which M. Hiriyanna describes as the 'climax of speculative thought' or atheist thought that the ultimate being—Tat Ekam or That One—is a dynamic and self-evolving entity with no outside power and thus no God. Charvak or Lokayata was a school of materialism which rejected religious rituals and supernaturalism and is described by Hiriyanna as 'restricted to the common experience'. And the Buddha was perhaps the world's most famous atheist who did not believe in Hinduism's gods.

In Hindu tradition, there is no belief in a single God or a single church or a single religious authority or 'the single truth' or in 'blasphemy'. How can there be a concept of blasphemy when there is no holy cow beyond human scrutiny? 'India has always been marked by richness and heterogeneity in religious, intellectual, moral, literary and artistic traditions,' writes Srinivas, with every major religion represented in India except Confucianism. 'Heresy-hunting has been unnecessary because rebels have in the course of time become a caste.' Concepts like 'blasphemy' simply do not exist in Hinduism. Writes Radhakrishnan: 'No country and no religion has adopted this attitude of understanding and appreciation of other faiths so persistently and consistently as India and Hinduism.'[76] But Hindutva nationalists, enamoured of Semitic religions, determined to imitate them and create a Semitized Hinduism, are creating an atmosphere of fear in which debates about traditions can hardly take place.

Those who project a monolithic Hindutva are deeply unaware of how false their project is. For example, Vinayak Damodar Savarkar, the icon of Hindutva, and his followers, today's Hindutvavadis completely differ on the subject of the cow. Savarkar was staunchly opposed to cow worship, saying 'while worshipping the cow, the entire Hindu nation became docile like the cow'.[77] 'If the cow is a mother to anyone, it's a bullock. Not to Hindus. Hindutva, if it has to sustain itself on a cow's legs will come crashing down at the slightest hint of a crisis . . . when humanitarian interests are not served in fact are harmed by the cow, and when humanism is shamed, self-defeating extreme cow protection should be rejected.'[78] Savarkar also said, 'I criticised the false notion involved in cow worship with the aim of removing the chaff . . . it is improper to forget the duty of cow protection and indulging [sic] only in worship.'[79] In fact, according to Savarkar, the symbol of Hindutva should not be the cow but the man-lion or Narasimha.[80]

Hindutva outfits also ignore other significant differences of opinion with their icons. They claim Bhagat Singh as one of their guiding lights, when Singh was a socialist and an atheist and even wrote a tract titled 'Why I am an Atheist'. Political Hindus claim Buddhism and Sikhism as part of Hindu unity. But they ignore the fact that these faiths arose as protests against rigid orthodoxy, ritualization and discrimination within certain Hindu communities and practices. The only way to claim all these traditions for a single canon called 'Hinduism' is to acknowledge the diversity and variety within Hinduism, a religion which is defined by difference.

Yet, bans, diktats and sedition charges are issuing like thunderbolts from a vengeful, enraged orthodoxy of political Hindus, an orthodoxy unknown in that glorious multiplicity known as sanatana dharma. These orthodoxies are shaped more by a Semitic interpretation of what it means to be a Hindu rather than any understanding of fundamental Hindu values. This campaign seems intent on making Hindutva a mirror image of radical Islam. The public beheadings by the Islamic State (IS) terrorist group can be compared to a Hindutva activist hacking his victim to death and then filming it to proudly proclaim his barbarity, as happened in Rajsamand. Political Hindus, in their obsessive Islamophobia, are making Hindutva a mimic of extremist Islam, copying everything they apparently criticize in extreme versions of Christianity and Islam.[81] Hindutva voices criticize these religions for being rigid and expansionist, accuse them for adopting the sword and offering inducements to spread their faith.[82] Yet, by pursuing campaigns such as 'ghar wapsi', 'love jihad' or 'gau raksha', political Hindus are adopting exactly the same strategies.[83]

Given this Semitization of Hinduism, Hindus are no longer free to delve into their traditions or to ask questions. They are no longer allowed to ask, for example, why so many festivals are male-centric or if certain hymns like the Purusa Sukta sanctify caste hierarchy.[84] How can the killing of Meghnad by Ram be interpreted in a modern way? Would the gatekeepers of so-called 'Hindu pride' ever permit an opera like *Jesus Christ Superstar* on the Mahabharata or the Ramayana? Would they permit a complex reading of the figure of Ram? Dalitbahujan scholars have asked questions about the way Ram killed Vali in order to win the loyalty of Sugriv and the monkey army, his treatment of Sita, where he chose to placate the mob rather than do the right thing by his beloved wife. Are these moral questions embedded in the Ramayana no longer open to reinterpretation? Hindu traditions created gods and avatars in their own mould, which is why gods reflect the high and low values of man through the epics and puranas. The epics are classic examples of not just morality plays showcasing the triumph of good over evil but constantly laying bare the dilemmas and choices, the inner wars, that confront both good and bad people. 'The Mahabharata and Ramayana,' says Gandhi, 'describes the eternal duel that goes on between the forces of darkness and of light.'[85] Gandhi further writes, 'The Pandavas and Kauravas are the forces of good and evil within us. The war is the war between Jekyll and Hyde, God and Satan, going on in the human breast.'[86]

In the Ramayana and the Mahabharata, there are few black-and-white characters. Instead there are constant reminders to be humble and seek knowledge. Exploring, questioning Hindus are being prevented from enlivening and reinterpreting their traditions in exciting new ways by the political armies of the Hindutva persuasion. The phrase 'Ekam sat viprah bahuda vadanti' (There are many roads to God) animates almost the entire Hindu tradition, in which vaad, vivaad and samvaad have always had a primary role.

The fixation on the extremist Islamist threat has meant that religious activists are now agitating for blasphemy laws and public punishment of crimes. Some are even issuing fatwas. In 2017, during the Karni Sena's distasteful protests against the film *Padmaavat*, the then Haryana BJP media coordinator offered a Rs 10 crore bounty for beheading actor Deepika Padukone and director Sanjay Leela Bhansali. Few Bollywood stalwarts spoke out against these threats. The singer Sonu Nigam had already revealed the proclivity of the leading lights of the entertainment industry to blow with conservative winds. He tweeted on 16 April 2017: 'God bless everyone. I am not a Muslim and I have to be woken up by the azaan in the morning. When will this forced religiousness end in India?'

A few minutes of the sounds of the azaan has for decades been part of plural India's sights and sounds, the religious multiplicity that Hinduism rejoices in. In fact, the issue is not so much the azaan but the civic problem of the use and abuse of loudspeakers, indulged in by every outdoor social or religious event, despite clear noise pollution guidelines. That celebrities from the entertainment world now choose to echo orthodox Hindutva views shows they too want to match extremist Islam, intolerance for intolerance.

In January 2015, several members of the Paris-based satirical weekly *Charlie Hebdo* were killed for 'insulting' the Prophet. Political Hindus too like to deliberately manufacture 'insults' to Hinduism, such as their campaign against cricketer M.S. Dhoni for being featured as Vishnu on a *Business Today* magazine cover in 2013, or their rage over a few seconds of the azaan or imagined slights to Hinduism in books and movies. Hindutva brigades constantly declare how much they loathe Pakistan, yet are striving hard to turn India into a 'Hindu' Pakistan by constantly keeping the religious-political pot boiling, thus politicizing both religion and society.[87]

In August 2014, Justice A.R. Dave of the Supreme Court asserted, 'Had I been the dictator of India, I would have introduced Gita and

Mahabharata in Class 1.' For Justice Dave, the Gita is perhaps the supreme holy book. However, for some sects of Vaishnavites, the Bhagwat Purana occupies a place even higher than the Gita. Anyone who attempts to impose the Gita forgets that even Krishna could not impose it on Arjuna but had to reason with him. As we have seen, the Bhagavad Gita in itself was influenced by the Rig Veda and the Upanishads and is not often mentioned in later scriptural texts.[88] In fact, there are innumerable interpretations of the Gita, many of which contradict each other. Gandhi looked upon the Gita as a guide for his ahimsa, while others have found in it inspiration to go to battle and sacrifice their lives. To seek uniformity in the Gita is itself a supreme delusion. To impose it, by the order of a dictator, goes against the spirit of the text itself.

Hinduism's inherent religious democracy has created many reform movements such as the Arya Samaj (founded 1875), Brahmo Samaj (founded 1828) and even the Swadhyay movement of Pandurang Shastri.[89] The insistence on a single God, Ram, and a single holy book, the Gita, is profoundly at odds with the dizzyingly varied Hindu inheritance, shaped crucially by individual choice. India's reform movements have been open to global influences. As Srinivas notes, many Hindu reformists emulated Western missionaries by establishing schools, colleges and hostels.

Radhakrishnan points out that because the principle of the individual soul, the 'atma', lies at the heart of Hindu Vedantic philosophy, no religion is as steeped in individualism as Hinduism. There is no evidence of any Hindu ever finding a way for collective or group moksha; in fact, moksha remains the most individualist quest possible. Writes Radhakrishnan: 'It is by turning inwards, towards an inward silence, that the individual consciousness, through introspection and reflection, that the self confronts the Supreme Self.' To awaken the moral and spiritual sense within, the human being needs only her own individuality.

The atma chooses his own route to brahma and is therefore invincible. The individual has the power to shape his own religious universe; thus, the individual is provided with an unprecedented religious freedom. It is this religious freedom that has made Hinduism virtually unconquerable. A single shrine is open to assault but millions of little shrines are too diffuse, too inward, too deeply buried within the soul to subdue. Many other civilizations underwent great cultural and religious transformation with every foreign conquest. But Hinduism survived political turmoil because the essence of Hinduism with all its diversity lay within each Hindu. Hinduism has never needed political patrons to protect it from anyone. In Vivekananda's words, 'Thus we understand why Hindus have survived inspite of numerous calamities and foreign invasions. Our ancestors in the past, finding that the quest for the secret of Nature through external investigations is useless, turned their attention inwards.' He also says, 'The real thing for Hindus is spiritual independence—Mukti . . . the Hindus will stand any trials and tribulations as long as their aspiration for Mukti is not affected.'

To quote scholar and author Jonardon Ganeri: 'The essence of Hinduism is that it has no essence. What defines Hinduism is its polycentricity, multiple centres of belief and practice . . . Hinduism is a banyan tree . . . under which a great diversity of thought and action is sustained.'[90]

Banning the books of Wendy Doniger and A.K. Ramanujan's essay in the Paula Richman volume, and prohibiting English and Urdu phrases in textbooks are seen as acts defending 'Hindu pride' or 'Indianizing education'. But can a book, any book, which Hindus traditionally touch to their heads as manifestations of Saraswati, ever be, for a true Hindu, a focus of contempt? In fact, you have to be quite un-Hindu to kick, stamp or disrespect and destroy a book.[91]

Indianizing education should surely mean to recreate and reignite the questioning spirit of Gargi, of Arjuna, of Kabir, who wrote: 'It's all one skin and bone, one piss and shit, one blood, one meat. From one drop, a universe. Who's a Brahmin, who's a shudra?'[92] Swami Vivekananda, whom the Hindu Right has adopted as one of its icons, was one of the fiercest critics of blind rituals and evil social customs which masquerade as manifestations of Hinduism. 'Superstition may be a great enemy of man, but bigotry is worse.' Vivekananda hailed Jesus as a supreme spirit, and said, 'According to Hindu teachings as embodied in the Gita, "wherever you find a great soul of immense power and purity struggling to raise humanity, know that he is born of my splendour and that I am there working through him. Let us therefore find God not only in Jesus of Nazareth but in all the great ones that have preceded him.'

Hinduism has always stood for intellectual freedom. It is a freedom that has led to super-achievers both at home and abroad. It is in fact decidedly un-Hindu to ban, exclude and suppress any form of knowledge, because Hindu traditions have always honoured those who embrace intellectual striving and forge new ways of reform, change and devotion. Tagore and Gandhi debated frankly on a range of issues, on nationalism, democracy and culture without ever losing respect for each other.

Strident voices who claim to speak for Hinduism, war-like fundamentalists who have captured the 'Hindu' space and call for a holy war against other religions, are not voices the liberal Hindu identifies with. These voices are calling for war not only against other religions but against the beliefs and practices of other Hindus as well.

Hinduism has never been a domineering force. The Hindu sings qawaalis, bhajans and Christmas carols, and enjoys kababs without guilt. The Ramakrishna Mission celebrates Christmas. Hindus have never been ruled by a religious police or been asked to prove their Hinduness through political loyalty to a particular party.

Hindus are being asked to hate when the religion they were born into teaches freedom, inclusion detachment and introspection. The mark of a true Hindu, as Mahatma Gandhi said, is, above all, a generosity towards others. Hindus are being asked not to question, not to reinterpret, they are being asked to be perpetually angry. But Hinduism's gods have always been playful, genial, unpredictable and mercurial. Krishna, Ganapati, Parvati, Saraswati—do these deities embody hatred and rage? It is the gentle playfulness of many Hindu deities that makes them so welcome in so many homes.

An amiable religion entwined with family folklore, in which each god is almost a family member whose story often mirrors an identifiable human drama, is suddenly now a fear-inspiring doctrine to be spoken of only in hushed tones. Yes, caste and superstition created terrible injustices within Hindu society. But from within the ranks of Hinduism itself rose the great social reformers who challenged these evils: Anti-caste campaigners Jyotirao Phule[93] and Rammohan Roy, Vivekananda, Tagore, Guru Nanak, Dayanand Saraswati in the north. In the south, Periyar and his inspiration, the early twentieth-century reformer Narayana Guru of Kerala, the great campaigner against caste and for social and spiritual awakening. The Bhakti movement made a deep impact on the non-Brahmin castes of south India and reformers like Roy went back to the Vedas to attack Hindu social evils, as Dayanand Saraswati did when he sought to reject all post-Vedic additions to Hinduism.

Hinduism of the ages has been about a culture-soaked joie de vivre, of sindoor, jasmine and marigolds: a feast for the senses and a balm for the soul. 'Bhagwan ek hain, alag naam hain', is a dictum heard across the land. Chandidas, a Vaishnavite poet saint of the fourteenth century, is believed to have said, 'sabar upare manus satya tahar upare nai' (The supreme truth is man, there is nothing more important than he is).

This quiet aesthetic, often spiritually atheist, set of beliefs is being sought to be transformed into a force that rages about insults, sedition, blasphemy, reconversion, love jihad and murder in the name of the cow. Political Hindus want to make Hinduism a doctrine that inspires terror and a quaking acceptance of mob rule. The axe murder of a Muslim on the excuse of 'love jihad' as an act of so-called 'Hindu vengeance' is meant to intimidate and quell protest. A multifarious spiritual tradition is in danger of being transformed into a justification for violence, a source of accusations, legal cases and FIRs, with section 295 (A) (Deliberate or malicious acts to insult religion) increasingly invoked.

A tradition comprising centuries of innumerable free thinkers like the fifteenth-to-sixteenth-century Bhakti leader Chaitanya Mahaprabhu and Ramakrishna Paramahamsa in the nineteenth century, has always stood for an open embrace of diversity and pluralism. Those who killed Mohammad Akhlaq in Dadri in September 2015 or Pehlu Khan in Alwar in April 2017, those attacking lovers, movie directors, meat eaters, artists or writers or rationalists (see Chapter 4), can those attackers really represent a religion which places the freedom to be different at the very centre of spirituality?

As we have noted, Hinduism has always been about belief in an individual pursuit of moksha: the seeker meditates alone and finds his own way. Why did Hinduism never need to proselytize? Because every path to god was seen as valid, Hinduism respects all. As Ramakrishna Paramahamsa said, 'Jato math tato path'—there are as many paths as there are opinions. The diversity of paths means they are all legitimate spiritual pursuits. The Hindu mind is marked by a 'noble scepticism', said Vivekananda. 'The Hindu mind is demanding of intense realization.'

A true Hindu has no reason to be fearful or feel threatened. This is because there is space even for those who reject Hinduism in the Hindu fold. Guru Nanak provided strong reasons for rejecting Hinduism primarily on the grounds of rituals. Srinivas sees Sikhism as a fusion of Hindu and Islamic thought as well as an avenue for upward mobility in a caste society. The coexistence of Hinduism and Sikhism is seen in the manner in which elder sons of Hindu families in Punjab often became Sikhs. The Upanishads can easily be considered atheist texts as they do not speak of God but of the brahma and the atma. 'Fire is His head, the sun and moon His eyes, space His ears, the Vedas His speech, the wind His breath, the universe His heart. From His feet the Earth has originated. Verily, He is the inner self of all beings.'[94] The self leads to God and self-knowledge to realization.

At the Kumbh Mela, there are no priests to mediate between the individual and his relationship with sun and river. The pilgrim comes in solitude. No wonder Hinduism didn't seek to capture political power. There was no reason to wield the sword for a religion that was simply unconquerable precisely because it was so undefined and varied. Who would a Hindu take up the sword for? For the Shaivite? For the Vaishnavite? For the tantric? For the Naga sadhu? 'As soon as India accepts the doctrine of the sword, my life as an Indian is finished . . . the ancients of India that the true thing for any human being on earth is not justice based on violence . . . but justice based on yajna and kurbani,' said Gandhi.

Whoever ruled on earth, whether British or Mughal, Hinduism has been indestructible. It has survived, and always will, because its domain is within. India is perhaps the only civilization that has experienced so many foreign conquests, yet, the broad contours of Hinduism with all its diversities have survived, in fact, assimilated many of the conquerors' belief systems too, without dissolving their own identities. That's why Tagore's song 'Hey more chitto' (Quoted in Chapter 1) ought to be the theme song of Liberal India as it is a paean to free spirit of the eternal Indian.

Should Hinduism be about Political Power?

Political Hindus seeking political power are destroying precisely that quality of inwardness that makes Hinduism so enduring. The Christian world struggled for centuries to separate church from state.[95] The Islamic world has been beleaguered by theocrats who used religion for legitimacy. Hindutvavadis want India to repeat the same tragedies that befell Christian and Muslim societies, which have had to wage bloody battles to separate political chieftains from holy men. Today, pan-Islamism as a doctrine has failed, and warring sects now fight blood feuds across the globe. In India, pan-Hinduism has never existed even as a cultural or religious phenomenon at any time in history, because an idea that is so open to diversity cannot be threatened and therefore there has never been a social or political need for any Hindu Rashtra–type phenomenon. This is a faith historically defined by its coexisting sects, perfectly at home accepting Buddhism, Christianity, Islam or atheism as just another sect.

Paradoxically, by politicizing Hinduism, political Hindus are taking away its unique power and seeking to merge it with politics. Hinduism has never needed protection from politicians. This is a religion which, even after assaults like when Mahmud of Ghazni so brutally ransacked the Somnath temple,[96] lived on in hidden shrines and homes, so adaptable, so much a 'little tradition' that it was unconquerable. Without a visible church or an established clergy, what tangible entity is there to conquer? Today, with demands to make the Bhagavad Gita into a 'rashtriya granth', the Gita as a philosophy is being overthrown for the sake of the Gita as a political weapon. What the conservatives ignore is that the allegorical battle in Kurukshetra tore apart the two sides, although both shared the same religion. Today's Hindutva warriors seem bent on make Kurukshetra a reality, even at the cost of destroying the essence of Hinduism and the idea of India.

It's time for liberal Hindus to reclaim their religion. It's time to assert that the Hindu inheritance is far greater than the building of a Ram Mandir at a particular spot. The Hindu meditates under trees and in high mountains, beside rivers and forests, the natural world is her temple and god resides in puja rooms in almost every Hindu home. To quote Vivekananda's famous lines:

Bahurupe sammukhe tomar
chhari kotha khujicho Ishwar,
Jibe prem kore jei jon
Sai jon sebichhe Ishwar

[Where are you looking for God,
when he is in front of you,
in every living thing.
Those who serve/worship any living thing
are serving/worshipping God.]

And nor did Vivekananda's notion of 'jibe prem' make him a vegetarian!

The attempt to create a homogeneous religious loyalty to only one set of deities (Ram and Sita), the insistence on a single form of worship (temple visits), a single set of dietary preferences (vegetarianism), a single racial type (Aryan), a single language (Hindi) and a single temple (the Ram Mandir at Ayodhya) is a repudiation of the faith of generations who lived in ease with dizzying diversities. Hinduism is the religion that the whole world, from scholars to hippies, once fell in love with. Voluntary choice is the basis of a liberal and free society and voluntary individual choice is the basis of Hinduism. The liberal Hindu is thus the adversary of the political Hindu, bent on using Hindutva for a political strategy to capture power.

Using Hinduism for the Ballot Box

For political Hindus, it is as if the Muslim defines their religion. They seem to be always spoiling for a fight with the Muslim 'enemy'. They seek to constantly reinforce their own victimhood and propagate the myth that they are victims in their own land. A piercing question was once asked: *Are political Hindus pro-Hindu or are they simply anti-Muslim?* Think about it!

In July 2017, Amarnath Yatra pilgrims were attacked in Anantnag. A familiar narrative flared up: Hindus are the targets in their country. According to this line, Hindus suffer in silence while only attacks on Muslims are highlighted. From Paris 2015 to Manchester 2017, every time Islamist terror strikes a Western city, it is used to put the entire Muslim community in India on notice, even though as George Bush famously said, 'India is a country which does not have a single Al-Qaeda member in a population of 150 million Muslims.'[97]

The Hindu victimhood narrative is nothing but an Islamophobic war cry against minorities. Like all claims to victimhood, the Hindu-as-victim line is also a manifestation of a sense of impotence and lack of self-esteem. Yes, innocent Hindu pilgrims died in Amarnath and their killers may have been motivated by a radicalized Islam that spurs violence. But is that reason enough to spin a comprehensive story that all of India's Hindus are at the mercy of Islamic terror?

Political Hindus refuse to accept that Muslims are the worst victims of Islamist terrorism. In 2011, the BBC reported that in cases where the religious affiliations of terror casualties could be determined, between 82 per cent to 97 per cent of terrorism-related fatalities over the last five years have been Muslims.[98] The Shia–Sunni conflict has resulted in the Muslim community turning on itself, and in Kashmir the overwhelming majority of the thousands killed in militancy have been Muslims (see Chapter 1). So who's the real victim here? In 2017, communal clashes broke out in Basirhat in Bengal, sparked by a teenager's Facebook post. Images of Muslim groups targeting Hindu shops were troubling, but more sinister were the fake photographs circulating on social media, designed to push a strategic campaign that Bengal had become a hub of hatred for Hindus.

Hindus were not victims in Bengal, which is why the fake photos on social media found no resonance among the citizenry. In fact, across India, the Hindu experiences no fear at all from the Muslim, however relentlessly victimhood campaigns are pushed.

The Justice Rajindar Sachar Committee report commissioned by the UPA and presented in Parliament in 2006 showed horrifyingly low levels of education and healthcare among Muslims,[99] a falling rate of Muslim representation in bureaucracy and police, female literacy lower than that of Scheduled Castes (SCs) and Scheduled

Tribes (STs). It showed that only one out of twenty-five students in undergraduate colleges and one in fifty in post-graduate colleges are Muslims. The average Muslim is falling behind in most social and economic parameters.

If Muslims have been 'pampered' and 'appeased' by successive generations of 'secularists', as Hindutvavadis allege, why doesn't this show with a rise in incomes and education? Or are we confusing the political patronage of regressive imams with the average Indian Muslim? Political patronage is a tool used to create a favourable impression of the party or government among religious communities and is a manifestation of identity politics. Political Hindus paint the patronage of Muslims as 'appeasement', but seek to leverage their own version of Hindu appeasement to create their own set of identity politics through government patronage.[100]

If 'Muslim appeasement' means granting a Haj subsidy or benefits to a madrassa, then frankly this has made no difference to the lives of ordinary Muslims.

Political Hindus fail to note how many Muslims, including the fiery Syed Shahabuddin, have spoken out openly against the Haj subsidy.[101] Hasn't Javed Akhtar repeatedly mocked Islamic fatwas?[102] Haven't Muslim feminists spoken in favour of the Uniform Civil Code on grounds of gender justice? (See Chapter 5.) Did almost the entire country not rally for a Hindu woman, Nirbhaya, irrespective of religion? (See Chapter 5.)

Today, the government has abolished the subsidy for Haj pilgrims on grounds of 'minority appeasement' but as columnist Swaminathan Aiyar pointed out, the Modi government has launched the Punyadham Yatra scheme, by which pilgrims to Puri, Vaishno Devi, Vrindavan, Ajmer Sharif and Mathura are all given subsidized transport and accommodation. In fact, even the Kailash Mansarovar Yatra is subsidized, and quite a few state governments have started subsidizing Hindu pilgrims.[103] As Aiyar asked, 'With what face can Modi abolish one pilgrim subsidy [calling it appeasement] but create others without calling them appeasement too?'[104]

Political Hindus spread the pernicious whisper campaign that Muslims are reproducing faster than Hindus and will soon outnumber the majority. However, the website IndiaSpend reveals through figures that fertility rates are higher among poorer communities, both Hindu and Muslim, and are not based on religion.[105]

There is also the narrative that Left-ruled Kerala is a killing field where RSS workers are being butchered by Leftist outfits (See instances cited earlier in the chapter). Yet, aren't Leftist and RSS outfits generally comprised of Hindus on both sides? Incidents of dowry-related violence, overwhelmingly inflicted by Hindus on Hindus, far outnumber the instances of love jihad by a wide margin. If newspapers decide to report crimes against women by religion or caste, the picture may not be very pretty for the Hindutva brigade.[106]

It was a sixteen-year-old Muslim boy, Hafiz Junaid, who was stabbed to death on a train in June 2017. In June 2017, sedition charges were slapped on youths allegedly celebrating Pakistan's victory in the ICC Champions Trophy. In July 2017, a Muslim family was attacked on a train in Mainpuri in Uttar Pradesh. Surely it is the Muslims, who, on a more regular basis than any other community, are the daily victims of the current spirit of muscular 'nationalism', a so-called 'nationalism' which has also fuelled efforts to humiliate Dalits. This muscular Hindutva nationalism does not distinguish between communal or caste identities.

When Hindu mythology, festivals, iconography and imagery are now the dominant themes in art, books, movies and TV shows, when the prime minister has himself once openly declared that he is a 'Hindu nationalist', why should the political Hindu feel as if he is cornered or spread this imagined fear?[107]

There have been innumerable attacks on Muslims in the name of the cow by gau rakshaks. Yet there's been little condemnation of gau rakshaks from the government. In fact, why just Muslims? Even Dalits and Christian carol singers[108] have not escaped the wrath of

Hindutva vigilantes. In a horrifying incident on 11 July 2016, four Dalit men skinning cow carcasses in Una, Gujarat, were tied to a car and brutally beaten with iron rods, leading to a nationwide outrage on this appalling attack on Dalit communities who have traditionally been engaged in the cattle trade.

An important question arises here: does this narrative of victimhood necessarily yield political rewards? In Haryana, Uttar Pradesh, Madhya Pradesh and Rajasthan, where most crimes against minorities are reported,[109] Hindutva activists feel enormously empowered by the 2014 general election win, even though the political returns on Hindutva victimhood may be waning. In the 2018 Karnataka assembly elections, the BJP scored impressive wins in the polarized coastal Karnataka belt, but failed to garner the fruits of Hindutva in other areas of Karnataka. The Modi-led BJP, with its unblinking eye on electoral benefits, finds it advantageous to ramp up Hindutva rhetoric at election time, such as the prime minister did during the Gujarat campaign in 2017. But although such rhetoric perhaps pulled the BJP back from the abyss of a defeat, the party still fell short of the psychological mark of 100 seats in Gujarat. In fact, the 2017 Gujarat campaign revealed that once political Hindutva reaches saturation point, it is then subject to diminishing returns.

In the 1990s, the Ram Mandir agitation served the purpose of temporarily uniting Hindus under one rallying cry.[110] Yet, the political dividends from the campaign were rather limited and Vajpayee slowly moved away from it post-1998, after forming the NDA coalition government. After 1991, the BJP lost power in Uttar Pradesh, regaining it only after two decades. The Ram Janmabhoomi movement brought only temporary political gains. After the demolition of the Babri Masjid, the BJP was in fact pushed to the margins of Uttar Pradesh politics until it returned with a bang in 2017.

An excess of violence or intimidation either in the name of cow protection or on other Hindutva issues runs the risk of destroying the uneasy social coalition that the Ram Mandir movement had helped nurture. During the mandir campaign, the common 'enemy' was the Muslim, as seen in the targeting of the sixteenth-century mosque and a focus on 'Babur ki aulad' as the common enemy. This strategy allowed the Sangh to accommodate within its fold Other Backward Castes (OBCs) and Dalits who had so far stayed away from the BJP because of its 'Brahmin–Bania' image. Will a future court judgement on the Ram Mandir issue once again replicate this Hindutva mobilization, serve a political purpose and turn the 2019 election into a referendum on whether India should be a Hindu Rashtra?[111]

In contrast to the Ram Mandir movement, in the gau raksha campaign, the 'enemy' often lies within Hindu society and not outside: poor Dalits, even OBCs, who may be engaged in the cattle trade, leather work and allied businesses. The immediate target may have been 'beef-eating' or 'cattle-slaughtering' Muslims, but the larger gau raksha campaign is driven by the Hindutva ideal of 'purifying' Hindu society into a homogenous, vegetarian force opposing all meat-eaters.[112]

In fact, the murders and attacks by gau rakshaks alienate the very backbone of Indian society: the *kisan*. Farmers' associations in Punjab have pointed out that the cattle trade today is suffering severe losses.[113] There is the menace of stray cattle. Many farmers say they are spending nights in their fields trying to fend off cattle that have been abandoned by their owners because many now consider them too risky to keep.

Turning an economic asset like the cow into a liability that cannot be traded or sold is a severe blow to farmers for whom the cow was akin to a bank loan or a fixed deposit to be encashed in times of emergency. A movement that alienates millions of kisans, as well as a middle class anxious that its personal freedoms are not tampered with, makes no political sense. Harish Damodaran, agriculture editor at the *Indian Express*, writes: 'The farmer is ultimately under no obligation to bear the responsibility for protecting the gau mata without any compelling economic rationale. The message is clear:

you cannot save gaumata unless the farmer has the incentive to keep cattle . . . and at this rate the cow has a future only in states that permit selective culling.'[114]

Thus, the gau raksha campaign can't be the new Ram Mandir movement. In any case, the Ayodhya campaign was useful to the BJP only while it was centred on the temple and the target was a clearly defined group, the Muslims. This target—the Muslims— have been increasingly retreating from the public space, thus denying Hindutva forces the kind of political rallying cry they had hoped for.[115]

Once the Ram Mandir movement became violent and riots broke out, the issue lost momentum. Vajpayee and Advani both regretted the Babri Masjid demolition, Advani calling 6 December 1992 the 'saddest day of his life' although neither of them directly criticized the kar sevaks. It is in this way that extremism gets normalized: when mainstream leaders do not condemn extremist and militant tendencies strongly enough.

The use of state power by the Big State becomes crucial when the idea is to create a monolithic Hindutva vote bank. Political Hindus always disseminating perceptions of 'minority appeasement' are themselves playing vote-bank politics and 'majority appeasement' in trying to convert Hindus into a monolithic vote bank by policies designed to appeal to the group identity 'Hindu'. Yet, the nature of Hinduism is that a Hindu vote bank cannot, by definition, exist. The 'Hindu' vote bank is thus a myth in the long term.

From 2014 onwards, Hindutva outfits embarked on 'ghar wapsi' programmes or reconversion ceremonies to bring back non-Hindus into the Hindu fold. 'Love jihad' was another campaign in which Hindutva activists began to attack inter-faith couples on the suspicion that Muslim men were luring away Hindu women. These initiatives as well as the bans on cattle slaughter, curbs on beef-eating and attempts to stop trade in cattle were attempts to create political unity among Hindus. In fact, cow politics goes back to the nineteenth-century campaigns of Dayanand Saraswati and the Arya

Samaj in their attempts to weld nationalist Hindu forces against beef-eating imperialists.[116]

After Independence, when demands were raised to ban the slaughter of cattle, Gandhi, the true liberal Hindu, held: 'I have long pledged to serve the cow but how can my religion also be the religion of the rest of the Indians? It will mean coercion against those Indians who are not Hindus. We have been shouting from the house-tops that there will be no coercion in the matter of religion. How can I force anyone not to slaughter cows unless he is himself so disposed? It's not as if there were only Hindus in the Indian Union. There are Muslims, Parsis, Christians and other religious groups here.'

In fact, after decades of cow politics, cow protection has failed to become a relevant political issue and has never garnered votes. How can this shop-worn agenda possibly work now in an electorate grown wise and weary of religious polarization? We have already noted Hindutva ideologue Vinayak Damodar Savarkar's views on the cow. Savarkar did not consider the cow worthy of being worshipped as the mother of Indians. Let us again listen to Savarkar on the cow: 'Animals such as the cow and buffalo and trees such as banyan and *peepal* are useful to man, hence we are fond of them; to that extent we might even consider them worthy of worship . . . When humanitarian interests are not served and in fact harmed by the cow and when humanism is shamed, self-defeating extreme cow protection should be rejected.'[117]

A purely Hindutva agenda centred on the cow generally doesn't win elections. Modi's 2014 victory was in no small measure due to his smartly repackaged 'Development Man' image. Historically, if the Hindu–Muslim question and cow issues were so politically powerful, would the Hindu Mahasabha not have dominated electoral politics in the post-Partition years, Partition being the most incendiary 'communal' issue in the history of post-Independence India?

If there was indeed a 'Hindu vote bank' even in the early decades of Independence, given the bloodily fresh memories of Partition, would a Hindu party, the Jana Sangh, not have reaped the benefits instead of remaining only a marginal force? The Jana Sangh was able to taste national power only post-1975 when it aligned with the anti-Emergency movement led by Gandhian socialist Jayaprakash Narayan.[118]

The Akhil Bharatiya Ram Rajya Parishad founded in 1948 was another Hindu party committed to cow protection. It won only three seats in the 1952 elections, two in the 1962 elections and eventually merged with the Jana Sangh.

If there really was a 'Hindutva' vote bank, would there be scope for any other political party in India, other than Hindu ones, given that India is 80 per cent Hindu? In actuality, attempts to create a Hindutva vote bank always lead to sharpening caste and even class divides, as instruments of mobilization like the cow or the Sanskrit language are in danger of being perceived as threats of upper-caste dominance against the interests of Dalits and backward castes. Lalu Prasad Yadav's statement that there are Hindus who eat beef is an astute articulation that for many Hindus the beef ban is a Brahminical upper-caste obsession.[119] The beauty and strength of Hinduism is that it can so easily accept the idea of the holy cow as well as those who eat cows.

Perhaps Hindutva activists know that a 'Hindu' vote bank is maya, an illusion. That's why they are inevitably pushed to frustrated violence in their polarization campaigns.

Why Soft Hindutva Is a Bad Idea

In the early 1980s, faced with the prospect of losing power and a uniting Opposition, Indira Gandhi began to play what is called the 'soft Hindutva' card, particularly in the Kashmir elections of 1983 and during the Khalistan agitation in Punjab in the 1980s. After her, this line was not only pursued by other Congress prime ministers like Rajiv Gandhi, when he allowed a shilanyas puja in the disputed Babri mosque in 1989, but also by P.V. Narasimha Rao when he allowed the BJP's rath yatra to proceed unchecked in 1991.[120]

Congress president Rahul Gandhi has continued this tradition by offering what is called 'soft Hindutva' as an alternative to the hard Hindutva of the BJP through his own recent well-publicized temple visits and pujas. Rahul visited at least twenty-five temples during his Gujarat campaign in 2017. He also visited a range of temples and maths during the Karnataka election campaign of 2018. In a similar strain, Congress MP Shashi Tharoor recently published a book titled *Why I am a Hindu*, claiming the traditions of Hinduism for the Congress.

Liberal political leaders—as the Congress claims to be—should *not* ordinarily invoke religion publicly or participate in religious functions if they truly believe in the essential tenets of Hinduism and constitutional values. In fact, Tharoor's book doesn't quite tell the whole story, since in the Vedanta the non-believing, non-practising Hindu is also a Hindu. The atheist, the beef-eater, the concept of inter-caste or intercommunal marriage are all part of the concept of Hinduism, precisely because no one born into the Hindu fold has to declare himself or herself as one. Charges of 'minority appeasement' or Sonia Gandhi's recently voiced fear that the Congress is perceived as a 'Muslim party' cannot be countered by speaking an anodyne version of the Hindutva language. This will only lead to deeper polarization and more politicization of religion and society.

How should politicians in India engage with religion? The Mahatma himself was criticized for bringing religious metaphors into politics, for adopting the dress of a Hindu fakir, for using bhajans like 'Vaishnava jana to' for his satyagraha campaigns. Yet, it must be pointed out that Gandhi, a truly spiritual being, never needed to establish his devotion through rigid religious rituals, and his support of inter-caste marriages, not quite approving at first, changed dramatically over time. There are few photos of Gandhi with any deity or idols. His moral mission was more spiritual than religious. Nehru, as historian Sunil Khilnani writes, was a politician without a religious faith but a highly developed moral sense. For Nehru, religion was mired in bigotry and superstition.

In the West, the separation of church and state came with a widespread acknowledgement that the representatives of God do not automatically reflect the goodness of God's values. There was also a growing recognition that rituals are not necessarily a reflection of one's devotion to religious values. Therefore, secularism grew out of a desire to preserve essential moral values without the rituals and restrictions of the church. When politicians visit holy places, are they necessarily upholding the *values* of religion or simply engaging in meaningless rituals which convince no one?

The first time Indira Gandhi was sworn in as prime minister in 1966, she refused to take the oath of office in the name of God. In her later years, however, she became ardently religious or ritualistic, visiting dozens of shrines and religious leaders, although it is doubtful whether this stance helped her politically.[121]

Today, the Hindu-oriented political stance of the Congress only further reinforces religion in the political space and legitimizes and normalizes Hindutva. To quote the writer Vivek Shanbhag: 'Rahul Gandhi is being foolish by visiting temples . . . he cannot counter the BJP's narrative by the same narrative . . . people support Congress for its idea of India, its idea of society, its idea of development . . . people know what former prime minister P.V. Narasimha Rao did for the economy.'

Soft Hindutva cannot outcompete hard Hindutva. To argue with Tharoor, there is no doubt that liberals need to reclaim Hinduism. But Tharoor fails to distinguish between spiritual or religious *values* and religious rituals. Secularism in the Western context meant exactly that, separating the government from religious rituals, not from moral values. This is the reason why politicians should not use public institutions to perpetuate religious rituals, either the Ganga aarti or Haj. This is why Nehru, an agnostic or even an atheist, could be so close to Gandhi, a firm believer. Neither Nehru nor Gandhi believed in public rituals. By contrast, Modi celebrated his win in 2014 by a Ganga aarti in Varanasi and a puja at Kashi Vishwanath temple.

Nehru didn't need to exhibit any public religiosity because of his tall stature as a popular and credible leader, both in office and outside. Gandhi made it a point to have multi-religious prayer meetings as part of his effort to reach out to all religions. The Mahatma didn't see any conflict between the essence of various beliefs.

The public display of religiosity is a consequence of diminished political status and credibility. When politicians lack moral stature and credibility and a convincing set of policy prescriptions, religious rituals become part of political tactics in a misguided belief that it will provide political credibility and legitimacy. Across the world, almost every effort to mobilize populations by invoking religion has had diminishing returns over time. The novelty of the effort, in the context of a prevailing political vacuum, succeeds in the initial years, but decays over time once the feet of clay of deified leaders' get disappointingly exposed. There is then the danger of a degeneration of values in both religious and political spheres, as we have seen in many Islamic countries today.

The campaign to add a religious tinge to icons like Subhas Bose or Bhagat Singh, both of whom had no truck with public religiosity, is another attempt by religious activists to try and capture these leaders' credibility. Vivekananda is projected as a Sangh icon, but as we have seen, while he was a Hindu monk, he believed deeply in the truth of all religions, not in denigrating any religion or any belief system as the spiritual 'enemy'. It is as if political Hindus want to legitimize public religiousness and rituals by linking them to credible icons who themselves had nothing to do with religious rituals.

When leaders possess genuine credibility, they can choose to be personally and publicly religious, or atheist and irreligious, a la Gandhi or Nehru. Audience and voters quickly grasp the difference between genuine personal beliefs and mere public pretence. Politicians of genuine credibility and known integrity don't need public rituals and ostentatious religiosity.

The Hindu religion, as we have been emphasizing, has survived political turmoil precisely because it constantly tried to accept, adapt and be inclusive, thus absorbing hundreds of sects with almost no friction. Throughout history, political divisions in the subcontinent never succeeded in preventing the intermingling of religious sects of all kinds. The authors of a fascinating book called *Beyond Turk and Hindu* delve into literary, architectural, biographical and administrative material of the five centuries before colonial rule to try and illuminate, indeed rescue, aspects of the subcontinental identity that later came to be cast in stone by British colonial census-takers, identities that were irrevocably cast as 'Muslim' and 'Hindu'. A transactional, local, patchily integrated world of 'Islamicate' and 'Indic' emerges which, while no 'secular' idyll, was an inter-linked space of memory, artefact and written text. This world created identities in which 'the categories Hindu and Muslim were largely subsumed in more intermingled and localized structures of devotion'.[122]

Most of the time through the history of South Asia, cultural practitioners or religious pilgrims had access to sites and shrines of their choice. It's only in the past seven decades, in the post-Partition years, that the movement of people, goods and ideas has become restricted across South Asia to an unprecedented extent.

Political Hindus seek to exclude and restrict, and if liberals play the same game they too will cease to be seen as inclusive. Radical Hindutva outfits already have a free run even in INC-ruled states, as seen in the murders of Gauri Lankesh (5 September 2017) and rationalist Narendra Dabholkar (20 August 2013. See Chapter 3). A supposedly 'soft Hindutva' or 'soft Islamic' political line only opens the gates for radical extremists to gain legitimacy. India's politicians would do well to follow the advice of Infosys founder N.R. Narayana Murthy. 'I am very religious,' he once said. 'But I keep my religion at home. I don't practice any religious activities outside the home, not even breaking coconuts, however dire the warnings of bad luck.'[123]

The Tragedy of Illiberal Secularism

Liberal Hindus continue to pay the price for 'secular' governments who have failed to be liberal and sadly played politics of what is called 'minority appeasement', identity politics and soft Hindutva. It was the so-called 'secular' prime minister, Rajiv Gandhi, who overturned the Shah Bano judgement in 1985, banned Salman Rushdie's *The Satanic Verses* in 1988 and, as we have seen, unlocked the gates of the Babri Masjid and allowed the shilanyas puja in the mosque. By appeasing Muslims on the one side and Hindus on the other, Rajiv Gandhi took illiberal secularism to its administrative heights, creating the grounds for a massive backlash of rampaging identity politics. As Hindu consolidation began to gather force, political secularists sought to appease identity-driven instincts of Muslim communities, and India is still paying the price for this tendency.

Illiberal secularism has almost become the norm for the Congress and almost every other party since the 1980s. So-called 'secular' parties have hardly been liberal because they have failed to uphold equality before the law for all religions, nor been able to demonstrate total neutrality in administration towards all religious groups.

Yet, a word here about the rights of religious minorities. Minority rights are fundamental to India. Democracies are known by how well they protect the rights of minorities, be they minorities of religion, class, gender, food habits or sexuality.

Political Hindus who want to create India as a Hindu Pakistan don't understand why the Indian state is fundamentally different from Pakistan. The Indian state's partiality towards minority rights was the direct consequence of Partition. Pakistan opted for an Islamic state, India repudiated the very idea of a religious state. The liberal secular mission was to resist a Hindu Pakistan or a Hindu Rashtra by asserting that religious minorities must feel a sense of equal citizenship in India. Yet those ideals have degenerated over the years. Genuine justice delivery was denied and vote-bank politics was resorted to in the Indira Gandhi–Rajiv Gandhi years.

Indira Gandhi's use, as we have seen, of the 'Hindu card' was a betrayal of the secular liberal values claimed by the Congress and was a prime example of illiberal secularism. The Congress has played communal politics both with Hindus and Muslims, seeking political and religious solutions, where the solutions lay in a neutral upholding of the law.[124]

Politician must not use state power—the power of the Big State—to push religious beliefs. Gandhi fervently believed in vegetarianism, prohibition and celibacy but did not seek to impose these values on others through state power. Ambedkar became a Buddhist but did not seek state support for Buddhism. If we follow their example, we must accept that a personal religious belief in cow protection can't be imposed on all of society—many sections of which may not regard the cow as sacred—through state power. Iftar parties, Diwali parties and Christmas parties must take place in the personal space and not in public and not by using taxpayers' money. Is it necessary for the prime minister of India to repeatedly visit temples? Are iftar parties by politicians, paid for by the tax payer, necessary? Liberal politicians should not be anti-religious by any means but must draw a clear *lakshman rekha* between the private and the public when it comes to religion. It is justice, compassion and morality, the true *values* of every religion, which count. If Hindus and Muslims receive impartial, merciful justice, there is no scope for the grievance industry to build on either side.

In 2014, on a trip to Japan, Prime Minister Narendra Modi gifted a copy of the Gita to Emperor Akihito, later saying our 'secular friends will create a toofan, he has taken a Gita with him, that means he has made this too communal'.[125] By mockingly stating that 'secular' people would object to the Gita, Modi echoed what has become a caricatured version of secularism, namely as an un-Indian cult decrying anything remotely 'Hindu'. In the early 1990s, the late Congressman V.N. Gadgil hit out at Congress-style secularism. 'Every time the Shahi Imam makes a statement, the party reacts as if God himself has spoken. Do minorities only mean Muslims? What about Buddhists, Sikhs and others? When thirty-six Sikhs were killed in Kashmir, not a single Congressman condoled their deaths. In Jammu and Kashmir, there is not a single Buddhist working in the state secretariat . . . We cannot go on ignoring the sentiments of 82 per cent [Hindus].' Today, this perceptibly illiberal secularism has laid the foundations for religious mobilization on an unprecedented scale. 'Secular' politicians have become discredited not only because they pussy-foot around Islamic militant groups but because they do not reject Hindu extremism unequivocally enough.

Yet, an important caveat here. Those who argue that illiberal secularists treat Muslim fundamentalists with kid gloves must also recognize that so far no Hindutva Right-wing politician—be it the late Bal Thackeray or Pravin Togadia—has ever spent extended periods in jail despite their incendiary speeches. This has given space to fringe groups to slowly acquire greater appeal, resulting in the growing clout of political Hindus.

The years of the Congress's illiberal secularism haunt today's politics. They provided an opportunity for BJP leader L.K. Advani to first coin the lexicon 'pseudo secularism' that pointed to this distorted illiberal secularism. Liberal Hindus cannot afford to be blind to the pitfalls of this illiberal secularism.

As we noted in the earlier section, Rahul Gandhi, while seeking to establish his credentials as a believing Hindu, as a way to meet the challenge of Hindutva, is actually further normalizing the role of religion in politics. Rahul seems to have chosen the path of his grandmother and father despite the tragedy that befell the nation in their misguided attempts to harness religion for their political projects. A far better example for Rahul is his great-grandfather, an atheist–agnostic, who teamed up with many liberal Hindus and successfully withstood the challenge posed by the Hindutva forces of his time.

Liberals must uphold the view that faith—religious, agnostic or atheist—is an entirely personal matter which should not be imposed through the political power of the Big State. In a magnificent judgement in January 2017, the Supreme Court held: 'The relationship between man and God and the means which humans adopt to connect with the almighty are matters of individual preferences and choice . . . the state is obliged to allow religious practice but can forbid interference of religions and religious beliefs with secular activities such as elections.'[126]

Although a dissenting opinion argued that such a law could mean that any questions, for example, on injustices on religious minorities, can't be raised, the court held up an ideal: in India, governance must at all times be secular and liberal and protect the rights and freedoms of the individual from being suppressed by any collective majorities.

The apex court courageously stated a philosophical position and boldly censured politicians, even so-called secular ones, who have freely used religious platforms and slogans through the years. In the 2017 Uttar Pradesh polls BSP leader Mayawati had called on Muslims not to divide their votes.[127] In 2017, Maulana Noor-ur-Rahman Barkati, head of the Tipu Sultan mosque in Kolkata, who had been seen sharing the stage with TMC leaders—TMC is a supposedly secular party—issued a fatwa offering Rs 25 lakh for violence against the prime minister.[128]

Liberal secularism implies insulating the state or government from religion of all hues. Yet, it was illiberal secularism that began the practice of dubbing as national enemy any belief system antithetical to the Congress, a tendency which reached its apogee in the Indira years and one which the BJP seems to be faithfully imitating.

Both cults—self-appointed champions of illiberal secularism and self-appointed champions of Hindutva politics—feed off each other. It suits the Hindutva agenda to project secularism as an elite, irreligious Marxist fad. It suits secularists to castigate any policy that does not make a special place for minorities as immoral and wrong.

In an article in the *Tribune*, political analyst and activist Yogendra Yadav argues that secularism must be distinguished from minorityism, that while special leave should not be given for Friday prayers, at the same time strict action should be taken against Hindutva groups trying to disrupt namaz. If jagrans and kirtans can be held in public places, why not namaz? 'The distinction between pro-minorityism and secularism, between special symbolic concessions to a community and equal constitutional rights of all citizens, should serve as a compass to guide secular politics.'[129] At the core of liberal secularism is to restore and reanimate a sense of justice. The focus for the liberal at all times must be the rule of law, irrespective of religion or heritage.

When Bengal chief minister Mamata Banerjee attempted to dole out honorariums to imams[130] she may have been practising the same Rajiv Gandhi form of illiberal secularism which inevitably leads to a backlash of majoritarianism, as may be happening in Bengal.[131] The SP's secularism too has often been is illiberal. When the party ruled in Lucknow, the joke was all you needed was a beard and a skullcap and you would be able to obtain a 'lal batti' car from the Akhilesh Yadav government. Posts for clerics are no substitute for real justice, welfare and security for all Muslims. Overt tokenism only encourages competitive identity politics. Secularism also gets discredited when it becomes a cover for corruption; that convicted Bihar chieftain Lalu Prasad Yadav makes the claim to being a secular hero gives secularism an unfortunate image.

Liberal secularism has to become something other than the dogmatic official folly of the past. Secularism should be renamed as a doctrine of just and righteous administration. Righteous administration is independent of any particular cult; it rises above the clashing cultist dogmas of secular vs Hindu. Righteous administration means not only scrupulous religious neutrality in public but upholding the law at all times through tough executive action. This means bringing to justice those attacking Wendy Doniger and M.F. Husain, as well as those attacking Salman Rushdie and Taslima Nasrin.

Righteous administration must be rooted in the liberal thinking of our liberal ancestors—Tagore, Gandhi and C. Rajagopalachari.

All were deeply learned in the scriptures, but respected religious differences equally deeply and placed the individual above the Big State. Tagore was a humanist with a strong sense of the Vedas and the Upanishads; Gandhi and Rajaji were practising pragmatic politicians, rooted in liberal Hindu beliefs. Theirs is the dharma that the modern pluralist must espouse, a dharma that passionately believes in a multiplicity of faiths, in confessional neutrality on the part of the state, a dharma that respects the philosophy of the Bhagavad Gita but rejects the use of the Gita for party politics.

The ancients sometimes need to be respectfully left alone. The phrase 'Chanakya niti' is often used to legitimize a modern abuse of power. This is a terrible disservice to the great acharya who did not live in a democratic milieu, who was not a theorist of democracy but instead an adviser to a despot and whose over-2000-year-old prescriptions such as politics through 'saam, daam, dand, bhed' are deeply anti-modern and anti-democratic.

How did Rajaji define his dharma? '[The Swatantra] Party stands for the individual to retain his identity and his motives for honest endeavour and for his serving the community with a willing heart and not out of compulsion . . . if we have no faith in our people, if we do not trust one another, democracy will be a poor make-believe and will break down with anarchy into rule by force . . . Social cooperation has always been our Dharma. The State should recede into comparative insignificance.'[132]

Social cooperation, justice, rule of law and minimum government should be the true dharma or religion of liberal politicians. Not empty rituals, temple visits or tokenist iftar parties.

Dilemma of the Muslim Liberal

In 2014, the Nobel Peace Prize was awarded jointly to India's child rights campaigner, Kailash Satyarthi, and Pakistan's icon of bravery against violent bigotry, Malala Yousafzai. 'The Nobel Committee regards it as an important point for a Hindu and a Muslim, an Indian and a Pakistani, to join in a common struggle for education and against extremism,' said the committee after announcing the award.

With the rise of extremism and the discrediting of tolerance, there is surely a need to find a common agenda of modernity. In times of religious mayhem, both within India and outside, at least in our republic of 'hurt sentiments', Hindus and Muslims need to build a new modern contract with each other. But only liberal Hindus and liberal Muslims can do this, not a government that constantly appeases its own religious ideologues, nor a Muslim community in the grip of narrow-minded clerics. In the words of Hamid Dalwai: 'Unless Indian liberals, however small they are as a minority, are drawn from all communities and join forces on a secular basis, even the Hindu liberal minority will eventually lose its battle with communalist and revivalist Hindus.'

Such a contract is impossible unless there are avowedly liberal leaderships in both communities.

A new Hindu–Muslim contract must be based on the common aim of modernity, access to market, business and economic ties on the ground, made possible by neutral platforms that facilitate merit and talent. An artificial unity imposed by administrative diktat and affirmative action, as shown by the experiments of previous 'secular' dispensations, will not create long-lasting coexistence.

It could be argued that electoral politics itself in many ways prevents the emergence of a liberal Muslim or a liberal Hindu leadership, both animated by the desire to challenge extremism and further the cause of modernity. Electoral politics premised on state patronage, with its in-built winner-takes-all syndrome, fragments society, giving extremists on all sides the incentive to capture a larger share of the pie. An example of this is the 2013 Muzaffarnagar riots, which brought massive electoral dividends for the BJP. (In the 2014 general elections, the BJP swept Uttar Pradesh, winning a staggering seventy-one out of eighty seats.) While Hindu and Muslim politicians privately may speak a surprisingly rational language, when rallying rival constituencies for votes, they invariably fall back on communally charged fire-and-brimstone religious rhetoric.

The blistering language often used by the SP's Azam Khan,[133] the rhetoric of Badruddin Ajmal of the All India United Democratic Front (AIUDF[134]) or even of Akbaruddin Owaisi of the AIMIM, the brother of Asaduddin,[135] reveal that it is extremely difficult for these Muslim leaders to take an openly 'liberal' stand and seek votes from the community. Besides, when Hindutva trumpets victimhood, why should Muslim politicians give up that victimhood claim easily? Electorally, the success of an openly liberal or atheist Hindu or liberal Muslim is limited: no saffron-clad neta will advocate unity with Muslims on education and health, no Muslim politician will openly advocate unity with Hindus on gender justice. How then can bridges be built?

For political Hindus, Muslims must be made into second-class citizens, eternally grateful recipients of the condescending goodwill of a benevolent Hindu Rashtra. They must be willing to pay the price of separation to achieve coexistence. In Gujarat, Muslims can become affluent and educated but must remain segregated in their Juhapura ghetto. A liberal Muslim leadership cannot emerge if Hindutva politicians keep targeting the community, pushing their backs to the wall and forcing them to take similarly sectarian positions.

Yet, Hindu–Muslim coexistence in India has come a long way since Yusuf Khan and Mahjabeen Bano had to change their names to Dilip Kumar and Meena Kumari to succeed in Hindi cinema. Today, the King Khans rule Bollywood; Irfan Pathan and Zaheer Khan are cricketing stars; Azim Premji and Yusuf Hamied are towering figures of Indian business and Sania Mirza is the Indian nation's collective pride.

These are not success stories made possible by patronage and sops, but by hard work and talent that in turn depend on the neutral platforms provided by cinema, sport and business. In Ahmedabad, even after the 2002 riots, Hindus still pack into Dhalgarwad garment market to buy from Muslim sellers. In Varanasi, Muslim weavers and Hindu sellers have worked together for centuries in the Benarasi sari industry.

What is the liberal way to create a new Hindu–Muslim contract? First, equal access to justice and a strictly neutral police. If the police proceed on the basis of religious prejudice, the cause of harmony is irretrievably lost. Also a mixed force recruited on the basis of talent tends to be a balanced force. Second, a common rational pursuit of civil codes where the law weighs in on gender justice and social equality without making the Uniform Civil Code a political stick to beat Muslims with. Third, mass establishment of government schools adhering to constitutional values as alternatives to madrasa education. Conservative Hindus attack madrasas, yet patronize Saraswati Vidya Mandir schools of the RSS variety.

While the liberal Hindu welcomes these measures of coexistence, Hindutva nationalists only look for ways to keep positioning the Muslim as the enemy. They do not want to find a solution, nor do they believe that a new equal relationship needs to be forged between Hindus and Muslims as individuals. They only want a relationship in which Hindus dominate. The Hindutva notion of equality is one where they are more equal than others. Open-mindedness is difficult when victimhood tugs at the Muslim and majoritarianism constrains the Hindu.

The liberal solution is this: an open, competitive economy is the best way to deliver unity. A patronage-dispensing Big State that treats Muslims either as secular tokens or as unwelcome guests cannot create a Hindu–Muslim relationship suited for the twenty-first century. Politicians operating in the gladiatorial ring of electoral politics may not be willing to create this modern liberal partnership but it can be achieved in civil society if bridge-builders come forward. Modern, liberal, secular Hindus and modern, liberal, secular Muslims must make common cause.

Identity-oriented Islamism in India seems to be a consequence of appeasement, where promises were constantly broken in order to nurture the grievance industry for political and vote bank purposes. Many Muslim leaders pandered to this, in a syndrome similar to what has happened with caste or tribal groups. The Dalit leadership did at some point try to move out of the special privileges compartment, for instance, when Mayawati forged her highly successful cross-caste alliance when for a brief while she abandoned the earlier slogan 'bahujan samaj' and instead propagated 'sarvajan samaj', in the process scoring a remarkable victory in Uttar Pradesh in 2007.[136] But there have been no similar movements from within tribal and Muslim leaderships, who have preferred to remain in their identity enclosures.

Many Muslim leaders, like the firebrand TV ulemas and maulanas, have created this situation for their own political agenda. They and the Hindutva leaders are dancing in tandem, both are hoping to benefit from greater polarization. In many instances, a short-sighted Muslim leadership has not helped the Muslim cause, instead, only heightened the sense of Muslim grievances and separateness.

Like the liberal Hindu, the liberal Muslim faces sustained criticism and attacks from her own community. In the 1990s, when academic Mushirul Hasan stated that although he found Salman Rushdie's book, *The Satanic Verses*, offensive, he did not believe the book should be banned, Jamia Millia Islamia, where he was a professor of history, erupted in outrage and he was attacked by his own community, just as Raja Rammohan Roy had once faced the wrath of his fellow Hindus. Today, there is another danger: by reposing her trust in secularism, is the Muslim's cultural identity, already under siege in the Hindu Rashtra, in grave danger? When perceptions of injustice and discrimination increase exponentially, there is a tendency to cling to identity ever more tenaciously.

Still, even in dreadful circumstances many believing Muslims are tenaciously upholding the liberal way of thinking. Scholar and activist and former Planning Commission member, Syeda Hameed has often argued that the best way to defeat the maulanas is to awaken the true spirit of Islam,[137] as have reformists like Maulana Wahiduddin Khan. 'Islamic law does not recognise violent protest,' Khan has often said. 'Islam recognises the right to spread your ideas in a peaceful manner.' Today, among Muslims there's a desperate need to believe in the secularism of the Indian nation-state. There is also a growing resolve that liberal Muslims need to speak out in alliance with other minority groups and strongly articulate a minority viewpoint. The late Syed Shahabuddin, who left the Indian Foreign Service to join politics, believed that it was the Indian state system which made the liberal Muslim into a hardliner by marginalizing the liberal and making space only for those who can deliver Muslim vote-banks and stand forth as Jinnah-type sole spokesmen.[138]

As we have noted, Big State patronage fragments society and gives birth to identity politics. This kind of politics inevitably spirals towards extremism, producing hardliners who specialize in splitting identities and creating narratives to consolidate divisions. The Indian state's search for Muslim tokens echoes in the words of Dr Zakir Husain, president from 1967 to 1969, who said, 'It is easier to elect a Muslim to the Rashtrapati Bhavan than to appoint a Muslim clerk in the Central government.'[139]

The identity of the liberal Muslim, rooted in the poetry of Mirza Ghalib or the Kitab-e-Nauras,[140] in Kathak, in Ustad Bismillah Khan and in Ustad Vilayat Khan, has not only been subdued because of electoral politics, but is being daily attacked by political Hindus, who are also attacking liberals in their own religion.

Thus, the political system itself marginalizes both the liberal Hindu and the liberal Muslim. A political system that relies on vote banks has marginalized the voices of those who don't have access to the voting public. In the words of the late veteran reformist Asghar Ali Engineer: 'Because the mullah has the platform of the mosque and greater powers of manipulating people and because politicians in the quest for votes seek alliances with priests, democracy ends up working in favour of the conservative and reactionary voice rather than the liberal one.'[141]

How many times do we see a saffron-clad priest and a bearded maulana on TV face each other down in a so-called debate, as 'representatives' of Hindus and Muslims? A maulana is no more a representative of a Muslim than a saffron-clad pandit is a representative of all Hindus.

For many Hindus and Muslims there is a genuine religious search. Liberalism, as we have been repeatedly emphasizing, need not mean forsaking religion. However, for Hindu and Muslim liberals, a public and vociferous rejection of all violence and discrimination in the name of religion and accepting the Constitution of India as the primary supervisor of public life, is key. Mounting a defence of sharia law or the codes of Manu can't be the preoccupation of Hindu or Muslim liberals.

Today, the sixteenth Lok Sabha had the lowest number of Muslims ever since the first general elections of 1952. There are just twenty-four Muslim MPs, down from thirty in the previous Lok Sabha, who constitute just 4.4 per cent of the House. For the first time in an Indian Parliament, there's not a single Muslim MP from Uttar Pradesh as the BJP did not field a single Muslim candidate across the vast swathes of north and west India with the sole exception of Shahnawaz Hussain, who is in the Rajya Sabha.[142] In the 2017 Gujarat assembly polls, the BJP did not give a single ticket to a Muslim. The prime minister may have once criticized gau rakashaks as 'anti-social elements', but not one member of the ruling party has vigorously prosecuted the cow criminals; Union minister Jayant Sinha has even been seen garlanding those accused in a mob lynching in Jharkhand. Meanwhile, the attackers of Pehlu Khan in Alwar have not been punished.[143]

Muslims seem to be disappearing from politics. They are often under siege in society. Wrongful incarceration of Muslim youth in cases like the Mecca Masjid blast case[144] only reinforce perceptions of injustice and discrimination at the hands of the law courts and the police. In this situation, the Muslim is being pushed into a rejection of 'secular' truisms even as the ghetto remains a refuge.[145]

Yet, throughout Indian history, Indian Muslim leaders have been staunch in their patriotism for India: Tipu Sultan fought the British in Seringapatam in 1799, Siraj-ud-daulah fought the British in the Battle of Plassey in 1757, it was under the figurehead Bahadur Shah Zafar, the last Mughal emperor, that the rebellious sepoys of 1857 rallied. Yet, these facts of the long tradition of Indian Muslim patriotism are being sought to be erased from public memory.

Which is why the community is in desperate need of a liberal, progressive leadership (just as Hindus are) that will encourage it to push for its due space in the national mainstream. The community needs a leadership which doesn't prey on fear, but offers hope— hope of a social and economic transformation, hope of a liberal, modern yet rooted identity that can challenge the narrative of the extremists within.

Such a leadership is unlikely to emerge when illiberal secular parties seek votes in return for 'protection' and offer only sops. Or when Hindutva forces are dominant and offer no hope of equal citizenship.

Yet, beyond the visible yelling bigots, there's a silent, invisible, more welcoming truth: Indian Muslims would not be the second-largest community in the world if the true Hindu was anti-Muslim. Of course, this question is even more pertinent for Hindus. In a country which is about 80 per cent Hindu, why has the victim card become the calling card of the Hindutva brigade? As long as political Hindus dominate politics, a 'liberal' Muslim leadership is unlikely to emerge.

Liberal Bridge-builders, Arise!

To tar India's entire secular liberal class with the illiberal failures of the Congress Party would be an injustice. Liberal bridge-builders have always existed in India and continue to toil for inter-community reconciliation and understanding. But liberal bridge-builders need to understand that the Big State, whether Hindutva or socialistic, is inherently violent because of its monopoly over the legal use of violence. Coercion and thought control is the natural impulse of the Big State. Thus, liberals must not seek state patronage or official sanction. This is a waste of time and effort.

During colonial rule and subsequent secular regimes in independent India, violence became institutionalized because the scope of Big State patronage kept expanding. Liberal bridge-builders must keep their work focused on civil society and citizens groups and not seek Big State patronage, which would only weaken their cause. If proponents of the Hindu Rashtra seek state power to enforce their own ideology, liberals must be distinguished by their mistrust of the Big State or centralized government power. Instead, they must campaign for a greater role for 'small government' or local government.

The Big State or expansive government rampages in areas where it should not, such as economy or patronage, and fails to act where it should, such as crime and violence against minorities. That's why Gandhi, India's greatest liberal, was so prescient in calling for restraining the Big State and demanded increasing doses of devolution of state power to localities.

Yet, while politicians failed liberalism, citizens have kept it alive. During the 1984 anti-Sikh riots, many liberal jurists, lawyers, writers, journalists and human rights activists exposed the murderous intent of Congress-led mobs. These same liberal voices challenged the manner in which riot victims in Gujarat were denied justice.

The agenda for liberal bridge-builders should be real equality before the law. The majoritarian backlash against Muslims and Dalits is a consequence of selective application of the law, with the law itself having been compromised by recognizing different legal standards for different sections of people. Differences in personal religious laws are only used to demand more inequality from the law in the form of special privileges.

Rather than seeing 'secularism' through the prism of religion (since that has been so discredited) liberal secularism should locate itself in equality before the law and highlighting prevalent hypocrisies and inequalities. For instance, if the beef ban is designed to protect the sentiments of some Hindus then equality before the law may require that pork be banned, too, to protect some Muslim sensitivities. Liberals must emphasize that the paramount aspect of good governance is to ensure justice, which cannot be delivered without equality before the law.

Yet, we can draw inspiration from the fact that liberal voices campaigned and protested against the Hashimpura massacre, which took place under the watch of a Congress government. When Bangladeshi origin author Taslima Nasrin was hounded out of Bengal, yes, a few Bengali Left intellectuals did cave in meekly, but many others openly supported her, including the writer Arundhati Roy. In 2012, when Salman Rushdie was prevented from attending the Jaipur Literature Festival, a group of authors read from *The Satanic Verses* at the festival as a riposte to the Islamist zealots.[146] The liberal's task is to ensure the law applies evenly to all religious groups. For the liberal, the mantra is the law in public and religion only in private. In order to achieve this we liberals must get to work!

Liberal Hindu = True Hindu

The true Hindu is a true liberal and the liberal Hindu is the true Hindu. Hinduism sits easily with liberalism because of its rejection of authoritarian power. The liberal's scepticism of the Big State, faith in individual conscience and action and belief in enlightened individualism, finds many echoes in Hindu traditions which have never subscribed to a single belief system or a single church. The ideological Left, as seen in Left-ruled Bengal, has sought to hugely expand the role of the Big State by erecting a vast bureaucratic machine made up of apparatchiks, thus also encouraging violence which, as we have seen, is embedded in such state expansion. The Right leverages massive state power for its own ideological goals. The Big State in the hands of ideologues recognizes no democratic limits on its power, imprisons citizens and blunts the rule of law. Society then becomes emptily idolatrous where religion degenerates into rituals and set customs, which kill the spirit and values of religion. Democracy is stifled by the rise of illiberal values. Street thugs, either of the Left or Right, call the shots.

The essence of religion, as Gandhi keeps reminding us, is devotion to truth, the commitment to search for truth. Today, religion is being equated with rituals. Communalism is the manifestation of a battle for the supremacy of rituals, sacrificing the quest for truth. The eternal quest, the inner journey towards self-realization through questioning, is now about the external quest to eliminate anyone who poses a question to oneself! Political Hindus care little for this philosophical quest. They are restless only to use Hinduism to capture political power.

A basic civic and political initiative is needed, critiquing the Big State and Big Government and placing its faith in civic individual action and morality, as Hindu traditions do. The liberal puts her faith in four elements: (1) the rule of law and equality before the law, (2) restraint on the state's use of force and state's power, (3) a limited government and (4) maximum space and liberty for citizens action.

In Hindu traditions, there is maximum faith in the individual and maximum respect for diverse cults and preferences and a premium on individual choice. But Hindutva is the very opposite of these traditions. It is trying to create a single authority, a single God, a single, unified nationalist belief system and a big structure— which is a law unto itself—supervising citizens' daily lives in the way Hindu traditions have never done. In protecting the pluralist and diverse inheritance of Hinduism, in being unthreatened by successful Muslim citizens of India and reaching out to them in a common liberal charter, in telling the truth about attacks on minorities, in championing the cause of individual freedoms over an authoritarian ruling regime or church, in being able to create governance that lessens the control of the state, it is the liberal

Hindu who keeps alive the iconoclastic, self-criticizing, knowledge-based philosophies of Hindu traditions.

The political Hindu is doing a terrible disservice to Hinduism—a religion that places the individual and individual choice at its centre. Political Hindus are politicizing Hinduism in order to unleash the power of the Big State on citizens and enforce their particular vision of Hindu society. This process was once used to establish Red hegemony. It is now being imitated by saffron hegemons. Let's end this chapter with the Bhagavad Gita: 'The drive of desire must be displaced by the knowledge of right action, but when the supreme end of the freedom of spirit is attained . . . the individual acts from insight . . . from deep insight into the spirit of all life.'[147] Thus, the prompting of desire, the guidance of law and the spontaneity of individual spirit are the three stages of action. Individual freedom, individual spirit, individual action: how beautifully the Gita celebrates the anarchic chaos of individuality harnessed through the power of law to become one with the Cosmic Being. Need one look to a greater inspiration than the Bhagavad Gita in order to be a true liberal?

[3]

The Liberal Thinker

Why the liberal who believes in enhancing the power of the individual is a better democrat than the liberal who believes in increasing the power of the government or state

The needle probes for the artery,
Enemies of poetry gather in your city . . .

India Gate:

Over there, the Rashtrapati Bhavan.
How ruthlessly has this city been combed and groomed!
White elephants sway at the gate of the past . . .

Armed regiments on alert;
The showy itch of culture . . .
Parading cavalry;
Anti-aircraft guns . . .
The President accepting a salute from those hanging between the sky and the earth . . .

Bravo!
What a spectacular festival.

—'New Delhi, 1985', Namdeo Dhasal[1]

D oes the government have the right to decide what citizens should eat, wear, read, write or what kind of films they should watch?

Should the government use the law and state and government institutions to push its own party ideology and impose this ideology on citizens?

Should the government keep increasing its own power and its capacity to use violence through too many harsh laws and centralized schemes?

Is the government's freedom more important than individual freedom?

Should citizens hero-worship elected representatives who depend on their vote?

Why the Big State or Big Government Is Very Dangerous

Citizens of India, why should you choose to be a liberal supporter of individual freedom instead of a believer in a big powerful government, the Big State seeking to restrict individual freedom, either for the sake of Hindutva ideology or socialist ideology?

As we have seen, individual freedom, free speech, debate, dissent, argument and counter-argument is the very essence of Indian traditions. A freedom-loving liberal is intimately linked to the prevailing age-old ethos of the subcontinent. India, as we have seen in the previous chapter, has always been a land of iconoclasts and free-thinkers. As C. Rajagopalachari has reminded us, Indians need a second freedom movement, this time not from the British raj, but from sarkar raj and neta raj. Citizens need to push back, push the encroaching government back, raise red flags and demand that the government cede control to citizens in key sectors. Infosys founder N.R. Narayana Murthy believes governments in India have a 'controlling mindset'. He says this mindset is 'changing slowly but as a nation we still think that poverty is a virtue. Anybody who has acquired some wealth is looked at with a level of scepticism and suspicion. The reason for this is that the pay of politicians and bureaucrats is very low compared to the pay of CEOs, etc., who go to them for approval. So naturally, there's always a little bit of hostility. I can understand. This doesn't happen in countries like Singapore because there bureaucrats and CEOs get similar salaries.

'But on the role of the government, I would say we have to move away from the current method of control to a different method of regulation. In developed societies, there is strong regulation but there's no stifling of businesses due to excessive controls. Anybody who violates any law is punished heavily. That is required. But until one is proven guilty, the others should be allowed to conduct their business effectively . . . I do think a lot of progress has to be made in making it easier for businesses to grow. The controlling mindset continues, that's the problem.'[2]

Individual freedom in the economy can only really take off if there's individual freedom in society. For example, the first start-ups in America, the innovative entrepreneurial ideas that transformed the economy, did not bloom under the aegis of government power in Washington, DC. Instead, Silicon Valley—home to some of the world's most exciting businesses such as Apple, Facebook and Google—which did benefit at first from some government support, blossomed in the state of California, the land of hippies and flower power. It was in California where in the late 1960s authority was rejected and individual freedom was embraced and California is noted for its liberal spirit.[3] 'Talent and energy [must] find scope for play without having to cringe and obtain special individual permission from officials and ministers, their efforts [must be] judged by the open market in India and abroad . . . statism must go . . . and Government reduced to its proper functions.'[4] The idea of India stands for freedom. Statists who want to increase government power stand for repression. India stands for a cacophonous clamour of voices. Rajaji said, 'Burke said he liked clamour. I am not of the opinion of those gentlemen who are against disturbing the public repose. The fire-bell at midnight may disturb your sleep, but it keeps you from being burned in your bed.' Statists only want the monotonous single drone of a single voice. India stands for the ability to disagree without violence. Ideologues enamoured of the Big State want to silence those with whom they do not agree, with a gun if necessary. Have you ever heard of a liberal take up the sword or a gun?

The liberal's upholding of the creed of non-violence would have been her greatest moral advantage. But sadly, as we have noted, political liberals or self-proclaimed 'seculars' have often failed the cause of liberalism as in the cases of Salman Rushdie, Taslima Nasrin or Shah Bano. Political liberals have on occasion been guilty of selective outrage. Unless we liberals face up to our mistakes and failures of the past, we will not be able to rescue the liberal argument or renew it with fresh energy.

'The word liberalism,' writes Masani, 'comes from liberty. The individual is at the centre of the picture and society is there to serve the individual, not the other way around.'[5] He also writes, 'governments are there to keep law and order, do justice, protect people, protect the country from attack. That's where the functions of the government stop.' Importantly, he points out, for the liberal, 'ends and means are interlinked. If we want a decent society, our methods must be decent.' For example, those who commit electoral fraud or use violence to win votes or buy votes or coerce legislators and thus secure a majority are only showing that that so-called electoral 'majority' is illusory. They are only pretending to abide by democratic norms. When the focus is only on the ends and not on the means then norms don't matter. That's why the liberal focuses on *means-oriented, norms-oriented* democracy and not just on majoritarian democracy, which involves securing a majority any which way. The liberal believes in a principled moral crusade for justice and the material benefits such a crusade brings, since such a crusade also believes in protection of personal freedom and personal property. Both the ideological Left and the ideological Right seek to leverage state power for their own priorities while the liberal seeks to restrain state power to safeguard individual freedoms. Civic and citizen initiatives need to focus, as Gandhi did, on why the government or state is taking over so many aspects of our lives and increasingly using force to coerce citizens into certain types of actions. Citizens need to push for, firstly, rule of law, secondly, restraint on the Big State or government's ability to use force, thirdly, a limited government and fourthly, campaign to maximize the public space available for citizens' actions.

Today, there's a lack of genuine political ideology (the BJP talks of 'vichaardhaara', yet religious or nationalist majoritarianism cannot really be considered a modern democratic political ideology). There is an absence of inspiring ideals, leaving only the free play of identity politics and the cultivation of different vote banks of identities to seize political power. When it comes to rule of law, liberals must be clear: rule of law means due process, investigation and an impartial police. It does not simply mean loud demands for instant retributive justice such as calling for death threats every time there is a rape while refusing to introspect that in the majority of crimes against women the accused is *known* to the victim. What then are the reasons for these crimes? That is where we as a society need to introspect. Retributive howls for vengeance are only war cries, where the crucial principle of liberal democracy—innocent until proven guilty—is sought to be reversed. The Supreme Court has upheld the death sentence for the Nirbhaya convicts.[6] But without systematic reform of police investigations and fast-tracking of justice, can the death sentence for a single crime be a deterrence for the future? We have already noted the rise in crimes against women in the post-Nirbhaya period.[7] The crucial pursuit for liberals is to ensure the delivery of real justice. And if all this sounds very self-righteous, then it must be admitted that liberals, for too long have remained in ivory towers. Liberals now need to venture out, to find wider support to engage people as equals.

'Leave people free,' pleads Masani, emphasizing 'trusteeship: those who have wealth must use it for the good of the community . . . while we have a good time on what we have, we must not be devoid of a social conscience or social obligation.'[8] For Rajaji, 'There is a moral obligation of those who possess wealth to hold it in trust for society. [We believe] in a doctrine of life based on that moral obligation as distinguished from seeking to establish a socialistic structure based on legislative sanctions . . . [we must not have] loss of incentive for the individual to work and increased dependence on the State and its officials in every walk of life.'[9] Those who have the good things in life must use it for the poor. Of course, nobody can force them to do so, but if he or she has a good conscience, the rich man or rich woman will do so voluntarily.

Yet, trusteeship is much more than bursts of charity and the whimsical generosity of the wealthy. Trusteeship primarily means ensuring the integrity of society's value-based liberal democratic institutions so that they don't end up oppressing or suppressing the poor and vulnerable. In reality, many rich people support and perpetuate injustices by not doing enough to, for example, bridge the health and education gap between rich and poor. They don't do enough and then offer charity as meagre compensation for victims. This is not trusteeship in the sense Rajaji meant because trusteeship also means a stake in creating a just society. For Gandhi, those with wealth cannot be devoid of social conscience. While no one should be able to take away a rich man's wealth, the rich must use their wealth with a good conscience towards those less fortunate.

Gandhi sought complete devolution of power at the bottom, to the level of village republics. The Mahatma was impressed by the nineteenth-century American philosopher and anti-slavery campaigner Henry David Thoreau's view: 'that government is best which governs the least.'[10] Gandhi's swaraj was not mere self-rule as 'Indians', but swaraj as self-rule of the moral individual over his own affairs in a just and good way. It wasn't the racial and nationalist category 'Indian' who would participate in swaraj, but the conscientious, active individual citizen.

For Gandhi, 'The logic behind decentralization is not just about weakening the central authority or about preferring the local elites to central authority, but is fundamentally about making governance at the local level more responsive to the needs of the large majority of the population.'[11] Thus, the Mahatma wrote, 'The end to be sought in human happiness [is] combined with full mental and moral growth . . . I use the adjective moral as synonymous with spiritual. This end is to be achieved under decentralization. *Centralization as a system is inconsistent with a nonviolent structure of society.*'[12] [emphasis added] Thus, Gandhi says, 'I suggest that if India is to evolve along non-violent lines, it will have to decentralize many things. *Centralization cannot be sustained and defended without adequate force.*'[13] [emphasis added] For Gandhi, 'I look upon an increase in the power of the state with the greatest fear, because while apparently doing good by minimizing exploitation, it does the greatest harm to mankind by destroying individuality, which lies at the root of all progress.'[14]

For Gandhi, 'Democracy cannot be worked by twenty men sitting at the centre. It has to be worked from below by the people of every village.'[15] To quote an analyst, Gandhi believed, 'Decentralization brings decision-making closer to the people and therefore yields programmes and services that better address local needs.'[16]

Gandhi had little faith in the centralized all-powerful Big State and unlimited confidence in the innate good sense of the individual. True democracy is only possible when state intervention—the dreaded Big State—is at a minimum and the individual's space for action is at a maximum. Gandhi was always terribly apprehensive about the abuse of state power to suppress the individual.

In contrast to Gandhi, Nehru had a great deal of faith in the power of a benevolent state and not as much faith in the power and capacity of the individual. At the same time, Nehru deserves much credit, though, for remaining a liberal democrat through his life. During his rule, the abuse of state power was limited because of his own consensus-building personality and his accommodative leadership style, as seen, for example, in his fortnightly letters to chief ministers in which he spoke about governance challenges with candour and honesty.

Despite being the overwhelmingly dominant politician of his time, Nehru did not believe in centralizing authority, instead he sought to decentralize. Once he passed from the scene, though, the institutions he shaped were misused by leaders who didn't share his commitment.

Gandhi did not believe in using the power of the Big State to push or impose his personal ideologies. He believed in a kind of politics where the people would govern and not be represented by over powerful representatives. Gandhi's idea of swaraj as a real democracy, was where all power ultimately rested with the people. For Gandhi, the British parliament was like a 'sterile woman'[17] and 'good government was no substitute for self government'.[18] For Gandhi, my individual rights exist because yours do too. For example, I may not like people who throw lavish parties. Does that mean there should be a law banning such parties? No. I may not like people who eat fish. Does that mean there should be a law banning fish-eating? No. The laws of a land can't be instruments to push personal choices as laws and rules are based on accepted constitutional values that are commonly accepted. The Indian liberal combines Western ideas of individual liberty, democracy and individual rights with Gandhian thought.

Liberalism means not just an abiding belief in the freedom of the individual but also, as Gandhi kept emphasizing, a belief that 'ends' and 'means' are linked. The ends refer to what we may want, while the means refer to how we intend to get our ends. What do 'decent means' imply? It means, basically, a rejection of violence, in which dominance by an individual is also seen as a kind of violence. Violent thoughts and violent speech beget violent action. This is why using violence, particularly coercive actions or impositions or threats or use of physical force, to achieve our ends is simply not acceptable. Violence is a manifestation of the failure to accept dissent and failure to respect a diversity of opinions and practices. The liberal is steadfast in her belief in the legitimacy of dissent, but not in violent means to express it. Gandhi believed the Big State, or centralized government, because of its very nature will always use coercion and violence to get its way and impose its will on citizens. We see this, for instance, in the manner in which the Maharashtra government has used the harsh UAPA law, the stringent Unlawful Activities Prevention Act 1967, to arrest five activists who participated in the Elgaar Parishad on 31 December 2017 and accused them of 'Naxal' links.[19] The manner in which the UAPA law was used to arrest five rights activists, namely Arun Ferreira, Sudha Bharadwaj, Gautam Navlakha, Varavara Rao and Vernon Gonsalves, on 28 August 2018 has also been strongly criticized.[20]

That's why, traditionally, liberals have always been against a Big State armed with massive and arbitrary powers. The liberal is a believer in the power of the individual and not in the unrestrained power of the government. The recognition of the capacity of the Big State or government for inherent violence and therefore the need to restrain the state into a very narrow limited sphere of action is fundamental to liberal philosophy. Modern liberalism in India is thus social and political resistance to the arbitrary and expansive Big State or government machinery which recognizes no democratic limits on its power. Gandhi was a determined enemy of this kind of Big State and its inevitable corollary: the legitimization of violence.

Liberalism also means not having a government that as Masani writes, 'expropriates, liquidates or engages in social engineering.'[21] The liberal opposes any socialist-style nullifying of private property or a Hindutva-style railroading of personal liberties.

India's Big Bosses

Political leaders who believe in massive state or government power—as Indira Gandhi did in the 1970s and as Narendra Modi does in the 2000s, are eager to capture the levers of state institutions so that they can impose their own ideology on citizens.

Such leaders believe that they as individuals know what is in the best interests of lesser mortals. The common man or woman, they believe, is afflicted by many vices and therefore must be 'cured', 'purified' and set on the right track. In their view, institutions of the state or government institutions must shape the mass of common citizens for a party's political and social purpose. Citizens are mere cannon fodder for these politicians who believe their world view is the only truth. The consequences of such leadership— for instance, manifest in episodes like the Emergency of 1975, enforced sterilization during the Emergency, bans on cattle trade enacted in May 2017, the rapid imposition of GST in July 2017 and demonetization announced in November 2016—have been, in many ways, tragic. Narendra Modi is often called a 'disruptor' by his fans but in fact he is an implacable supporter of his own dictatorially imposed order. Modi has certainly not been a disruptor of India's decades of post-Independence statism or ever-tightening control of the citizen by the Big State.[22]

Illiberal leaders swear by government power. Liberals value the individual. The liberal cherishes diversity, embraces different ideas and recognizes that each individual is free to follow their own ideology—liberalism or socialism or conservatism. Illiberal leaders believe only in themselves. The liberal does not believe in imposing any ideology on others as the 'ultimate truth'. A true liberal restricts the role of the government to upholding commonly agreed upon constitutional values and the law. Liberal citizens thus oppose illiberal politicians who impose their individual beliefs through government power.

As we have seen, the liberal does not believe that an absolute similarity of views is necessary for coexistence. Two of the founders of the Swatantra Party, Masani and Rajaji, held completely opposite religious views. Masani was an atheist who perhaps became an agnostic. Rajaji was a religious believer. Liberalism brought them together without disrupting their personal beliefs. Rajaji often mounted a critique against irreligious dogmatism, often quoted from the Sermon on the Mount and the Gita. The writings of Rajaji and Masani reveal that Indian liberals have always stood against all orthodoxies, whether the orthodoxies of Hindutva nationalism or those of dogmatic secularism. Above all, the liberal places her faith in an impartial application of the law.

As Rajagopalachari wrote: 'Law is not whatever is enacted by the majority community, it is something that rests on permanent principles and is inherent in the conscience of a community. The Sanskrit word "dharma" denotes it best, the root of dharma being to sustain . . . the authoritarian notion that the will of the majority in parliament is a law . . . is a debasement of the rule of law.'[23]

A blind belief in the will of the majority is also a debasement of democracy. Democracy as majority rule can only mean enslavement and silencing of the minority. Justice and laws (not legislation) have always been cornerstones of liberal ideology and should always be. The focus on rule of law, implies focus on means rather than on ends.

The Swatantra Party, a party led by intellectuals, had extremely important liberal ideas yet its presence on the ground was thin.[24] It flourished in the period of Nehru's decline, when Indira had not yet consolidated her power. However, it wilted once the gale-force winds of Indira Gandhi's personality cult began to sweep through India. In the 1962 general elections, the Swatantra Party won eighteen seats; by 1967 it jumped to forty-four seats and was the single largest opposition party in the Lok Sabha. But it was able to win only eight seats in 1971. The Swatantra began to decline rapidly after Rajaji's death in 1972. In electoral politics in India, the liberal, with her emphasis on individual rights, is always up against the more seductive power of group rights and identities—that is the power of caste identity or religion or language. However, it's possible that over time, as economic and social mobility increases, group identities will begin to crack and there will be growing demands for performance and accountability from leaders. This could create a shift away from identities based on groups and may set India on a path of politics based on individual freedoms. You never know, a liberal party might just win elections sometime in the future!

Pushing Citizens Around

Turning its back on India's liberal founders, today the Hindutva nationalist Big Government (and its non-state actor affiliates in society) is barking out a volley of instructions to citizens and encroaching upon individual freedoms in fundamental ways in the pursuit of its own ideology.

Don't eat beef!

Don't shout slogans we don't like!

Don't put up social media posts the government doesn't like!

Don't dissent on government policies!

(The government is deemed as the 'nation' and therefore any dissent is necessarily seen as 'anti-national'. Such an assumption ignores the fact any government in a democracy is temporary! The nation and society lasts far beyond any particular government.)

Get an Aadhaar card and make sure it is linked with your bank account, passport and PAN card!

If you're a girl, dress 'modestly'!

Learn Sanskrit!

Do yoga!

Snatch up a broom and sweep!

Go cashless, stand in long queues and prove you don't have black money!

Remember, the state is always watching and the government has the right to your personal data!

Why do you want privacy anyway? Are you a thief, a criminal or a terrorist or some other form of 'anti-national'? Do you have something to hide?

Citizens are being asked to be completely transparent and accountable to the government. Yet, the government is claiming secrecy and avoiding accountability.[25] This can be illustrated in the new scheme announced by the Modi government to 'cleanse the system of political funding in the country', or the new political party funding law. The Modi government has proposed the introduction of electoral bonds apparently to promote transparency in election funding.[26] But while donors will remain publicly anonymous they will be known to the government, thus potentially scaring off those donating to the Opposition. This law has been challenged in court.[27] Such a law is the latest illustration of how those in power are seeking secrecy. Yet they demand that citizens shed their privacy and constantly come clean before the government. For example, citizens are not allowed to ask who travels with Prime Minister Modi in his plane.[28] The prime minister himself has not held a single open press conference in his tenure so far.[29]

Yet, the list of dos and don'ts for the citizen is seemingly endless, systematically attacking personal freedoms from all angles. This attack on personal freedoms has perpetuated economic controls. The rhetoric of a so-called business-friendly environment has only become a façade to mask cronyism, while curbs on personal freedoms, including freedom of speech and expression, aims at preventing citizens from exposing the nexus. The Modi government's imposition of a range of import duties and raising protectionist walls has been called a 'return to socialist protectionism' and a continuance of Nehru-style economic controls.[30] With the Punjab National Bank (PNB)–Nirav Modi banking fraud, the ICICI Bank fraud and the less-than-ethical practices at private hospital chains, columnist T.N. Ninan notes that because the private sector is increasingly beset by cronyism and wrongdoing, all talk of economic reform is fading.[31] A controlling Big State inevitably ends up encouraging crony capitalists instead of creating a level playing field. It pushes business into sharp practices by the lack of open, transparent regulation.

Demonetization: A Purification Ritual

On 8 November 2016, Prime Minister Modi suddenly announced that all Rs 500 and Rs 1000 currency notes would cease to be legal. They would be in the prime minister's words, 'worthless pieces of paper'. Citizens had little more than a month to deposit these old notes back into banks.[32]

Demonetization was an act of rampaging Big State power. A super-powerful prime minister issued a diktat from on high, compelling citizens to act in a certain way—and to hell with the personal consequences for individual citizens. What about the severe psychological blow of referring to hard-earned money as 'worthless pieces of paper'? Who cares!

In an address on 31 December 2016, on the eve of the New Year, Modi described demonetization as a 'shuddhi yagna',[33] a drive against 'kala dhan' and 'kala mann', a curative ritual against black money and black minds. By likening the holy war against black money to a drive against evil sinners, and by referring to demonetization as a quasi-religious purification yagna, the government was attempting to use government power as a holy weapon to coerce every citizen into becoming a so-called holy warrior for honesty, a bonded religious slave, a worshipper at the economy-purifying 'yagna'. Citizens were now forced to become blind bhakts, devotees of a prime ministerial command, which was not just mere economic policy but something like a theocratic pronouncement from the summit of a highly centralized government. At that moment the government assumed not just overweening temporal power but also a certain sacred power.

Thus, demonetization was a state-enforced 'puja' to clean India of the 'sin' of black money by a gruelling endurance test. Citizens stood in endless queues in banks to return their useless notes.[34] Millions suffered acute daily hardship. Forget economic reforms, this was about *paap* and *punya*, a rigorous pilgrimage, a phase of spiritual torment and suffering, like an arduous trek to the Badrinath shrine, to atone for past immorality. Importantly, the Reserve Bank of India announced less than two years later, that almost all the demonetized currency, 99.3 per cent in fact, was returned to banks. Analysts pointed out that not even 0.01 per cent of the black money was extinguished.[35] What did all that suffering achieve?

Demonetization was an epic announcement that affected the life of every Indian. Yet, reportedly, the decision was made with little consultation with anyone outside a small group. Reportedly, no one, not even the chief economic adviser, had the chance to disagree.[36] Demonetization was thus the apotheosis of state power in India, the Big State flexing its muscles over citizens, commanding a national 'purification' ritual that assumed every citizen was a sinner and needed shock treatment to prove her innocence and love for the nation. It was a flamboyant spectacle of the power of a supreme authority. In actuality, demonetization changed nothing on the ground, denting neither corruption nor black money. It was, in the end, a brazen demonstration of government power.

Demonetization can be criticized from the liberal point of view as expropriation. It was a move that took away the individual right to property, since legal personal cash is private property. It was also a campaign that viewed every citizen with mistrust as a possible hoarder of black money unless they proved otherwise. The burden of proof of innocence lay on the citizen. Every citizen was guilty until they proved their cash was legal. Every citizen was a potential crook, asked to account for their cash, without first establishing their guilt. Demonetization was a reversal of a fundamental tenet of modern jurisprudence: 'innocent unless proven guilty'. Demonetization held every citizen to be guilty unless they could prove their innocence.

According to this mindset, citizens don't pay taxes because they are essentially quasi-criminals. It doesn't cross the statist's mind that perhaps citizens evade taxes because they have no confidence in the government's ability or desire to deliver on promises after collecting taxes.

Fans of Big Government exulted over this apparently thrilling flourish of power. Many saw it as an act of 'disruption'. Many were entranced by the sheer irrationality of it all, an exciting demonstration of the power of Modi's fifty-six-inch chest, enthralled by a prime minister who could simply appear on TV and kapow! Make an announcement that would change lives and overturn rules. Wow, what power! What decisiveness!

As Harvard professor Yascha Mounk puts it, all over the world voters are seduced by the rule-breaker. Weary of a discredited political class that breaks its promises, the lure of an individual who promotes himself as a system-changer is high. The tragedy is, those who promote themselves as system-changers are often upholders of the same old system to the nth degree.[37]

Demonetization was propagated by an authoritarian Supreme Leader appealing to people to make sacrifices for Bharat Mata. In the 1990s, the BJP used religious nationalism and the mandir–masjid issue to consolidate the Hindu vote. In the twenty-first century, a populist appeal in the name of kala dhan sought to create a new generation of 'cashless' nationalists. In this context, going cashless actually implied surrendering privacy, first to finance companies and then to government.

Societies that value privacy prefer cash because there's less fear of leaving an electronic fingerprint. And societies where people voluntarily go cashless are those where the fear of government intrusion is minimal.

Citizens of India, ask yourselves, today the government commands you to give up cash, tomorrow it may order you to only use a particular credit card, or only use certain banks. Why should citizens grant so much power over their lives to the Big State over their personal choices—whether to use cash or go cash-free? Going cashless may be a good thing but should it not be a free choice? Should the individual not have the right to decide whether to live in a cash economy or in a cashless one?

The traumatic dislocation and travails caused by demonetization have been well documented.[38] However, in the Uttar Pradesh elections close on the heels of the 'notebandi' announcement, the BJP swept the polls, winning 325 out of 403 seats in the March 2017 elections. In the light of the UP results, Modi the 'strongman' was seen to have triumphed.

Illiberal Strongmen (or Strongwomen) in India

A centralized government, addicted to statist initiatives, inevitably contributes in the long term to disillusionment when tall promises are not met. The supreme delusion and hankering grows that a 'reformer' riding a white horse can charge in and restore an imagined golden age. The truth is, this white-horse-riding system-changer actually ends up expanding the Big State even further, further squeezing the space for citizens. To quote Yeats:

> 'Hurrah for revolution and more canon shot!
> A beggar upon horseback lashes a beggar on foot.
> Hurrah for revolution and canon come again!
> The beggars have changed places, but the lash goes on.'

Strongmen triumph when rules and processes are considered rotten to the core, when the 'sab chor hai' mentality prevails, when, as Mounk tells us there is widespread cynicism about 'the system'. A so-called 'outsider' prime minister like Modi, who at first glance does not play by the old rules, is bound to be appealing, particularly to restless youth and an impatient middle class. The irony is that Modi plays exactly by a shop-worn rule book, which holds that the government—the Big State—knows everything and can do anything. Modi is in fact a very old-fashioned 1970s style leader attempting to resurrect the 1970s style Big State.

Why do we Indians hero worship a dictator-like single leader who flaunts power, as Indira Gandhi was once worshipped and as

Modi is, perhaps to a lesser extent, today? It is because Indians as a people are deprived of power and individual agency in our own lives because the government has taken away so many of our freedoms. That's why we Indians worship power, we worship idols come to life. The Dabangg, the Baahubali, global comic superheroes like Superman, Batman, Spiderman and Ironman, are awesome, terrifying figures who, because they wield awesome power, enjoy high approval ratings. Lost in admiration, we remain unaware that these all-powerful figures we admire so much are actually seriously curtailing our individual freedoms and steamrolling our personal liberties to build their own cult.

The superhero cult extinguishes the difference between means and ends—that important liberal prescription. They reinforce the belief that since only the superhero is good and powerful, they will, by their own power, save the world. Hero worship of politicians is in fact a highly religious belief. It's a belief that gods will descend from heaven, perform miracles and save devotees.

Nehru, for example, India's longest-serving prime minister and the unchallenged colossus of his time, is hardly ever referred to as a 'powerful' prime minister. This is because Nehru never felt the need to pose as a power-flaunting strongman. Neither did prime ministers like Atal Bihari Vajpayee or P.V. Narasimha Rao, although one ran a remarkably successful coalition government and the other, while heading a minority government, dramatically initiated the freeing of India's economy from socialist controls.

For those whose basic consciousness is the drive for power embodied in mythological figures like the Mahabharata's Duryodhana or Kamsa, the tyrant of Mathura, rules, norms and laws soon become expendable. The awesome and spectacular display of power keeps people spellbound, like a show of dazzling fireworks, magnified by twenty-first-century reality TV, in which the worst-behaved individual always gets the highest ratings. We see this tendency on TV already: the most foul-mouthed party spokesperson, the rudest anchor, is inevitably the most watched. Yet the stronger the grip, the more fragile power becomes and suddenly slips through the fingers. Those blinded by power cannot see the dark clouds in the distance, because when the aura of power begins inevitably to reduce and legitimacy leaks away, authoritarianism begins to judder upwards like a rapidly building typhoon.

Leaders who pretend to be demi-gods will always need to imagine and invent an 'enemy', 'asuras' or demons they can then seek to ceremoniously slay to proclaim their greatness before their devotees. Indira Gandhi invoked the 'foreign hand', and Narendra Modi and his followers, as we have already noted, invoke a wider range of enemies: 'anti-nationals', 'secularists', 'half Maoists', 'jihadists', 'urban Naxals' or 'presstitutes' (journalists) are among their chosen asuras.[39]

So-called 'powerful' leaders from Aurangzeb, Louis XIV, Hitler, Stalin, Mao and Indira Gandhi who ruled with an iron hand generally caused misery and havoc.[40] The hell for leather drive for power leads almost inevitably to political turmoil. The response is then to divide and rule or cultivate different vote banks, which results in class war or war between communities. Class war sometimes takes the guise of a culture war.[41] Let us apply this to today's conditions. The Hindutva 'revolution' in many ways is posited as a class war against the privileged elite represented by the Congress. Modi's supporters claim Modi is a humble 'chaiwallah', an outsider in Delhi's elite circles.[42] Modi has often referred to himself as the 'kaamdaar' (working man) vs the 'naamdars' (privileged dynasts) of the Congress.

The war for Hindutva is thus often posited as mortal combat between non-elite, first generation, urban, upwardly mobile folk versus the entitled elite. It's the born-to-privilege snobs who are seen to uphold elitist, disconnected liberalism while the non-elite are marked by rooted authentic Hindutva. In history, powerful regimes have a tendency to create class conflicts. This class battle has the potential to easily escalate to street violence. With so much in-built violence in rhetoric, language and attitude, and in the inclination to take arbitrary actions against opponents, so-called 'powerful' regimes are, if history is our guide, liable to soon experience a noisy collapse.[43]

Writes Mounk: 'Until recently, liberal democracy reigned triumphant and citizens seemed committed to this form of government . . . but now citizens have grown disillusioned, restless, angry and disdainful and authoritarian populists are on the rise around the world . . . elected strongmen have succeeded in turning fledgling democracies into electoral dictatorships . . . destroying the free media, undermining independent institutions and muzzling the opposition.'[44]

Mounk points out from a survey that while more than two-thirds of older Americans say it is essential to live in a democracy, less than a third of younger Americans feel the same way. Many young Indians seduced by the Modi cult are similarly scornful of democracy. In a fast-paced news 360 universe, where the daily news cycle and 24x7 television dominate life, who cares for slow, tortuous democratic processes when short-circuiting those processes is so much more thrilling? When a psychedelically lit-up, media-powered 'feel good' guru performs magic tricks and stupefies by the power of his personality?[45]

Mounk believes that for democracies to work, all major political actors must adhere to the basic rules of the democratic game most of the time. 'Winning an election is less important than preserving the [liberal democratic] system.' Mounk quotes Michael Ignatieff, former leader of the Canada Liberal party: 'For democracies to work politicians need to respect the difference between an enemy and an adversary. An adversary is someone you want to defeat. An enemy is someone you have to destroy.' This tendency of Hindutva nationalists to destroy the enemy is seen in the BJP's slogan of 'Congress-mukt Bharat', and the way it has used fair means and foul to stop the Congress from forming governments, notably in Goa and Manipur.[46] In this, the BJP has adopted the worst instincts of the 1970s Congress, which similarly tried to wipe out all opposition with disastrous results for itself and India, particularly in states like Punjab and Jammu and Kashmir.[47]

Yet, leaders who are chipping away at liberal democracy are gaining support across the world from Vladimir Putin in Russia to Recep Erdogan in Turkey to Modi in India. Mounk describes these leaders as the new 'elected autocrats' of the twenty-first century, leaders elected by democracy who are now adversaries of democracy.[48] They are destroying liberal democracy by ensuring that state institutions are no longer neutral and are captured by their own ideology, that the media is silenced and that the separation of powers between institutions is undermined.

A Pew Research Survey showed that support for a 'strongman' unchecked by judiciary and parliament is highest in India at 55 per cent.[49] Almost half the population of India, 53 per cent, say military rule would be a very good thing. Former director of BBC News, James Harding pointed out in a lecture that democracy is in retreat across the world, authoritarianism is on the rise, press freedom is widely curtailed and propaganda is commonplace.

Harding quotes Amartya Sen to say 'democracy is not just majority rule. Democracy has complex demands, which certainly include voting and respect for election results, but it also requires the protection of liberties and freedoms, respect for legal entitlements and guaranteeing of free discussion and uncensored distribution of news and fair comment.' Sen's constant reiteration of individual freedoms is a warning to statist autocrats.[50]

Mounk points out that illiberal democracy is a much more insidious threat because earlier the threat to democracy was geographically and ideologically from the outside. Communism and fascism grew in societies where liberalism had not taken root.[51] Today, the threat of populism and the prospect of illiberal democracy has emerged within liberal democratic societies. This is because illiberal strongmen leaders think they can get away by bending the norms, and an adoring public often encourages them to do so.

Does the popularity of the elected autocrat endure, though, if his governing style continues to restrict the individual freedoms of citizens? The context in which belief in a strongman is sustained is important. If that context is changed, that is, if the 'strongman' reveals himself to be calamitous for personal freedom, there is a chance these beliefs may rapidly change. During the 2014 election campaign, Narendra Modi proclaimed himself as India's 'chowkidar'. Yet, this single, all-powerful chowkidar could not prevent a gigantic banking fraud such as the Rs 12,600 crore PNB fraud allegedly pulled off by businessmen perceived as allegedly close to the prime minister: Nirav Modi and Mehul Choksi. The liberal would argue here that a sole chowkidar can never be a watchdog of democracy. Instead, the real watchdogs in a democracy are functioning value-based autonomous institutions like the Central Bureau of Investigation (CBI), the Central Vigilance Commission (CVC), the judiciary, et al. The seeming inability of a strongman prime minister to prevent wrongdoing by cronies has somewhat affected Modi's popularity.[52] Modi promised 'minimum government, maximum governance' but suddenly the Hindutva nationalist state seems to be a monster state, its finger in every pie from education to culture to yoga to food choices. This is an even larger government structure than the one created by Indira Gandhi.

The Modi years have seen the growth of a massive government whose every new initiative is bringing ever more layers of officialdom, inspectors, permits and rules. It has been called 'saffron socialism' in full bloom, a Big State unwilling to let go of, say, the banking sector or even properly set Air India free from control even as it offers it for sale.[53] The disinvestment record of the Modi government— ostensibly a 'Right-wing' government—has been called 'pathetic'. Out of thirty state-owned companies approved for sale under the 'strategic sale' plan, only one—ONGC's acquisition of HPCL—has happened.[54]

But why blame only Modi? Strongmen or strongwomen illiberal leaders may be found in 'secular' regimes too. Illiberal leadership cults don't emerge only on the Hindutva nationalist side. In Bengal, for example, these cults have emerged in the CPI(M) and in the TMC. 'Where the mind is without fear and the head is held high,' wrote Tagore. Today, in Tagore's native Bengal, a violent political culture has created deeply entrenched fear in society.[55]

Ambikesh Mahapatra, a Jadavpur University chemistry professor, was arrested in April 2012 for circulating cartoons about the chief minister. Mahapatra's neighbour Subrata Sengupta was also arrested simply because Mahapatra used his email. Another academic, scientist Partho Sarothi Ray an assistant professor at the Indian Institute of Science Education and Research, and others were arrested in 2012 for taking part in a protest against the displacement of slum-dwellers.[56] In the panchayat polls in May 2018, TMC cadres were accused of using violent tactics against the opposition.[57] Bengal, once famous for its iconoclasts, is now thoroughly politicized, providing little space for independent thought, aside from two bitterly divided camps.

Three decades of Left dominance has created a numbing politicization of education, administration, police, civil society and even art, and has almost wiped out the independent thinker. The intellectual vacuum has in turn spawned a political vacuum.

The lack of intellectual diversity means that all politics ultimately becomes personalized. Without a contest of ideas, without clashing doctrines, politics becomes just rival gangs of toughs or equally foul-mouthed people on both sides who prefer to let their fists talk rather than their words. This could become the fate of India if illiberal strongmen leaders use governments to force party loyalties to the exclusion of all else—as the Left did—thus stamping out free thinking and a free battle of ideas.

Gopal Krishna Gokhale famously said over a century ago that what Bengal thinks today, India thinks tomorrow. In a tragic way, Bengal's politicization of society and lumpenization of politics, which has been growing since the late 1960s, were adopted at the national level in the 1970s when a violent politics took hold. Today, these methods have been normalized across the nation, with the current ruling party at the centre zealously adopting and upholding these traits.

When the grammar of politics is violence, the educated tend to stay away. Those who do join, lend legitimacy to the politics of 'us vs them' by providing an intellectual veneer to crass anti-intellectualism. The Left ruled Bengal for three decades through a structured arrangement to perpetuate fear and deprived the Bengali of the right to think aloud. Bengal chief minister Mamata Banerjee is victim, inheritor and perpetrator of the same fear-inspiring machine.

In many ways, Bannerjee's is a 'strongwoman' personality cult similar to that of Modi at the Centre. Mamata believes that she is the 'true' Left and the CPM and others are mere pretenders. Narendra Modi and the Hindutva brigades too are convinced that they are the only 'nationalists' and those who disagree are by definition 'anti-national'. The ghosts of Stalin and Mao would be proud to see the success of their methods, so vociferously adopted by self-appointed Right- and Left-wing political parties in India!

Bhakti, Bhakti Everywhere

As we have noted, our society is prone to hero worship. But the liberal must always be wary of hero-worshipping anyone. Instead, the liberal lives by her power to reason. But because of 'democratic authoritarianism'[58] taking hold, not just at the centre but in the states, the Indian mind is closing and reason and rationality are at a discount. This closing of the Indian mind might end up destroying the economic future of India too. A vibrant economy needs an open and critical intellectual environment in order to question currently dominant economic actors, and find newer and better ways to satisfy consumer demands. A free mind is a necessary precondition for a free market. Illiberal sycophancy can take a toll on a free economy too. 'If subservience and slavish adulation take the place of independent thinking and criticism is never resorted to but with fear and trepidation, the atmosphere breeds political diseases . . . careerism, intrigue and various types of degrees of dishonesty,' warned Rajagopalachari.

Today, many take pride in being 'chamchas' of a big political boss. Dev Kant Barooah, Congress president during the Emergency, once declared, 'India is Indira. Indira is India', and this has become a standard template for many wannabe Barooahs in different political parties. The previous Congress regime with its feudal impulses set the trend for rewarding loyalists. After all, wasn't Pratibha Patil chosen as India's twelfth president because of her uninterrupted loyalty to the then ruling party? Patil's symbolic value was the same reason Ram Nath Kovind was chosen to be India's fourteenth President in 2017 by the ruling party today.

'I am proud to be a Modi chamcha,' former Censor Board chief Pahlaj Nihalani once declared.[59] Vice President Venkaiah Naidu, when he was a Union minister, said that Narendra Modi was 'god's gift for India';[60] at Mamata Banerjee's swearing-in, ministers bowed to her in a way Bengal politicians have rarely done, and in Tamil Nadu, All India Anna Dravida Munnetra Kazhagam (AIADMK) members would prostrate themselves at the late Jayalalithaa's feet in servile loyalty.

Politics has turned presidential. Towering personalities are like absolute monarchs in their parties. He or she wields so much clout that they attract a swarm of ambitious hangers-on, all jostling for posts and appointments from this single Caesar. For these darbaris, politics is not a vocation for independent-minded public service but simply a means to better their prospects. These personality cults are a reflection of the lack of political ideals and the revival of feudal mindsets. They are an overthrow of democratic norms and rules. The destruction of democratic norms in politics and the closing of the mind to discussions and debates undermines democracy itself.

Writes Mounk: 'There is something performative about authoritarian populists to break democratic norms . . . their recklessness is no less dangerous for all of that . . . once some members of the political system are willing to break the rules, others have a big incentive to follow suit . . . there are spectacular attacks on basic democratic norms [from newcomer populists] and the representatives of old established parties have also become increasingly willing to undermine the basic rules of the democratic game.'[61]

Today, politics is so heavily personalized that there are few institutional checks on executive authority if the electoral mandate is large enough. A hefty mandate brings licence to wreak havoc on democratic norms. Yet, without those norms democracy cannot survive.

India's political parties choose sycophancy over meritocracy for three reasons. First, because of the rise of the High Command culture where an authoritarian individual at the top demands complete loyalty. Second, the breakdown of party structures— organizational structures within parties are almost defunct so there are no open and transparent ways for an individual to rise, apart from becoming a 'chamcha'. Third, the decline of ideological vibrancy— ideological effervescence is not possible if any difference in opinion is immediately deemed to be 'anti-party' or anti-national. Since there is barely any debate within parties, there is no focus on those able to think afresh. Thus, the party leader is not someone who argues his case or wins over detractors through debates. He simply has to be powerful enough to impose his writ. Gandhi would call this kind of imposed leadership a manifestation of violence.

Parties are afraid of open and honest debates because they are convinced that any new idea could lead to the loss of vote banks. Parties see the state or the government as a source of power, and seek to bribe or coerce citizens as a way only to retain power. When vote banks are the only prisms, individual citizens disappear from view. Only vote banks are visible, individual citizens are invisible.

The Modi government has declared its commitment to creating a start-up culture. But in politics, deadening sycophancy is killing the space for political start-ups. Politicians who have new marketable ideas can't hope to be heard within the established party structures. Instead, they have to set up their own outfits, as Arvind Kejriwal did with the AAP in 2012. Over time, the AAP too has developed its own High Command.

In an illiberal democracy, personal loyalty has become a substitute for political ideas. The High Command structure of parties is reflexively resistant to talent because talent is a disruptive force and implies a threat to the illiberal Supreme Leader. The politician who arguably sank the Congress in the Assam polls of 2016, Himanta Biswa Sarma, is regarded as a talented politician. He was once in the Congress. However, he claims that 'blue-blooded' dynasts who surround Rahul Gandhi forced him out.[62]

Since there is no space for debate and dialogue within parties, anyone who questions the party line is seen as a rebel, be it Yogendra Yadav[63] in the AAP or Biswa Sarma in the Congress. Discordant voices are stilled in the name of 'party discipline'. This culture impacts processes in Parliament as much as it affects every family and every business, reinforcing hierarchy and discouraging open debate. New ideas therefore cannot emerge and parties remain in a time warp.

B.R. Ambedkar wrote: 'In India, "Bhakti" or what may be called the path of devotion or hero-worship plays a part in politics unequalled in any other [country] . . . "Bhakti" . . . or hero-worship in politics is a sure road to degradation and to eventual dictatorship.'[64] Ironically, the legatees of Ambedkar are the worst offenders of bhakti. The supporters of Mayawati have furiously built statues of her, as if to etch their loyalty in stone.

Patriarchal societies tend to yearn for a strong man at the top. Democratic leaders who rule by consensus or are seen to be part of a team, like Manmohan Singh, suffer perceptionally because they are not dominant macho personalities. In fact, not just in politics but in society as well, we seem to be reverting to a culture of unquestioned blind loyalty to a leader required to be an alpha male. Grafted on this yearning for a roaring 'Dabangg', are media and PR campaigns that professionally manufacture 'greatness' 24x7. Any criticism of these super-heroes can be dangerous. For example, if you criticize film star Rajinikant or cricketer Sachin Tendulkar on social media, you might be cast almost as a blasphemer against God.[65] Similarly, ask questions about Modi and the 'Modi bhakts' will start a vociferous vilification campaign far more effective than official censoring or banning. Non-state censorship, or outsourcing bans to the hooligan mob, has become a unique feature of the post-2014 years.[66]

The cult of Narendra Modi is based on remarkable personal popularity. Yet, in India, the office of the prime minister has always been more poetically mystical than ruthlessly political. The prime minister controls no specific territory, he's the court of last resort, the place where differences are settled. Prime ministers have generally been inclusive, accommodating figures carrying parties along, reaching out to adversaries at critical junctures and setting a high national tone through verbal signals and public images.

Modi is different. He is a pugnacious, battle-ready, combative prime minister fighting bitter political wars, seeking to demonstrate overweening political power. He has often directed slurs at his political opponents, saying, for example, 'This is a 10 per cent commission government', about the then Siddaramaiah-led government in Karnataka, and 'there is something wrong in Nitish Kumar's DNA' when the latter split from the BJP.

He insists on personalized executive action such as sweeping streets or leading the nation in yoga, but is impatient with parliamentary procedures and rarely attends Parliament.[67] This confrontational, rather menacing political style has left the government's allies disenchanted. The Telugu Desam Party (TDP) exited the NDA on 16 March 2018, and ally Shiv Sena not only fought against the BJP in the Maharashtra by-poll in Palghar in 2018 but also termed the BJP its 'biggest enemy'.

'Where power is allowed to be centralized in a few hands in government, democracy shrinks. That is why, in all written democratic Constitutions, there is provision for a division of power or functions,' writes Masani. The 397-member Prime Minister's Office under Modi has been called 'the most powerful PMO in Indian history', with major decisions like demonetization and the roll-out of GST on 1 July 2017 taken by the PMO. It is significant that it was Prime Minister Modi who journeyed to France to finalize the purchase of the Rafale aircraft in 2015 rather than the then defence minister. The Pradhan Mantri Ujjwala Yojana to distribute LPG to poor households, was launched by the prime minister on 1 May 2016, not by the minister for petroleum and natural gas. The prime minister generally fronts all major executive actions of this government.[68]

Yet, B.R. Ambedkar and India's Constituent Assembly designed India's Constitution as more federal than unitary. 'India, that is Bharat, shall be a Union of States,' declares Article 1 of the Constitution. To gain the confidence of the states, the prime minister needs to stand for reconciliation, magnanimity, and inclusivity even with adversaries.

While sitting on a perch of supreme state power, how successful has the Prime Minister's Office been in drafting original public policy for the future? Let's rewind to when Narendra Modi was Gujarat chief minister. At that time, we did not really see any new legislative or policy initiative emanating from Gujarat. The Jyotigram scheme or electrification of rural households has been hailed. Yet, Gujarat had always had significant amounts of installed capacity in power although Modi for his part did create a parallel rural electricity grid, giving farmers a choice between erratic, low-cost supply and higher-priced regular supplies. Few unknown public policies originated from Gujarat in Modi's term. Tamil Nadu had its mid-day meal scheme, Kerala's claim to fame was basic education and health services, Andhra Pradesh's its Rs 2 rice, Rajasthan had its RTI initiatives and Bengal its land reforms. Good or bad, at least Operation Barga in Bengal was an original policy contribution by the Left. We may debate these initiatives, but can't deny their lasting imprint. In 2014, Modi campaigned with the slogan 'government has no business to be in business'. But we have seen little original policymaking in this direction. As *The Economist* points out, only one in 200 state-owned enterprises has been sold and that too to another state-owned enterprise. No private player was interested in buying Air India because of the government's insistence on a 24 per cent stake and no one was sure that the government would not keep interfering.[69] So, transforming the economy through intelligent policymaking? Not really.

The Gujarat model—if there is one—is one of ruthless authoritarianism through the centralization of power. Two draconian Gujarat laws originated in Modi's time. The Labour Laws Bill of Gujarat[70] (now passed) and the Gujarat Control of Terrorism and Organised Crime (GCTOC) Act, still awaiting presidential approval. The Ahmedabad edition of the *Times of India* was charged with sedition in 2008, and the Gujarat police carried out several 'encounter' killings, such as those of Ishrat Jehan, Tulsiram Prajapati and Sohrabuddin Sheikh. The marginalization of the media and NGOs and the crushing of labour unions were seen as the hallmarks of the state's so called 'efficiency'. As Prime Minister, Modi similarly cracked down on NGOs. Over 4470 NGOs lost foreign funding licences. Greenpeace India's registration was cancelled[71] and the Ford Foundation was placed on a watch list.[72]

But can the 'Gujarat model' be applied at the all-India level? Indira Gandhi could be a supremo cult at a time when the Congress was dominant in most states. Today, when half a dozen powerful regional leaders dot the landscape, why should they obediently line up behind a supremo prime minister?[73]

In fact, in India it is actually coalition governments which uphold the Constitution's federal spirit more than governments led by supremos. Coalition governments have tended to be more liberal, more consensual and more respectful of federalism than governments with massive mandates. In a way, coalition governments remain the last institutional check on illiberal leadership cults.

The Janata coalition of 1977 and those led by H.D. Deve Gowda and I.K. Gujral were indeed shaky. Yet, the coalition government led by Vajpayee and the minority government led by Narasimha Rao were highly successful. Former RBI governor Y.V. Reddy recently said that coalition governments produce better economic growth than majority ones, pointing out that India saw the highest growth from 1990–2014 during coalitions.[74]

The Vajpayee coalition government of 1999—the first to last a full five years—was a remarkable experiment in political cooperation that saw growth rates pick up, tough decisions on disinvestment, a new relationship with the US and a drive towards infrastructure. It showed that if there was a consensus-building leader as the glue, it was possible to provide purposeful governance even if no party had an absolute majority.

Both Rao and Vajpayee were old-school, broadly liberal, low-profile practitioners of realpolitik who saw the need to carry others along. It was Rao who brought in the non-political technocrat Manmohan Singh[75] to take charge of the economy. Vajpayee conveyed a sense of reconciliation, among allies and opponents alike.

If Vajpayee was the reconciler, Narasimha Rao was the crafty political manager who, while heading a minority government, pulled off the most dramatic transformation India had ever seen post-Independence, namely, the 1991 reforms. With stealth and statecraft, Rao initiated the liberalization of the economy, carrying with him a divided Congress and hostile opposition. Yet, the lack of political conviction in reforms came at a price. Economic reforms at that time, never quite received popular legitimacy. Instead, the impression went around that a weak government had succumbed to the alleged 'Washington consensus' or World Bank–IMF diktats on liberalization, privatization and globalization, thus damaging the country. This is the reason why today no political party dares to campaign openly on the plank of economic reforms.

As a group of liberal analysts have put it, 'The benefits of [economic] reforms need to be felt by the largest section of the

people who are in the rural areas. This brings popular endorsement
and political support to the reforms agenda . . . yet economic
reforms which began in the 1990s focused only on non-farm
sectors . . . 3 decades after initiation of economic reforms every
aspect of agriculture is tied up in red tape . . . so there is little
popular appreciation or support for 'economic liberalisation'. We
will explore the liberal agenda for farmers in the next chapter.

A word of caution here on the liberalization of 1991. Even
as the liberal, above all, values private enterprise and minimum
government, the role of the government in India requires detailed
debate. Since the liberal rejects dogma of any kind—whether
of the market or of socialism—and is ultimately a pragmatist,
she recognizes that the government cannot abjectly surrender its
responsibilities. The journey to prosperity through the market may
need to be balanced with government responsibilities in education
and public health, in the form of the democratic welfare state. The
liberal is open-minded on the need for the government to shoulder
its responsibilities. Pure market economics, as pragmatic liberals
understand, could in some instances drastically widen inequality
without, as Amartya Sen points out, accompanying public investment
in health and education. 'Given that one of the worst features of
social injustice in India is the continued exclusion of a large part of
the population from basic facilities, the struggle against injustice has
to be connected with constructive demands for basic entitlements.'[76]
The delivery of these basic entitlements do need to be addressed by
governments. To paraphrase Rajaji again, the government must be a
catalyst in stimulating economic development, providing highways,
roads, waterways, communications and foster private enterprise and
self-help among individuals. Manmohan Singh, a liberal centrist,
once quoted John Maynard Keynes: 'If the rich had spent their
wealth on their own enjoyments, the world would have long ago
found such a regime intolerable. But like bees, they saved and
accumulated . . . to the advantage of the whole community . . . the
duty of saving became nine tenths of the virtue and the growth of

the cake the object of true religion.' Not only the growth of the cake but also the equitable distribution of the cake is also what Rajaji meant when he spoke of the 'trusteeship of the rich'.[77]

Let us return to our focus on coalition governments. Contrast the Rao and Vajpayee coalitions with India's majority governments. Indira Gandhi's thundering mandate in 1971 led within three short years to a descent into socialistic protectionism and the 1975 Emergency. Rajiv Gandhi's huge victory in 1984 soon collapsed amid perceptions of influence-peddling coteries around an all-powerful prime minister.

Modi has ruled with a massive majority, repeatedly proving his electability. Modi's style is highly centralized, bombastic and self-centred—one that alienates significant sections of the political class. The TDP's angry estrangement and the Shiv Sena's attacks reveal the flaws in a decision-making structure concentrated overwhelmingly around the PMO in Delhi. The manner in which Federal Front leaders have ganged up against the Modi-led BJP reveals how supremo-centred, illiberal politics tends to drive away regional allies.

Illiberal democracy thus means an incapacity to deal with those who may differ and an immersion in one's own echo chamber. The increased centralization of political power erodes the capacity of the economy to devolve, decentralize and deliver. Today, despite the hype and rhetoric of economic growth and the claims of transformational changes, little has changed on the ground. This shows how a centralized government fails and a decentralized government works.

The market works precisely because no economic actor can claim omniscience or claim to know exactly what all consumers want. Therefore, the entrepreneur seeks to find incremental improvements to a product here or a service there. The open, competitive market makes it possible to test the many products and ideas that different entrepreneurs may have by providing a level playing field for all.

In contrast, a centralized government may boast about its powers and trumpet its knowledge. But in reality, it becomes completely disconnected about the working of the economy and society at the grassroots because it functions, as Gandhi said, 'as twenty men at the top'. This is actually not even a centralizing of power but a centralizing of an ignorance of reality and a recipe for increasing social and economic conflicts. A centralized, know-it-all authoritarian government simply imposes its will. It does not bother to create dialogue at every level of society or involve as many stakeholders as possible before taking a final decision.

Banned, Banned, Banned!

How many bans are there today anyway? How many aspects of our behaviour are policed?

Want to eat tenderloin in Maharashtra? Sorry, it's banned.

Want to read Salman Rushdie's *The Satanic Verses*? Sorry, it's banned.

Living in Gujarat and want to read the book *Great Soul* by Joseph Lelyveld? Sorry, it's banned.

Want to see the movie *Fifty Shades of Grey*? Sorry, it hasn't been cleared by the CBFC.

Living in Gujarat and want to see the film *Fanaa*? Sorry, that was also banned in Gujarat.

Want to see the play 'Mi Nathuram Godse Boltoy'? Sorry, that was once banned too.

Does Priya Pillai of Greenpeace want to voice her views in London? Sorry, she was once banned from travelling.[78]

Want to see *India's Daughter*, a documentary on the Nirbhaya rape case? Sorry, that's banned from TV telecast.[79]

Bans are an entirely un-Hindu thing. Think about it, is anything banned in Hinduism? Almost nothing. What's common between liberal democracy and Hindu philosophy? A constant search for answers, a quest for knowledge, a starting assumption that we don't—we cannot—know everything. However, governments which are stubbornly convinced that they possess *absolute* knowledge implement policies through bans and diktats. People of goodwill may on occasion differ on answers and on specific public policies. Democracy provides a platform to legally and formally negotiate a common ground in a particular context, which is open to change as the context changes. Hindu philosophy is full of such debates and in these debates there is little *absolute* knowledge or any *absolute* certainty of truth.

The epics (as we saw in the last chapter), particularly the Mahabharata, are tales of heroes (and some heroines) constantly plagued by self-doubt. They constantly debate the right course of action. The Gita is a treatise of Arjuna's tryst with self-doubt. The Upanishads are question-and-answer sessions on philosophy. The Ramayana's heroes are as flawed as they are noble.

Yet, those who believe in supreme government power believe they have all the answers and are the sole repositories of knowledge. They believe they have seen the light. Self-doubt does not trouble them. The Big State believes it has ultimate knowledge about what's good for the people. The people have to simply be goaded and herded into obeying the mai-baap sarkar's wishes. Any questioning or disagreement is not only plain wrong or agenda-driven but equivalent to treason.[80]

Is the strength of a so-called strong government to be defined by how brutally it demolishes citizens' personal freedom, privacy and personal choices? Yes, the benefits of yoga are undeniable, but should the taxpayer's money be spent on yoga events on a national scale?[81] In 2016, in the aftermath of demonetization, Prime Minister Modi praised a Surat couple who chose a low-cost wedding and managed to marry by paying only Rs 500.[82]

Don't citizens have the choice about whether they want meagre or extravagant weddings? Can citizens in a democracy be forced into austerity as a moral command? Why should citizens be instructed by the prime minister on their behavioural choices? It is as if only the government and the prime minister know what is in the best interests of over a billion mindless children who apparently believe they are citizens of India! It is an infantilizing of an electorate empowered to vote! To quote Masani, 'The government should not be like the mother who told the nanny, nanny go and see what the child is doing and tell him not to. The child should only be stopped when he is really doing something which he shouldn't.'

But then, the Hindutva nationalist government—a nanny Big State where the nanny is also a fierce ideologue—recognizes no limit on its power. An important way in which this was manifest was the manner in which the government introduced rules on cattle slaughter.

Citizens, What's Your Beef? Just Obey the Big State's Command!

In 2017, the government banned the sale of cows and buffaloes for slaughter in animal markets, saying it was aiming to prevent uncontrolled and unrestricted animal trade.[83] This, in spite of the fact that India had fast expanded its beef exports by 12 per cent annually, boosting its share of world beef exports from 5 per cent to 21 per cent.[84] According to the new rules, cattle could only be sold to a person who had documents showing he was an agriculturalist. Selling non-milch or ageing or 'unfit' cattle was banned. Only farmland owners were allowed to trade in animal markets. Cleverly, the rules were notified under Prevention of Cruelty to Animals (PCA) Act of 1960, which gives the central government power over animal welfare. This was perhaps designed to blunt liberal protests by disingenuously professing a commitment to protect animals from 'cruelty'. The notification was titled 'Prevention of Cruelty to Animals (Regulation of Livestock Markets) Rules 2017'.

The Kerala government called the ban 'fascist and anti-federal', with the chief minister saying, 'cattle slaughter becomes illegal at a time when manslaughter happens in the name of the cow.'[85]

The Supreme Court has now suspended the controversial ban on trade of cattle for slaughter, although cow slaughter and beef consumption is banned in several states.[86]

In Maharashtra, the Animal Preservation (Amendment) Bill passed by the BJP–Shiv Sena government in 1995 already makes the sale and consumption of beef punishable by Rs 10,000 and carries a jail term of five years. In Gujarat, cattle slaughter carries the punishment of life imprisonment. However, a blanket ban across would have broken the supply chain for the meat and leather industry, worth more than an estimated $16 billion a year in annual sales. Let's face it, the laws and bans on cow slaughter and trade are only an ideological proxy war against Muslims and Dalits, the communities mostly employed in the leather and cattle-culling industries. Hindutva groups opposed the suspension of the ban, saying 'sentiments of Hindus should be respected.'[87]

Think of the hundreds and millions of cattle in India, including cows and buffaloes. Should farmers not be free to sell them once they have reached the end of their productive period? Are these rules not an assault on the property rights of farmers? Modi had once promised to double farm incomes in five years.[88] Can farm incomes be doubled if the economic assets of farmers are tampered with? Why should a farmer be restricted by law in how he chooses to use his cattle, perhaps as potential capital to be sold at short notice when in need of quick ready cash?

A spate of cow-related killings and lynchings have stained India's earth with blood since 2015. In September 2015, Mohammad Akhlaq was lynched in Dadri. In October 2015, sixteen-year-old Zahid Bhat was killed in Udhampur. In 2017 Pehlu Khan was attacked and killed in Alwar.[89] All these attacks were carried out by so-called 'gau rakshaks' or cow vigilantes and were only half-heartedly condemned by the prime minister.[90] As a result of these cattle-protection-related attacks, many innocents died at the hands of vigilantes and scores were injured. In a belated recognition of how badly the ban on cattle trade and slaughter hit the farmer and the livestock and leather industry, cattle-trade rules have now been diluted and some of the restrictions on animal trading in markets have been done away with.[91] But does the mob care about these changes in rules? No. Cattle-related attacks continue well into 2018.

The imposition of the cattle-trade rules was an example of the Big State in dangerous action, using government power to limit individual constitutional liberties such as the right to life, right to livelihood and right to live with dignity. Judging from how vociferously Hindutva groups supported these bans, clearly considerations of Hindutva ideology (rather than any scientific policy on cattle welfare) was uppermost for the government. Hindutva leaders have been the most vocal about the bans on cow slaughter. In April 2017, RSS chief Mohan Bhagwat called for a nationwide ban on the slaughter of cattle.[92] In the same year, Chhattisgarh chief minister Raman Singh said that those guilty of cattle slaughter should be hanged.[93] The municipal chairman of Hoshangabad in Madhya Pradesh even gave a call to make Hoshangabad 'pure vegetarian' by putting up a Facebook post asking if meat, fish and mutton should be banned in the holy town of Hoshangabad.

Should an Indian citizen in the twenty-first century be forced to be vegetarian? Or be forced to choose his diet by the government of the day? Is it for the government to decide what citizens of India should eat? Or not eat? The fact that there was hardly any consultation or dialogue before the announcement of the cattle rules highlighted arrogance, limited knowledge and ignorance of history. That a cattle-trade ban which affected the livelihoods and eating habits of millions of Indians was announced overnight, with no warning, again shows how the attainment of the so-called 'Hindu Rashtra' means a fundamental restriction on the individual freedoms so carefully enunciated by our liberal Constitution.

After the announcement of the cattle slaughter rules, there were protests from Kerala and states in the north-east and some colleges even held beef-eating festivals. In May 2017, R. Sooraj a PhD student at IIT Madras and a member of the Ambedkar Periyar Study Circle, was badly beaten up by Right-wing student groups for participating in a beef-eating festival.[94] Dissenting voices are irrelevant and must be cowed into submission; Hindutva majoritarianism trumps any other consideration. Journalist Gauri Lankesh squarely blamed Prime Minister Modi for cow-related crimes. She wrote: 'Modi is the prime cause for these attacks and murders . . . during the 2014 election campaign, Modi kept bragging about cow protection . . . he said the Central government has started a Pink Revolution[95] . . . cow goondaism has increased phenomenally . . . the main food of Muslims and Dalits is being snatched away and those who live on cattle skin are on the streets. Cow goondas have created a fear psychosis.'

For two days in 2015, during the Jain festival of Paryushan, the sale of meat and slaughter of even chickens and goats was banned by BJP-ruled states. This was done ostensibly to protect sentiments of the Jain community.[96] Again, the question arises of whether governments exist to 'protect sentiments'. If the state can ban goat slaughter for mutton, is this one step away from hypothetically banning the azaan in mosques because 'sentiments of Hindus' are being hurt, or hypothetically banning Durga Puja celebrations because 'sentiments of iconoclasts' are being hurt, or banning the sale of alcohol because 'sentiments of teetotallers' are being hurt? Is the Big State, a guardian of sentiments?

This is a profoundly illiberal idea! Liberals must unitedly oppose the usurpation of these enormous powers by the Big State. The real goal here is not the welfare of cattle or goats or chickens but to legitimize the expansion of the government by using the levers of religion and so-called religious sentiments. Once citizens accept the ever-expansive government (which is expanding its power using religion as a cover) it is only a matter of time before citizens entirely lose their capacity to hold governments accountable. It's the most dangerous game in town, folks!

Just as the ban on meat was only a cultural euphemism and proxy for asserting Hinduness versus Islam, the ban on Maggi

Two-Minute noodles in 2015 was a means of asserting pure Indianness versus foreign multinationals. After a long court battle and several food tests, the courts set aside the ban a few months later. The war against Nestle and Maggi noodles smacked of a nativist anti-MNC, Hindutva nationalist campaign to protect the 'pure' Hindu kitchen from the polluting influences of western multinationals in the case of Maggi. It was yet another 'demonetization-style yagna' to cleanse the country of 'dirty' foreign influences.[97] Paneer, chilli, potatoes, all came to India from abroad, but Hindutva statists yearn for a return to a 'pure' Vedic idyll not through persuasion or debate but a ferocious use of state power. Interestingly, just a week after Maggi relaunched its instant noodles, the Baba Ramdev–promoted Patanjali launched its instant atta noodles with the tagline 'jhatpat banao, befikar khao'. Today, even though the ban on Maggi has been struck down, the enormous popularity of the once-beloved fast food has taken a hit. It has been subtly conveyed that Maggi may be legal but it's not-quite-acceptable, it may be eaten but not celebrated. The court battle has left behind a detritus of misgivings about Maggi, almost as if to say 'eat it at your own risk'. Maggi exists and occupies shelves in stores but Brand Maggi is no longer appreciated as eagerly and with the same enthusiasm, its place in the popular palette and culture shoved aside. The votaries of 'be Indian, buy Indian' have scored a moral win.

Louis Dumont observes in *Homo Hierarchicus*[98] that 'purity' and 'pollution' is central to the Hindu world view (and to notions of caste). It seems as if the government has taken it upon itself to protect the 'pure' Hindu kitchen from 'unclean' 'polluted' influences. In the household hierarchy, after the temple, the kitchen is the purest, where 'pure' (but poor) Brahmins were often employed as cooks.

The fixation on diet is thus to keep the kitchen pure and by extension keep the nation pure and free of 'foreign' influences. Thus, meat—associated with Muslims—or instant noodles associated with a foreign brand are supposedly anti-'purity'. Should modern urban kitchens be policed at a time when the Indian palate is being thoroughly globalized by all kinds of cuisines, from Italian to Mexican? Citizens, if achieving the Hindu Rashtra means giving up on spaghetti bolognaise or mutton biryani, is it really worth the sacrifice? Certainly not for a hardcore non-vegetarian like me!

Jammu and Kashmir has never been much of a beef-eating state. Many Kashmiris have pointed out that beef is even culturally looked down upon by most Kashmiris.[99] In fact, a loose ban on the slaughter of bovines and sale of beef has been in place in the state from the pre-Partition era. However, in 2015, the Jammu and Kashmir High Court, echoing the sentiments of the time, directed the government to strictly enforce the beef ban across the state.[100]

Imposing the ban on the sale of beef in Jammu and Kashmir, when it was never much of an issue anyway, was more 'nationalist' muscle-flexing intended as a message to the rest of India about the 'taming' of Kashmir under the umbrella of the Hindu Rashtra. It led to protests and shut-downs and was attacked by separatists as an 'interference in religion'. An inherently violent order carrying the potential of Big State power saw an inevitably violent fallout. In October 2015, a truck driver Zahid Bhat was killed in Udhampur on the basis of cattle slaughter rumours. Reacting to his death, then chief minister Mufti Mohammed Sayeed said in anguish: 'I have no words to condemn this dastardly act which consumed the life of a young boy for no fault of his.' The political polarization that the ban intended took place. Then Peoples Democratic Party (PDP) leader Mehbooba Mufti was forced to assert that there would be no change in policy in Jammu and Kashmir towards beef.

The Hindutva obsession with beef-eating and meat-eating is food politics, which is also identity politics. It is part of the massive cultural and social engineering the Hindutva-oriented Big State is attempting to carry out by sending out the subliminal message that eating meat is a political act against an imaginary Hindu sanskriti.

Yet, there are many instances of meat-eating in the Ramayana and the Mahabharata. As author Mrinal Pande points out, in their sojourn in the Dandakaryanya forest, Ram, Sita and

Lakshman are supposed to have eaten 'mamsambhutdana' (rice cooked with meat and vegetables) and the Mahabharata refers to roasted meat. The grammarian Panini had even used the word 'goghna' for killing a cow. The 'vegetarian' message is either ignorance masquerading as Indian culture or, more probably, an attempt to amass political power in the name of protecting an imaginary Hindu culture. This is nothing but a pursuit of power, using the levers of an imagined Hindu vegetarian tradition. We have already noted Vivekananda's reference to meat-eating in Valmiki's Ramayana and Vinayak Damodar Savarkar's (who incidentally coined the term 'Hindutva') near-complete rejection of cow worship.

For BJP governments to impose meat bans is at odds with the mandate of 2014, given for a vikas-oriented India, not for a return to an imagined Vedic paradise. The Sangh's cultural mission has to take second place to the constitutional duties of a government. Good governance is not food governance! Article 48 of the Directive Principles of the Constitution, which calls for a prohibition on cow slaughter, is claimed by cow vigilantes to cover themselves with legitimacy. But the cow warriors are failing to realize that Article 48 is only a constitutional guideline and not a law and couched in very careful language. To quote Article 48: 'The state shall endeavour to organise agriculture and animal husbandry on modern, scientific lines and shall, in particular take steps for preserving and improving the breeds and prohibiting the slaughter of calves and other milch and draught cattle.'[101] A broad moral guideline, hedged in with the words 'modern' and 'scientific' is being sought to be made into a diktat imposed by force.

The kitchen is a private space where individual choice is supposed to flourish. The right to eat as one wants is a basic democratic right which falls under the ambit of freedom of choice. An authoritarian illiberal government is attempting to take away the right of citizens to make food choices. The government thinks it is protecting 'Hindu culture' but is unaware that the Taittiriya

Upanishad, for example, which describes what 'food' is, never speaks of any form of vegetarianism. Far from attributing any divine aspects to cattle, it even says, as S. Radhakrishnan comments, 'animals are marked by the inadequacy of the principle of life'. Says the Taittiriya Upanishad, 'From food are beings born. When born they grow up by food. It is eaten and eats things. Therefore it is called food.' Sinlce food eats things, it follows that the eating of a living thing is quite acceptable.[102]

Bans on meat-eating have little to do with Hinduism, and everything to do with RSS ideas of nation-building through thought and lifestyle control. Vegetarian Brahminical Hinduism is mostly a Hindi belt phenomenon, even though former prime minister and Uttar Pradesh Brahmin Atal Bihari Vajpayee was famously non-vegetarian. Maharashtrian Brahmins who founded the RSS[103] might be strictly vegetarian but Maharashtra as a whole has large meat- and fish-eating populations. Bengali and Kashmiri Brahmins are non-vegetarian, as are coastal Brahmin castes like the fish-eating Saraswats.

According to a 2006 CSDS survey on food, not only are a whopping 60 per cent Indians non-vegetarian but 45 per cent Brahmins are also non-vegetarian. So why is a narrow vegetarian, Brahminical, so-called 'food sanskriti' being selectively imposed as a pan-Indian cultural norm? And how can any government be so bold as to enter citizens' kitchens? They are so bold because creating a common Hindutva identity has nothing to do with philosophical Hindu belief. It is only an instrument to grab power in the name of so-called Hindu belief and expand the scope of Big State power.[104]

Mistakes Secularists Made

Secular dispensations, as we have seen, helped to legitimize the culture of bans. In Indira Gandhi's time, as we have noted, the socialist Big State assumed immense powers over the lives of individuals. After

Indira, successive 'secular' dispensations have not stopped the process of arming governments with huge powers. Indira Gandhi once pushed the 'Indira revolution' by attempting to clamp government control on the press, judiciary and the civil service. Indira's so-called 'committed' bureaucracy ('committed' meaning a bureaucracy bent to the will of the prime minister) only paved the way for similar allegations of 'committed' institutions today.

The brilliant P.N. Haksar was Indira Gandhi's principal secretary and the most powerful bureaucrat in her time. Commenting on Haksar, journalist Karan Thapar writes, 'Haksar had no compunction whatsoever that a civil servant must not indulge in politics or trespass into the political lives of those he serves.' Haksar intervened unashamedly and undisguisedly in the politics of Indira Gandhi, drafting her political resolutions, finalizing manifestos and advising her on how to handle MPs. Thus, Haksar's behaviour as a civil servant was an 'unforgivable breaching of the red lines'. If Indira Gandhi's top babu played politics, how can we complain if the same thing happens today? As we are continually arguing through this essay, the illiberal Big State untethered by democratic norms was invented by so-called 'seculars' and has now been taken to its maximum height by Hindutva nationalists.

There are several important instances where liberals themselves have devalued democratic institutions, enhanced Big State power and thus contributed to the manner in which Hindutva demagogues and populists have so easily taken over these institutions. Nehru created the intellectual and policy space for massive state or government intervention in the economy. Indira Gandhi nationalized entire industries and initiated gargantuan state-led redistribution schemes in the name of the poor.

The massive expansion of Big State power (which is basically embodied in the over-powerful politician, while the liberal dream is of a time when politics counts for little and individual freedom counts for more) over the economy squeezed civic and political freedoms in an unprecedented manner. The massively expanded

Big State legitimized its own use of violence to secure its ends, so that violence has now been adopted both by government and social groups as the first line of action rather than the last resort. Officials, professionals, academics, businesses, the media today all need to seek access to politicians or government power to push their respective causes. The use of violence is so widely accepted that the violence of non-state actors and lynch mobs today is actually celebrated in certain quarters. It is the Big State which has legitimized violence in the first place.

Indira Gandhi's Big Statism was inherited by her son and successor Rajiv Gandhi. It was the Rajiv Gandhi government, for example, that set up the gargantuan HRD ministry in 1985, pushing the tentacles of government control into cultural bodies, museums, textbook-writing bodies and art, vocal music and cultural institutes. So much government control over cultural institutions is bizarre and in fact there is a strong case that the HRD ministry should be swiftly disbanded and shut down.[105] There are reports saying that from October 2018 to March 2019 the Ministry of Culture is preparing a 'One Calendar' cultural extravaganza in Delhi. When the Big State directs culture, politics is uppermost. When politics directs culture, culture is hardly free instead ironed into politically correctness, shrinking the space for genuine cultural diversity.

There has been a great deal of debate on the usefulness of the Ministry of Information and Broadcasting as well. It was set up in the aftermath of Partition, when the Nehruvian state felt that messages of communal harmony needed to be broadcast to a divided populace. However, as former information and broadcasting (I&B) minister Jaipal Reddy points out, Nehru believed that in course of time All India Radio (AIR) should be given the same autonomy as the BBC.

In fact, two former I&B ministers, Jaipal Reddy and Manish Tewari, have both argued that the ministry should be immediately abolished. Writes Reddy: 'It is important to note that no advanced democracy, be it in Western Europe or in North America, has a Ministry called I&B. Those democracies instead have independent commissions. In the U.S., for example, the Federal Communications Commission has been effective in regulating the functions of television companies for more than a half a century . . . Public broadcasting services are autonomous in every democracy, though private channels are as prevalent as they are in our country. If a Minister is there for the portfolio, he/she cannot sit idle; they poke their nose into the functioning of such institutions by way of self-employment. Hence, the urgency to abolish this portfolio.'

Recently, when the Modi government found itself in an acutely embarrassing position after sending out a circular on 'fake news',[106] another former I&B minister, Manish Tewari, asked if the time had come to shut down the I&B ministry for good.

How can this be done? Writes Tewari:

> Carving out pieces of the ministry, reforming them and liberating those areas one by one. By way of example, the film remit is the most low-hanging fruit. The Cinematograph Act can easily be repealed, CBFC—the dreaded Censor Board—abolished and replaced with a Programme and Advertising Code as it is for the television industry…the current self-regulatory frameworks are a bit of a joke for the lack of a better word.

Similarly, if Prasar Bharati has to become a truly public broadcaster, it has to be 'liberated from the apron strings of the I&B ministry'.[107] A crucial way that the supposedly 'liberal' UPA could have strengthened the mainstream media was to liberalize the media sector and permit the entry of foreign investment and competition. This could have helped the media as a whole emerge stronger. However, most media houses opposed the entry of foreign players. In 2015 the government said foreign companies could own up to 100 per cent of cable and direct-to-home satellite operators but separate regulations on cross-media ownership regulations prevent diversified international media companies from being able to benefit from this opening up.[108]

Governments of all hues have consistently legitimized blows to individual freedom. It was not the government's remit to ban Salman Rushdie's *The Satanic Verses* as it did in 1988 or to ban the play 'Mi Nathuram Godse Boltoy' in 1998. Protecting identity, culture or sentiments is simply not the Big State's job, which also moved to control the intelligentsia during Nehru's and Indira Gandhi's regimes. To quote Masani again, '. . . the control of the State over universities . . . the institution of Sahitya Academies and other Government institutions . . . have undermined the independence of writers, artists and other members of the intelligentsia.' What are the various Akademis but tentacles of Big State power threading their way through civil society?

The essentially liberal Indian Constitution contains Articles 14, 19 and 21 guaranteeing freedom of choice and free speech to the citizen. However, legal scholar Abhinav Chandrachud points out, today the fundamental right to free speech is meaningless against the thuggish might of mobs and vigilante groups who act as 'non-state actors'. These groups enforce the Hindu nationalist state's self-proclaimed goal of protection of Hindutva sentiment.[109] When the government and its agents play moral and cultural policemen, all forms of vigilantes are encouraged to take it upon themselves to propel their ideology forward.

Bans and witch-hunts have simply not been resisted by so-called secular governments as staunchly as they should have been. It was during the UPA government that renowned painter M.F. Husain was forced to live outside India because of the threats he faced from Hindutva vigilante groups. Movie directors in Mumbai have been targeted when they showed Hindi films with Pakistani stars.[110] Today, censorship by mob is being normalized. In February 2017, a seminar at Delhi University had to be cancelled because a vigilante mob of Hindutva nationalists, namely, the youth wing of the BJP, the ABVP, took objection to it.[111] It must be pointed out here that the Left has often got caught in its own orthodoxies: in JNU, there have been instances of intolerance towards those who do not share an ideological affinity with Left-wing opinion, such as when JNU students protested against a lecture by Baba Ramdev, which was ultimately cancelled.

Today, an unelected group, the RSS, founded as far back as 1925, the mother-ship of Hindutva nationalist ideology, is at the zenith of its political power since Independence. Its 'guidance' of the Modi government is often openly demonstrated, as seen in the three-day 'baithak' that the RSS held in September 2015 to assess and review the performance of Prime Minister Modi and his government, a baithak in which all senior ministers as well as the prime minister were present.[112] But even though the RSS enjoys unprecedented political influence, its cultural likes and dislikes cannot become prescriptions for modern governance. However, given that so-called 'secular' regimes have for so long fed the appetite for bans, witch-hunts, repression of creative freedom and identity politics, Hindutva is only taking a sadly well-trodden path.

On 24 August 2017, the Supreme Court delivered a landmark judgement on the Indian citizens' right to privacy. The case had begun when then Attorney General Mukul Rohatgi had declared in court, in the context of the Aadhaar card, that citizens had no absolute right to privacy over their bodies. 'Citizens cannot refuse to give iris scans or fingerprints for Aadhaar because the concept of the citizens' absolute right over their bodies was a myth.' In this historic judgement the apex court held that: 'The Right to Privacy is an integral part of the Right to Life and Personal Liberty guaranteed in Article 21 of the Constitution.' This crucial judgement gives the citizen legal recourse in the protection of her personal data, food choices, sexual choices and entertainment choices.

But do the street mobs know about this judgement? Do they care? Does this judgement keep the citizen safe from the freedom-and-individual-rights-destroying mobs? The mobs don't care. So whatever the freedoms guaranteed by the law, the institutional decay of law enforcement, namely, the absence of neutral tough policing, leaves individual freedoms more vulnerable than ever before in the face of 'non-state actors' professing loyalty to the Big State.

Big Brother Is Watching

The fact of the government being the regulator of citizen behaviour is seen not only in the beef and mutton bans but also on a proposed ban on 857 porn sites, which was attempted in 2015.[113] The government justified the ban as a drive against child pornography. But surely on issues such as child morality, social campaigns and citizens' awareness drives must take over where government ends. Why should governments decide whether citizens have a choice on whether or not they want to consume porn? Is it the government's job to ban porn? Or instead, is it to catch those who commit crimes and enforce the law, if a crime is being committed against women or children. Consuming porn is no crime, however unacceptable puritans of the Hindutva nationalist variety may find it.

In fact, Indians are believed to be among the world's third-largest consumers of pornography in the world.[114] After widespread outrage, the porn ban was reversed but the government has still banned the film *Fifty Shades of Grey*, as well as *India's Daughter*, a BBC documentary made by film-maker Leslee Udwin on the Jyoti Pandey (Nirbhaya) rape case of 2012.[115]

As mentioned, illiberal banning cuts across party lines. The film *Kissa Kursi Ka* was banned by the Congress in 1975 for making fun of the Emergency. Certain newspapers were banned from public libraries by the TMC.[116] The CPM in Bengal routinely banned material not sympathetic to the party line. The Congress attempted to prevent the circulation of Javier Moro's book *The Red Sari* (apparently a fictionalized account of the story of Sonia Gandhi), although the book was released in India in 2015. In 2008, ABVP activists launched protests against A.K. Ramanujan's essay 'Three Hundred Ramayanas', and Delhi University dropped the essay from its syllabus in 2011. In 2010, Rohinton Mistry's book *Such a Long*

Journey was dropped from the Mumbai University curriculum after protests by the Shiv Sena. In 2004, the self-styled Sambhaji Brigade ransacked the Bhandarkar Oriental Research Institute (BORI) library in Pune after protests over James Laine's book *Shivaji: Hindu King in Islamic India*. In 2010, Dina Nath Batra led the attack on Wendy Doniger's *The Hindus*.

In 2015, the CBFC, then headed by Hindutva sympathizer Pahlaj Nihalani, suddenly came up with a list of words that should be banned from films. In fact, the CBFC has over the years arrogated to itself the role of government-appointed cinema policeman when its limited ambit, as its name implies, is simply to *certify*, that is, decide which categories of films are suitable for viewing in which age groups. It has also taken upon itself to blur alcohol labels in its crusade to ensure cultural 'purity'. The list of cuss words the CBFC tried to ban included: 'bastard', 'son of a bitch', 'haramzada', 'gandu', 'madarchod', 'behenchod', etc. The list of cuss words has now been withdrawn but those words are apparently being removed anyway. This shows that even when a ban is withdrawn its purpose is served: to create a climate of fear that either encourages self-censorship or outsources enforcement of the non-ban-which-is-still-a-ban to others, namely, street mobs of moral policemen, to bring so-called 'rebels' back in line.[117]

Should government agencies take away a film writer's freedom to use swear words if he's writing a story where they are demanded? Is a man about to be killed in a thrilling climax supposed to say 'aapki meherbani' or 'kya main aapko maar sakta hoon'? Interfering with the right to curse is the same as interfering with the right to speak, imagine, get angry or indeed be human! 'Nationalist' statists, in their quest for a pure Vedic dreamland, are not just ignorant of the notion of individual rights, they are trying to reduce 'Indian' culture to fantastical cartoons of what they imagine this culture is.

This basket of bans—meat ban, beef ban, porn ban, cuss words ban—are all actions of an ideologically driven illiberal government determined to stamp on individual freedoms in order to expand the scope of the state for a future Hindu Rashtra.

Diversity, the essence of Hinduism, is being demolished by the Hindutva forces in the name of protecting Hinduism! With friends like these, Hinduism hardly needs any enemy!

Today, so widespread is the ban culture that anyone can call for a ban—the 'ban band' includes anyone who can shout loud enough. Every identity group, be it a religious group, a feminist group, caste-based or professional groups such as doctors or the police, have all called for bans on something or the other, at some point or other. The Big State, in its never-ending quest for votes, keeps giving in to sectional identities without ever thinking of that ideal of liberal democracy, namely, the 'common good'.

Social media's role in censuring or extending bans into free speech by snooping on citizens and compromising their privacy exploded with the Channel 4 sting on Cambridge Analytica in March 2018.[118] Now, Prime Minister Modi was once Facebook CEO Mark Zuckerberg's close ally, becoming the first head of government to be hosted on the Facebook campus in September 2015 and sharing the stage with Zuckerberg at a town hall meeting. After the Cambridge Analytica exposé, the Modi government in March 2018 issued notices to Facebook over the misuse of data. But it has been intriguingly less protective about citizens' data than other democracies. For the government to express its outrage at data leaks by Facebook is convenient. The greater the outrage at the 'foreign hand', the better the diversion away from the government's own complicity in profiling its citizens. As a liberal theorist, writes, 'technology in the hand of the government is very different from those operating in an open competitive market . . . governments can monitor and search a citizen's transactions and interactions without any legal safeguard, such as a warrant. Citizens are not the property of the government to identify and account for, but are the real sovereigns and the government is their servant . . .' India's culture of bans in a way eerily complements rather than contradicts social media. Social media provides the perfect platform to the army of 'nationalist' cyber trolls with allegiance to the ruling party to serve the government's purpose by targeting, threatening and terrorizing those who dare to dissent.

Internet shutdowns are another way the government tries to control the spread of information. Instead, what governments should do if faced with a crisis is counter bad information with good information. In 2017, the Internet was shut down sixty-nine times, the maximum number of shutdowns taking place in Jammu and Kashmir.[119] On the one hand, there are regular clampdowns on the Internet, on the other, fears of state surveillance through digital technologies is growing. In fact, as *The Economist* comments, 'technologies that once seemed a friend of freedom, allowing dissidents and dictators to communicate and organise more easily, now look more Orwellian letting autocrats watch people closely.'[120]

Fears of the surveillance state are particularly strong in the manner in which the government is pushing the Aadhaar card, an intrusion into citizens' privacy, of which liberals must be deeply wary and about which many have expressed deep concern.

Where Are We Going with Aadhaar?

Citizens were made to feel guilty during demonetization, and about using swear words, eating meat or surfing porn. A prime source of citizens' guilt is if you don't have an Aadhaar card. In fact, there are many ways a citizen can be guilty these days.

Have you not yet linked your income tax documents with your Aadhaar card? You're guilty!

Are you finding it difficult to fill complicated GST forms? You're guilty!

Did you ever keep cash in the house? You're guilty!

Do you eat meat? You're guilty!

Do you read Mughal history or books on Marxism? You're guilty!

Do you crave a tenderloin? You're guilty!

Do you watch porn online? You're guilty!

Do you feel the national anthem need not be played in movie theatres? You're guilty!

Are you a woman who dares to drink in public? You must be of low moral character and should feel guilty!

Are you insisting on a right to privacy? You must be guilty!

Not guilty? Prove it on a daily basis.

Our liberal ancestors, Gandhi and Rajagopalachari, would be shocked at the manner in which the government is using its brute majority in Parliament to make laws, using numbers in parliament to muzzle the cut and thrust of parliamentary debate. In March 2016, amendments to the Aadhaar Bill were pushed through as a money bill (which requires only a yes in the Lok Sabha) without a proper debate in Parliament. The Modi government had clearly already made up its mind and was in no mood to listen or introspect or, if need be, change course. The Union Budget of 2018 too was pushed through without any debate. Why should a crucial law like one related to the Aadhaar not have been fully debated? Why should the Union Budget not be fully debated? Don't citizens need to know how the government intends to use their personal data and where their hard-earned tax-payer money is going? Do they not have a right to know? When a government believes a massive mandate gives it the power to ride roughshod over parliamentary processes and individual rights, is that government democratic? No, it's behaving like an elected dictator.

The manner in which the government pushed the Aadhaar card as the ultimate proof of identity has justifiably raised fears about why it wants to gain access to the private details of citizens' lives. Former finance minister P. Chidambaram has said the UPA only intended Aadhaar as a means to make sure that government transfers to citizens reach the intended beneficiaries. But linking Aadhaar to everything under the sun was seen to have 'serious consequences' that could have turned India into an 'Orwellian state . . . compromising the ideals of a liberal democracy and an open society.'[121]

To quote Chidambaram: 'If a young man and woman want to have a private holiday, they may not be married, what's wrong with that? If a young man wants to buy condoms, why should he disclose his Aadhaar identity? Why should the state, that is, the government, know what medicines I buy, what cinemas I visit, what hotels I stay in, or who my friends are?'

An important article by economist and social activist Jean Drèze needs to be quoted here because of the graphic manner in which it spells out the slow but inexorable interference of the government in every sphere of life: as national and cultural ombudsman, as tone-setter, as policeman and as super-snoop.

'India is at risk of becoming a surveillance state, with faint resistance from libertarians, intellectuals, political parties, the media, or the Supreme Court. Very soon, almost everyone will have an Aadhaar number, seeded in hundreds of databases. Most of these databases will be accessible to the government without invoking any special powers. Permanent surveillance of all residents becomes a possibility. Only a simpleton would expect this possibility to remain unused.

'With everyone on the radar, dissent is bound to be stifled. As it is, many people and institutions are anxious not to get on the wrong side of the government. NGOs are afraid that their registration might be cancelled if they antagonise the authorities. Vice-chancellors and principals are unable to stand up for their students' right to hold public meetings on sensitive issues. Newspapers treat the government with kid gloves, especially on security matters. Investigative agencies target or spare Opposition leaders at the government's bidding. Nationalism is confused with obedience to the state. With Aadhaar immensely reinforcing the government's power to reward loyalty and marginalise dissenters, the embers of democracy are likely to be further smothered.'

Drèze points out various fallacies over Aadhaar: (1) It does not help welfare because scores of stories are pouring in about citizens being turned away from services because they lack an Aadhaar number, (2) The 'money goes to the right person' line is a myth, (3) Savings are not enabled by Aadhaar, (4) Its technology is not flawless.[122]

However, on 26 September 2018 the Supreme Court in a crucial judgement put the brakes on the dictatorship of Aadhaar and cut to size the BJP-led government's unrestrained use of Aadhaar. While upholding the constitutional validity of Aadhaar, the apex court fundamentally restricted its scope to primarily being a provider of welfare and not a universal verifier of identity. While accepting Aadhaar for beneficiaries of PDS and direct benefit transfer schemes, the court struck down any Aadhaar requirement for a range of facilities, from phone connections to bank accounts and students appearing in examinations.

Equally crucial for the liberal was the fiercely dissenting judgement of Justice D.Y. Chandrachud. Justice Chandrachud struck down the Aadhaar law as wholly unconstitutional, stating that the way the government pushed it as a money bill 'constitutes a fraud on the Constitution'. In a powerfully worded judgement, Justice Chandrachud held: 'Dignity and the rights of individuals cannot be made to depend on algorithms or probabilities . . . Constitutional guarantees cannot be subject to the vicissitudes of technology.'[123]

Chandrachud's wise words offer a reminder of how the Big State can misuse an enabling technology to potentially spy on citizens. We must also remember that there is no guarantee that a future government will not bring in legislation permitting commercial organizations to harvest citizens' personal data. There is also no guarantee that even as a welfare instrument the poor will not face harassment from state functionaries in the use of Aadhaar. The poor may still be confronted with the tortuous ordeal of authenticating their Aadhaar information.

The liberal does not regard technology as a silver bullet for social ills, or technology as the only means to fight corruption in the delivery of welfare. Corruption arises from misdirected incentives because people feel they can gain more from looting the system rather than following the rules. Technology is the Big State's drive for efficiency, but if the incentives to be corrupt remain then the technology will only be misused to create new opportunities for power brokers. As Justice Chandrachud opined: 'Aadhaar allows constructing profiles of individuals, which is against the right to privacy and enables potential surveillance.' Justice

Chandrachud's dissent is a highly significant check on any rampant use of Aadhaar by future governments. Even for the moment, liberals must remain vigilant about the use of Aadhaar by governments.

It must be pointed out here it was the UPA and previous Congress governments that came up with instruments that gave rise to these fears of a state that could subject citizens to surveillance. Aadhaar had been criticized by privacy activists even during the UPA years. The UPA had then insisted that the Aadhaar, launched by Manmohan Singh in 2009, was never meant to be an instrument of fear or a device to dominate citizens' lives. It claimed that the limited aim was improved delivery of welfare schemes. Yet, if this was the aim, then the UPA could have introduced a bill to clearly stipulate the limited role and scope of Aadhaar and drafted another bill on citizen data privacy. Without these safeguards, the UPA (only slightly less statist than the NDA, mind you), left the door open for a rampaging statist government like the Modi government to make Aadhaar a vehicle of surrendering private information.

The Aadhaar issue is yet another instance of a statist measure introduced by 'secular liberals' taken to a maximalist dictatorial height by Hindutva nationalists.

A liberal opposes Aadhaar if it interferes in the individual's right to personal preferences and choices. There is always a serious danger that an ideologically driven government may use this data to pursue its own political goals. However, now with the Supreme Court judgement as well as the supremely liberal judgement of Justice Chandrachud, the 'function creep' of Aadhaar from welfare delivery to possible surveillance and being a necessity for dozens of other activities has been halted.

Let us rewind a little here to the agitation that Aadhaar caused before the apex court delivered its final judgement. In November 2017, the Supreme Court stated that there was panic among the public and asked telecom companies and banks to stop harassing customers with warnings about Aadhaar linkage.[124] But should the Supreme Court not have sounded the alarm earlier? The Supreme Court's delayed hearings on Aadhaar meant that this particular sword of Damocles hung over citizens' heads in the form of threatening deadlines of Aadhaar linkages. How many of us received messages from banks telling us to link our Aadhaar cards to our bank accounts or the accounts will be blocked?

The official line on Aadhaar was that it aimed to collect as much information about citizens as possible, using retina scans, fingerprints, each digital transaction the person makes, and keep a record of bank account numbers, cellphone numbers, income tax and voter IDs. All this was being done apparently in a technologically 'perfect' way to check corruption in the delivery of services.

But dozens of reports are still pouring in about how the most vulnerable are suffering because of Aadhaar. In December 2017, a Jharkhand girl reportedly died because she could not get rations due to the lack of an Aadhaar card.[125] There have been cases of the poor being turned away from hospitals because of their missing Aadhaar card details.[126] Even American whistleblower Edward Snowden has said that so much private data can be easily misused by companies and governments.[127] Data leak stories too have been surfacing regularly.[128] For the moment, though, the unrestrained free run of Aadhaar over the Indian people has come to an end.

Government Knows Best

Like the religious fanatic who lives by absolute certainties, the Modi-led government believes its knowledge is absolute, that it is omniscient like the gods it wants to imitate. As a Big State also begins to become a super-snoop surveillance state, with news TV as its shrill stormtrooper, liberal democracy's basic principle—innocent until proven guilty—is being turned on its head. As we have noted, every citizen is now potentially guilty and has to prove her innocence, her patriotism and her commitment to the newly launched moral crusade to 'purify' India. As former prime minister Manmohan Singh said, the attitude of suspecting everyone to be a thief is damaging to the democratic discourse. 'By questioning bullet trains, does one become anti-development? Does questioning GST and demonetization make one a tax evader? This attitude of suspecting everyone to be thief or anti-national . . . low level rhetoric is damaging to democratic discourse.'[129] The more sinister question arises, if citizens are deemed to be guilty by default then can the Big Government really respect the freedoms and choices of citizens at the ballot box? An omniscient and omnipotent government is the antithesis of democratic government in a citizen's republic.

India's Constitution puts individual rights first but increasingly it is individual citizens who are the focus of suspicion. In certain authoritarian quarters, wielding the danda has long been argued as the way to bring notoriously lawless Indians to heel, but India's greatest resource has always been its liberal-minded, freedom-loving people. Indians can do without almost anything, said Vivekananda, but they can't do without their mukti (freedom).

If Indians are subject to endless surveillance, checks and identity searches and become the target of perpetual government mistrust and suspicion, the question arises, can the Indian people realize their full potential?

The regimented Indian is the unsuccessful Indian. It is the free Indian who is the soaring thinker, innovator, business builder and high achiever. The phenomenal success of Indians in the US shows how well the Indian genius thrives in the land of the free. When the Indian is browbeaten and cowed, how can she be a super achiever?

Our liberal founders dreamed that India too would be a republic of the free but today it's not citizens but the Big State that is free to do exactly what it wants.

Governments across India are dictating how 'nationalist' feelings must be expressed. In November 2017, Jaipur mayor Ashok Lahoty ordered employees to sing the national anthem in the morning and 'Vande mataram' in the evening in order to instil 'patriotism and love for the country' and anyone opposing this order should 'go to Pakistan'. Government teachers in Haryana have been ordered to double up as priests in temples and distribute prasad and undergo priest training sessions. In Uttar Pradesh, social media posts against the ruling party can get you arrested.[130] In late 2017, rumours surfaced that *khichdi* was about to be declared a 'national dish'. Such reports contained an important subliminal message: if India ever gets a national dish it will be a vegetarian one that gets the official stamp.

The drive across the world is how to make governments more transparent and accountable to citizens. In sharp contrast today the reverse is true in India. It is citizens who are forced to be more and more transparent and accountable to governments. The animating spirit of this government seems to be: that citizens are by nature corrupt, they're hiding personal information, they evade taxes, they're slothful, lawless, don't do enough yoga and must be reined in and made accountable to the government. The government in so-called 'New India' is laying out a new ethical code for its citizens—'Disclose everything if you have nothing to hide'. Yet at the same time the new code for the government is 'disclose nothing' to citizens, since they are simply not worthy of trust.

Why this mistrust? Precisely because the remaking of India according to the ideological Hindutva blueprint is such a priority. Individual rights are an obstacle to the creation of the Hindu Rashtra. That's why the citizen must repeatedly be subjected to a patriotic examination.

When the prevailing mindset is 'everyone is guilty', even the guilty are easily normalized in politics. The 'sab neta chor hai' is a highly anti-democratic sentiment. Equally anti-democratic is the belief by a government that every citizen is guilty of something.

Citizens of India, you are *not* guilty just because you lawfully exercise personal choices. Just because you happen to disagree with the government does not make you guilty. You are guilty only if you break the law, not if you offend the government's ideological certainties or refuse to be a cheerleader of the government of the day.

But those engaging in free speech are often seen as enemies by the Hindutva nationalist Big State. All citizens must therefore be made transparent and accountable to the government. But government itself, with every policy from Swachh Bharat to Start-Up India, to

Skill India is setting about enhancing its own power and patronage over citizens through humungous schemes and 'yojanas'.

Why We Should be Proud to be Liberal and Indian

The liberal view is the state exists to safeguard the individual. The individual is not a soldier of state power. The rights of the individual therefore become the supreme consideration because liberty is the supreme good. Those street mobs who are trying to take away this freedom are not protectors of identity, they are just terrorists peddling fear. Should these violence-using terrorists be guardians of culture in India, as they are in parts of the Muslim world? Intriguingly, the RSS, which today is helping to create the Hindutva Big State, was once a great opponent of the Nehruvian Big State. Delegates of the RSS' Akhil Bharatiya Pratinidhi Sabha resolved in a declaration in March 1959: 'The tendency of the Government to establish its control and monopoly . . . over various spheres of social life is becoming more and more pronounced. Concentration of power in the hands of the government is growing at a fast pace and individual freedom is getting curtailed . . . this all round onslaught on people's liberty is a grave crime against all human values . . . [we must] stand up in the defence of the freedom and dignity of the individual.'[131] Today, the RSS is supporting the extinguishing of individual liberty in the quest to build the Hindu Rashtra.

Defending personal freedom is also, in many ways, a defence of Indian traditions. Attacking personal freedoms is profoundly anti-Indian. If identity warriors set themselves the task of hypothetically demolishing the Taj Mahal, as the Taliban once blasted away the Bamiyan Buddhas, it will be because citizens did not protect freedom as strongly as we need to. The essence of Indian spiritual and cultural heritage is the ultimate individualistic pursuit of self-realization. Recognition and respect for personal freedom in a modern polity is an extension of that age-old wisdom.

Those who are attacking the mainsprings of Indianness, who are hacking away at the deep roots of liberalism in our soil and flying in the face of generation upon generation of free thinkers and iconoclasts are ironically posing as the so-called defenders of 'Indian' identity. It is the free minds who are being attacked by fearful minds.

The liberal spirit of the Constitution of India is thus far more authentically 'Bharatiya' than the manufactured outrage of those who worship at the altars of the extremist and violent versions of Islamist and Christian extremism. The deep respect for the individual, the long tradition of tolerance, of locating the universe itself in the core of individual anarchism or the atma, that is the spirit of generations of poets, philosophers, fakirs, women wanderers, pirs, sanyasis, naked sadhus and bohemian rebels who have lived and died in the Indian subcontinent. Today the mimic men of the Taliban want Indians to shun that dizzying procession down the ages, of unconventional free spirits, and follow in the steps of the violent orthodoxy-upholding Hezbollah or ISIS.

No, we subcontinentals are no pale imitators of Semitic extremists. How can we be when hovering over our heads, there in the Himalayas, is Shiva, the cosmic rebel, disdainer of convention and orthodoxy, Bholenath, the ultimate liberal individualist?

And if Shiva's single descent into violence in the tandav nritya does not exactly fit our liberal tenets of non-violence, then we need to recognize that in our midst sits an even greater liberal. Who better than the amiable Ganesha? Ganesha has no violent streak at all, instead, he is the god of peaceful trade and business and the deity of justly acquired profit. No god is seen as so playful and non-threatening, sitting easily and comfortably in his own place co-existing happily alongside Shiva temples or Vishnu temples. Ganesha is the god of the aam aadmi and khaas aadmi. From film star Salman Khan to millworkers in Mumbai's Lalbaug,[132] Ganesha is the mascot of the great Indian workforce. Ganesha's not a VIP, he doesn't come with much pomp and show. He's the companion in need, the fisherman's friend, the taxi driver's soulmate, painted gaily on newly acquired cars or homes, sitting peaceably in households. Ganesha fights with no one and instead goes all out to bring peace, freedom and wealth to all. A true liberal indeed.

[4]

The Liberal Dissenter

Why the liberal dissenter is not a traitor and why free-thinking intellectuals are crucial for a nation's progress

Hum dekhenge
Lazim hai ki hum bhi dekhenge
Wo din ki jis ka wada hai
Jo lauh-e-azl mein likha hai
Jab zulm-o-sitam ke koh-e-giran
Rooh ki tarah ud jaenge
Hum mahkumon ke paaon tale
Jab dharti dhad dhad dhadkegi
Aur ahl-e-hakam ke sar opar
Jab bijli kad kad kadkegi . . .
Jab taaj uchale jaenge . . .
Jab takht girae jaenge . . .
Hum dekhenge, Lazim hai ki hum bhi dekhenge.

—Faiz Ahmad Faiz

[We shall witness
It is certain that we too, shall witness
The day that has been promised
Of which has been written in the slate of eternity

When enormous mountains of tyranny
Will blow away like cotton
Under our feet, the feet of the oppressed
The earth will shiver and shake
And when above the heads of our rulers
Lightning will strike and thunder will roar . . .
When the crown will be tossed
When the thrones will be brought down,
We shall witness
It is certain that we too shall witness.]

Is an individual who dissents or who criticizes the government of the day a traitor?

Are farmers not deserving of liberal, market-friendly policies?

Must students be punished if they are free thinkers and freely raise slogans?

Are intellectuals enemies of the nation?

Should school and university curriculum be decided by the ruling political party of the day?

The Politician Is King of the Ring

The liberal, as we have been emphasizing, argues for a limited government—a limited role for the state—for the primacy of individual freedom and individual enterprise to create welfare, uphold justice and to awaken society's moral sense. The argument here is that the ills of our time—communalism, identity politics, scarcities of justice and opportunities—are all a result of the Big State expanding its role in citizens' lives and politics taking over every aspect. The Big State means politicians and when politicians have a killer grip on civil society, they seek only to expand their own patronage and kill individual initiative. 'Politicians do not have the incentive to press for systematic reform,' writes former

RBI governor Raghuram Rajan, 'for that would eliminate a key function they provide. They would prefer the government to be indifferent to the general public while being responsive [only] to politicians, so they can offer patronage. In return, they expect the public to ignore the thievery that goes on as they join hands with big business. And the few honest middle-class bankers and entrepreneurs who try their hand at politics soon find they get few votes if they cannot promise their constituents patronage. No one wants a Don Quixote who will tilt against the system if it means their needs will be ignored while he is attempting systemic change.'[1] That's why a 'profusion of well-connected billionaires' flourish, and the general public has little basic access to education, health and finance, or even in having their own property rights clarified. As the government structure expands, it not only squashes individual freedoms but also creates the 'connections' culture. This is a syndrome 'where proximity to government is a huge source of profitability', where what you get depends on who you know in the government. As the Big State expands, politics grows ever important. Today, politicians are everywhere. Their faces are on billboards. They are chief guests at functions, they give or receive awards and bask in citizens' applause, simply because they control access to government. They control the supply of facilities, from water connections to media advertising, even the supply of justice. The basic individual rights of those who are not perceived as 'loyalists' become precarious in the connections culture, as those who *are* loyalists become more equal than others. That's why the liberal presses for a limited government.

However, where the government must exercise a primary and fundamentally important role is in the maintenance of law and order. Without the law, citizens cannot exercise their constitutional rights. In the murders of four individuals who did exercise their constitutionally guaranteed freedom of speech, we have seen governments fail woefully in their all-important duty to uphold the law.

Dissent in the Time of Murder

On 20 August 2013, sixty-seven-year-old doctor Narendra Dabholkar, an atheist and a rationalist, was out on a morning walk in Pune. Suddenly, two men appeared out of nowhere, shot him at point-blank range and zoomed away on a motorbike. Dabholkar had been a lifelong opponent of blind faith, ritualism and superstitions. In 2003, he had drafted the Maharashtra Prevention and Eradication of Human Sacrifice and Other Inhuman, Evil and Aghori Practices and Black Magic Act of 2013. This law was promulgated in Maharashtra after his murder. It criminalizes black magic, human sacrifice and exploitation resulting from superstition. Dabholkar also founded the Maharashtra Andhashraddha Nirmoolan Samiti (MANS) or society against blind beliefs. 'The call of religion was (once) morality,' he wrote. 'But it very soon changed into a matter of convenience. It was the convenience of the king, of the wealthy and of the priestly class that mattered . . . to be moral, it's not necessary to observe meaningless rituals and rites . . . the foundations of [the] new morality are freedom and responsibility of every individual . . .'[2]

Dabholkar's views and influence clearly enraged his enemies enough to want him dead. Hindu extremist outfits like the Sanatan Sanstha and the Hindu Janjagruti Samiti have been accused in the murder, but the conspiracy has not been fully unravelled, nor have the ringleaders of the Dabholkar murder operation been caught and punished.

On 16 February 2015, another rationalist, the eighty-one-year-old communist Govind Pansare, was out for a morning walk in Kolhapur with his wife. Once again, two men appeared on a motorcycle and shot at them both. Pansare died from the gunshot wounds four days later on 20 February. Pansare had endorsed Dabholkar's campaign against black magic and superstition. After Dabholkar's death, Pansare had exhorted the former's followers to continue Dabholkar's work. In his well-known Marathi book

Shivaji Kon Hota?[3], Pansare argued that Shivaji was not a Hindutva icon but a secular leader who gave top posts to Muslims.

On 30 August 2015, seventy-seven-year-old M.M. Kalburgi, scholar and Sahitya Akademi Awardee, was shot dead at his home in Hubli–Dharwad in Karnataka. On that Sunday morning, two men came knocking at the door of his house in a quiet, leafy enclave of Hubli–Dharwad. Kalburgi was speaking on his cellphone at the time. As he answered the door, the men shot him at point-blank range. Kalburgi slumped dead on the front verandah, while the murderers escaped by motorcycle. His wife, Umadevi, recalls, 'I thought they were students when they came. My husband lived in the world of ideas. Until today I don't know why anyone would want to kill the professor.'[4]

Kalburgi had been engaged in a lifelong study of the twelfth-century Bhakti reformer and Lingayat philosopher Basavanna and his beliefs that the Lingayat community constituted a separate religious identity distinct from caste-based Hinduism. 'Kalburgi was a scholar to his bones,' recalls fellow academic and former English professor G.N. Devy, 'and believed that the Lingayats had no belief in an external God.'[5] Kalburgi specialized in Vachana literature or Kannada writings centred around Basavanna and his teachings. Like Dabholkar and Pansare, Kalburgi was sceptical of idol worship and criticized blind belief.

On the evening of 5 September 2017, fifty-five-year-old journalist Gauri Lankesh, a fearless and outspoken critic against Hindutva majoritarianism who published her own bold and radical weekly, 'Gauri Lankesh Patrike', in Bengaluru, drove home from work. As she entered her house, she was shot dead at her doorstep by a murderer who again escaped on his motorbike. Investigations into Lankesh's death have led to police probes on extremist Hindutva outfits.[6]

In their investigations into the killings of these four fearless intellectuals and dissenters against Hindutva beliefs, the police are focussing on members of Hindutva Right-wing groups like the

Sanatan Sanstha and the Hindu Janjagruti Samiti. In the course of investigations into the murders of Dabholkar and Pansare, the CBI in 2016 arrested an ENT specialist linked to the Hindu Janjagruti Samiti, Virendra Tawde, described by the CBI as 'a force behind the Sanatan Sanstha and the Hindu Janjagruti Samiti in Kolhapur'. However, Tawde was released on bail in 2018.

Who or what was the common enemy of intellectuals and activists like Dabholkar, Pansare, Kalburgi and Lankesh? The needle of suspicion points to those spreading superstition, blind faith and militant religious majoritarian beliefs. The intellectuals who spoke out against these extremists, armed with nothing but raw courage, were cut down, so mortally threatened were the bigots by the power of their rationalist and liberal arguments.

The heterodox diverse nature of Hinduism has created a deep liberal tradition that guns can never silence. But the murders of the four activist-writers show the grave dangers of free speech in an India where the mob enjoys immunity from the law even as the state structure fails to protect free thinkers or even looks away from the citizens' rights enshrined in the Constitution.

Each of these murders drove a knife through the heart of those who value free thought. The murders represent an attack on every citizen who holds a free opinion and believes in expressing it—whether one is vegetarian or loves beef, loves sarees or jeans, Sanskrit or English, whether one believes in singing the national anthem or not, whether one cherishes religion or wants to denounce it. Suddenly, it appears that anyone who holds a different view could be targeted by a mob wearing the false colours of a so-called 'religious' and 'nationalist' cause.

When it comes to allegations about 'saffron terror', not since Nathuram Godse, who assassinated Mahatma Gandhi on 30 January 1948 in New Delhi and stood waiting to be caught, has an allegedly Hindutva-inspired assassin openly taken authorship of an act of murder. While Islamist or Maoist extremists generally claim responsibility for their killings, the hand of 'saffron terror' has been suspected and investigated, arrests have been made but so far there have been no convictions.[7]

On one occasion, however, a Hindutva-inspired murderer did take proud ownership of his act. This was in December 2017, when Shambhu Lal Regar hacked and burnt to death a Muslim labourer from Bengal, Mohammed Afrajul in Rajsamand, Rajasthan, apparently to save his Hindu 'sisters' from 'love jihad'. Regar got his teenage nephew to take a 'before' and 'after' video of his grisly act and posted it on social media. In March 2018, a tableau of Regar was taken out during a Ram Navami procession in Jodhpur.[8]

The 'cow-protecting' hooligans who have been on a lynching spree since 2014, attacking and murdering those they suspected to be guilty of cattle slaughter, often take proud ownership of their bloody acts of 'gau raksha'. Many such lynchings have been filmed and circulated on social media.

I have been maintaining a list of such attacks on Muslims and cattle traders on my public Facebook page. Here are some instances of heinous attacks motivated by 'gau raksha' from my list.

1. September 2015: Mohammad Akhlaq lynched in Dadri on suspicion that he was storing beef.
2. October 2015: Zahid Rasool Bhatt, sixteen years old, dies in a bomb attack on his truck in Udhampur. He was attacked because of rumours that his truck was carrying beef.
3. March 2016: Suspected cattle traders Mohammed Majloom and Azad Khan hanged in Latehar.
4. April 2017: Suspected cattle traders Abu Hanifa and Riazuddin Ali beaten to death for allegedly stealing cattle in Assam.
5. April 2017: Pehlu Khan dies of injuries after being attacked in Alwar.
6. May 2017: Two meat traders thrashed in Malegaon, Maharashtra, for allegedly storing beef.
7. May 2017: Cattle trader Mohammad Naeem and three others beaten to death in Jharkhand.

8. June 2017: Ainul Ansari attacked in Dhanbad, Jharkhand, on suspicion he was taking beef to an iftar gathering.

9. June 2017: Tamil Nadu animal husbandry department officials transporting cattle in trucks attacked in Barmer.

10. June 2017: One lynched, three thrashed over beef rumours on a train between Delhi and Ballabhgarh, Haryana, leading to the death of sixteen-year-old Junaid.

11. June 2017: Three men killed in Dinajpur in Bengal on suspicion of stealing cattle.

12. June 2017: Hundreds beat up a Muslim man in Jharkhand after finding a dead cow in front of his house.

13. August 2017: Anwar Hussain and Hafizul Sheikh, both nineteen years of age, beaten to death in Jalpaiguri, Bengal, on suspicion of cattle smuggling.

14. June 2018: A mob lynching in Hapur, Uttar Pradesh, led to the death of Qasim and another Muslim man, Samiuddin, being badly injured. The mob was apparently motivated by rumours that Qasim was slaughtering cattle. The police later said this was a case of 'road rage'.

While mob lynchings have been filmed and circulated, the assassination of rationalist intellectuals has been met with triumph in some quarters. After Gauri Lankesh's murder, social media handles describing themselves as 'proud Hindus' or 'nationalists' on social media expressed open jubilation at her slaying. 'A bitch died a dog's death and now all the puppies are wailing in the same tune,' posted Nikhil Dadhich, a Surat-based textile trader, on 5 September 2017 in Hindi. Another Twitter user, Ashish Mishra, posted on the same day, 'Jaisai Karni, Vaisai Bharni' (as you sow so you shall reap). His Twitter bio declares: 'I am Hindu and Team PM Modi.' Social media handles professing loyalty to Prime Minister Modi and abuse at opponents instead of arguments, preferring diatribe to discourse and adopting the tactics of the hammer and not the pen.[9]

The fact that abusive social media handles pretending to be 'nationalists' took pride in openly abusing a journalist who was murdered for her so-called 'anti-national' views reveals the dreadful extent to which free speech is in danger today. Right-wing news TV plays a sinister role here. Those advancing liberal arguments are not only in danger of being murdered on the streets, but they are also often harassed, demonized and terrorized on television for their views. Several 'nationalist' TV anchors take the lead in these vilification and abusive campaigns against liberals, branding them 'traitors', 'anti-nationals' 'jihadists' and 'Naxalites'. On 7 June 2018, Republic TV ran a programme with the headline: 'Arundhati Roy–Jignesh Mevani Plot to Divide India Exposed'. Arundhati Roy was called 'anti-India' and a 'separatist sympathiser' and pictures were shown of Roy with Hurriyat hardliner Syed Ali Shah Geelani. She was accused of being funded by Pakistan with the hashtag #AntiIndiaEcoSystem. Photos of Arundhati Roy with Geelani were shown and she was referred to as part of the 'tukde tukde gang'. At one point, the anchor shouted: 'How can you call Arundhati Roy oppressed? She represents Lutyens' Delhi.'

An atmosphere is being created for violence. The fever pitch of TRP-driven accusations on TV often builds to such a crescendo that the individual against whom prime-time fingers are pointed ends up becoming the equivalent of a criminal for the 'nationalists', an enemy figure vilified on TV every night with a metaphorically blackened face. As she is attacked by shrill anchors, a gladiatorial mob looks on and voices on social media howl for her blood.[10]

As we have noted, violent minds, violent language beget violent acts. Violence of speech and thought is legitimized, endorsed and even seen as the fastest way to creating a loyal and wide TV audience and even an electoral constituency. In this situation, the actual act of murder of an 'anti-national' becomes part of a 'righteous war' against those liberals who insist on the fundamental right not to be 'nationalists' of the Hindutva kind, or to be atheist or rationalist, or to criticize superstitions, or to eat beef, or to wear mini-skirts, to be homosexual, to criticize government policy on Jammu and Kashmir, or to speak in support of JNU students. The witch hunt against these so-called members of the 'tukde tukde' gang is often so intense on the media that their very lives are put in danger. The Kashmiri journalist Shujaat Bukhari, editor of the Srinagar-based newspaper *Rising Kashmir*, was murdered on 14 June 2018. Before his killing, he faced days of attacks on social media from hardliners for his alleged 'pro-India' stance as well as from Right-wingers for his apparently 'pro-separatist' stance. Shujaat was trapped in the middle ground between extremists on both sides. One of his last tweets on 2 June 2018 was: 'For last 24 hours I am being trolled as I posted pic of Srinagar youth being mowed down by CRPF. While they have every right to defend CRPF as they think #JammuandKashmir is just a piece of land, dey will have to realise why this fear of death is missing in #Kashmiri youth.' Often, attacks on social media are a prelude to a physical attack, signs that certain groups are intent on silencing the dissenter in body and mind. In Bukhari's case, investigations have led to accusations against Pakistan-based militants.[11] The online mob now has a fearsome offline avatar as well.

Why is it that those who hold certain views or write certain articles face the danger of their very lives being snuffed out? This is because of the toxic divide which has been created between 'nationalists' and 'traitors'. Lankesh had strong ideas and lived by her beliefs. She spoke out against Hindutva politics, attacked caste discrimination, pushed for Naxals to abandon the gun and argued passionately for the sexual liberation of women. She wrote trenchantly against the Modi government's ban on the cattle trade. 'The lives of farmers and dairy owners are going to be draconian under the Modi government,' she wrote in 2016.

In a conservative regional milieu, her voice may have been offensive to some, but instead of mounting counter-arguments or writing strongly disparaging articles against her views, someone decided her voice had to be forever silenced. Since when did the land of the Upanishads, the Bhagavad Gita, Ambedkar, Gandhi and Nehru become a land where people are killed, yes, killed for their views? What happened to 'vaad, vivaad, samvaad'? Lankesh and Bukhari were labelled at both ends of the political spectrum. Lankesh raised her voice against Hindutva majoritarianism, Bukhari against militant separatism in the Valley. Both occupied the middle ground of independent views and paid for their beliefs with their lives.

In 1951, Prime Minister Jawaharlal Nehru introduced the First Amendment to the Indian Constitution, subjecting freedom of speech and expression to 'reasonable restrictions'. This amendment restricted the scope of freedom of expression and was widely regarded as 'Nehru's folly'. Nehru did it chiefly to counter the extreme voices opposing Partition and giving vent to communal rhetoric.[12] The main vociferous voice of opposition against this amendment was Shyama Prasad Mukherjee, the founder of the Bharatiya Jana Sangh and the former head of the Hindu Mahasabha, who pointed out 'the irony that while the First Amendment in the United States Constitution created the right to free speech, the First Amendment to the Indian Constitution was seeking to restrict it'.[13] Nehru, in his defence said, 'No state in the name of freedom can submit to actions which may result in wholesale war and destruction.' During Partition, the logic of prohibiting incendiary speech perhaps had a rationale. Yet, ironically, Nehru's belief in a state-imposed clampdown is being imitated today by those who pride themselves on being his ideological adversaries. The self-proclaimed 'Hindutva' followers of Mukherjee are seeking to imitate the not-so-edifying chapter of Nehru's administration while discarding the free speech legacy of their own political ancestor.

Gauri's killers may have used a gun, but don't we also see a symbolic gun pointed at the heads of student activists like Kanhaiya Kumar and Umar Khalid in the manner in which they are publicly vilified and attacked?[14] Doesn't the gun loom large when hit lists are circulated, naming women journalists and activists as the next targets after Gauri?[15] The cult of violence is breeding faster than the Aedes Aegypti mosquito and infecting many with the fever of blood lust against those they disagree with. None other than Paresh Rawal, a BJP member of Parliament, has called for author Arundhati Roy to be strapped to a jeep.[16] Noxious, foul-mouthed abusers get strength and even legitimacy from the fact that they are 'followed' by the top political leadership, who seem to echo their views.[17]

Journalists have been threatened, intimidated and murdered before, especially in far-flung areas where telling the truth means risking all. But today, it seems as if attacks against journalists are being tacitly endorsed by supporters of the ruling party when only perfunctory condemnations of Gauri Lankesh's murder are issued. When the government itself takes pride in an anti-media stance, when certain media organizations are boycotted by ruling party ministers (certain BJP members and ministers do not appear on the news channel NDTV), when critical journalists are censored and labelled 'news traders' by the political leadership,[18] when lawyers who assault female reporters are not censured,[19] then is the government itself creating an environment that encourages violence and stifles free speech? India ranked 133 among 180 countries in the World Press Freedom Index in 2016, and this ranking has fallen further to 138 in 2018.[20]

A preponderance of illiberal religious ideology in politics inevitably creates violence in society. Those rulers who practice 'soft Islamism' or 'soft Hindutva' must introspect as they tend to open the gate for more radical extremists to gain legitimacy. Today, the divide between Hindus and Muslims is being catastrophically sharpened, with every new issue like the calling of the azaan, the beef ban, the singing of 'Vande Mataram'[21] or even the so-called competing claims of 'shamshans' and 'kabristans'[22] becoming tacit political signals for violent goons to take over the discourse and physically attack the targets of their rage. (We see examples of increasing religious strife in the way SP member of the Legislative Assembly (MLA) Abu Azmi said, 'A true Muslim will never say Vande Mataram.'[23] The slogan 'Bharat mata ki jai' has also caused conflict. AIMIM MLA Waris

Pathan refused to chant 'Bharat mata ki jai' and was suspended from the Maharashtra assembly.[24] AIMIM leader Asaduddin Owaisi said he would not say 'Bharat mata ki jai' even if a knife is put to his throat.[25])

'Shout, don't shoot' is supposed to be the mantra of democracy. Yet, when democracy becomes entwined with irrational religious ideology, 'shout' becomes tacit permission to 'shoot', all norms of liberal democracy brushed aside by those motivated by blind faith. In many ways, this is only a use of religion for a naked power grab and to muzzle all opposition. Ironically, in another example of how the Hindutva brigade imitates the seculars in dictatorial impulses, the Modi-led BJP government is following in the footsteps of former prime minister Rajiv Gandhi, who brought in the anti-defection law, a legislation that wiped out the possibility of 'vaad, vivaad, samvaad' in India's temple of democracy: Parliament.[26] The anti-defection law is another instance of 'illiberal secularism'—how secular governments have often taken illiberal actions.

'The broadness of the anti-defection law has hit at the heart of legislative operations in India. Because no member can act "contrary to any direction" issued by her political party, legislative deliberation and voting risks becoming a mere ornamental exercise,' writes lawyer Madhav Khosla.[27] Members of Parliament thus cannot give independent, impartial views, they cannot speak their minds, they have no freedom of thought or the right to dissent within their parties.

To quote columnist Aakar Patel, 'The anti-defection law essentially removed the conscience of the elected representative and is thus a blow against democracy and constitutionalism. It also takes away the agency and freedom of the legislator. The law fails us, the citizens, in two most important ways. First, the loyalty that a legislator must have towards his voter and his constituents as opposed to his party. And secondly, the false assumption that the party is always right. The history of independent India shows that no party is perfect, and all their leaderships are capable of mistakes. The anti-defection law blunts the resistance to such actions.'[28]

The assault on freedom has been gathering strength for a long time. Have liberal citizens woken up too late to the dangers of freedom in India? In June 2017, sixty-five retired IAS officers wrote an anguished open letter about the manner in which a 'bludgeoning binary' was being created between 'nationalists' and 'anti-nationals', and about the bulldozing of debate.[29] They wrote about the growing 'climate of intolerance', 'bullying of independent thought', 'troll armies silencing dissenters' and how 'NGOs are being intimidated' by being charged with violating the Foreign Contribution (Regulation) Act (FCRA) and the Income Tax Act.

The former civil servants raised extremely important questions. Yet, it must be asked: why have things come to such a pass in the first place? Where were these conscientious former civil servants when 'reasonable restrictions' on free speech were incorporated into the Constitution in 1951, when Indira Gandhi suspended fundamental rights and conducted Parliament with most opposition members in jail; when Rajiv Gandhi enacted the anti-defection law; when the UPA put in place the draconian Section 66A in the IT Act?[30] The BJP-led government is building on this highly controversial legacy of Big State power unleashed by so called 'liberal' parties of the past. As far as the civil servants are concerned, if while warning of clear and present dangers at the same time they fail to acknowledge past follies, the seriousness of the message may get lost. The credentials of the messenger are then open to accusations of partisanship. Freedom was abused then, it is being destroyed now.

In times when the prime minister himself talks the language of 'shamshaan' vs 'kabristan', it's worthwhile to recall the wise words of actor Meryl Streep, who said at the Golden Globes award ceremony in Los Angeles in December 2017: 'This instinct to humiliate, when it's modelled by someone in the public platform, by someone powerful, it filters down into everybody's life, because it gives permission for other people to do the same thing . . . Disrespect invites disrespect; violence incites violence. And when the powerful use their position to bully others, we all lose.'

While attacks on anyone who dissents or deviates today are justified and even endorsed by sections of the top echelons of the political leadership, the liberal always takes the opposite stand. Respect for dissent is the hallmark of the liberal. In fact, the liberal needs to stand for *all* dissent that is peacefully and democratically expressed. Liberals need to be able to stand up for the constitutional rights of 'communists' and 'conservatives' alike, because unlike the 'nationalists', they cannot seek only to protect their own rights and instead must protect *all* peaceful expressions of individuality. Yet, the tragic question looms, in the death of the four rationalist intellectuals, are we all collectively guilty? Should we as a society have risen against the threats to freedom much earlier?

Stop Laughing

Another assault on freedom of speech and expression can be seen in the attacks by politicians and vested interests on comedians and satirists. In January 2016, comedian Kiku Sharda was sent to fourteen days judicial custody for mimicking Gurmeet Baba Ram Rahim Singh, the Dera Sacha Sauda godman now jailed for rape. Before this, in February 2015, a 'roast' video by the AIB comedy group was banned and FIRs filed against all those who were part of the show. They also faced obscenity and criminal defamation charges in 2017 for posting pictures of the prime minister with a 'dog filter'. The picture carried the hashtag #wanderlust.

How absurdly ironic that India's law enforcement which seems so helpless against billionaires who siphon away crores from public sector banks (in February 2018, a billion-dollar fraud involving Punjab National Bank came to light in which the prime accused is billionaire diamond trader Nirav Modi) or against debt-ridden tycoons who flee from Indian legal proceedings are busy filing FIRs against comedians! In Umberto Eco's thrilling book *The Name of the Rose*, set in a Benedictine monastery in the fourteenth century, monks are mysteriously murdered because they begin to read Aristotle's hidden book on theories of comedy, laughter and pleasure. So dependent was the medieval church on suppressing the subversive power of laughter that the mysterious mass murderer in the book was prepared to kill to stop monks reading a book teaching them how to laugh. To quote Eco: 'Laughter kills Fear and without Fear there can be no Faith.' Those who attacked and killed the staffers of the Paris-based magazine *Charlie Hebdo* for publishing satirical cartoons in 2015 and the violent attacks and riots that resulted from the publication of cartoons by the Danish newspaper *Jyllands-Posten* in 2005 are similarly intolerant of all humour. This kind of intolerance of humour or satire has manifested itself in India in the various legal cases against cartoonists and stand-up comics.

Laughter is the best protest. Laughter is an escape from political control. The playwright Bertolt Brecht used comedy to create powerful plays questioning social inequality. Charlie Chaplin's *The Great Dictator* was a send-up of Hitler with Adolf satirized as Adenoid Hynkel. *Dr Strangelove* was Stanley Kubrick's brilliantly satirical film on the Cold War. Joseph Heller's book *Catch 22* was a comic masterpiece on the absurdity of war. As the saying goes, if you want to tell people the truth, make them laugh, else they might kill you.

When war can be the subject of a joke, why can't godmen and prime ministers be laughed at? In fact, there's a comic revolution taking place today. Apart from the AIB roast and many comic videos on social media, there are stand-up comics like Kapil Sharma, satirical cartoons like 'So Sorry' (an animated feature on India Today TV) and sharp political cartoons in newspapers. Desi humour seems to have outgrown the gentle 'Yeh Jo Hai Zindagi' variety and become more biting. Indian cartooning, whether R.K. Laxman's well-loved Common Man or Mario Miranda's Miss Nimbu Paani fall in the playful gentle genre, even Shankar's takedowns of political figures in the 1950s were mischievous rather than vicious. Today, the humour and satire in cartoons, on stand-up shows and on social media, is more irreverent and far closer to the bone, as they should be.

Humour can be one of the most effective battering rams against the powerful. The British magazine *Private Eye* was a pioneer in trenchant satire against politicians. Veteran journalist and editor Khushwant Singh's satire in his column 'With Malice Towards One and All' was funniest when it was the most intimate. As Ron Jenkins wrote in *Subversive Laughter: The Liberating Power of Comedy*, comics use their art to combat social and political oppression in everyday life.

The crackdown on humour and satire has taken place across political lines, and 'secular' governments have been as repressive as 'nationalist' ones. In 2012, the cartoonist Aseem Trivedi was charged with sedition and jailed for two weeks by a Congress government in Maharashtra. In the same year a Jadavpur University chemistry professor, Ambikesh Mahapatra, was arrested by the Mamata Banerjee government in Bengal for circulating cartoons about her via email. 'The appropriateness of a cartoon should be judged by the people, not by the police,' the India Against Corruption group asserted at that time.

The Medieval Queen's Loyal Mob

Let's turn our attention now to one of the most horrendous instances of freedom of expression being stamped out because of so-called 'identity' politics. This was the episode around the movie that was first called 'Padmavati' and later released as *Padmaavat*, to make it clear that it was based on the sixteenth-century poem of the same name written by Sufi poet Malik Mohammed Jayasi on Padmavati, the queen of Chittor, and Sultan Alauddin Khilji.[31]

The film met with explosive protests by the Rajput Karni Sena, which objected to how their 'queen' had been depicted in the film.[32] Agitations took place in several cities, including Ahmedabad and Mumbai. Buses and malls were vandalized, effigies of director Sanjay Leela Bhansali were burnt, and in Gurugram even a school bus was attacked. Politicians were unable and unwilling to stand up to the wrath of the Sena, fearing the melting away of their all-too-precious vote banks; state chief ministers from Rajasthan, Madhya Pradesh and Maharashtra all quailed before these identity warriors.

Are we in the twenty-first century? Do we as citizens, democrats or political leaders not need to resoundingly condemn these acts of violence against a film? Why is this so-called 'cultural identity' so violent that it leads thugs to attack a school bus?[33] Why is this 'cultural identity' so weak that it is liable to be destroyed by a mere movie? Why is this attachment to culture so blindly unthinking, so moronically feudal, so regressive and so primitive that it cannot tolerate any individual creative expression?

There needs to be an urgent recognition across the board that all liberal-minded citizens have to strongly and vociferously defend individual artistic expression and say a firm 'no' to violence. Asserting individual rights in times saturated with an enraged sense of identity may be foolhardy. But unless we citizens courageously defend the ideal of peaceful freedom of expression, we will soon not be able to speak of anything that is not 'officially sanctioned'. The areas of art, culture and innovation will become ever more woefully restricted. Can this kind of fearful, scared-to-open-our-mouths version of India ever make a leap into the twenty-first century, into innovation and into the exploration of newer creative vistas? With the closure of the mind, creativity will perish and walls will inevitably be erected in a vain attempt to protect 'culture'.

The Karni Sena cannot be denied its right to protest. But these protests should take place lawfully in courts or through petitions and arguments, above all peacefully and without violence or public arson. Calling for bans and censoring of movies and books is not a protection but in fact a destruction of so-called 'identity', a destruction of a proud and enduring Indian tradition that has survived and grown strong precisely because it was always unafraid of reinterpretation and reinvention.

How are traditions kept alive? Traditions are kept alive precisely by new imaginings, by new modern interpretations of

old texts. Think of the musical *Jesus Christ Superstar* or the film
The Last Temptation of Christ. Despite controversies, Semitized
Christianity in the West didn't stop such reinterpretations, even
when they offended the sensibilities of many.

Today, identity warriors are turning their backs on their
own culture, on their Indianness; they are in fact destroying the
uniqueness of Bharatiya sanskriti and its capacity for endless
exploration. The Big State has always sought to stifle the freedom of
the intelligentsia. As we have already noted, through the nationalized
universities and various Akademis, governments have undermined
the independence of India's artistic and intellectual community.
India's post-Independence intelligentsia, as Masani and other
liberals point out, has been weakened by too much dependence on
government patronage. Liberals have thus not been able to create
robust civil society networks that can stand up strongly to violent,
identity-oriented politicized outfits. Liberals should have early on
stopped themselves from gravitating too far into the arms of the Big
State and governments. They should have striven to create platforms
reflecting a wide range of views and institutions of independence and
credibility that could stand as sentinels for individual freedoms.[34]
Liberals should have denied politicians any kind of stranglehold
on the arts and worked to create autonomous institutions with a
collective, dignified voice, which could have mounted a strong
counter-argument against politicized street thugs.[35]

Yes, Indian liberals, artists and thought leaders have raised
vociferous voices supporting free art, for example, M.F. Husain's
paintings. They have by and large stood for the freedom to
reinterpret and reinvigorate tradition and protected creative
expression, be it the Kama Sutra, the Khajuraho sculptures or even
quoted and popularized writings on homosexual love, like the story
of Madho and Hussayn in the seventeenth-century poem 'Haqiqat-
al Fuqara'. The reason why many of these works still survive in the
public sphere is because liberals have protected them from attack.
But liberals should have done more. Liberals could have followed

Tagore's example and set up many more private universities like the Visva Bharati University. But, sadly, many liberal voices have been heard campaigning for a government takeover of Tagore's dream university.

The Free Speech of Students and Dalits

On 30 July 2015, Yakub Memon, convicted in the Mumbai blasts case of 1993 was hanged in Nagpur jail. Following Memon's execution, on the same day, students at Hyderabad Central University held a prayer meeting and a debate on capital punishment. Most of the students belonged to the Ambedkar Students Association or ASA. This event led to a clash with the Hindu Right-wing student organization, the ABVP. Weeks of student agitations followed, which incurred the wrath of the high grandees of the Modi government in Delhi. In the midst of protests and what some have called the harsh punishment of the protesting students by the University, on 17 January 2016, postgraduate student Rohith Vemula hanged himself in a campus hostel. He and other students had been barred from living in the hostel by the university as part of the disciplinary proceedings. Rohith's monthly stipend had also been stopped.

Should the students of Hyderabad University have been as harshly punished as they were? Why does a student group not have the right to protest a hanging? In a letter to then HRD minister Smriti Irani, then labour minister and RSS ideologue Bandaru Dattatreya wrote on 17 August 2015 that Hyderabad University had become a 'den of casteist, extremist and anti-national politics' and how the university administrator had become a 'mute spectator' to these events.

In Dattatreya's letter, the free-thinking student is being made into a clear 'enemy' of the Hindutva nationalist viewpoint. The free-thinking student, cherishing the principle 'where the mind is without fear', is valuable, not because he or she necessarily holds universally correct views, but because he or she is exhibiting the courage to explore, to ask, to be proven wrong and to evolve from possible errors. Admittedly politicized students have sometimes demonstrated their own version of intolerance, such as when JNU students campaigned to cancel a lecture by Baba Ramdev in 2015.[36] Yet, in the Hindutva nationalist view, there is simply no space for any other opposing point of view, for student protest of whatever hue, no space for a diverse range of political activities. Only those student activities that are considered 'Hindu' and 'nationalist' pass muster.

In his suicide note, Rohith Vemula wrote: 'My birth is my fatal accident . . . I loved people without knowing that people have long since divorced from nature. Our feelings are second handed. Our love is constructed. Our beliefs coloured. Our originality valid through artificial art . . . the value of a man was reduced to his immediate identity and nearest possibility. To a vote. To a number. To a thing. Never was a man treated as a mind. As a glorious thing made up of star dust.'[37]

Rohith Vemula's tragic yet lyrical suicide note reveals how many young minds are increasingly finding their individualities stifled. It reveals how many find it difficult to give full rein to personal freedoms in a society forcing conformity at every level, how many suffer in loneliness as they experience social discrimination and hatred, and the toll it takes on their spirit.

Vemula's is the letter of a young man crying out against injustice and misunderstanding. Did such a young mind deserve to be evicted from his hostel room, deserve to have his fellowship suspended, simply because he was an activist of the Ambedkar Students Association and thus dubbed a potential 'anti-national'?

This is what happens when India's liberal atmosphere is replaced by a censorious illiberalism that makes enemies of every free-thinking student at universities where debate, dissent and freedom of expression is supposed to be the daily diet. Students' perceptions and conclusions may not be necessarily valid or politically correct, but it is precisely these free explorations that make education meaningful. Education itself would be meaningless if students were not free to err, learn from mistakes and move forward. Calling student protestors 'anti-national' is not only an assault on youth, but a frontal attack on India's Constitution. Free thought creates the enlightened citizenry that Rajaji held to be the very basis of liberal democracy.

In fact, for our liberal Constitution-framers, the key to making democracy successful was individual growth and moral transformation. For Ambedkar, democracy and constitutional morality were alien to India and the spirit of democracy had to be cultivated in every citizen. Without a democratic society and a social revolution, political democracy is, according to Ambedkar, impossible. 'How long shall we live a life of contradictions where we have inequality in social and economic life and equality in politics?' For democracy to succeed, every individual has to imbibe the notions of liberty, equality and fraternity. The struggle to overcome personal and social rivalries and jealousies is an essential part of becoming a citizen and a democrat.[38]

'Social and economic democracy are the tissue and fibre of a political democracy,' said Ambedkar. Democracy is meaningless if a government only claims a massive mandate and then proceeds to hamper and hinder the workings of social democracy—tolerance for difference, freedom of speech and individual liberty—among citizens. In this sense, Gandhi and Ambedkar were one: the struggle for a better country was a struggle for one's best self, for a democratic transformation within, for the true realization of individual conscience, which is the calling of the atma.

Whose 'Quota' Is It Anyway?

A word here on the vexed issue of affirmative action, reservations or quotas. Where does the liberal stand? After Rohith Vemula's suicide there was a debate on whether he was in fact a born Dalit or had been admitted to the university on merit. Without delving into the specifics of Rohith's birth, what should be the liberal's stand on affirmative action? For the liberal, as Rajagopalachari points out, the individual is the smallest minority in any society or group. If an individual has legal protection, everyone will enjoy the same. Ethnic, religious or other minority groups and those who have been deprived through social and political customs or practices may need special privileges.

But if the *thrust* is on special privileges, sooner or later a political or social backlash may be inevitable. It's much more rewarding and sustainable, therefore, to focus on the injustices that caused the deprivations in the first place and seek to minimize those. Instead, the typical Indian syndrome is first to demand reservations and privileges and then continue with the same practices and customs that caused the discriminations and injustices. And when the problem continues, we comfort ourselves by saying we have compensated the victims by giving them special privileges.

To quote Rajaji: '. . . statutory and other concessions given for the uplift of backward elements are prescribed on the basis of caste . . . this is basically erroneous procedure being in conflict with the no-caste ideology of the nation . . . caste wise approach should be given up and a secular economical test substituted for all state assistance and concessions . . . if the individual should be benefitted by a subsidy or a concession on account of his caste, it becomes a new privilege which is not good policy to create or perpetuate.'

'Reservations should not last for more than ten years, but the device has become a habit,' writes Masani. 'Every ten years Parliament prolongs its life because by now the spokespersons of reservations have become a vested interest. This has become one of the main points of corruption in public life and an easy way to professing to provide social justice.'

This is evident in the predicament in higher education in India, where there is a permanent shortage of seats as well as a decline in quality because of rigid regulatory and legal restrictions. When institutions claim to admit students on the basis of merit, most seats inevitably go to children from privileged backgrounds. We then throw crumbs at those who are deprived in the form of reservations. In fact, what is needed is to dismantle the entire system of controls which is creating and sustaining these disastrous shortages in the supply of quality higher education. When the supply of higher education is left entirely to the government, how can there be equality of opportunity given that demand far outstrips supply? For example, take the case of the cut-throat competition in medical examinations and the desire for lakhs of candidates to qualify for admission in a quality institution like AIIMS. Both the UPA and NDA governments committed to creating more AIIMS-like institutions, but the promises have not been met. The UPA set up six new AIIMS in 2012 (Bhopal, Bhubaneswar, Jodhpur, Patna, Raipur and Rishikesh) but these are nowhere near the standards achieved by the original AIIMS set up in 1956.

The Modi government's failure to meet its promise is even more glaring. Upon the completion of four years the government bragged that it had approved thirteen new AIIMS but an India Today investigation revealed that not a single one has been started.[39] The way to address the shortfall in seats is clearly to increase supply. The way to increase supply is not just through government projects but to encourage progressive-minded citizens to set up such institutions on the basis of open, transparent regulations. Yes, education is a sector from which the government cannot and should not escape responsibility. But relying on reservations to deliver education has become far too much of a habit, an easy recourse for politicians and an all-too-easy way for politicians to pose as sole spokesmen of the deprived or messiahs of the poorest. For politicians, quotas are the easiest way to prove their commitment to social justice. For the liberal, however, true social justice means creating enough supply or ending the huge shortfall in the supply of quality education. Rampant quotaism can be phased out if there are enough seats to go around. The Big State, always in the hands of some political party or another with its own motives and ideologies, should not run all activities that are needed for peoples' welfare as a monopolistic charity paid for by taxes. This is where Rajagopalachari's notion of trusteeship of the rich comes in which means the wealthy must set up institutions out of a sense of social conscience. Let us note here that the Ivy League universities in America were set up by wealthy private entities and do not count as US government institutions. The universities of Oxford and Cambridge were established by religious orders and private benefactors and not by direct government funding and support. The trusteeship of the rich in creating centres of excellence in India cannot be discounted, as seen in the highly successful Ashoka University or the OP Jindal Global University as well as in the Manipal Academy of Higher Education.

It may be interesting to note here that Kaka Kalekar, the chairman of the Backward Classes Commission appointed by the Government of India to determine the criteria of backwardness, which submitted its report in 1955, was himself sceptical of quotas. M.N. Srinivas quotes a letter Kalekar wrote to the President of India where he said, in Srinivas's words, 'The whole line of investigation pursued by the Commission is repugnant to the spirit of democracy since in democracy it is the individual, not the family or caste, which is the unit. Kalekar recommended that the state regard as "backward" and entitled to special educational and economic aid all those whose total family income is less than Rs 800 a year, regardless of caste or community. Kalekar himself opposed reservation of posts for backward classes in the government services which was recommended by the Commission.' For the liberal, caste quotas in perpetuity spur greater injustice and also fuel the politics of group identity.

Freedom for the Dalit Voice

The Dalitbahujan critique of Hindutva nationalism as articulated by so many Ambedkarite students like Rohith Vemula and the Dalit intellectual's attack on hierarchical Brahminical Hindutva has been met by attacks. Dalitbahujan scholars like Kancha Ilaiah, the author of *Why I Am Not a Hindu*,[40] criticize Brahminical Hindutva from many angles. He asks why most Hindu gods and goddesses are depicted as aristocrats, as wealthy kings and queens seated on thrones, when Jesus and Mohammed are depicted as poor men and shepherds. He asks why Dalitbahujan deities Pochamma, Kattamaisamma and Polimeramma are marginalized in the 'Hindu' pantheon. He asks why hymns like the 'Purusa-sukta'[41] are not cause for introspection, why even are they not rewritten or reinterpreted. And he questions a nationalism centred on the white cow, preferring instead a 'buffalo nationalism' with the black buffalo rather than the 'white cow' as its symbol.

In September 2017, Ilaiah was violently attacked in Telangana. His car was surrounded as mobs threatened to chop him into pieces. The assaults and death threats were a result of his most recent book in which he referred to the Arya-Vyasa caste as 'social smugglers'.[42] Dalit poets like the radical Namdeo Dhasal (who was part of the Dalit Panther movement of the 1970s) have directed searing attacks against Hindutva: 'Who are these people, you usurpers of yore who seized my country . . . Yesterday they murdered Gandhi. Now they want to put the whole nation to death . . . How many stories of alien invaders shall I tell them? . . . My original ancestors were dark Dravidian non-Aryan.'[43]

While Hindutva nationalists seek to appropriate B.R. Ambedkar as one of their heroes, they are deeply insecure about the free speech of assertive, articulate Dalits whose intellectual activism pierces Brahminical injustices and whose political activism threatens to split a united 'Hindu' vote bank. Both the BJP and Congress may have succeeded in the short term in gaining Dalit support during elections but the Ambedkarite mission of a frontal challenge to caste Hindu society is unpalatable to both mainstream parties, and in fact shows their illiberalism in refusing to directly attack caste and caste prejudice.

Jignesh Mevani is the young Dalit leader from Gujarat who made his debut as an MLA from Vadgam in the Gujarat polls of

December 2017. Mevani sparks fury among 'nationalists' and is denounced as divisive and anti-national. In January 2018, teargas and water cannon armed police attempted to stop a youth public rally he had called in Delhi. FIRs were registered against him for violence on 1 January 2018 at the Bhima-Koregaon rally near Pune even though Mevani wasn't even at the site.[44]

In a culture of fear and suppression of free speech, Mevani dares to openly and audaciously mock Prime Minister Modi. And he brings the sharp Dalit critique of caste Hinduism into politics, posing a frontal ideological challenge to Hindutva. Mevani combines a caste battle with a wider class war; he attacks the very foundations of so-called Hindu unity while seeking to unite humanity across all identities. He emphasizes the Dalit ideological challenge and counter-culture to hierarchical Hindutva—beef-eating and cattle trade as Dalit ways of life, English education as a Dalit right, the right to wear Ambedkar's prescribed modern dress of trousers and shirt. He is holding up a mirror to society. He is once again reminding us, as Ambedkar did, that governments must work for the liberty, equality and fraternity of all and not be a state in the grip of a political party that pushes only the liberty of a few, in this case those whom Mevani challenges as vegetarian, north Indian, upper-caste Hindus.

The Dalit challenge to caste Hindu society has been met by outrage, mockery, dismissal and only grudging respect. When Dalit leader Kanshi Ram bellowed, 'tilak, tarazu aur talwar, inko maaro joote chaar', in the 1990s, it sent shivers down the spines of upper-caste elites. The party that Ram founded in 1984, the BSP, soon got absorbed into the power elite but the Dalit critique of 'Hindu' society has always been a challenge to the statist, elitist orthodoxies among which there is still little introspection on caste. It's important to note that in the light of these entrenched attitudes on social superiority, at least the inhuman plight of manual scavengers, drawn mainly from Dalit castes, has been highlighted by the mainstream media.[45]

Youths like Rohith Vemula who saw themselves as part of the Ambedkarite mission have continued to spread awareness about Ambedkar on campuses. Dalit intellectuals like Chandra Bhan Prasad praise the British Raj for liberating Dalits from 'Manuwad'. Prasad has even built a temple to the 'Goddess English' in Banka village in Uttar Pradesh, the goddess shown wearing a British-style sola topi.[46]

'They say Adani–Ambani, we say jobs, they say love jihad, we say love zindabad,' Mevani yells. He represents the new wave of educated Dalits committed to a no-holds-barred attack on Brahminical Hindutva icons like Ram and Dronacharya. It is a critique that liberals need to embrace as a crucial part of the universal right to free speech. Should we condone Dronacharya for demanding Ekalavya's thumb? Should we see Surpanakha as an evil witch or 'rakshasi' simply because she professed her love? Writes Ilaiah, 'the famous Shambuka was killed and his kingdom usurped. The major opposition to Ram's aggression came from Kishkinda, a tribal king called Vali. The Brahmins befriended Vali's brother Sugreeva and his nephew Anjaneya and, aided by their treachery, killed the powerful Vali. When a beautiful Dalitbahujan woman Surpanakha wanted to marry Ram, the latter said she should ask Lakshmana. But Lakshmana in response cut off her nose and earlobes.'

Gail Omvedt points out that the anti-caste movements of Jyotiba Phule, E.V. Ramasamy or Periyar and Narayana Guru have always attacked Hindu nationalism by arguing that Hinduism in essence was Brahminical and exploitative. 'Phule tried to formulate a new theistic religion, Periyar promoted atheism, Ambedkar turned to Buddhism, Narayanswami Guru's radical follower Ayyappan asserted, 'no religion, no caste, and no God for mankind'.[47] A social and religious critique of Hinduism was fundamental to generations of reformers in India, with whom the liberal finds common cause because as a modernist and progressive she respects tradition but also seeks to build real change on the basis of reinterpreting traditions. The liberal rejects those traditions that do not fit with constitutional values. In fact, anti-Brahmin, anti-caste, anti-orthodox and anti-clerical traditions are as strong and as powerful in India as conventional Brahminical ones.

Attacks on Dalits are increasing.[48] The assertive Dalit is now daring to keep a pointed moustache, a practice which reportedly enrages the upper castes.[49] Dalits who own or ride horses again reportedly arouse upper-caste wrath and resentment.[50] Chandrashekhar Azad Ravan, the fiery and highly popular leader of the Bhim Army, was jailed in May 2017, after being arrested following caste clashes in Saharanpur. Chandrashekhar, who calls himself 'Great Chamar', has only recently been released after being held under the harsh National Security Act for a year. One of the most horrifying attacks on Dalits took place in Una, Gujarat, on 11 July 2016, when four Dalit men skinning a cattle carcass were brutally beaten with pipes and sticks by cow vigilantes. The Una attack became a mobilizing moment for Jignesh Mevani's campaign for Dalit rights.

Casteism has taken and continues to take particularly virulent forms across the Vindhyas. Tamil author Perumal Murugan, who has spoken out strongly against attacks on Dalits, has been as much a victim of Hindu orthodoxy as Wendy Doniger. In 2015, Murugan faced so many attacks in Tamil Nadu over his book *Madhorubhagan* (*One Part Woman*) that he declared his own death as a writer.[51] The Madras High Court ruled in his favour in 2016, saying, 'The author Perumal Murugan should not be under fear.'

Diversity Ki Jai

From Rohith Vemula to Jignesh Mevani to Perumal Murugan, liberals must embrace difference and plurality. From the Dalit beef-eater to the OBC meat-eater, from the Naga Christian to the Ambedkarite Buddhist, from the Bengali Vaishnava to the Maharashtrian Shaivite, the existence of numerous sects and streams and intellectual belief systems are all accepted by liberals as the truth of India. The liberal cannot stand silent over the closing of the Indian mind. In fact, most Indians subconsciously accept these pluralities, illustrating how deep liberal roots run in our country, how the pursuit of truth and tolerance for diversity are embedded in the earth of India.

The question is, what is it that fuels the need on the part of the 'nationalist' Hindutva warriors to constantly assert their identity as part of a collective, and why does it often degenerate into assertions or claims against some other identity? If we accept that 'identity' means an assertion of self-hood against another identity—such as Hindu means anti-Muslim, upper caste means anti-Dalit—then there will only be a downward spiral further into identity politics, leading to continuous fissures and fragmentation, with communities engaged in perpetual warfare against each other. We will then never be able to cherish and celebrate the diversity that makes India, a common identity acceptable to all citizens. As we have seen (in Chapter 2), identity and identity politics tend to easily lead to a dead end, as with the mandir and mandal agitations in the 1980s and 1990s. For instance, if the Hindutva identity was so powerful, would the BJP have come so close to defeat in the so-called 'Hindu laboratory' state of Gujarat in 2017? In the end, justice and liberty for all is the only possible sustainable politics that provides a permanent dividend.

Today, a plethora of economic regulations and social controls have restricted free choice. They have perpetuated scarcities and retarded voluntary economic and social interactions. This syndrome is leading to political mobilization based on one identity or another as each group lays claim to a larger share of the pie, material or cultural. Each of these claims is presented clothed in their own perception of injustices, sometimes real, at times imaginary.

The Dalit protests at Bhima-Koregaon in January 2018 or during the Bharat Bandh on 2 April 2018 are not only the result of upper-caste attacks on Dalits by militant casteist forces emboldened by the advent of the Hindu Rashtra. They are also the result of real economic deprivation and shrinking opportunities. A recent statistic is deeply revealing: in Haryana, almost 15,000 applied for eight peon jobs in a Jind court, many of them graduates and postgraduates.[52] Even in so-called 'developed' Gujarat, some MCom and BEd degree holders are running paan and tea shops.[53] In 2015, 23 lakh people, among them PhDs and engineers, applied for 368 peon posts in Uttar Pradesh.[54] In a restricted economy with too many scarcities, identities are running amok, and nominating a Dalit as president of India (Ram Nath Kovind, appointed as India's fourteenth president on 25 July 2017) seems not to have lessened caste discrimination, possibly even blinding us to the severe scarcities fuelling identity politics.

* * *

In this frenzy of identity politics, or the politics of group identity, there is a need for a social and political leadership that appeals to our highest instincts, inspiring us all to seek new heights, both personal and public. Gandhi epitomized that kind of leadership, inspiring his followers to be their best selves and follow his example in the struggle for truth and non-violence. His was a devotion to an ideal in the real sense, not a caricature of devotion that is only empty ritualism and which degrades the essence of religious and spiritual ideals. Youth today are hungry for inspiring idealism. If liberals can't provide it, power-brokers will fill young minds and use them as cannon fodder for their own narrow political games. In the mad rush to capture political power by every political party there is simply no space to discover the importance of articulating a coherent political ideology beyond a crafty, calculating instrumentalism, of just seizing the throne any which way.

The prevailing sense of delegitimization of politics and disenchantment and mistrust of government is a consequence of gross government overreach. Tall promises are made. Politicians fail to live up to them. In the prevailing disillusionment, the government falls prey to capture by vested interests. This kind of maximum state intervention is also corroding commonly held ethical values, both public and private. The Big State is dehumanizing us, preventing us from being moral beings. The liberal first has to become aware of what the Big State is doing to us as human beings. Then the liberal must see the need to control the Big State's powers and champion clear limits in how far governments can extend themselves. If the government and politicians remain determinants of our cultural and moral values, individual morality will disappear down the drain, as is happening all around us. Party politics should not be the only avenue of public life. Participation in local self-governance, citizen initiatives and independent civil society networks should be of equal salience.

Public life doesn't begin and end with elections but also involves impacting the political process by creating a narrative of active, engaged citizenry, so that no matter which party wins, it can't ignore this narrative from citizens. This is a narrative that constantly pushes for transparency in government, delivery of real justice and politics as a pursuit of higher ideals. Liberals must work for a widespread understanding that democracy is NOT about majority rule, but moral principles and social commitment to play by the rules of the game and uphold decent means. As a suggestion to political VIPs: instead of portraits of 'great men' in their office rooms, why not install portraits of R.K. Laxman's iconic Common Man?

Farmers: A Liberal Agenda

Are we aware of who some of the most liberal sections of Indian society are? Those who have been campaigning long and hard for their individual freedom? No, these are not feminists or JNU students, writers, journalists or activists. These are instead certain communities of farmers, the humble kisans. In March 2018, the Kisan Coordination Committee released an eight-point charter of demands calling for open markets and just prices.

The charter was released by followers of the late farm sector leader and liberal Sharad Anantrao Joshi. Joshi spent most of his life exposing the injustices heaped on farmers by caging them in all manner of laws and restrictions. The charter calls for the liberalization of agriculture, the end of government intervention in the farm economy, scrapping of the National Food Security Act, direct benefit transfers to the poor, free trade in farm products and the removal of restrictions in creating rural land markets.[55]

Joshi was one of India's pioneering liberals. He was an urbane, brilliant Sydenham College and Switzerland-educated United Nations diplomat who returned to India to become the most vocal economic liberal of the farm sector. He founded the farmers' union, the Shetkari Sanghatana, in 1979. Joshi had always advocated free enterprise in the rural economy and while in Parliament famously tabled a private member legislation demanding that the word 'socialism' be deleted from the Representation of the People Act, 1951. The liberal must indeed ask: why should a political party seeking registration in India swear to uphold the principle of socialism? Does every party have to uphold the same economic ideology? Don't the people of India have a right to choose whether they want to be ruled by a socialist party, capitalist party or liberal party? Joshi believed this clause effectively bars liberal parties from contesting elections.[56] Interestingly, the Janata Party was Indira Gandhi's sworn enemy but was ideologically almost exactly on the same page as her uber-socialism. While Indira's Congress had moved to dilute property rights to actively intervene in the private sector, the Janata Party in 1978 deleted the fundamental right to property altogether.[57] The socialism clause in the Representation of the People Act is yet another illiberal aberration inserted by the Rajiv Gandhi government and needs to be debated. It effectively bars all those who do not want to swear allegiance to socialism, from contesting elections.[58]

Joshi set up the Shetkari Sangathana to oppose farm subsidies, demand remunerative prices for farm produce and gain access to markets and technology. Why is it, Joshi asked, that while finance and industry were deemed worthy of liberalization, agriculture was not? Agriculture is the largest private sector in India. Yet, it is completely ignored when it comes to economic liberalization and ease of doing business!

For too long, the kisan has been trapped in a time warp of the statist politicians' imagination. He is seen as a figure seated calmly and wisely next to fields of waving paddy, wearing colourful clothes and uttering profound and simple phrases—the constant 'Other' of city folk. The 'kisan' is seen as a representative of an unchanging rural idyll which must be cossetted and protected by successive governments, preserved in a glass case like a museum piece. The ideal underlying 'Jai jawan, jai kisan' has degenerated in the hands of successive generations of politicians who pay lip-service to both groups, only to keep them dependent on state handouts, robbing them of their basic dignity.

Liberals, on the other hand, argue that the farmer must be set free. The farmer must be freed from land ceiling laws and land conversion laws. The absence of clear titles and deeds means that there can be no free buying and selling of land and there is still no proper market for land. Thus, a farmer cannot maximize his holdings or farm his fields productively as he cannot freely buy and sell. If he builds his own ponds and check dams he could violate drainage laws as per the Northern India Canal and Drainage Act of 1873. If he takes his produce across state boundaries he could be in violation of the Agriculture Produce Marketing Committee Act (APMC) or Mandi Act enacted almost fifty years ago, which states the requirement of separate trading licences for every mandi. Farmers can therefore sell to traders only with a licence for a particular market.[59]

While the fruits of liberalizing industry are clear, no thought is given to liberalizing agriculture. An arsenal of legislation prevents farmers from realizing their productive potential because statist policymakers cannot set them free and instead only make them the target of populist hand-outs.

Why is it crucial to recognize farmers' individual rights? Joshi campaigned for politicians to respect the farmers' right to trade, sell and make a profit. Joshi wanted FDI in the farm sector, along with the latest seeds and technology. He also wanted to give farmers the option of exiting the farm sector if they want to. Joshi's key realization was that the woes of farmers were the result of a gross misperception that farming was an ancient lifestyle rather than a serious modern profession. This mindset has led to the desire on the part of the Big State to 'protect' farmers. Endless red tape has been offered as a lifeline, but it has only bound their hands and legs.

Instead of individual freedom, farmers have been trapped in government policy and are always subservient to the government. The Modi government promised to double farm income in five years by 2022.[60] Yet there have been a spate of farmer suicides.[61] In April 2017, farmers from Tamil Nadu stripped naked in front of Prime Minister Modi's office and even consumed their own faeces. A mammoth protest march poured into Mumbai in March 2018, in which 35,000 farmers across Maharashtra covered 180 km on foot over five days.[62]

A range of controls bears down on the Indian farmer. Not only is he unable to freely buy and sell land, but the prices of his crops are fixed by the government.[63] His wherewithal to farm (such as water, fertilizers and seeds) is either unavailable or of poor quality, and he is thus perpetually tethered to poverty. Writes columnist Swaminathan Aiyar, 'Farmers should be treated as producers with internationally competitive potential, not as objects of charity . . . a national strategy on agriculture should include, creating good land records, financial infrastructure and moves to give cash grants per acre per year.'[64]

Joshi's cry was always to set the farmer free from all the controls he labours under, as if to argue, don't keep us trapped in a home like a bride. Let us come into the world and see what we can do. He said: 'We don't want alms, we want the price of our sweat and toil.' To reiterate a quote from a policy paper written for a Round

Table Conference held by a group of Indian liberals in Deolali in June 2018:

> The economic reforms which began in the 1990s focused only on non-farm sectors, and agriculture was overlooked once more. Indian agriculture is the largest private sector in the country. Yet nearly three decades after the initiation of economic reforms, almost every aspect of agriculture, from land, to crops, inputs, credit, prices, access to market, logistics, value addition, to domestic and international trade, remain captive in a regulatory maze. Consequently, the largest sections of people have experienced little benefit from so-called reform policies, and not surprisingly there is little popular appreciation or support for 'economic liberalization'. Therefore, each small step can only be taken stealthily or surreptitiously, often by sugar coating through subsidies and handouts, which ends up opening new doors for corruption and cronyism, deepening the popular disenchantment with the political process. The farmer is chained to poverty and then offered charity from the government.[65]

Just as the student must have the right to protest, the writer the right to write, the film-maker and poet the right to creative expression, the farmer must have the right to free trade and the right to make a profit. In many ways, the depth of intellectual corruption and hypocrisy in India is reflected in the devaluation of the term 'profit'. We are a culture that traditionally celebrates profit, where good wishes for the Indian new year are expressed as a wish for 'shubh labh'. We even have a God of profit, Ganesha, and a goddess of prosperity, Lakshmi. Yet, we oh-so-righteously preach service without profit, for farmers, teachers, doctors and almost all other professions. Manuwant Choudhary writes, 'the Swatantra Party with its slogan, Farm, Family and Freedom . . . wanted a liberal free market economy and an end to the license permit quota raj where a few businessmen were favoured and others denied permission to set up enterprises, was lent much support by Sharad Joshi.'

Liberals, always siding with individual freedom against an overpowering government, believe in the power of the individual and the rights of the peasant proprietor. As Rajagopalachari puts it, 'The peasant proprietor stands for initiative and freedom and is interested in obtaining the highest yield from the land . . . we must promote modern production without interfering in the cultivator's rights of ownership, management and cultivation of land. Regulation must be limited to requirement and not expanded to the point of killing individual incentive.'[66]

A new policy orientation towards farmers requires independent thinking and a readiness to shake off the baggage of the past. Independent thinking is difficult for statists on both sides, whether secular socialist statists or Hindutva nationalist statists. Independent thinking is particularly difficult for Hindutva nationalists and identity warriors who see any deviation from their assumed norm as acts of national betrayal. But what are we without free thought? Without free thought there can be no functioning democracy.

Yet, how can there be independent thought when there is an ideological mission to stamp it out for the sake of building the Hindu Rashtra? The Hindu Rashtra tolerates even less independent thinking than the Indira Gandhi Rashtra. The secular state under Indira Gandhi may have frowned on deviations from its party line but with the exception of the Emergency years, the 1970s secular Big State, which set the tone for the destruction of individual freedoms, still did not push as hard at individual freedoms as the Hindutva Big State does.

Attack on Intellectuals

Threats to academics and intellectuals have become commonplace. What is the motive in attacking, even killing, intellectuals? To spread fear and create a chilling effect. In February 2017, a shocking incident took place at Jodhpur University. JNU professor Nivedita Menon was invited to speak. This led to protests by the ABVP and Menon's denouncement as an 'anti-national' from JNU. The professor who invited her to the conference, Rajshree Ranawat was suspended by Jodhpur University. This was by no means the only instance of victimization of academics and intellectuals. Author Arundhati Roy and academic Ashis Nandy have faced sedition charges.[67] Idealistic physician Binayak Sen was held guilty of 'rajdroh' (see Chapter 1).

In 2015, Nobel Laureate Amartya Sen spoke out on the serious threats faced by academic institutions from the Modi government. In the same year, Sen himself openly stated that he was 'ousted from' the post of chancellor at Nalanda University.[68] In a forceful essay in the *New York Review of Books*, Sen pointed to the Modi government's 'extraordinarily large' interference in academia and the aggressive and hostile attempts to seize control of academic institutions, from TIFR to ICHR to even the IITs:[69] 'The Delhi IIT director Raghunath Shevgaonkar resigned, the IIT Board chairman Anil Kakodkar expressed that he could not help the government with anything in the future . . . instead of having effective power, this becomes direct control.'[70]

Sen wrote in his *New York Review of Books* essay how the then head of ICHR, Yellapragada Sudershan Rao, was not regarded as a serious scholar and that the famous writer Sethumadhavan was asked to step down from the National Book Trust. The manner in which historian and scholar Mahesh Rangarajan was forced out of the Nehru Memorial Library in 2015 and replaced by a bureaucrat again shows the extent to which independent, liberal academic inquiry is being brought to heel under the writ of the Hindutva nationalist cultural identity.

To quote Sen: 'Governments must understand that winning a Lok Sabha election does not give you permission to undermine the autonomy of academic institutions, or for that matter, the courts or the upper house of Parliament. Universities don't have the power of courts or the upper house so they are easy prey. You can go through them like a sword through butter . . . academic freedom is based on the government understanding the limits of its formal power as opposed to its actual power and what they are expected to do: they are expected to listen to the voice of the professoriate and the voice of the people in the university.'[71]

Yet the liberal must also raise the question: isn't first nationalizing education and then expecting that the autonomy of those nationalized (or government-controlled) educational institutions will be respected a bit of a pipe dream? Particularly in a country where independent institutions have all too often degenerated under political pressure? The lesson of the Modi years has been: once you allow the government in everywhere, you can't then choose between good government and bad government. Instead, the lesson for liberal-minded citizens is to not allow the government to encroach unnecessarily, else what the seculars once did the Hindutvavadis will only take to newer heights. The founder of the ICHR and the Indian Council of Social Science Research (ICSSR) was S. Nurul Hasan, a distinguished historian but also a member of the Congress and the minister for education in the 1970s. Was this not a blurring of the red lines between being a professional historian and expanding political influence into the writing of history? A secular interference in history is as political as a Hindutva interference and there is a danger of the party line being imposed in both situations.

India has taken pride in the age-old gurukul tradition. Yet in that system, teachers and students enjoyed complete freedom to choose each other. The reputation of the teacher was the sole criterion, and discussion, debates and respect for dissent were the norms. It was the belief that if the student didn't appropriately compensate the teacher, his education would not be complete. 'The Indian philosophical tradition,' writes Srinivas, 'was rich in diversity, and public debates between members of different schools were an established institution. A teacher's greatest success was believed to be a student who defeated him in argument.' In the gurukul tradition, a real guru actually takes pride in the shishya who is able to reach even greater heights than the guru. The completely discursive nature of most Indian scriptures underscore the prime importance they attach to education by a process of debate, learning through a battle of wits and scholarship.

Premodern India didn't really have any institutions of higher learning beyond the gurukul, and some gurus were seen to be at a higher level than others. But in the highly competitive world of the knowledge gurus, liberal values of open-mindedness and the spirit of enquiry prevailed, since no one had any intellectual authority or administrative power to impose their own versions on others. 'The word 'upanishad', writes Radhakrishnan, 'is derived from upa [near], ni [down] and sad [to sit], that is, sitting down near. It implied, 'groups of pupils sit near the teacher to learn from him the secret doctrine, in the quietude of the forest hermitage.'[72] It is only Nalanda University, founded in the fifth century BC, that sought to institutionalize higher learning. Such a centre of excellence came about with the great intellectual churn of Buddhism, which emerged to challenge the orthodox Hindu doctrines of the time. In fact, the intellectual traditions inherited by Indians have been marked as Srinivas notes, by 'a continuous self-criticism and self-questioning that goes back to later Vedic times'.

Today, self-appointed custodians of that argumentative, self-critical, debate-oriented gurukul culture, the Hindutva statists, are telling teachers, students and parents that they cannot think. That the government must choose and decide what is good for them. Students must follow what the Big State decides should be in their textbooks, from certain teachings of history to Sanskrit. The education minister has even voiced his rejection of the scientific theories of Charles Darwin.[73] The modern-day, self-appointed custodians of gurukul culture are overthrowing its fundamental tenets.

Hindutva nationalists target Amartya Sen but have any twentieth-century Hindutva thinkers such as Vinayak Damodar Savarkar, author of the book *Hindutva*, or RSS ideologue Madhav Sadashiv Golwalkar, author of the book *Bunch of Thoughts*, been distinguished by the global renown of scholars like Amartya Sen, Romila Thapar, M.N. Srinivas or Ashis Nandy? India's Right wing lacks internationally influential intellectuals because the Hindutva movement puts the brakes on free thought in its obsession with avenging historical wrongs and settling historical scores. Hindutva, in fact, is a reflection of a prevailing fashionable anti-intellectualism, a mindset that leads to banning books, as well as marginalizing intellectuals like Sen.[74] Intellectual pursuit is a reflection of the culture of 'vaad, vivaad, samvaad' and requires recognition of debate and dissent. A conducive environment for debate calls for the recognition of freedom of expression as a basic minimum. A line of enquiry may turn out to be futile, or a criticism may not seem justified, but it is the *freedom* to pursue an independent line of thought, unrestrained by dogma or blind faith, that enables the debate to move forward, indeed makes civilizations progress. Anti-intellectualism is an attempt to halt the march of civilization itself.

Scientific progress thrives in an atmosphere of uncertainty and relishes honest intellectual jousts. Rigid beliefs, on the other hand, promise certainty. The prospect of uncertainty rocks the world view of believers to their foundations. Yet, as we have seen, Hindu philosophy has always accepted a massive diversity of beliefs: atheists, agnostics, materialists, monotheists, dualists and believers in multiple deities. That's why it did not feel culturally threatened by conquests, political upheavals or scientific revolutions. Generally, societies and cultures that progressed at different historical periods did so when they were able to open their doors and absorb diversity. Civilizations veer towards collapse when they close their doors, in the belief that they are the 'chosen' people, 'chosen' on the basis of race or religion. The liberal champions openness, an open society and open minds. The nationalists want to close minds and close societies because they are so threatened by differences. Wrote the great Marxist historian Eric Hobsbawm on his Jewish background and on Israel: 'I have no emotional obligation to the practices of an ancestral religion and even less to the small, militarist, culturally disappointing and politically aggressive nation-state which asks for my solidarity on racial grounds . . . if there is any justification that the Jews are "chosen" or special people it rests not in what they do in the ghettos or special territories but on the remarkable contribution made to the wider world by those who have been allowed to leave the ghettos and choose to do so.'[75] Whether you are 'chosen' or 'special' does not depend on your religion, race or background, but how much you can contribute to humanity.

India's Hindutva Right also lacks intellectuals of global stature because it has never faced global competition. Cocooned in an insular world, Hindutva nationalist writers or activists have not had to compete for global professional stature against international scholars the way Left and liberal intellectuals and scholars have had to. The RSS, in my opinion, being an authoritarian line and command organization like the army, hardly encourages original thinking or fresh ideas. Those who view Hinduism in an iron silo will not even aspire for global stature or the need to be intellectually open to exploring the world.

Hindutva supporters espouse 'vasudhaiva kutumbakam' but seek to ostracize or silence all voices that differ or dissent. They claim the world, but can't conceive of anything beyond their own well or echo chamber. So they remain unquestioning and non-self-critical and believe they don't need the world, just as they believe that at home they need to hammer all diversity into a single pattern of robotic thinking.

Followers of Hindutva do not believe in challenging the master, when in fact this challenge was the principle of Upanishadic thought and of the gurukul system. Instead, within Hindutva outfits, mantras are handed down without question or interrogation. But while Hindutva brigades have a vested interest in projecting an unquestioning version of Indian tradition and sanskriti, that kind of rigidity is clearly not what the scriptures and mythologies show at all, each placing interrogation at the centre of their philosophy. Free thought can only happen in cultures and institutions that are not based on command and control. But modern-day Hindutvavadis obsessed with ideological enemies can hardly create a free-thinking intellectual tradition. Hindutva nationalist identity warriors, seeking only to prove their own set prejudices and certainties, lack the element of doubt or self-doubt that propels new thinking forward.

Liberals are open-minded, plural and unafraid of questioning and argument. Like Gandhi, they are unafraid of self-doubt. That's why they can achieve great heights of intellectual enquiry. The Gita, in fact, is solely concerned with the individual's search for his own path. But since individuals make up the family, community, society and country, generations of thinkers and leaders have tried to interpret the Gita in a wider social and political context. The Mahabharata comes close to providing a narrative where governance and justice are at the core.

In the Shanti Parva (the twelfth book of the Mahabharata) there is a long section on the challenges and dilemmas of government. Over many days, as Bhishma, the patriarch lies dying on a bed of arrows, Yudhisthira asks him many questions to which Bhisma replies, illustrating his point with stories. Each story shows, in different ways, that in Indian traditions good individuals hold the key to good and benevolent institutions.

For example, the Bhagavad Gita does not contain specific tenets of governance. Instead it is predominantly concerned with the good and bad conduct of the individual. On the other hand, Western systems of thought sought to create independent value-based, virtue-based institutions to preside over impersonal relationships. For the modern Indian liberal, these two elements, good individual conduct and virtuous institutions, must necessarily complement each other. Otherwise, individuals will not trust institutions and those manning institutions will not be able to be just and fair to citizens. Many current social and political conflicts in India stem from a breakdown of the relationship between individual citizens and those in charge of institutions. Gandhi wrote in detail on these principles. We have noted how urgently he sought devolution of governance, local self-government and conceptualized swaraj as self-rule, which brings ultimate authority to the individual. Ambedkar and the writers of the Constitution sought to create institutions of integrity. But as Ambedkar had warned, if those individuals who followed the founders of 1947 failed to preserve the integrity of democratic institutions, 'then democracy would not be successful in India. Public conscience made up of individual morality is an essential condition for the successful working of a democracy; without public conscience democracy cannot be sustained or be successful. Only when each individual is democratic and is able to accept the liberty of others which he claims for himself can there be good government.'[76]

When governments begin to lose the intellectual argument, they tend to attack those who are perceived to be winning it. Liberals seem to be winning because the intellectuals ranged on the liberal side are relatively powerful. But liberals won't win for very long until they realize the reasons for their fall from grace.

Totalitarian governments from Stalin's Soviet Union to Mao's Communist China targeted intellectuals. Stalin sent political opponents and writers like Alexander Solzhenitsyn, author of *The Gulag Archipelago*, to the gulag or forced labour camps. Maoist China attacked intellectuals and 'reactionary academics' during the Cultural Revolution. In some cases, brainwashed Maoist children often killed their own parents for 'disloyalty' to Mao.[77]

In Cambodia, the Khmer Rouge slaughtered the educated.[78] Nazi book-burning campaigns in the 1930s consigned to flames all so-called communist and 'un-German' books. In December 2015, in the Lok Sabha, BJP MP Kirron Kher, among others, turned her ire against intellectuals and jholawallahs, saying they were 'politically motivated' and only returning awards to embarrass the

Modi government. Historian Ramachandra Guha has accused the Hindutva nationalist government of being the most anti-intellectual government India has ever had.[79]

Yet, whether on social and religious reform or big government excesses, India's intellectuals have not only been at the forefront of change, they have also been impartial critics. Renowned novelist Amitav Ghosh has spoken out against the Gujarat riots of 2002 but has also written a trenchant critique of the anti-Sikh riots of 1984.[80] Amartya Sen and Arundhati Roy may be critical of this government but does that make them 'anti-national'?[81] Nayantara Sahgal is castigated as a leading dissenter to Hindutva yet she was also a fierce critic of the Congress dispensation under Indira Gandhi. Krishna Sobti has also been attacked but she is a formidable writer who blazed a trail in Hindi literature. Both Sahgal and Sobti have been caricatured as 'biased' against the Modi government and accused of being part of the 'manufactured protest' by 'anti-nationals'. This was when writers returned their Sahitya Akademi awards in 2015 as a protest against the growing 'culture of intolerance' marked by the murder of M.M. Kalburgi as well as the government's silence on the lynching of Mohammed Akhlaq in 2015.[82]

Instead of branding all thinkers as 'politically motivated' or 'urban Naxals', should their views not be debated? Should intellectuals not be intellectually answered in a verbal duel, instead of resorting to name-calling? Perhaps the reason why 'nationalists' hate intellectuals is because they cannot defeat them in argument or they have no answers to intellectual opinions. But Hindutva nationalists do not realize that threats or acts of violence are futile against the power of ideas.

Ideas can only be countered with better ideas. The Left lost the plot by refusing to acknowledge its critics, by labelling and branding all dissenters as 'class enemies' and refusing to dialogue. Now the Right is following the same slippery path. They don't hesitate to silence their critics, but forget that ideas can't really be erased so easily. The enduring appeal of India's epics and mythologies and the basic values they communicate testifies to the power of ideas. Ideas cannot be erased just by demolishing a mosque or a statue or even killing the ideator. The ideas of Aristotle, Karl Marx and Adam Smith have outlived them because ideas are immortal. When former President Pranab Mukherjee visited the RSS headquarters in Nagpur on 7 June 2018 and delivered a speech extolling the virtues of the Congress vision of patriotism to an RSS audience, it was a positive move by the secular class to engage in a battle of ideas with the Hindutva side.

There is a problem, though. Secular intellectuals generally have had an addictive propensity to hobnob with political power centres. They are drawn almost with a magnetic force towards powerful politicians. Thus, they have often let themselves be used by successive generations of politicians. The politician has wanted to patronize the intelligentsia to claim legitimacy and the intelligentsia has let itself be patronized. This tendency is coming back to haunt intellectuals. By now Indian intellectuals should have been able to shape and propagate a mass acceptance of the ideas of diversity and pluralism. They should have put their shoulder to the wheel to propagate the cause of pluralism at the grassroots. Yet they failed to give ballast to these ideas either by bowing too much to the political bosses of the day or remaining hidden in ivory towers. Gandhi was killed not just by the bullets fired by an extremist, but by bigoted extremist ideas. Those ideas needed to be challenged robustly, fiercely and powerfully, at all levels, all the time, 24x7. But India's secular intellectuals did not join the battle enthusiastically enough even as they let themselves be co-opted by the Big State.

The appeal of state power attracts various shades of opinion across the ideological spectrum. Despite the obvious failure of Big States—communist, socialist or Hindutva—political actors and members of the public keep seeking and thirsting for more and more state power. The power of the Big State lies in handing out patronage which members of Indian civil society are all too eager to accept. By doing so, they only weaken themselves.[83]

However, Hindutva 'nationalists' who rubbish or wreak violence on liberal intellectuals are only demonstrating their own weakness. When you attack the literate class, it means you have no counter-argument. Gandhi's analysis on violence centred on the fact that violence in the end always turns against the so-called revolutionaries because violence is, in essence, self-destructive. The pen is the foremost enemy of the sword because the sword does not have a solid case against the pen.

The Battle for History: Secular vs Nationalist

It must be admitted that through the decades of the post-Independence years, Left liberals have exercised the heavy hand of state sponsorship on academia and often not allowed deviations from the party line. In their own way, they have stamped out dissent in universities and isolated any fledgling Right-wing academics. State control over education and universities tends to inevitably stamp out dissent and diversity or any line of thought that questions the government-ordained status quo. The illiberalism of Leftist orthodoxies has led them in the past to dismiss those on the 'Hindu' side.[84] This has now led to a furious backlash.

In many ways, this is the crux of the problem. The government intervenes in education and then seeks to micromanage the direction of education to suit its ideological proclivities. History is particularly problematic because of the propensity of the Big State to buttress its legitimacy by suitably tailoring history to meet its own political needs.

Today, it is clear that both sides, 'secular' and Hindutva nationalist parties, have been illiberal in their desire to rewrite history. Nationalists have always believed that for too long history-writing has been in the clutches of 'Congress-friendly Leftists' who allowed no space to Hindu nationalist history. When the government set up the ICHR in 1972 it did become a patron of historical research and 'nationalists' claim that Left-leaning scholars like R.S. Sharma and Romila Thapar kept them out.

However, Left-leaning historians have pointed out that the Hindutva Right has simply not produced globally renowned historians comparable to Thapar. The galaxy of formidable historians designated as 'Left-liberal' are far more accomplished and distinguished by international recognition. Sumit Sarkar is called a 'Leftist', yet he is one of India's most distinguished scholars. Although he uses Marxian analytical methods, he has been stringently critical, for example, of the Tiananmen Square massacre of 1989. Nor are his pursuits all 'Leftist'. Sarkar is the author of an acclaimed paper, the *Katham Amrito of Ramakrishna Paramhansa*, which was appreciated at the Ramakrishna Mission. Although intellectually 'nationalists' have been no match for Left-liberals, the former have more than made up for their lack of intellectual heft by attempting to delegitimize voices on the other side. Sadly, Leftist scholars have often let themselves get too closely identified with rather pathetically performing Left governments, thus becoming 'guilty by association'. Left-leaning scholars have been somewhat discredited for enjoying the patronage of Leftist regimes whose legitimacy was sharply questioned by the public. (Indira Gandhi patronized intellectuals and even drew them into her own 'Kitchen Cabinet', CPI[M] in Bengal too had its own following of intellectuals, many of whom later switched to the TMC).

The writing of history textbooks has tended to be politicized in India because of far too much government interference. The Right argues that the Left has misrepresented its role in the Gandhi-led freedom struggle of 1947. Yet, Left liberal historians have marshalled immense historical data to show that indeed the role of the RSS and the Hindu Mahasabha in the pre-Independence period must be objectively probed as these outfits had little role in the freedom struggle because they regarded their real enemy as the Muslim and not the colonialist.[85] The Hindutva side for its part, has kept up a war against the dominance of Leftist versions of history texts. As far back as 1977, Nanaji Deshmukh's note on education led to the withdrawal of R.S. Sharma's textbooks from schools. On the secular side, the painting of Akbar as a sort of sixteenth-century Nehru was criticized as Congress official hagiography.

Left and Right historians have clashed down the years. Historians clash when intellectual pursuits are coloured by state patronage. Had the Indian education system been open to anyone who wanted to set up a school or university, scholars and institutions would have had to compete to earn their reputations and status. In an open, competitive environment, the divergence of ideologies would reflect in the diverse conclusions and theories of an eclectic range of scholars. As a result, discourse as a whole would perhaps have been enriched. Such openness would also provide an incentive to all students to think on their own and draw their own conclusions. Extreme statism in higher education has inevitably drawn historians into party politics.

'Vivekananda was a revivalist,' says the Left; he was a 'nationalist', says the Sangh. 'Indian history must be seen through the prism of Hindu–Muslim conflict,' says the Right, 'Indian history is the history of "subaltern" against "oppressors"', says the Left. The culprit as usual is the meddlesome Big State which has arrogated to itself the power to write textbooks, set curricula and decide on what is correct history. The stated mission of successive Congress regimes was to create a secular state and they used history to legitimize their agenda. Today, 'Hindutva nationalists' are adopting the same strategy to establish their own claims.

Should governments be in the business of writing history textbooks in the first place? Should governments be in the business of supporting centres of historical research? Once more we see a familiar syndrome: secularists created the intrusive state which the Hindutva ideologues have inherited and taken to new heights. History is, in fact, in need of disinvestment by the government and textbook-writing is in need of disinvestment by the government. As a solution, the government should set up institutions that are then made autonomous so that they can be run professionally without being burdened with any ideological preferences of the state. Or they should not be set up by the state but by local government bodies, or collectives of schools and universities. In India the social and institutional capacity of institutions to maintain their autonomy is in severe doubt, particularly if the government is powerful enough. In this scenario, it is best if the writing of history textbooks is opened up to a range of professional historians and schools are allowed to make informed choices on which texts they will use.

One of the obsessions of the Hindutva nationalists, one on which they disagree sharply with liberal historians is the 'Aryan migration theory'. The nationalists attempt to show that Hindus are the original inhabitants of the subcontinent. Such an interpretation would challenge the theory of Aryan expansion, established by historians like Thapar, that Central Asian or Aryan tribes streamed into the subcontinent thousands of years ago. As a result, India became a diverse melting pot of numerous cultures and races. The nationalist project to conflate 'Hindu' with 'Indian' makes a nonsense of the many great faiths, languages and cultures that have coexisted in easy pluralism for centuries in the subcontinent.

The Aryan migration theory would mean that Indians have diverse gene pools and histories and therefore there is legitimacy in recognizing that subcontinental diversity is of ancient provenance. Hindutva nationalists, however, need to disprove the Aryan migration theory by asserting that Indians as a 'race' originated in India and therefore there is a basic homogeneity in genes and culture. Thus, 'racial' and religious identity are tied to the land and science is pressed into service to buttress their beliefs, beliefs that trump knowledge. In many ways, the social and political debate in India over the history and science of Aryan migration is similar to the debate in the US between evolution and creation, between the abortion and anti-abortion camps. The debate illustrates the power of beliefs and how identity politics is rooted in such beliefs. Since politics is rooted in creating a suitable history, the role of history writing in reshaping narratives becomes of paramount importance. Romila Thapar believes that to create a Hindu Rashtra, there is a need to show that Hindus by historical record were original inhabitants of the subcontinent and thus have a primary right to being first-class citizens.[86]

'There is a kind of division of labour between the RSS and its ex-pracharak prime minister,' points out Pranab Bardhan, academic at University of California. 'Incremental economic reform [some of it a continuation of the policies of the UPA regime] will not be objected to by the populist-nationalists in the RSS, as long as the latter are given a free hand in controlling the agenda of education, culture and history. In India, there's always been an unhealthy amount of state control over education and culture but the current regime has mobilized an unusually large number of bigots and charlatans for this job. If the economy doesn't do well and young people get frustrated, they can always ratchet up the cultural stuff—cows, love jihad, beef, and the rest of it.'[87] Rewriting history is of enormous importance to those who want to build the future Hindu Rashtra on the basis of past tales of imperial glory and racial superiority.

Journalists and the Big State

The liberal journalist is the prime enemy of the Hindutva statist nationalist. Social media is the happy hunting ground where so-called 'libtard'(a mix of the words 'liberal' and 'retard') journalists are repeatedly attacked as 'anti-national', 'Pakistani', 'Congi', 'sickular' people. Hatespeak on social media as well as fake news and propaganda, are serious enemies of liberal democracy because they divide society into hostile, hyper-polarized camps where annihilating the enemy and not defeating the opposition in argument becomes the primary objective. The ruling BJP and its social media force dominates Twitter and Facebook and efficiently pushes government campaigns and propaganda drives although the Opposition is now more active than it ever was. But Hindutva nationalists, trolls and 'bhakts' attack liberal journalists, indeed all liberals, in unison.

Right-wing social media activists propagate aggressive 'Hindutva nationalism' to apparently counter a 'Left-liberal' bias in the mainstream media. Hindutva remains the dominant narrative on social media platforms in India. During writers' protests, social media took the lead in demonizing those returning various state awards by making the hashtag #Awardswapsi trend, a phrase used by the media as well. After the mob lynching at Dadri, social media successfully campaigned for the news media to give equal space to the killing of a Bajrang Dal activist in Moodbidri, Karnataka (see Chapter 2 for more on Hindutva 'victimhood' campaigns). Social media thus crucially impacts the mainstream media and often sets the news agenda.

Fake news, fake videos, fake memes and trends are created to drum up potentially explosive communal situations. During the July 2017 riots in Basirhat, videos from a Bhojpuri film were circulated via social media. During Eid in 2016, fake photos of streets running with blood were shared, designed to show the 'barbaric' nature of minorities. Social media tends to be dominated by ultra-illiberals, making it an echo chamber of baser anti-democratic prejudices. These haters use a platform for free speech to target and muzzle those who have different or dissenting opinions. The common strategy is to use vulgarity, abuse and threats of violence and mount a coordinated assault to try to overwhelm or coerce liberals into silence. Lately, interviews have surfaced of workers of the ruling party's IT cell who have divulged how they are tasked with systematically attacking those perceived to be liberal.[88]

The control of the BJP-led government over the media has been unprecedented in the history of post-Independence India, except during the Emergency period when press freedom was suppressed by law.[89] The Modi years have seen an undeclared Emergency on the media, in which journalists who do not toe the ruling party's line face threats of being removed from their jobs or ostracism by government functionaries. Many mainstream journalists are deeply censored and sadly tamed by the government, with influential sections of the press reduced to touting the 'Hindutva nationalist' line without question.[90]

There are important contrasts here with the American press. American President Donald Trump is perhaps as flamboyantly anti-media as Prime Minister Modi. But the press in the US has revealed itself to be institutionally far stronger. During the US elections, for example, American media houses often openly endorse their preferred candidate, just as the *New York Times* backed Hillary Clinton in the 2016 campaign. It was an accepted norm that while the newspaper's editorial position was in favour of Hillary (editorial pages after all always take a position), its news pages would provide news without opinion. Being able to transparently endorse a candidate reflects the institutional strength of the American press. Equally, it reflects the independence of US institutions, where its Supreme Court bats for the protection of constitutional rights.

Consequently, the US government is restrained within the four corners of the Constitution. This is one of the key reasons it cannot impose its diktat on the media or anyone else without a clear legal provision.

The current attempts by the Modi government to control and censor the media without any legal provision but through various rules and regulations controlling business, such as the threat of denying government advertising, actually illustrate why India is still ranked 100 on the Ease of Doing Business index of the World Bank. Every media house, like almost every Indian business, feels the presence of the government directly or indirectly. During the Emergency, Advani had famously said that when the media was asked to bend, it crawled. Today, without a legal Emergency, while the government outwardly preaches the virtue of free press, it also expects the media to fall in line behind the government.[91]

Journalists in the US may be called names by President Trump but they need not fear violent reprisals or being 'silenced' as there are several detailed checks and balances against politicians attempting to intimidate the media. In India, it would be unthinkable for a media house to openly endorse a particular candidate. Can you imagine what would happen if the rival won? The Indian press, unprotected by rule of law, has always been a victim of arbitrary political authority.

Journalists today are timid and have become deeply fearful because there is an asymmetry in the power equation with the government. Journalists have become used to being pulverized by politicians, denied access and advertising if they push too hard. If a media house does endorse a politician then it is likely that its opinion is determined by partisan loyalty rather than a free editorial choice.

Be it the often violent clampdown on the 'bourgeois' press by the Left, or the denial of newspaper advertising to hostile newspapers by the Bihar government[92] or the slapping of sedition charges on the Ahmedabad edition of the *Times of India*, regimes of all hues have sought to snatch away press freedom. The notorious 'fake news' circular issued by the Modi government in April 2018, a directive that a government-appointed committee had the power to take away the accreditation of journalists 'found guilty' of publishing 'fake news', an order that was subsequently hurriedly withdrawn, was nothing but an attempt to bring the press to heel, crack and whip and show who's boss.[93]

In 2016, the Modi government ordered a ludicrous one-day ban on the Hindi news channel NDTV India for its coverage of the attacks on the Pathankot army camp on 2 January 2016, apparently for revealing 'sensitive details'. The Supreme Court intervened and the ban was ominously put 'on hold'. However, the fact that it was even announced was yet another instance of government muscle-flexing over the media. BJP president Amit Shah even said 'nationalism'—the ruling party's current battle-cry—could not be questioned under the guise of freedom of expression. If the act of asking questions is criminalized then the day is not far when journalists will be treated as law-breakers for simply doing their jobs. They are already in danger of being stigmatized as such. Long before journalists, ordinary citizens and RTI activists have been hauled over burning coals for criticizing or questioning the government.[94]

In my opinion, when a government wants to see itself as the embodiment of the 'Nation', anyone, particularly the media, who questions the government, is sometimes deemed 'anti-national'. This empowers non-state actors (that is, mobs) to threaten the media or violently assault media persons to secure obedience, while government agencies tend to look the other way.[95]

Banning a media house for providing the wrong sort of information during a national security crisis is hardly a solution to the challenge of creating a rational and accurate information flow. If channels broadcast wrong or 'sensitive' information, it is the job of the government to undertake regular briefings during a security crisis and provide more credible information that journalists can use. The information war can only be fought by more credible information, not by forcibly shutting down sources of information, because every rumour and speculation will come out anyway in some form.

Attempting to control information in the age of social media is stupidly futile. In spite of the Madhya Pradesh government's loud defence, the video of the 'encounter' of alleged SIMI activists in Bhopal[96] went viral. Hizbul commander Burhan Wani (see Chapter 1) did not need the TV or newspaper media to spread his message; he gained an enormous following by using only social media. In a furiously competitive media environment, governments will have to compete to provide truthful, accurate and credible information of the actions they undertake in the name of the citizen. If they don't, they'll be overtaken by multiple news sources. Banning NDTV India for a day may gratify netas and babus and satiate their egos, but rumours and viral videos will keep spinning in cyberspace. Indira Gandhi defeated the news, but even she couldn't defeat the rumours that eventually contributed to her downfall.

Some channels may have broadcast irresponsibly during the 26/11 terror attack,[97] the reason the Cable Act was amended in the first place. But if such violations cause the muzzling of the press then bad reporting and rumours will only be driven underground. Attacking the media is the illiberal politicians' favourite blood sport, as if the media is responsible for their political fortunes. Yet, a free press is the infrastructure of a liberal democracy and any attempts to ban it or censure it will take a terrible toll on the freedom of all citizens. As journalist and author Bee Rowlatt puts it, 'Today if you want journalists to shut up, there will come a time when somebody will ask you to shut up and there'll be nobody to speak for you.'[98] Besides, censoring the press doesn't necessarily deliver political rewards. Indira Gandhi censored the press for two years. The people at large saw and heard only massive Emergency propaganda hailing her. Did it stave off her defeat in 1977? The BJP launched a gargantuan publicity campaign during the 2015 Bihar assembly polls. Did it bring victory? No, it brought crushing defeat.

Yet, today, every politician feels free to abuse journalists. 'Presstitutes', tweeted General V.K. Singh, then minister of state for external affairs in the Modi government. Prime Minister Modi has called journalists 'bazaru'. Today, the adversarial and combative interview is almost dead. No politician feels the need to face a genuinely probing no-holds-barred interview any more. Nor does illiberalism towards the press rest only with 'nationalists'. It was the secular Congress who in Indira Gandhi's time imprisoned 253 journalists and Rajiv Gandhi, who tried to bring in the Anti-Defamation Bill.

Since the 1980s, India's press has been co-opted by the state, either through a friendly owner, or through patronage, such as government awards. And India's media under the 'nationalist' BJP has continuously slipped. In the World Press Freedom Index 2018, it ranks 138 out of 180 nations. The India Freedom Report: Media Freedom and Freedom of Expression 2017 by media website Hoot shows eleven journalists murdered, forty-six attacked and twenty-seven cases of police action in 2017.

For liberals, a huge, diverse, chaotic, clamorous and largely uncontrollable media still provides a rough check on the system.

To quote Raja Rammohan Roy again 'The existence of a free Press is equally necessary for the sake of the governors and the governed.' In fact, as the US Supreme Court held, the press must always stand in an adversarial position to those in power 'because the press exists to serve the governed, not the governors'.[99]

Sanjaya in the Mahabharata was perhaps the subcontinent's first journalist. He was given a boon for long-distance vision, so that the blind king Dhritarashtra could hear an honest account of developments on the battlefield. Clearly, even the Mahabharata recognized that a ruler needed to have true information to be able to judge a situation properly. Equally, citizens benefit from a free press providing accurate news and a diversity of views so that, empowered by news and views, citizens are able to hold the government accountable at every turn.

Liberals, Don't Fall Silent!

So-called 'nationalism' rages on in swathes of Indian society. An aggressive anti-modernity has taken hold, leading to unparalleled cultural and political regression. When individual freedoms simply do not matter, why should press freedom be regarded as remotely worth defending?

These are years which have seen the axe murder of Mohammad Afrajul in Rajsamand,[100] the death of sixteen-year-old Junaid on a train[101] and of activist Zafar Khan in Pratapgarh, who died while trying to protect the dignity of a group of women who were being photographed as they answered nature's call in the open.[102] We have seen attacks on carol singers.[103] In the communal outbreak in Kasganj in January 2018, a Hindu was killed and a Muslim was blinded in one eye.[104] Law and order, the primary and fundamental responsibility of the government and so essential for a liberal climate of entrepreneurial innovations and business confidence, does not seem to exist when religious and 'nationalist' identity is so terrifyingly dominant.

How can intellectual freedom and openness flourish, if the government does not maintain impartial law and order, but at times instead even provokes violence? Political populism leverages the public's baser emotions like anger and hate for votes. Populist ideologies also massively expand the scope of the government, trapping citizens in a cage. Despite differing ideological veneers, populism of all shades is united in its unbridled statism. How can citizens driven by hate and trapped in a government cage, create a dynamic entrepreneurial country?

The liberal alternative instead believes in the capacity of people. In the people's inherent ability to aspire for the best within themselves and be inspired towards freedom, peace and prosperity. It's the enterprise and moral sense of every individual that can roll back the menacing Big State and its agents, which are politicians armed with dictatorial powers, always trying to curb people's individual freedoms, economic opportunities as well as cultural preferences.

As we are arguing through this essay, the seculars first created the Big State, the Hindutvavadis took it to its maximum heights. A similar process can be seen in the way the 'soft Hindutva' of Indira Gandhi only paved the way for the subsequent hard Hindutva of the BJP. The 'soft' Big State of an earlier Congress era increased government power through Aadhaar and laws like 66A of the IT Act. But because it was a soft Big State it still tolerated, for example, the informal sector and the cash economy. The new hard Big State of the Hindutva regime is a much more remorseless Big State moving to crush individual freedoms in fundamental ways. An example of this is the demonetization decision and how the entire cash-based informal sector of the economy was overnight made illegal! The soft version of Aadhaar implemented by the UPA has given way to the harder version of the Hindutva Aadhaar which is its use as a weapon of guilty-until-proven-innocent.

Gandhi, India's best liberal, believed India had a special mission in the world: to spread the doctrine of the individual and his moral conscience: 'I believe that the ancients of India, after centuries of experience have found out the true thing for any human being . . . justice based on sacrifice of self, yajna and kurbani.' Gandhi led from the front, with conviction in his principles and an unshakeable confidence in the people's ability to rise to the occasion. Gandhi's politics was in sharp contrast to the crop of politicians who only repackage the same set of policies. Today's politicians prefer to lead from the back following the baser instincts of the crowd. Politicians are barely driven by ideology and conviction—religious fanaticism hardly being a democratic ideology—but only by immediate political tactics and point-scoring against each other. They are street smart, not wise, self-promoting rather than transparent.

For Gandhi, in the face of injustice, discrimination and authoritarianism, the individual had to respond with his own conscience and sense of morality and create a satyagraha against injustice. Gandhi placed the power of the individual at the centre of his political philosophy. It is the genius of Gandhi that created an utterly brilliant political mobilization movement like the salt satyagraha.[105] The salt campaign didn't need to use any easy gimmicky religious-based tactics. It actually created massive public support for policy reform based on fundamental principles. When Gandhi called for the British to 'Quit India', it was a call to the British Raj to quit ruling India as a colonial power, not a call for the British people to leave India on racist or religious grounds.

Yet, Gandhi endlessly explored. He sought knowledge. He tried to learn from contrarian views. He grappled with the many challenges of his time. Who else but a Mahatma would invite his enemies to the highest positions, asking staunch critic Jinnah to be prime minister of India or suggesting to Nehru that another implacable detractor, B.R. Ambedkar, be appointed as chairman of the Constitution's drafting committee? Could there be a greater difference in views between Gandhi and Ambedkar? While Gandhi was a declared devout Hindu, Ambedkar declared, 'There is no Hindu consciousness of any kind. In every Hindu, the consciousness that exists is the consciousness of his caste. That is the reason the Hindus cannot be said to form a society or a nation.'[106] Gandhi, on the other hand, believed that caste has nothing to do with religion and the essence of Hinduism was its 'enunciation of one and only God as Truth and its bold acceptance of ahimsa as the law of the human family'.[107] That Ambedkar and Gandhi's Congress worked so closely to create the Constitution shows how differences in views and dissent were accepted and treated with respect by India's liberal founders.

Gandhi realized that the human condition was based on the words 'I don't know, I don't have complete knowledge but am trying to know and trying to find out'. It is with the same spirit that Hindu scriptures debate endlessly and provide India's liberal tradition of discourse and debate. Krishna had to explain to Arjuna the need to go into battle through argument and persuasion in the face of Arjuna's constant questioning. Arjuna questioned God himself. Did Krishna simply command Arjuna to do his bidding? Did he issue a diktat and demand it be instantly obeyed? No, in Indian Hindu traditions, even divinities must dialogue, debate and persuade. And listen to opposing points of view.

Today 'Hindutva nationalists' believe they have a monopoly on the truth. That there is no need for any course correction. To them every differing point of view is illegitimate and intolerable. This attitude turns its back on the Gandhian inheritance, even as the Hindutva nationalist government seeks to appropriate Gandhi's charkha and spectacles for its various schemes.

But then, how many governments post-Independence have truly imbibed Gandhi's spirit? Gandhi kept admitting his mistakes and searching for what he called the truth. He started with the assumption that he did not have all the answers. Instead, he sought dialogue with as many people as he could to find the answers. Hindutva nationalists in their belief in a monopoly on the truth, in the power of their own certainties, in their intolerance of any disagreement and counter-argument, are profoundly anti-Indian, profoundly anti-liberal and profoundly against the founding ideals of India.

The Liberal Agenda

In order to change its illiberal Hindutva nationalist stance, the BJP must begin its full embrace of liberal modernity. It must forever forsake communalism and Hindutva extremism and instead seek to become a 'normal' conservative party with its identity in economic policy and cultural outlook rather than in violent Hindutva. Unless it forever abandons the Hindutva lumpen, the BJP will never become modern and the Indian Right wing will remain outsourced to the street fighters.

The conservative American writer E.J. Dionne has written of his despair at the conservative moment capitulating to Trump, ceasing to debate with its opponents and 'taking itself out of the game'. The BJP similarly will take itself out of the game if it capitulates to the Hindutva mob and does not debate with its opponents.[108]

In fact, this ought to be the prescription for any political party aspiring to win political office, not limited to the BJP. Right-wing or Left-wing parties all have their legitimate place in a democratic set-up, as do liberals. A particular political formation may be in office at one point of time, but that does not automatically make other ideological persuasions liable to be declared as 'anti-national'. Liberals generally don't feel threatened by cultural differences. In the same way, they must feel similarly unthreatened by political differences and always uphold the legitimacy of genuine ideological differences.

The liberal in India must never fall silent, however hard the Hindutva nationalists come at us. Whether protesting against capital punishment, voicing dissenting arguments on Jammu and Kashmir, supporting those who speak the language of Dalit empowerment and opposing Hindutva majoritarianism, liberals must never allow the government to shut their minds and mouths.

Hindutva nationalists believe freedom of expression is nothing but sedition, an insult to 'religion', an insult to the Indian nation, and the existence of the liberal who believes in free speech is a threat to the nation's existence. They believe in uniformity, in thought control, in a regimented policed citizenry which will only echo their own views.

'Hindutva Nationalists', from street mobs to social media gangs to politicians, are a ferocious army demanding loyalty to their culturally inadequate, militarist and politically aggressive cause. They are against anyone who disagrees and represent an engine of thought and social control that is harnessed firmly to authoritarian personality cults.

Instead of caricaturing all liberals as 'elitists' and 'anti-nationals', why don't Hindutva nationalists want to participate in a democratic debate? Why are they seeking to eliminate, shut down and silence all critics and the entire opposition in general? Any critic of this government is labelled a 'deshdrohi'; any hint of disagreement and you become an 'anti-national traitor' liable for sedition; any small critique means you are a 'minorities-worshipping', 'sickular' 'libtard', 'communist', 'dynastic Congi slave' who must instantly take up residence in Pakistan.

Why do Hindutva nationalists forget that liberal journalists questioned and exposed the Congress-led UPA too when it was in power? Was the government led by Manmohan Singh not torn apart on the 'coal scam', '2G scam' and 'the Commonwealth Games scam'?[109] But at least the Congress-led governments did not call all liberals names, the way 'Hindutva nationalists' do.

Why is debate not acceptable? Why is dissent not to be tolerated? Why are nationalists transforming social media from an important debating platform into a cacophonous echo chamber of thought control?

The religious 'nationalists' call themselves Right wing, but are they? 'Right wing' in the US and Europe implies parties who are socially conservative on issues like abortion and gay rights but zealously uphold the free market and business. Now, Hindutva nationalists may be socially conservative on Hindu–Muslim marriage and live-in relationships, but are they Right wing on the market or do they, instead of market, only believe, as historian Mukul Kesavan writes, in 'maar-kaat'?[110]

Of course, this is the traditional characterization of the Right wing—that is, socially conservative and economically market oriented. The Left wing is seen as socially liberal and economically state directed. But in recent years, with the rise of populism, originating from the Left and the Right, sometimes this division is not easy to sustain. Perhaps, in the current climate, ideology can't really be compartmentalized. Apparently, liberal positions in one sphere necessarily get compromised by illiberalism in another sphere. What we can safely say is that populist parties, whether of the Right or the Left, seek Big State governments, governments unrestricted by any democratic rules or norms and governments that seek to shut down any dialogue or give-and-take of ideas.

Why has the space for debate suddenly become so restricted? Lack of debate is also reflected in the economic sphere, constricting the economic space for entrepreneurship, employment and economic growth.

Let's throw the debate open. Let's work for a more vibrant democratic order based on respect for pluralism and diversity. The right to free speech must fundamentally include the right to dissent. Questions on policies and issues will inevitably arise. Let's not shut down all questioning. As we have been seeing throughout this book, Hinduism has always stood for freedom of thought.

From a muscle-flexing Big State on demonetization, to dictatorial cattle slaughter rules, to bans of various kinds, to the inability of the political class to stand up against vigilante mobs, to court cases and FIRs against writers and comedians, individual freedoms are imperilled to an extent that our liberal ancestors could never have dreamed of. The individual (and his freedoms) is under sustained attack from an ideologically driven state, bent on curbing freedoms to install the Hindu Rashtra.

That's why advancing and sustaining the liberal argument is more important than ever and standing up for individual freedoms is a crucial duty of public-spirited, civic-minded citizens. A rooted Indian liberalism, as fought for by Dabholkar and Pansare, has always existed. We need to fight for its open-minded cause with renewed vigour and energy.

Citizens of India, today your right to eat beef is being snatched away and you don't mind too much. Tomorrow, your right to own personal data could be snatched away. Your right to write or read all kinds of books is already censored but may be snuffed out altogether. It's a slippery slope downhill unless you act now and say that the rights and freedoms of the individual have always been sacrosanct in India. If you don't, more individual freedoms will be taken away.

In the Mahabharata, Yudhisthira asserts that it is the citizen who must be a 'prabhavi', who must have the ability, tools and space to impact governance. We must never lose our ability to reason, to argue and to express ourselves as citizens.

Democracy is not simply majority rule. Democracy is the rule of the enlightened civic-minded citizen. This is the time of the citizen. It is up to each one of us to realize why the values of openness, dissent, disagreement, individual freedoms and respect for each other matter if we are going to leave behind a sane, rational, compassionate and free India for our children and grandchildren.

Gandhi, Rajagopalachari, Ambedkar and Tagore placed enormous store by and gave enormous responsibility to the individual's own conscience and sense of morality, just as Hinduism does to the 'atma' or the individual sense of morality and God.

Liberal democracy is not rule by a raja. It's about participating and sharing in power. It's about constant citizen vigilance. Liberal democracy depends crucially on aware, brave and free-thinking citizens who speak up for their rights, for justice, for decency, for individual freedom and for non-violence. The liberal draws inspiration from the divine Krishna, who, even in battle did not seek to impose his authority on Arjuna, instead sought dialogue and persuasion. In subcontinental traditions, even the gods practice vaad vivaad samvaad. That's why we can justifiably say, garv se kaho hum liberal hain!

[5]

The Liberal Woman

Why the liberal must always oppose those who
discriminate against and stereotype women, crush
their freedoms and force them to be caricatures of an
imagined 'Indian culture'

Bidhir Badhon katbe tumi amon shaktiman
Tumi ki amni shaktiman
Amader bhanga gora tomar hate emon abhiman
Tomader emni abhiman
Chirodin tanbe piche chirodin rakhbe niche . . .

— *Gitabitan*, Rabindranath Tagore

[Are you strong enough to reverse the course of destiny
Do you think yourself strong enough
To rein in our ups and downs with audacity,
Do you think yourself audacious enough
To drag someone behind, to hold them down forever . . .]

I s the free liberal woman a threat to society?
    Is the free modern woman the enemy of religion, culture and family?

    Should women be obedient to men and elders about what they wear, when they go out and whether they use mobile phones?

    Should a woman in politics always be known as a wife, daughter or mother?

    Is a Hindu woman in perpetual danger from Muslim men?

Blind Traditionalism and Backlash against Modern Women: Whose Tradition Is It Anyway?

Citizens of India, why should you choose to be a liberal supporter of women's freedoms rather than a champion of some narrow-minded notion of 'Indian culture' or 'family values'? This question needs to be posed not just to women but to men too. Why should men—as much as women—not be inspired by the liberal cause of identifying the core aspects of injustice that affect most gender issues? Let's remember there are many social conservatives across religious and caste divides who are women. Kashmir has a burka-wearing fundamentalist women's group (the Asiya Andrabi-led Dukhtaran-e-Millat) and there are Hindu sadhvis of various hues who can be as prejudiced as any Hindutva patriarch.[1] The struggle for justice for women is not a conflict between men and women but between liberals and conservatives.

    A furious backlash against aspirational and empowered women is afoot. The backlash is part of a more comprehensive assault on women and girls in general.[2] It is part of a larger political and social campaign to ensure everybody knows their place, that society is organized into a patriarchal hierarchy and power is established over every 'other' identity—regional groups, caste and religious minorities and minorities of gender. The aim of this campaign is to marginalize these minorities (of religion, region, gender and even of sexual orientation) and establish the social and political dominance of a single ideology. Since the smallest minority is the individual, this is a project to establish dominance over every minority identity which may not conform to the dominating majoritarian collective.

Yes, there are government schemes like 'Beti Bachao, Beti Padhao'[3] and token celebrations on Women's Day. India at the moment has a woman defence minister, foreign minister and woman speaker of the Lok Sabha. But powerful women prime ministers or chief ministers, as we shall see, have not really helped improve the condition of women. Instead, they have only reconfirmed the notion that power is a great equalizer. The appeal of power reinforces conformity with the status quo and underscores the fact that power recognizes no equal.

Without real change in society, do women in high positions matter? Without a revolution in the mind, can gender justice ever be a reality? In the recent violent dance of bigotry over the film *Padmaavat*, apologists for jauhar, both among the Karni Sena and the Rajput community, stated that a woman's honour lay in leaping into flames instead of risking a possible assault. This is perverted logic. Is the suggestion here that rape victims have no right to live? If women have been victims of 'dishonour', must they sacrifice their lives? And what does this say about the men who failed to protect their women's 'honour'?

During the *Padmaavat* protests in 2017–18, the hysterical defence of the custom of jauhar actually implied that if women can't defend themselves, they should opt for death rather than survive the ordeal. The message was that women should not even try to defend themselves.

In January 2018, in a surreal coagulation of shallow modernity with an equally cock-eyed traditionalism, jeans-clad sunglasses flashing, Rajput women took out a march in Chittorgarh shouting slogans like 'Jai Jauhar, Jai Bhawani', glorifying ritual suicide. They warned that if the film was released they would all go to their deaths by throwing themselves into an inferno, since the film 'dishonoured' their cultural identity. Many even registered for mass suicide.[4] The demonization and then the celebration of Padmavati brought to the fore the extent to which women themselves can be among the greatest opponents of liberal, enlightened women.

Is this display of medievalism in campaigning *for* jauhar, not a complete reversal of the notion that modern India is a place where women are equal and rational beings, educated to reason and think as democratic-minded citizens? Don't such displays of irrational, frenzied traditionalism show a blind attachment to superstitions and rituals? Interpreting a heinous crime against women as a supreme display of cultural identity reveals a return to a nineteenth-century mindset when superstitious, ignorant orthodoxies attacked and campaigned against then colonial governor general of India William Bentinck for declaring sati illegal in 1829.

At the height of the Rajput Karni Sena's protests against *Padmaavat*,[5] it seemed as if India was hurtling back 200 years. Such is the crazily unthinking illiberal and dangerous fascination with 'culture' and 'identity' that even completely false rumours that the film suggested a possible 'romance' between a Muslim sultan and a Hindu queen spurred impassioned and enraged Islamophobia. Such was the religious hatred of the Muslim, that women did not mind declaring war on their own lives, bodies and individualities. What would Raja Rammohan Roy, a lifelong crusader against sati, have made of these protests?

The power of assertion of 'identity' is so dangerously bewitching that sleepwalking into the medieval era is seen as a return to one's roots, to authenticity, to being 'true' and 'pure'. That's why a socially conservative mindset has taken hold. The 'moral policeman mentality', which regards the free woman as Public Enemy No. 1, keeps revealing itself, frequently and angrily. Now more than ever before, to combat the hypnotizing power of a glitzy, repackaged, neon-lit tradition, or arcane backward values dressed up in Bollywood technicolour, liberals must be ranged with the struggling woman. Liberals should be at the barricades against those invoking regression as tradition and hara-kiri as sanskriti.

A model is being created where individuals are consumed by the collective. The immolation of an individual woman on her husband's funeral pyre is hailed as a victory of the collective embrace of so-called 'tradition', hailed as voluntary, hailed as a symbol of eternal wifely love and devotion. This triumph of a collective morality over the life of an individual woman has the potential to turn woman against hapless woman. The message is: in order to serve tradition, you have to die.

This collective triumphalism exemplifies power and greed. It is a willingness to inflict immense fear and pain to persuade victims to submit to the dictatorial will of the collective. When Bollywood movies which peddle downright regressive values become smash hits, it only shows how widespread is the social acceptance of these so-called misplaced 'virtues'. Why, in twenty-first-century India, was a crime against women like 'sati' or 'jauhar' being hailed as a tradition worth defending?

Citizens of India, it is time to recall that our liberal ancestors fought for women's freedom as much as they fought for India's freedom. Equality and progressive values as far as women are concerned are embedded in India's founding principles, in the very blood and sinew of the constitutional arrangement that presides, or is supposed to preside, over public life. Do we want to go back to a time when Jyotirao Phule and his wife were publicly ostracized for daring to speak about educating women? 'The Phules are out to destroy our religion!' the Pune papers wrote at the time, 'They want to educate our women! There will be chaos if women start reading and writing. They will read vulgar literature and write impish wayward letters to their husbands!'[6]

Today, there may not be open calls to stop women from being educated, but dress codes, behavioural prescriptions,[7] denunciations and even physical attacks[8] show that rising numbers of militant traditionalists want to push women back inside the lakshman rekha. The lakshman rekha patriarchally seeks to put the onus of protecting women on men. But over time this idea of 'benevolent' protection inevitably degenerates into men claiming women as their property and women's identities being seen solely in reference to men: daughter, wife, sister or mother.

The irony is that after having claimed ownership over women, when men fail to live up to their promise, the onus falls back on women to uphold the honour of men—by giving up their lives by committing jauhar or sati.

Let us put the Karni Sena in the context of our overall argument of the need to roll back state power and the power of the government from individual lives and civil society. The kind of identity politics that the Karni Sena represents is the outcome of a communalized Big State. As the Big State seeks more power, it begins to pander to communal identities or vote banks because as the state expands it reaches into every area of citizens' lives. The Big State seeks legitimacy by patronizing clients or different sets of clients, handing out patronage, quotas, sops and all manner of benefits to a range of clients (who invariably are all men). These clients could be Jats one day, Marathas one day, Patidars one day and the Rajput Karni Sena the next. Problems begin to arise because no state or government has the capacity to completely satisfy every whim and fancy of these groups, and soon this patronage system, or this network of state-sponsored identities, gets captured by vested interests who seek ever-larger shares of the pie of state patronage. After all, if Jats can get OBC status, why can't the Rajput Karni Sena hold the government to ransom for its particular identity-related demand?[9]

When the big government is a sponsor of identity, newer sets of political adventurers jump in, with newer demands, whipping up disenchantment and grievance along identity lines. All of these identity groups have their own flags and totems and they need 'enemies' and targets over which they can claim victory, never mind how many buses they need to burn or railway tracks they need to uproot in the process. For example, during the Jat protests in Haryana in February 2016, highways and railway tracks were blocked and damaged, showing that crucial public utilities don't matter when all-important 'identities' are at stake. Since the Big State needs more and more clients, no state government was able to stand firm against the regressive, obnoxious and lawless behaviour of the Rajput Karni Sena

or mount an argument against their version of woman's 'honour'.
Most state governments are now patronage dispensing machines to
minuscule identity groups. The government's tendency to intrude
into social identities and seek to co-opt them is the reason so many
group identities today have become so emboldened.

Rampaging group identities is the reason why no government
today can stand forth as a defender of liberal values. By expanding
its powers, governments have become defenders and champions
of varied identities, each free to espouse their own form of violent
illiberalness. So a government can make women's empowerment its
slogan, but at the same time not feel able or competent to put down
a violent agitation that champions a medieval notion of women's
'honour'. The possibility arises that the government never intended
to empower women, nor did it have any intention of defending the
individual woman. It is only interested in creating an image for itself
as apparently committed to gender justice.

The rise of identity politics provides a pretext to sacrifice
lesser identities, including that of the individual. Why is it that a
government can trumpet the slogan 'Beti Bachao, Beti Padhao'
but at the same time cannot strictly bring to justice those calling
for the beheading of a movie actor?[10] That's why the commitment
of governments to the official cause of 'women's empowerment'
rings so hollow and camouflages the lack of any decisive intention
to protect the rights of women. During the protests after Gauri
Lankesh's murder, the slogan was raised: 'Beti bachao, beti padhao,
par padh likh kar agar zyada bole, toh usse goli se udao.'[11]

The Big State or big government has a natural interest in
nurturing identity clients because identity-related demands help
legitimize the continuous expansion of the Big State, which as
we have seen increasingly intrudes into personal freedoms. These
identity clients help to perpetuate this interference by diverting
attention away from the government's misplaced intrusions, which
have, in the first place, restricted the individual's space in society.
For example, it is the government which has legitimized the culture

of bans. Once the government legitimizes bans, bans are then demanded by a myriad identity groups.

The continuous fragmentation of different identities illustrates the severity of government-generated scarcities. What are these scarcities? These are scarcities of delivering justice and scarcities of individual freedoms. Since there is no protection for individual rights, there is the resulting demand by different groups for more and more government largesse. Thus by chipping away steadily at individual rights, the Big State legitimizes its own expansion.

When the anti-woman, anti-freedom and anti-modern Karni Sena launched its 'war' against *Padmaavat*, very few actors or film directors spoke up for the beleaguered film or its team. The manner in which the film industry repeatedly capitulates before the government is again a result of India's expansionist state.

Rather than standing his ground, the film's director, Sanjay Leela Bhansali, repeatedly pleaded that the film did not offend Rajput sentiments. This was an acknowledgement that identity sentiments are so sacred that they should never be hurt. Logically extended, this means no work of fiction or film would be possible since all stories rely on bad people or villains in order to contrast and highlight the goodness of the protagonists. Every such negative character might necessarily offend some identity; therefore, the door would be opened for that particular aggrieved identity to assert its claim. No wonder caste groups, regional groups, linguistic groups and even professional groups like police and doctors have all protested their alleged negative depictions in films and other creative works.[12]

The American film industry, Hollywood, does not depend on government patronage. It does not get much financial support or any cultural endorsement or protection (since the law cannot be arbitrarily turned against them) from the government, nor is the fate of Hollywood movies reliant on a government-appointed censor board. This enables many artistes in Hollywood, from the time of the Vietnam War, from actors like Jane Fonda to Meryl Streep, to stand up to state agencies and political leaders without fear or favour. Can an Indian actor even think of making an anti-Trump speech like Meryl Streep did at the Golden Globe Awards in 2017, when she said that powerful people indulging in bullying and humiliation gives permission to others to do the same thing?[13]

In India, despite its enormous success and ability to raise finances without government help, the political context makes Bollywood constantly seek endorsement from and bend before the government of the day. Although the financial support of the government is quite limited, the indirect support, or lack of it, is much more critical. In the past couple of decades, the Big State has frequently refused to ensure law and order for film shows in the face of threats from various identities due to vote-bank considerations. Consequently, films which have met all legal requirements and been approved by the censor board have still not been screened in some states; for instance, *Fanaa*, which was banned in Gujarat in 2006. At times the state has not overtly prohibited a film but the owners of movie theatres themselves realized that the government is not inclined to provide them security and, therefore, as an act of self-censorship, they have chosen not to screen a particular film.[14]

Another more strangulating form of indirect control exercised by the government is through the censor board, or the Central Board of Film Certification (CBFC). The film *Kissa Kursi Ka* was famously banned during the Emergency in 1975. Since then there have been various diktats by the government-nominated censor board.[15] Although it is technically supposed to only function as a certification board and not a censor board, it is the censoring role rather than the certifying one that is to the fore. There is no parallel of a government-appointed censor board in Hollywood. It is a unique Indian monstrosity.[16]

Film-makers need protection from the government because of the constant possibility that gangs of goons nursing 'hurt sentiments' may at any time feel free to attack or burn down a movie hall. Where is the film-maker to turn to except to the government? Today, the government's power over films is enormous, which it enjoys precisely because identity politics enables it to play the arbitrator, with the prime objective being the enhancement of its own scope and role.

Former I&B minister Manish Tewari points out, 'The I&B runs all of the film business . . . myriad institutions ranging from film institutes . . . the CBFC under the Cinematograph Act 1952.' Here, the question may be asked of Manish Tewari: why are members of the Congress who ran the system when they were in power, suddenly discovering the virtues of liberalism and rolling back state power when in the Opposition? Once back in the saddle will they only revert to their anti-liberal ways, as patented by their statist ancestor Indira Gandhi? This underlies our argument through this essay that the groundwork for curtailing individual freedoms and expanding the ambit of the Big State was laid by the so-called 'secular' politicians, a state structure whose power has been inherited and maximized by politicians upholding Hindutva nationalism.

When the government's powers are so great, when its desire to keep every possible vote bank happy is so powerful, can the government, any government, protect the cause of women's freedom in the face of identity warriors as effectively as it should? The cause of women's liberation can be outsourced to mahila morchas and women's commissions and other bodies that uphold an official sarkari feminism, but these bodies are hardly forums of open, wide-ranging debates on issues of justice and equal opportunity. Nor can they tackle backward social and cultural mores that still stand in the way of modern women. By imprisoning women in the ladies' compartment or 'zenana dabba' of sarkari feminism, patriarchal tradition is only perpetuated and strengthened.[17]

Women Can be Both Kali and Sati-Savitri

India's liberal founders regarded a progressive and modern identity for women as one of their foremost missions. Misogynist ways have always been powerful and existed in strong competition with progressive values. The liberal founders were committed to the fight for progress, a fight which the present generation will need to fight too.

Rammohan Roy, the great opponent of Sati, whose efforts led to its abolition in 1829, and a lifelong campaigner for property rights for women, wrote movingly of the plight of the women he saw around him: 'At marriage the wife is treated as half of her husband, but (after marriage) they are treated worse than inferior animals. For the woman is employed to do the work of a slave in the house . . . if in the preparation or serving up of the victuals they commit the smallest fault, what insult do they not receive from their husband, their mother-in-law and the younger brothers of their husband . . . as long as the husband is poor she suffers every kind of trouble and when he becomes rich she is altogether heart-broken . . . when he takes two or three wives . . . they are subject to mental miseries and constant quarrels.'[18]

Gandhi believed that the liberation of women was necessary for the liberation of men, to escape from stereotypical notions of the dominant male, or what is today called 'toxic masculinity'. Wrote Gandhi: 'By seeking to interfere with the free growth of womanhood in India, we are interfering with the growth of free and independent spirited men.'[19]

Kamaladevi Chattopadhyay, the brilliant socialist who pioneered the revival of India's craft traditions, believed that even housewives were feminists. 'It is time society recognized that every housewife supports herself, though she may not scratch at a desk or run a machine, by the social labour she performs and the contribution she makes towards the maintenance of the home and its happiness,' she wrote.[20]

Yet today, after over six decades of independence, the lamp of progressive modernism for women is flickering. Sometimes it seems almost extinguished by a backward-looking society seemingly entranced by a treacherous romance with the past. It is not even so much of a genuine romance but a pretence to claim a legacy and legitimacy from the past so that militant traditionalists can pull off a power grab in its name.

A glorification of decrepit, discredited, old-fashioned mores, a seductive delusion of ancientness, commodifies and sexualizes women in unforeseen ways in the name of protecting culture. There is a harking to ancient tradition in order to try and justify the unjustifiable in the present, an effort at rationalization to claim a mythical legacy so that the horrors of the present can be erased.

In the quest to create a so-called 'pure' Indian culture, the purity burden is to be borne only by women. A society that cannot set women free of this burden of being the carrier of tradition, the eternal womb where the flame of 'pracheen Bharat' must burn, cannot be modern. In the past generations, many women have cried out against traditional texts like the Ramayana and voiced scathing criticism of Rama in the context of Sita's Agnipariksha. In fact, Hindu traditions provide myriad instances of non-elite women speaking up for liberal values which present-day bigots would like to ignore.

Should tradition be blindly imitated? In the epics, there are the Kauravas and Pandavas, there is both good and evil. Duryodhana and Dushyashana were as much a part of the Mahabharata as Yudhishtira, Bhima and Arjun. The figure of Krishna in the Bhagavad Gita illustrates that even gods have limited powers of persuasion over humans. Hindu mythological narratives typically show the eternal struggle between good and evil, and Krishna in the Bhagavad Gita shows that individuals must voluntarily choose to believe in what is just and voluntarily choose the righteous path.[21]

Stories from the epics show that to be human is to constantly make choices between good and evil. The present claimants to tradition have chosen to opt for Krishna's invincible army of state and government power instead of choosing Krishna himself, who reflected the good and the just and continually held up free moral choices.

Women's free choices are often seen as anti-tradition. In 2014, Haryana chief minister Manohar Lal Khattar suggested that the way women dressed was responsible for the crimes against them. 'If a girl is dressed decently, a boy will not look at her in the wrong way . . . if you want freedom, why don't they just roam around naked? Freedom has to be limited. These short clothes are Western influences. Our country's tradition asks girls to dress decently.'[22] Khap panchayats, according to him, 'make sure that a girl and a boy do not see each other in the wrong way'. But khap panchayats are known to be implacably against freedom for women! In Uttar Pradesh in 2014, a khap banned girls from wearing jeans and carrying mobile phones.[23] In 2007, another khap had ordered the killing of newlyweds Manoj and Babli. Given these unconstitutional primitive diktats, should a constitutional functionary like a state chief minister publicly applaud a khap world view?[24]

The social conservative is mortally terrified of 'free' women. Or perhaps militant traditionalists are terrified of their own powerlessness and inability to dominate independent women. Their own sense of potency seems to come from their ability to exercise arbitrary physical power over those who may not be able to defend themselves. This is the syndrome by which the Devi is worshipped and feared but the woman in real life is hammered into submission.

In 2017, Uttar Pradesh chief minister Yogi Adityanath wrote in a blog post: 'Considering the importance and honour of women . . . our scriptures have always spoken about giving her protection . . . As energy can go waste and cause damage if left free and uncontrolled, women power also does not require freedom, but protection.'[25] The potential damage that this feared female 'energy' can cause is not just to society, but also brings to the fore the visceral male fear of possible loss of social and sexual power. Shakti is typically depicted in intimidating female forms like—Devi, Durga, Kali. On the other hand goddesses like Lakshmi and Saraswati are depicted as demure and soft. To prefer one over the other is not only a distortion, but smacks of a vested interest. Why can't Durga, Kali, Lakshmi and

Saraswati exist as avatars of the same woman, possessed with the dignity of a complex individuality? Why this need to split women up as *either* nurturing *or* destructive figures?

In the same blog, Yogi quotes from Manu: '[Her] father protects [her] in childhood, her husband protects [her] in youth, and her sons protect [her] in old age.' A woman is thus never fit for independence. What a complete contrast from our liberal, progressive ancestors!

The social conservative is perpetually fixated on suitable behaviour and dress for women because he is convinced that crimes take place because women lure men into committing crimes. Mahesh Sharma, minister of state for culture in 2016, advised women visitors to India to not wear short skirts or go out at night to stay safe.[26] He did not think to advise Indian men not to harass, humiliate or molest tourists.

Sadly, Bengal chief minister Mamata Banerjee had also once voiced similar sentiments, showing women can also be influenced by illiberal ideas as men. That women of the Hindutva nationalist persuasion would be opposed to liberal, independent women is quite understandable. But that even women who have had to compete hard against men for top political jobs, as Banerjee has had to do, hold illiberal notions on gender shows just how deep the problem runs. When asked about rapes in Bengal, Banerjee dismissed them and famously called them 'shajano ghotona', or manipulated events. She also said crimes against women take place because men and women interact freely.[27]

Illiberalism towards women thus cuts across political parties. Most political parties are silent on khap panchayats.[28] On the Kathua and Unnao rape cases,[29] Congress president Rahul Gandhi, for instance, spoke out only when publicly exhorted to do so.

For the social conservative, the free, independent woman is a potential destroyer of their puritanical notion of Bharatiya sanskriti, or the puritanical notions of this so-called sanskriti. The free woman is seen as the destroyer of family values because she dares to assert herself against her husband's writ. Good Hindu women have a duty to not only be guardians of culture but also give birth to as many Hindus as possible. Can we forget what BJP MP Sakshi Maharaj said in 2015? 'The concept of four wives and forty children just won't work in India but it is high time that every Hindu woman produce at least four children to protect the Hindu religion.'[30]

Protect the Hindu religion from what exactly? After centuries of various forms of rule by Muslim rulers in different parts of India, Hindus never seemed to have felt as threatened as they apparently do today, at a time when Muslims have been the most marginalized politically and electorally than ever before.[31] There is a manufactured fear of what Muslim men can do to Hindu women. There is also a manufactured fear of what may happen if women venture out of the house too much. Perhaps because of the rising tide of conservatism, Indian women are increasingly choosing not to work. Contrary to global trends, women's participation in the workforce in India has been declining in recent decades, making it more difficult for women to seek independence. Today, India has one of the lowest rates of women's participation in the workforce in the world, with 65 per cent university-degree-holding women out of work. In other Asian countries, more women are working. In Bangladesh 41 per cent degree-holding women are out of work, in Indonesia the figure is 25 per cent.[32]

Assertive women sometimes even face blows from the police and insults from institution heads. In September 2017, when women students of the Banaras Hindu University (BHU) were lathi-charged for protesting the molestation of one of their classmates, the then BHU vice chancellor G.C. Tripathi—who had never masked his RSS identity—unleashed a volley of prejudice that glaringly laid bare the hatred the social conservative feels towards those referred to variously as 'modern girls' or 'Leftist-feminists' or 'bold women'.[33]

The BHU protests showed that even a premier educational institute in none other than the prime minister's constituency of

Varanasi practised institutionalized gender discrimination—on curfew times, non-vegetarian food and even access to the Internet.[34] The lathi-charge on the BHU girls protesting against sexual harassment was a reminder of just how panicky Indian state agencies and authorities becomes when faced with women aggressively demanding their rights. The physical violence unleashed by the police was matched by the verbal violence unleashed on social media by so-called 'nationalists' and even by the BHU vice chancellor.

Girls who talk about sexual harassment 'sell their modesty in the market', Tripathi told students, insisting in interviews that the molestation incident should be described by that quaint Victorian-era male fantasy phrase 'eve teasing', and was not a case of molestation or assault. When the girls met Tripathi to communicate their grievances about their hostel accommodation, they received a lecture on dharma and morality: 'Only those who have performed their own duty well have a right to talk about "dharma". Did you follow your duty when you sold the victim's modesty in the market?'[35] Men are excused from these standards of good behaviour because the 'boys will be boys' mentality runs deep. In this mentality, men are considered incapable of either duty or dharma.

The BHU vice chancellor's prejudice is hardly an exception. This prejudice is increasingly being legitimized as examples of a necessary assertion of 'Indian culture' or Indian mores, as a riposte to girls who are becoming too 'forward'. There is a widespread moral and cultural panic created by the publicly high achieving woman. Dress codes have been imposed by a range of educational institutions from Jammu and Kashmir to Tamil Nadu. Society celebrates women's achievements as pilots and engineers, but the public discourse is also marked by regular outlandish utterances from the powerful about how women must cover up or not venture into public spaces or be too 'forward'. An increasingly illiberal, religion-saturated society has begun to despise independent women, confusing independence and autonomy with promiscuity and licentiousness.

The Hindutva nationalist who is mostly also a social conservative likes to see women as perpetually confined within a Lakshman Rekha. She must always be seen as a traditional housewife in a sari, mangalsutra and sindoor as the flags of her unbending traditionalism and repudiation of western culture. As already noted, most women in mainstream political parties, notably in the BJP, dress in this way, presenting themselves as archetypal Bharatiya naris with tokens of Hindu culture emblazoned on their bodies.

In fact, the politicization of the sari was evident when actor Raveena Tandon tweeted the following in June 2017: 'A sareee day . . . will I be termed communal,Sanghi,bhakt,hindutva icon?if I say I love wearing the saree and I think it's the most elegant [sic].' Apparently, Tandon thought, entirely misguidedly, that by adopting the sari she was thumbing her nose at 'liberals', that she was being a Hindutva icon in the face of liberals' jeans-clad hipness. This is an absurd construct, showing that for social conservatives the sari is apparently a symbol of cultural and political assertion and a shriek against so-called 'Westernized liberals'.

Little do they know that India's so-called Westernized feminists liberals have more often than not worn saris. CPM leader Brinda Karat is always in a sari. Most Indian politicians from Sheila Dikshit to Mamata Banerjee always wear saris, and Indira Gandhi's saris were always on dazzling display as prime examples of Indian handloom traditions. Arundhati Roy, the arch enemy of Hindutva 'nationalists', wore a sari to receive her Booker Prize in 1997. It was the RSS, apparently the torchbearer of 'Indian tradition', which first chose to wear Westernized shorts and then full trousers, both foreign imports, even as it claims to be the gatekeeper of Indian traditions. To claim that the sari is a symbol of Hindu *sanskar* is as absurd and comic as to claim that the salwar kameez is a symbol of north Indian attire when it is widely worn in the south. It is as absurd to believe that the hijab, if worn as a personal choice, immediately identifies a woman as a fundamentalist (as opposed to a believing) Muslim.

Hindutva social conservatives have got it all wrong. They think it's 'Indian tradition' to cage and trap women, when Indian women like Rani Lakshmibai[36] and Raziya Sultana[37] cast off conventions of traditional women and blazed trails as monarchs and leaders in battle. Social conservatives fear the energy of the free woman in a country where Dalit viranganas like Jhalkari Bai[38] are known to have distinguished themselves on the battlefield. Do we find this fantasy of a 'pure', modest, caged, downcast woman anywhere in the Ramayana and the Mahabharata?

Kunti was the mother of five sons born from five different gods. Her first-born was Karna, born before her marriage due to her prayers to the Sun God, who she abandoned. Sita preferred to sink into the earth rather than live out the rest of her days with a husband who had forced her to take a purity test. Sita, one of the icons of the champions of Hindutva 'tradition', actually rebelled against patriarchal authority and raised her sons as a single woman[39]—sons who turned out brave enough to defeat their father in battle. Hindu traditional lore is full of bold, spirited and individualistic women who were unafraid to stand against social convention. Almost every famous woman from the Indian epics and mythologies is individualistic and heroic in her own way, including Sati and Savitri, the two names synonymous with the ideal Bharatiya nari.

Feminism Is Desi, Not Western!

We do not have to press the epics and traditional texts to our cause to argue why we need to constantly agitate for greater freedom for women. India's liberal founders comprised highly educated and adventurous women, unafraid to follow their hearts and embrace great causes outside the home. Our courageous foremothers, Aruna Asaf Ali,[40] Lakshmi Sahgal,[41] Rajkumari Amrit Kaur,[42] Sarojini Naidu,[43] Bhikaji Cama,[44] Kalpana Dutt[45] and Kamaladevi Chattopadhyay[46] were involved in a range of activities, from political participation to combat in war to revolutionary struggles to leading workers' protests. Pritilata Waddedar[47] joined 'Master da' or Surya Sen's band of revolutionaries, and was perhaps the only woman revolutionary who on being injured during a raid swallowed cyanide rather than face capture by the British police. There's even a statue of Waddedar in Chittagong, in Bangladesh. These are the stout-hearted women we are descended from.

Importantly, India can boast of an indigenous liberal feminism that is not simply a copy of Western ideas but one created by generations of women who have campaigned for greater opportunities in public life and for income generation and the right to livelihood for women.

The women's movement in India, its leaders castigated as 'the bindi brigade' by the Hindutva Right wing, has always been an ally of 'movements from below', women's movements rooted in India's soil.[48] Indian feminists of the 1970s may have been liberal and Westernized themselves but nevertheless allied with grassroots movements. For example, the anti-alcohol agitations by women in Shahada, Maharashtra, their feminist struggle rooted in the daily realities of women.

Liberal and Left feminists have marched against the Mathura rape case of 1972, supported the campaigns of the mothers of the dowry death victims of 1982, supported the women who stood up for their rights during the Chipko movement, campaigned against the terrible sati incident in 1987 and rallied for justice for Bhanwari Devi in 1992[49] and Shah Bano in 1985. These are not women who can be described as 'alien'—'Westernized', 'femi-nazis'. They were and are Indian women, rooted in their own milieu, asking for justice by following in the footsteps of countless women who fought for India's freedom in the 1940s and before that women who through the centuries campaigned for social reform. The struggle for women's freedom is centuries old in India. The public-spirited woman who is active outside the home is as much a tradition as the home-bound soul who chooses to nurture the family.

When Hindutva traditionalists demand that Indian women uphold 'Indian culture', what and whose culture are they talking about? The culture of Jhansi ki Rani? Gargi Vacaknavi of the Upanishads? Of Ahilyabai Holkar?[50] Of Sarojini Naidu and Lakshmi Sahgal and Kamaladevi Chattopadhyay? Of the marching, campaigning women of the post-Independence era? The so-called timid, shy woman caged in patriarchal protection, wrapped in a sari and bejewelled from head to toe, as if the gold bangles are her handcuffs and the necklaces her prison chains, exists only in the imaginations of the militant social conservatives.

Even in the nineteenth century, fiery Indian women cried out for freedom from stereotypes. To quote the Marathi writer Tarabai Shinde: 'Men, [you say] you're stronger than her when it comes to brains . . . women are whirled about many whims . . . women are the very abode of debauchery . . . women are a very city of thoughtlessness . . . women are ignorant, just like female buffaloes in a pen . . . women are the storehouse of all guilt . . . [on Sita] . . . it was that whore who really ruined Ravana. See what these wretched women get up to, destroying homes and kingdoms . . . it's all women's fault. Sita even took the fire ordeal, but people still went on blaming her. Did that make Ramchandra all the greater or something?'[51]

Tarabai's fearless critique of Ram, the 'Purushottam' or perfect man, shows that the spirit of freedom has long germinated in the hearts of Indian women. Liberal women have often chosen to risk opprobrium, stand up for what they believed to be right and exercised their right to express themselves in their chosen way, in the face of social norms, cultural preferences and political correctness. It is the imagined, cock-eyed love affair with some Vedic fantasia or a comic book version of tradition which is leading twenty-first-century Indians to shun their deeply liberal traditions.

The *Guardian* columnist Polly Toynbee writes how the traditionalists' perverted hatred of a woman's body places modern women on a collision course with religious conservatives of all hues, because 'to be modern is to set the woman free'.[52] Toynbee writes: 'Clashing against the modern world, religions founder on their sexual fetishes . . . sex always means women . . . religions define their identity through fixation on women's bodies—ritual baths, shaving heads, purdah, keeping unclean women from the altar.'[53]

The free modern woman is the prime enemy of religious orthodoxies, whether Hindu or Muslim. Eve, as Toynbee writes, is always the temptress, perpetually guilty for Adam's downfall because of her dangerous sexuality. Thus, she must be forever caged and, euphemistically speaking, 'protected', in order that men are kept safe from her evil ways.

The sarsanghchalak (head) of the RSS, (the RSS being the ideological parent of the current BJP-led government) Mohan Bhagwat has said that Hindu women should perform their household duties without getting 'distracted by anybody'.[54] The BJP leader from Madhya Pradesh Kailash Vijayvargiya once declared that women should dress according to Indian culture and not wear clothes that provoke others.[55] How different are these Hindutva voices from Islamic clerics issuing fatwas on Sania Mirza's tennis skirts or insisting women stay in purdah?[56] In fact, purdah among Hindu women continues to be practised in some parts of north India where women are seen with their *pallu*s pulled down to the chin. A century ago, purdah or veils pulled down below the face, was the expected norm across much of India.

For the militantly traditional, a woman is either virgin or whore, devi or dayan, bikini-clad vamp or sari-swaddled Sati-Savitri. It is a perverse sex-suffused binary vision that prevents a woman from ever attaining the status of either an individual or a citizen with equal rights, or even a human being.

The ongoing romance with traditional fantasies legitimizes the backlash against 'Westernized elitist feminists.' This means it's open season on any woman perceived to be liberated. The attacks on women journalists on social media, diatribes against women activists, howls against Arundhati Roy or Priyanka Chopra and the showering of blows on BHU girls are all part of a traditional society recoiling in fury against assertive modern women who insist on their rights as individuals.[57]

Pummelled by globalization and its popular culture, social conservatives yearn for the golden age of Bharat, an imagined pre-British, pre-Mughal 'authentic' and 'pure' Vedic homeland. This is actually a globalization-inspired love affair with ancientness which legitimizes the curtailment of a woman's democratic rights. There are two dimensions here: on the one hand, the hypocritical desire for a Sati-Savitri who will demur and quietly submit to everything a man may hurl at her. On the other hand, there is an incessant demand for sexual gratification in every form imaginable as seen in the rising demand for porn and commodifying women in entertainment media (see Chapter 4.)

The space to question traditions from the perspective of gender justice is shrinking. Male-centric festivals such as karva chauth, Shivratri or bhai dooj cannot be reinterpreted or reimagined, just as those campaigning for a clean Diwali or waterless Holi are cast as 'anti-Hindu'. The woman who seeks to interrogate traditions in the light of modernity is seen as going against tradition itself and also demonized as 'anti-Hindu'.[58]

In September 2017, in a judgement that was met with some outrage, the Punjab and Haryana High Court granted bail to three rape accused stating it was the rape victim who was apparently 'promiscuous' and 'voyeuristic'.[59] The judgement can be criticized as smacking of the traditionalist's dread of the sexually active woman. It's a mentality that implies that if a woman lacks unimpeachable Sati-Savitri-style virtue she's immediately asking to be raped. In the Mahmood Farooqui case,[60] the judgement dwelt on the woman's 'feeble no' and 'act of passion actuated by libido'.[61] These words seem to suggest that unless a woman is a 'pavitra nari' in the purest sense, unless she's a demure Sita shyly crouching inside her Lakshman rekha, there can be no violation or assault.

A similar mindset can be seen in the way the courts and the media viewed Dr Nupur Talwar, who, along with her husband Dr Rajesh Talwar, was convicted in the murder of their daughter Aarushi before being later acquitted.[62]

During the tortuous legal journey of the Aarushi Talwar murder case it became intriguingly clear that a morality play was afoot. Simply because the Talwar couple were professionals, worked late hours, kept alcohol in their home and that Nupur is a poker-faced, striding, tall professional woman betraying none of the stereotypical symptoms of a traditional falling-to-pieces grief-stricken mother, the Talwars were made out both in the media and in the language of judgements as examples of people living a depraved modern lifestyle, of the horrors that await when 'Indian values' are lost. So surcharged was the moral fervour against a young professional couple and their daughter that any defence of the Talwars became a defence of modern depravity where scantily clad adolescent daughters dallied with domestics in a world of rich people (when the Talwars, both doctors, are by no means super rich) who drink whisky and pursue swinging, partner-swapping lifestyles. At the now-infamous press conference after the murders, the inspector-general of police Gurdarshan Singh opined that the murder was an 'honour killing'. He told a deliciously shocking story about how not only was father Rajesh having an affair with mother Nupur's friend, but also that Aarushi, as 'characterless' as her parents, was also having an affair with the domestic help, Hemraj. Thus, said the police, the enraged, licentious father first killed the help; then, after a few pegs of whisky, turned his wrath on his daughter for betraying the honour of his family and killed her too. As author Avirook Sen puts it, 'people watched Gurdarshan Singh tell his tale of murder and debauchery . . . in TV ratings terms it was astounding . . . and the press went wild with stories of an adulterous father and a sexually precocious daughter.' Wrote journalist Vir Sanghvi: 'Most worrying of all is the IG's obsession with sex. Every possible motive leads back to sex . . . this is not a sex crime. So why is the Noida police going on and on about sex?'[63]

The newspapers spoke of Nupur almost as a nameless horror figure in their reports, referring to her as a nameless 'she'. 'She' read the Hanuman Chalisa in jail and 'she' ate vegetables in jail.[64] When she was denied bail, the CBI court order read like a hysterical moral indictment: 'The legal history is replete with instances of matricide and fratricide. Everything is possible in these days of modern era where moral values are fast declining and one can stoop to the lowest level.'[65] Another court judgement pronounced the Talwars as 'freaks'.[66]

The widespread anxiety about the 'loss' of culture and loss of values leads to women being perceived, as Nupur Talwar was, as capable of any wickedness, including murdering her own child. A sensible rational defence has now rubbished this lurid morality play that was continually broadcast by the media, and the Talwars were acquitted by the Allahabad High Court in October 2017.

The woman who does not fit stereotypes is likely to be demonized as a she-devil. As women cast off the hypocritical robes of male-defined purity, patriarchs are resorting to misogynist stereotypes, shrieking out abuse against those they call 'shameless' women. Shades of these 'impurities' are suggested against women in the public eye, who happen to be either glamorous or high-profile. While on the campaign trail in 2012, then Gujarat chief minister Narendra Modi made the following remark about Congress MP Shashi Tharoor's then new wife, the late Sunanda Pushkar: 'Wah, kya girlfriend hai. Apne kabhi dekha hai 50 crore ka girlfriend?'[67] The '50 crore girlfriend' satisfies every stereotype of so-called 'modern' women: valueless, purchasable, lacking morality, just one shade away from whore. The subject of Pushkar's tragic demise has now become a controversy for Tharoor.

Crimes against Women and the Women's Magna Carta

On the evening of 16 December 2012, a twenty-three-year-old physiotherapy intern and her friend Awinder Pratap Pandey went to watch the film *The Life of Pi* at a Saket theatre. On their way home, they boarded a bus. In the bus, the driver and five others raped and assaulted her with such ferocity that the attack became a kind of ritual dismemberment, with one of them yanking out her insides with his bare hands. Stripped and bleeding, 'Nirbhaya' (as she was called in the media) and Awinder were dumped on the road, where they lay in the cold, screaming for help but receiving only curious stares. They were taken to hospital only an hour later. After eleven days, Nirbhaya was moved to a Singapore hospital, where she died on 29 December 2012.

Her death led to a powerful protest movement. She was dubbed 'Nirbhaya' because of the courage she had shown in fighting off her attackers. The Nirbhaya moment seemed at the time to become a turning point for India's women, particularly for young women living in urban surroundings. As Nirbhaya lay dying in hospital, crowds poured on to the streets in Delhi and other cities, grieving, enraged, braving the cold and police lathis. Wrote a lawyer about Nirbhaya's days in hospital: 'Over the last few weeks we watched with amazement your courageous epic struggle.' Those words seemed to echo in thousands of ears as citizens swarmed into the lawns around Delhi's India Gate for the extraordinary protest movement that began in those chilly weeks of December. To this protest came women, young and old, mothers and fathers, bikers, guitar-playing students, activists, all saying 'enough is enough, women will not tolerate more violence'. It was an unusual, radicalizing moment for Delhi, a time when priorities were reordered and preconceptions were challenged. It was a surreal awakening; it seemed like a game-changing time.

Television played its part. Protest and coverage became a self-perpetuating cycle. Crime is always good television but this was not just any old rape story. This was a sudden mesh of youth, citizenship, anger and desire for change that coalesced into a mini-revolution. The Nirbhaya protest movement became a symbol of liberal citizenship, a movement where citizens led the courts and Parliament towards real change in law and policy.

Out of that public anger around India Gate at Nirbhaya's death rose one of the finest institutions India's liberal democracy has seen. Three wise liberals strode into the fray, took responsibility for the future and took on the task of framing legal guidelines to protect future generations of women. The late Justice J.S. Verma, late Justice Leila Seth and former solicitor-general Gopal Subramaniam, in a record time of twenty-nine days, produced the comprehensive, thorough and pathbreaking J.S. Verma Committee report on justice for women which broke new ground in giving an expanded definition of rape, even proposing a Bill of Rights for women.

Reigniting the dreams of India's liberal ancestors, the report declared, 'every woman has the right to express and experience complete sexual autonomy including with respect to her relationships and choice of partners'. Calling for police reforms, the report recommended, 'a standard of policing which is based upon a positive and co-operative relationship between civil society and the police service.'[68] Parts of the Verma Committee report were incorporated into the Criminal Law Amendment Bill of 2013 which has enhanced punishments for assaults against women. On 9 July 2018, six years after the crime which the apex court had described in May 2017 as 'brutal, barbaric and diabolic' and a crime that had created a 'tsunami of shock', the Supreme Court upheld the death sentence for the Nirbhaya convicts.

Tragically, though, despite changes in the law, brutal assaults on women and girls continue. It is almost as if the Nirbhaya moment had never happened. Tough laws have not stopped crimes against women. The Thomson Reuters Foundation 2018 survey has stated that India is the most dangerous country in the world for women in terms of sexual violence, trafficking, forced marriage and labour and sexual slavery. After the rape and murder of an eight-year-old Bakherwal girl in Jammu, the government passed an ordinance enhancing the punishment for rape from seven years to ten years. Earlier, women and child development minister Maneka Gandhi had announced the death penalty for anyone found guilty of raping children under twelve years. However, less than 3 per cent of reported crimes since 2012 have seen convictions.[69] Given the poor quality of investigation, indifferent or callous prosecution and a judicial system dogged by delays, merely strengthening the law is unlikely to either deter or secure a better conviction rate; instead, it may even open new avenues for misuse.

The important question is: have mindsets changed? No, they haven't. In 2013, former CBI chief Ranjit Sinha provoked outrage when he apparently joked that if you can't ban betting, you should enjoy it, just as you should enjoy rape if you can't prevent it.[70] In 2016, actor Salman Khan was widely criticized for saying that his schedule during the film *Sultan* was so gruelling that he felt like a 'raped woman'.[71] During the debate on the Criminal Law Bill in Parliament in 2013, Janata Dal (United) MP Sharad Yadav bellowed: 'Who amongst us has not followed girls?' Before him, another Yadav chieftain, Mulayam Singh Yadav had stated that rape was nothing but mistakes that boys make.[72] During the Nirbhaya protests, another MP this time from the Congress, Abhijit Mukherjee, none other than former president Pranab Mukherjee's son, said the protestors were only 'sundori, sundori mahila [beautiful women]' who are 'highly dented and painted', who have no connection with 'ground realities'. He also added: 'Walking in candelight processions, going to discotheques, we have also led student life, we have been students. I well know what a character of a student should be.'[73]

Deeply prejudiced mindsets, and politics will invariably colour justice delivery when the laws are crafted without regard to the problems of policing, investigation, prosecution and judiciary. In fact, this is precisely the intention of the political bosses. A stronger law creates an impression that something serious is being done. This then provides an avenue for legislators and politicians to avoid accountability by pointing a finger at everyone else, including the mindset of citizens. This is exactly how the Nirbhaya law or the Criminal Law (Amendment) Act 2013 and the POCSO law (Protection of Children from Sexual Offences Act) have played out over the past four years. Make a law, proclaim you have done something decisive, take the credit and leave it at that.

The Unnao and Kathua rape cases in 2017 and 2018 reveal how politics can overtake the course of justice when crimes are committed against women. In fact, only four months after Nirbhaya's death, newspapers ran headlines like 'Nirbhaya All over Again' when a five-year-old girl was locked in a room and sexually tormented for three days with candles and glass inserted into her vagina. Five years after Nirbhaya, India was once again confronted with that terrible sense of déjà vu, with the Kathua rape and murder case and the Unnao rape case. The statistics have remained chilling. In 2016, four rape cases were reported every hour in India; the number of reported cases increased by 88 per cent to 38,947 in 2016 from 20,737 in 2007.[74]

In the Unnao rape case of 2017, the victim was repeatedly turned away from police stations, which refused to register her complaint as the accused was a powerful BJP MLA, Kuldeep Singh Sengar. Desperate, she was driven to attempting suicide at the gates of the chief minister's residence to draw attention to her case—most shocking of all, the victim's father died in police custody, pointing towards shocking police complicity in protecting the BJP MLA. After a media outcry, the police finally arrested Kuldeep Singh Sengar and the CBI has confirmed the rape charge.[75]

The appalling Kathua rape case when an eight-year-old in a village outside Jammu was raped, mutilated and murdered in January 2018 aroused fury and horror in citizens across India. The fact that a fragile, flower-like, angelically smiling child was assaulted in so gruesome a manner sent shockwaves of revulsion and remorse through the country. Protests and marches were held and a cry went up: why was it that even members of the ruling party were sheltering those accused of this ghastly crime? After the attack on the eight-year-old, the Hindutva outfit Hindu Ekta Manch took out a march in support of the accused.

The child, belonging to a family of Bakherwals, had been watched for weeks by locals. Her abduction and murder were meticulously planned to allegedly drive her family and the entire community of Bakherwal nomads from the area. Not only was the crime shocking, more shocking perhaps was the defence mounted by elements within the ruling BJP. It was almost as if the ruling regime and its political affiliates were active participants in shaping the narrative over ghastly tragedies for their own political gain. The lawyer for the Kathua victims' family, Deepika Rajawat alleged that she was being threatened on Hindu communalist grounds by the Jammu Bar Association for taking up the case. 'I can be raped, killed,' Rajawat told the media.[76]

The Unnao and Kathua rape cases revealed that from the criminalization of politics, India has today descended into the politicization of crime, when religious and nationalist ideology is used to somehow whitewash atrocious acts, when excuses are dredged up in the form of 'whataboutery' about other rape cases.[77]

When the prevailing standard is 'everyone is guilty' then the guilty are normalized as part of that standard. Indeed, the communalization of rape is one of the most horrifying examples of a collapse of the rule of law. Both in the Unnao and Kathua cases political interference was intense. In Unnao, it was revealed that the police were operating under the orders of powerful politicians[78] and in Kathua certain lawyers even sought to obstruct justice by preventing the police from filing a charge sheet.[79]

The rule of law, respect for human freedom, rights and dignity is what separates civilization from terrorism. The liberal must locate her campaigns in a fair and just application of the law—law without religion or politics, law which does not bow to any vote bank. Until the rule of law takes deep root in India, the free woman or girl, among others, is doomed.

Across India, in these deeply worrying circumstances, blithe womanly courage is up against those for whom assaulting women is a muscle-flexing flaunting of political and social power. In this milieu, the morality of the rape victim remains deeply conflicted. On the one hand, she is the victim but on the other, as seen in the case of the victim of the Park Street rape case (the woman assaulted in a Park Street pub in Kolkata in February 2012), she is often seen as someone of easy virtue. After the Park Street case, political voices rang out that the victim had left her two daughters at home to go drinking in a pub and only got the fate she deserved because of her moral lapses. TMC MP Kakoli Ghosh Dastidar even described the assault as not a crime but a 'misunderstanding between two parties involved in professional dealing—a woman and her client'. In fact, the misuse of rape charges is often cited by politicians and parallels are drawn with the many instances of the misuse of Section 498A or the anti-dowry law.[80]

Yes, instances of misuse of gender justice legislation do exist but given the brutal prejudices out there a tough law is at least some protection, even if it doesn't prevent instances of victim shaming by politicians and media.[81] Rape still exists in the realm of the lascivious and the forbidden, a woman's victimhood coexists with her guilt, rape is subliminally regarded as the result of female promiscuity or uncontrolled sexuality, almost always a taint on the woman. In illustrated media graphics of rape victims, the female silhouette is always a curvaceous bosomy figure with flowing hair fleeing, damsel-in-distress style, from oversized male hands. Rape is not seen as the crime against an individual that it is, but shot through with an almost tantalizing hint of guilty pleasure, wild lifestyles and secret obscenity. Women have to find a way to deal with and refuse to accept socially imposed guilt. There are some brave women who have attempted to walk that path, the Park Street victim being one of them. Sunny Leone, an actor in adult cinema, is another who has refused to be shamed or acknowledge any guilt imposed by social norms, conducting herself with dignity despite suggestive questions by the media.[82] Shaming and humiliating unconventional women is the easiest recourse of a traditional society seeking to obstruct their progress.

The liberal must use the Justice Verma Committee report as a blueprint of how we approach crimes against women. The liberal constantly tries to bring public attitudes in tune with constitutional values. The Verma Committee report which recognizes marital rape and the right to sexual orientation, sexual autonomy and bodily integrity is a crucial template for a progressive awareness of justice for women. However hard the conservatives may have denounced the Verma committee as 'femi-nazi', the fact is that it has, at least on paper, given more freedom to women and shown more awareness than any legislation so far. In a country where fatwas are issued against women tennis players, where dress codes for women are routinely prescribed in universities, where vigilante groups like the Sri Ram Sene take it upon themselves to act as moral policemen and assault women in a pub, a liberal, progressive document like the Justice Verma Committee report stands as a silent sentinel for women's rights, it is indeed a Magna Carta or a charter of rights for India's women. It is a report that harks to the liberal citizenship of India's founders in that it makes the quest for greater democratization a part of freedom for women and gender justice an integral part of the widening of democracy. Yet, while a useful guidepost, the report is still no substitute for the long battle to change prevailing social norms, which the current generation of women and men will have to undertake if we are to create real change.

Holding Hands or Drinking Beer? Watch Out for the Morality Cops!

So deep are the fears about 'Westernization' and of modern women that with the exception of eminent writer, late U.R. Ananthamurthy, who said that anti-terror laws should be enforced against the pub attackers,[83] almost none of Karnataka's galaxy of public intellectuals came to the defence of the young women attacked at Amnesia Lounge in Mangalore.

Days before Valentine's Day, on 24 January 2009, around forty members of the Sri Ram Sene barrelled into Amnesia and beat up a group of women gathered there, dragging them out of the pub by their hair while screaming that they were 'violating Indian values'. The founder of the Sene, Pramod Muthalik, later declared on television that the Sene was fully justified since girls going to pubs was not acceptable.[84] As we have already noted, Goa chief minister Manohar Parrikar commented, 'I have begun to fear now, because even girls have started drinking beer.' The minister later retracted his statement but it had already revealed a mentality: male moral policemen were attempting to shame women wherever they could. Patriarchal forces have become so emboldened that they are not only openly violent but also propagate that women who are not conventional enough must be publicly censured. In September 2018, a woman media professional was murdered in Indore by a stalker who confessed he killed her because she had a 'modern lifestyle and many male friends'.[85]

In her interview with one of the accused in the Nirbhaya rape case, film-maker Leslee Udwin, who made the BBC documentary 'India's Daughter', records how one of the rapists, Mukesh, was convinced he had done no wrong, that he had felt compelled to teach 'Nirbhaya' a lesson because she was alone at night with a man in a bus, that women should never be out of the house with men who were neither their husband nor brother. Mukesh felt, Udwin recounts, he was doing his duty according to India's age-old traditions.[86] He told Udwin: 'A decent girl won't roam around at 9 o'clock at night. Housework and housekeeping is for girls, not roaming in discos and bars, doing wrong things, wearing wrong clothes.' Mukesh also said he was quoting what he had heard from politicians.[87]

Yet Nirbhaya's short life reveals how the social conservatives are being seriously challenged at the grassroots. Liberated women in India don't come from elite, Western-educated backgrounds any more. Her parents, Asha Devi and Badrinath, are first-generation urban dwellers who sold their ancestral land to educate their daughter, so determinedly did they want her intelligence and free spirit to thrive. In her photos, Nirbhaya appears as an attractive young woman with a no-nonsense gaze, a square-shouldered forceful presence that seems impossible to ignore or repress. She was a girl, yet she occupied a central place in her family's life, and her family was centred around her ambitions. Within a modest, lower-middle-class family thrived an unexpected resolve, a vision that dreamed of Nirbhaya becoming a doctor and a professional high achiever and like any successful son, taking the family name to great heights.

So, if the militant traditionalists believe that only middle-class, privileged women are 'feminists', they must think again. They must recognize how many feminists are being born in Indian homes across regions and income groups and how many of them in villages or tiny towns are increasingly questioning the burdens of their gender. This is precisely why the liberal must ally with these million female mutinies, never give up the fight against discrimination and violence and never fall prey to arguments about a defence of Indian 'culture' to stall the spread of fundamental dignity of the individual, and his or her democratic rights.

The Holy Glass Ceiling

In 2006, women devotees began a renewed demand to enter and pray at the Sabarimala temple in Kerala. The Sabarimala shrine, where women between the ages of ten and fifty were strictly prohibited, is a shrine to male celibacy. It's the temple of Lord Ayyappan, said to be the god of the Brahmachari or the celibate. If women are allowed into Sabarimala, says the *thantri*, or chief priest, the underlying meaning of the temple will be destroyed and the purpose of the arduous pilgrimage to Sabarimala which men undertake will be nullified.[88] So, were the female voices who called for the entry of women into Sabarimala guilty of forcing an artificial modernism into a traditional place of prayer where the God's traditions have been kept alive for hundreds of years? No, they were not. As we have been arguing, traditions are best kept alive when they are reinterpreted for the times in which we live. We have noted that religious orthodoxies tend to be hostile to free women, but is it time this hostility ends? Should modern institutions uphold the old fashioned notion that menstruating women are 'dirty' and 'polluted' defilers of holy places? In its judgement delivered on 24 July 2018, the Supreme Court held that the ban on entry of women into Sabarimala would have to be tested on constitutional grounds. In its path-breaking judgement delivered on 28 September 2018, the Supreme Court held that the practice of barring women devotees to the Sabarimala temple was 'illegal, unconstitutional and arbitrary'.[89]

Haven't Indian traditions always freely re-interpreted women's role in religion and religious practices? The Bhakti cults around Krishna and Mirabai are very open to women, and many women over the years have joined the Vaishnav movement. The fourteenth-century woman mystic of Kashmir, Lal Ded, revered by both Hindus and Muslims and in many depictions shown as stark naked, was known for her devotional Shaivite poetry. If religion was truly confined to the private space, any apparent discriminations would have been accepted as legitimate private choice because liberals cannot police private preferences as long as they do not actually violate someone else's rights. But the issue here is different. Temples like Sabarimala are seen as public institutions, primarily because of the money and assets they have compiled from donations by devotees. And as public institutions, active in the public domain, they must abide by modern constitutional values. Thus, it is difficult to justify discrimination on the basis of gender at holy shrines, particularly as social and religious norms in the subcontinent have constantly evolved and changed over time.

The Catholic Church's ban on abortion and contraception has long placed it in opposition to feminists worldwide. Many largely Catholic countries have either tolerated violations of these bans or have legalized such deviations. Importantly, in May 2018, the Republic of Ireland voted overwhelmingly to overturn the ban on abortion after an Indian-origin woman in Ireland died of infection because she was denied an abortion.[90]

Many have suggested that the reason Dan Brown's *The Da Vinci Code* became a bestseller is that it revived an unconventional yet old belief among some Christians—namely the belief in a female apostle. After all, if Mary Magdalene was as close a companion to Jesus as Christian traditions show, is it not possible that she too could have been one of the carriers of the word of God, just like Luke, John and Peter were?

Women in Hindu traditions on the face of it, seem freer than in Abrahamic faiths. The Mother Goddess, the Shakti cults, the rampaging nude Kali, the avenging Durga, and the hundreds of little traditions of Lakshmi, Saraswati, Parvati and Santoshi Mata are all evidence of a plethora of female goddesses each with a dignified place in the sacred pantheon. In Hindu traditions there are no strictures against birth control; women participate in worship as equally as men, pilgrimages are undertaken as couples, and whether it's a Ganga *snan*, for the evening arti, or the Amarnath Yatra, men and women are relatively equal in the holy realm.

But gaze a little closer at several practices of Hinduism today and there are instances that women, for whatever reason (perhaps because of the sheer dominance of the Brahmin male or because women have perhaps never needed to assert themselves in a tradition that is regarded as seemingly open), have not played as vital a role as they could have, given the many existing role models in the form of goddesses. Deification, as even Ambedkar noted, is just about the most effective way to kill the idea underlying the appeal of the deity. So the pattern is, we say our prayers or pay our bribes to the deity, and then go about our usual business of 'eve-teasing' or harassment of women during public festivals. This is common in the puja pandals of Bengal, and in many public religious cultural gatherings.

We have referred to the debate between Yajnavalkya and Gargi in the Brihadaranyaka Upanishad. Gargi Vacaknavi was the ancient Upanishadic scholar who was seen to challenge the men of an elite Brahmin academy when she asked Yajnavalkya, the leading scholar of the time, to participate in a debate with her. But Gargi asked so many questions that Yajnavalkya soon shut her up with the firm retort.

Then Gargi asked him: 'Yajnavalkya,' said she, 'since all this here is woven, like warp and woof, in water, on what, pray, is water woven like warp and woof?'

'On air, O Gargi,' Yajnavalkya replies.

'On what, then is air woven like warp and woof?'

'On the worlds of the sky, O Gargi.'

'On what then, pray, are the worlds of the sky woven, like warp and woof?'

'On the worlds of the gandharvas, O Gargi'.

[She goes on questioning Yajnavalkya, until he finally answers]: He [Yajnavalkya] said, 'Gargi, do not question too much lest your head fall off. Verily, you are questioning too much about a divinity about which we are not to ask too much. Do not, O Gargi, question too much.'

Thereupon, Gargi Vacaknavi kept silent.[91]

Kunti was the mother of the Pandavas, one of the matriarchs in the Mahabharata. Yet her chief identity seems to be frozen as the errant mother of Karna, rather than as a woman with a complex relationship with divinity, as represented perhaps by the 'Sun', the 'Wind' or the various 'fathers' of her sons. In some legends, Aditi, mother of the gods, was so determined to win the battle of egos with her sons that she buried one of them under the earth with an elephant for company, although in the end her son triumphed over her. Savitri stared down Yamaraj himself but only to rescue her husband, Satyavan, from untimely death. Savitri's act was symbolic of her love and commitment to him that she dared even death to win her husband's life back. By contrast, on hearing of the death of Sati, Shiva became so enraged that he performed the Rudra Tandava, virtually threatening the destruction of the universe because of his own personal grief.

The sexuality of the Hindu woman in mythological traditions is neither apologetic nor hidden, yet, in many instances, the Hindu woman's path to God seems to always be through her husband or her son or her lover.

In a universe teeming with female goddesses, there are still very few women priests or women religious scholars today and most 'godwomen' exist outside the ambit of formal religion. The fact that they attract large numbers of followers, indicates that it's not religion itself that is discriminatory but the use of religion to exercise political and social power over others which is the issue—this misuse of religion either due to ignorance or vested interests.[92] Religion then becomes only a pretext in this power grab. According to Tulsidas: 'Dhol, ganwar, shudra, pashu, nari, yeh sab taadan ke adhikari' (Lower castes, animals and women should be shunned).[93] A negative interpretation of this phrase informs the mindsets of orthodoxies in several parts, where tradition is used to restrict women's freedom by seeking sanction from the scriptures.

The allowing of women into Sabarimala by the Supreme Court is an important reaffirmation of Hinduism's inherent spiritual democracy. Women have also won the right to pray at the Shani Shingnapur temple, a movement led by the jeans-clad, short-haired activist Trupti Desai.[94] Muslim women have also won the right to visit the Haji Ali shrine.[95] Discrimination cannot be camouflaged by tradition. When men have the right to visit any shrine of their choice, why should women not have the same rights? When men are able to undertake pilgrimages to places of their choice, why can't women?

Tradition is made relevant by doses of new interpretation. Liberals must support women's entry into Sabarimala, Shani Shingnapur and Haji Ali as well as women who wish to give full rein to spiritual callings, just as men. In fact, the temple entry debate should also be used to legitimize the decisions of some men and women not to enter any temple whatsoever, or even practice any religion without stigma. Social and political recognition of individual rights is independent of gender or religion or any other identity. The atheist who scorns religion is not less endowed with rights than the temple-goer.

Religion is a deeply personal journey and is not centred only on outward rituals. In Hindu traditions, rituals bend to the seeker and varied worshippers follow different rituals. If the seeker of religious truth happens to be a woman then surely manmade rules and rituals about who can or cannot enter shrines must give way to the spiritual quest, in the name of the spiritual freedom Hinduism has always stood for.

Love Jihad

Militant traditionalists invoke religion in other ways to deny women their freedom to fall in love or marry. The Hindutva nationalist cry of 'love jihad' is one such. Many reports have now shown that love jihad—or the so-called practice of Muslim men abducting, assaulting and making Hindu women convert to Islam—is a myth.[96] Yet, for those who think of the Muslim as the perennial, black-bearded foreigner bent on deflowering that patriarchal construct known as 'our women', love jihad is a delicious political fantasy, mixed with nasty voyeuristic impulses and mobilization campaigns. Like the term 'eve-teasing', the term 'love jihad' reeks of hypocrisy. It links love or friendship to male conquest, permanent enslavement of women and a life of perpetual shame. This is patriarchy working to entrap women in guilt and is emphatically not any kind of 'protection' of religious culture.

In 2010, Akhila Ashokan, an adult homeopathy student from Vaikom, Kerala, studying in Salem, Tamil Nadu, and the only daughter of ex-serviceman K.M. Ashokan, befriended two Muslim girls. In September 2015, she converted to Islam, repeatedly stating that she had done so of her own free will, and took the name Hadiya. She subsequently registered on a matrimonial website and met and fell in love with and married a Muslim man, Shafin Jahan, who was working in Muscat at the time. In 2017, the Kerala High Court, acting on a petition filed by Hadiya's father, annulled Hadiya and Shafin's marriage on grounds of love jihad and brainwashing; Hadiya was described by the court as 'weak and vulnerable'. 'A girl aged 24 is weak and vulnerable, capable of being exploited in many ways,' held the court.[97] Describing this infantilizing of Hadiya, historian Mukul Kesavan wrote, 'It was as if an adult Hindu woman who converted to Islam could be declared a ward of the State against her expressly stated wishes, have her rights as a citizen suspended and her marriage voided.'[98] The duly infantilized Hadiya was sent into the care of her parents, her marriage was invalidated and she was even placed under police surveillance. After the Kerala High Court judgement on an appeal by Shafin Jahan, the Supreme Court ordered a probe into the marriage by the National Investigation Agency (NIA) which usually tracks terrorism-related cases. 'The NIA's involvement is necessary to ascertain if this is really an isolated case or is there something more . . . something wider,' said the bench.[99] Meanwhile, Hadiya maintained: 'I was not forcibly converted nor was I forced to marry. I want to go with my husband and I should get justice.'[100] After repeated appeals, the Supreme Court in 2018 observed that the NIA can't probe the marriage of an adult woman 'who married out of her own free will' and set aside the Kerala High Court order annulling the marriage. In reaction to the judgement, Ashokan, himself an atheist, said he was 'pained' to see his daughter go with a 'terrorist'.

Hadiya is at last free of social humiliation and being thought of as a helpless mindless being whose life needs to be guided by state authorities. An adult citizen of India was denied her rights, first by her parents, then society at large, and treated as a helpless object who was lured down the path of religious conversion by a Muslim. It revealed just how inanimate, incapable and dependent women are still perceived to be, mere 'things' without free will who must be directed and controlled by seemingly benevolent elders, particularly if a Muslim man is involved. If women are indeed so incapable, then in the future, would questions be raised whether women can be equal citizens or even enjoy the right to vote?

In the Hadiya case, the Supreme Court held on 8 March 2018:[101] 'The right to marry a person of one's choice is integral to Article 21 (right to life and liberty) of the Constitution. The social values and morals have their space but they are not above constitutionally guaranteed freedom.' The court also inveighed against, 'patriarchal autocracy and possibly self-obsession with the feeling that a female is a chattel.'[102] How many identity warriors and militant traditionalists would agree to abide by the directions of the court that their so-called religious and social values do NOT rank higher than constitutionally guaranteed freedoms?

Love jihad is a pernicious concept, one that assaults religious freedom and gender justice, which sees women as chattel and Muslims as the perpetual enemy. Love jihad infantilizes women, allowing Hindutva vigilantes to oppress Hindu women and threaten Muslim women with retaliation.

When former Uttar Pradesh BJP state chief Laxmikant Bajpai asked, 'Have they got the certificate to rape girls because they belong to a particular religion?' or when Yogi Adityanath is heard in a 2009 video saying 'We will marry 100 Muslim girls for one Hindu',[103] these statements reveal a belief that communal polarization is good for politics and also reveals the prevalence of a mindset that sees any relationship that is not sanctioned by society (and the Constitution be damned!) as 'rape'. Any operation of free will of women is seen as 'brainwashing'. The real truth about rape is that repeated studies have shown that over 90 per cent of rapes happen where the victim and the perpetrators are known to each other. And within that category, a large number take place within the family, which is one of the reasons for the gross under-reporting of rapes.[104] So far from the political propaganda that it is Muslims who are perpetually plotting to deflower helpless Hindu women, it is the hidden violence within the home and within communities that is more threatening to women.

In 2014, in yet another saga of 24x7 media frenzy, a young woman in Meerut, Shalu Tyagi, and her boyfriend, Kaleem, were accused of love jihad. Even as Shalu and Kaleem kept insisting that they had fallen in love, she was allegedly forced by her father to

file gangrape and forced conversion charges, even as communal
tensions began to boil in the area. Rumours were spread that a
Hindu girl had been 'gangraped' by Muslims. Shalu later said that
her father was forced into politicizing her relationship because of
intense pressure from Hindutva militant outfits in the area. Today,
Shalu and Kaleem are happily married. 'In a free country people
should be free to fall in love with whoever they want,' Shalu later
told the media. Added Kaleem: 'Love jihad doesn't exist. It was
created by people to polarize and for political gain.'[105]

Love is rampaging through Bharat like never before.[106] Young
lovers professing the right to love, are inevitable enemies of
orthodox tradition, and traditional society is hitting out at them just
as it did against the star-crossed lovers from popular fiction, Heer–
Ranjha, Laila–Majnu and Romeo–Juliet. While urban living spaces
are becoming starkly divided along religious lines, old patterns of
coexistence persist in villages and in mofussil towns. Where mandirs
and masjids exist cheek by jowl, is it not but natural that love
should blossom even across the walls of religious separation? When
Indira Gandhi decided to marry Feroze Gandhi in an interreligious
marriage, Mahatma Gandhi said: 'As time advances, such unions are
bound to multiply with benefit to society.'[107]

Nowadays Cupid hovers in every tehsil and every *basti*. Love
is banging on the gates of tradition, demanding that either those
gates open on their own or be forced open. The *Manusmriti* may
thunder that a Brahmin who takes a Sudra wife to his bed will (after
death) sink into hell, but love knows no caste or creed and instead
breaks the status quo. Liberals are allies of love. Rajmohan Gandhi,
in his biography of Gandhi, tells the story of how the Mahatma as
a middle-aged married man once fell deeply in love. Gandhi wrote
to a friend about how he 'nearly slipped . . . after meeting a woman,
but was fortunately freed from a trance [discovered] passions lying
dormant within me.'[108]

Love is the emotion of the Bhakti movement. 'I am mad with
love, a cowherding girl . . . I am Pale with longing for my beloved,'

sang Mirabai.[109] Love infused the whirlings of the Sufi, or the mast qalandar seeking union with the divine. King Dushyant fell in love with Shakuntala even though she was a poor hermit's daughter. The seventh-century monarch Harshavardhana wrote several plays, two of them translated by scholar Wendy Doniger. In one of them, 'The Lady Who Shows Her Love', Harsha describes the intense love of King Udayana and the beautiful Vasavadatta.[110] In the Tamil text *Silappadikaram*, Kannagi continued to love Kovalan even though he betrayed her.[111] If there's one emotion that can smash religious and caste and class barriers, it is love. But in tune with the conservative momentum of the times, Bollywood seems to have turned its back on the theme of star-crossed lovers or the theme of lovers who defy tradition. Apart from the odd *Veer-Zaara*—a 2004 film about a romance between an Indian Air Force pilot and a Pakistani woman—the intercaste or interreligious romance is hardly a staple in twenty-first-century Hindi cinema, reflecting the conservative popular and political mood on love. Bollywood generally bows to the popular mood; the King Khans of the film industry only rarely play Muslim characters, nor has there been a modern version of the classic 1959 Bimal Roy film, *Sujata*, about love crossing caste and class barriers.

Traditionalists detest love. In 2014, the parents of software engineer P. Dipthi allegedly killed her for falling in love and marrying outside her caste.[112] In 2012 a Kolkata youth, Mehtab Alam, beheaded his sister for falling in love and eloping with her lover.[113] In another tragic story in Kolkata, twenty-nine-year-old computer graphics designer Rizwan-ur-Rahman, who romanced and married twenty-three-year-old Priyanka Todi, the daughter of industrialist Ashok Todi, was found dead on the railway tracks on 21 September 2007 in mysterious circumstances, with his head bashed in.[114] Khap panchayats have ordered the killing of lovers, as with the 2007 killing of newly-weds Manoj and Babli in Haryana by Babli's relatives. In September 2018, Pranay Kumar a Dalit man was killed in Telangana for falling in love with and marrying Amruta Varshini, not from his caste.

Yet, in a fast-changing, liberalizing India, there's no stopping love. The Shiv Sena and other moral policemen are the self-appointed adversaries of Valentine's Day.[115] In 2018, the Sena announced it would perform 'lathi puja' and use sticks against young lovers on 14 February.[116] The Sena has also said that Valentine's Day is not only 'vulgar' but should be observed as a 'Black Day' because it was on 14 February 1931 that the death sentence was awarded to freedom fighter Bhagat Singh.[117] But, unfortunately for the Sena, St Valentine is being celebrated almost every day by twenty-first-century Roopmatis and Baz Bahadurs, the sixteenth-century lovers, she a singer and he a musician. Today, however much the khaps, maulvis, militant Hindutva outfits and social conservatives may rage and fume against love, they are up against an unstoppable torrent which is as much a 'crime' as an avalanche or a deluge. The liberal must be firmly ranged with young lovers as they battle tradition because liberals seek to defend individual liberty and protect freedom of choice. The liberal is a steadfast defender of individual agency and dignity, irrespective of whether or not some romantic involvements eventually turn out to be enduring or successful.

Cultural intimacy between India's communities was an ideal for India's liberal founders. For Ambedkar, inter-caste marriage was an instrument of social democracy, a crucial step towards a discrimination-free society. 'The real remedy for breaking caste is intermarriage. Nothing else will serve as the solvent of caste,' said Ambedkar. He also said: 'Criticising or ridiculing people for not inter-dining or inter-marrying or occasionally holding inter-caste dinners and celebrating inter-caste marriages is a futile method of achieving the desired end.'[118] The Modi government, in typical Big State fashion, has sought to push for inter-caste marriages as a government initiative, by offering monetary benefits if an individual marries a Dalit. But it is genuine social transformation not engineering by state action that will break rigid barriers in the long run.

An extremely significant moment for liberal values, a moment when a long battle for individual freedom was won, occurred on 6 September 2018. On this date the Supreme Court struck down Section 377, the colonial era law that criminalized consensual adult homosexual sex. In a judgement that was widely applauded, the court pronounced, 'Section 377 is irrational indefensible and arbitrary. The majoritarian views and popular morality cannot dictate constitutional rights.'[119] The reason why this judgement has wide implications for liberal freedoms lies in the manner in which the apex court strongly laid down the difference between 'majoritarian views' and 'constitutional rights'. Yet while gay rights are of crucial importance, selective liberalism or fighting only against harsh laws like Section 377 but choosing to ignore other repressive laws and not standing against all forms of social discrimination, remains a danger for liberals. Just as liberals campaigned for gay rights, they must also campaign for the rights of all young lovers to fall in love with individuals of their choice.

The traditionalists' rejection of gay rights remains strong. BJP leader Rajnath Singh once stated, 'We believe in Section 377 because we believe homosexuality is an unnatural act and cannot be supported. The Court does not have to legalise or illegalise such a thing. It is against the order of nature.'[120] RSS leader Dattatreya Hosabale tweeted on 18 March 2016: 'Homosexuality is not a crime but a socially immoral act in our society. No need to punish but to be treated as a psychological case.' He also tweeted on 18 March 2016: 'Gay marriage is institutionalization of homosexuality. It should be prohibited.'[121] However, BJP leader and Union minister Arun Jaitley said in 2015: 'When millions of people world over are having alternative sexual preferences, it is too late in the day to propound a view that they should be jailed.'[122]

The existence of voluntary, consensual relationships across religions and castes is a modern ideal. Consensual adult relationships between Hindus and Muslims are fundamental to creating a new social contract away from politics and the temptations of religious extremism and mutual suspicion. Interreligious marriages not only help to build a new contract between religions and communities, they also empower the modern woman with the right to love.

The trishul- or fatwa-waving social traditionalist today is being boldly challenged by the jeans-clad female millennial equipped with her backpack and smartphone. And in times when soaring womanly achievement is defined by dashing figures like badminton player P.V. Sindhu, women's cricket team captain Mithali Raj, outspoken actor Kangana Ranaut, and the all-woman crew aboard INSV *Tarini* the Indian navy vessel which circumnavigated the globe from September 2017 to May 2018, it looks as if India's women are ready for the fight.

Beyond the Trophies

On 29 August 2016, the same day as Olympic champions Sindhu, Sakshi Malik and Dipa Karmakar received the Khel Ratna, culture minister Mahesh Sharma warned foreign tourists against wearing short skirts. We celebrate women power at the Olympics on the front pages of newspapers. In the inside pages, we read reports of how every fifteen minutes a woman or girl is raped. The success of Indian sportswomen has little to do with social empowerment across the board. Instead, it is the triumph of individual willpower. They have succeeded despite the system, not because of it, even though the system is now attempting to co-opt them. An active working life is almost impossible for most women in India. There has been a dramatic fall in women's participation in the Indian workforce, noted International Labour Organization (ILO). India ranks 121st in a list of 131 countries as far as percentages of women in the workforce are concerned. The female employment rate has hurtled downwards from an already low 35 per cent in 2005 to just 26 per cent in 2018.[123] Due to dismissive attitudes to women's safety, women working on night shifts still say they feel unsafe and little progress has been made on the safety infrastructure for professional women.[124]

It is through sheer individual grit and talent that Indian women succeed at the workplace and have broken the medal barrier in sport. The great P.T. Usha dazzled at the 1982 Asian Games in Delhi and missed the bronze by a whisker at the 1984 Olympics. No one has yet made a biopic on P.T. Usha as they have on the mighty Milkha Singh, who also finished fourth in the 1960 Olympics. What does the Flying Sikh have that the flying Usha doesn't? The emotional saga of Partition adds to the Milkha legend, but does that make Usha any less of an inspiring figure in her time?

There is a danger that 'women's empowerment' is becoming a Page Three entertainment machine, a celebrity procession or a prettily decorated Republic Day float that rolls along, disconnected from real life. Feel-good, glossily illustrated stories of women's success captivate us because we know that, like escapist cinema, the reality is darkly depressing. Wrestler Sakshi Malik wins a bronze medal at the 2016 Olympics but khaps continue. Badminton player Sindhu becomes the first Indian women's singles player to win a medal at the Badminton World Championships, but women continue being attacked in public (See crime statistics given earlier). Women sportspersons are talented athletes who are shining through sheer individual effort, even as the system and society around them conspires on a daily basis to keep them down.[125]

The same syndrome of succeeding-despite-the-system prevails in politics. Leaders like Mayawati, Jayalalithaa and Mamata have been phenomenally successful in breaking the glass ceiling in politics. Yet, they are hardly seen as icons of women's empowerment, and are not noted for women-oriented policies or attitudes.[126] Like Indira Gandhi, who said in an interview to *Life* magazine that she did not like to be called Madame Prime Minister and preferred 'sir', women politicians generally need to keep showing that they are more manly than any man. On the Kathua rape case, which outraged and angered women across

India, women belonging to the ruling party, the BJP, remained deafeningly silent.[127]

In the country of Indira Gandhi and pioneering social activists like Ela Bhatt, have women role models made any difference? No Bollywood female actor earns as much as male stars.[128] High-profile molesters and assaulters, like Manu Sharma, the son of Congress leader Venod Sharma, who shot dead model Jessica Lal, or former high-ranking Haryana police officer S.P.S. Rathore, convicted for molesting teenager Ruchika Girhotra who committed suicide, are perceived to have got off lightly for their crimes.[129] Sharma and Rathore were convicted, but only after protracted legal battles and intense media publicity.

In the Ruchika Girhotra case, on 22 December 2009, after nineteen years, forty adjournments and more than 400 hearings, the court finally pronounced Rathore guilty under Section 354 IPC (molestation) and sentenced him to six months imprisonment and a fine of Rs 1000. By this time, Ruchika, a talented tennis player, unable to bear the years of stigma and harassment of her family, had committed suicide.

Reservation for women in politics has been the subject of much debate but as we are arguing, the liberal must always reject the quota mentality or the group identity mentality, a mentality that undermines individuality for the sake of a narrowly defined collective. When quotas are given, the beneficiary tends to be looked down upon. The perceived losers in the general category take it as a licence to continue with discrimination now that the debt of underprivilege has been paid off through the quota. Beneficiaries of quotas become trapped in a scarcity mentality. They seem to cherish their new perks and privileges too much to bother much about the realities still facing those who have no prospect of ever enjoying that privilege.

One of the best examples of this can be seen in public transport, as I have witnessed. Today, it is not uncommon to see some women passengers often demand their reserved seats. Yet, very few women ever give up their own seat to other women, be it the elderly or pregnant women or mothers with small children. Quotas can become an entitlement that impedes genuine social justice, as Rajaji so presciently observed.

Yet it is hopeful that, for example, cabin crews on Indigo flights are all women. Or that the first woman solo fighter pilot, Avni Chaturvedi, has been inducted into her squadron.[130] But even in the prime minister's home state of Gujarat, 26.6 per cent of girls in the age group of fifteen to seventeen have either dropped out or never been to school.

Misogyny is rampant on social media. The trolling of publicly visible women is a daily bloodsport, with hundreds of social media users unleashing the choicest expletives against women perceived to be assertive or opinionated.[131] We mark Women's Day but repeatedly hear new strictures from politicians on how women must dress and behave.[132] Except among the Sikh and the Jain community, child sex ratios are at their lowest since 1961. The sex ratio means the number of girls per 1000 boys. According to the 2011 census, this was 927 in 2001 and fell to 918 in 2011. The sex ratio decline was the highest among Hindus—the sex ratio fell from 925 in 2001 to 913 in 2011.[133]

In fields where meritocracies are slowly emerging, like sport, talented women will inevitably succeed. But in terms of gender justice, violence and crimes against women, attitudes, language and the growing, neo-traditional self-image of women (as seen during the *Padmaavat* protests or the furious defence of festivals like Karva chauth), as well as the backlash from moral policemen, India's turning the clock back on justice for women.

Triple Talaq Is Gone but Is the Muslim Woman Free from Injustice?

On 22 August 2017, the Supreme Court struck down the practice of instant triple talaq, or the practice of a Muslim man being able to divorce a Muslim woman simply by uttering the words 'talaq

talaq talaq', sometimes even on the phone. The court held that the practice of instant triple talaq was 'unconstitutional, arbitrary and not part of Islam'. The provisions had been challenged by a group of Muslim women, among them thirty-five-year-old Shayara Bano. The court asked Parliament to come up with a new legislation in six months.[134] On 19 September 2018, the Modi government declared that the practice of instant triple talaq was a 'constitutional emergency' and pushed the law making instant triple talaq illegal through, without a debate in Parliament, as an ordinance. This ordinance has led to many protests about the lack of parliamentary debate on a crucial legislation.

The striking down of instant triple talaq was an important way in which discrimination against Muslim women in India was ended. Liberals must support a common set of laws for all communities, both in the interests of gender justice and individual freedoms. To quote Kamaladevi Chattopadhyay: 'All progressive elements in India have long dreamed of an establishment of a common national legal code, operating irrespective of caste or creed . . . laws have had to change under changing conditions . . . where it becomes a social injustice, the need for adjustment has to be recognized as imperative.'[135] It's important to note that for Kamaladevi, all societies—including Hindus—must recognize the need for modifications and changes in personal laws.

However, while accepting the cry for justice by Muslim women, we need to recognize that a universal civil code does not mean and should not mean a code favourable to any community, but one that treats every individual as equal. It could be argued that a simple marriage and divorce code would have been much more desirable rather than a code that makes divorce much more painful (with the ban on triple talaq) only adding to the agony of failed relationships. Ending triple talaq must not be seen as an attempt to brow-beat or criminalize the Muslim man under a political flag. Thus, liberals must also ask, when the BJP-led government celebrates the rights of Muslim women, is it upholding the democratic rights of Muslims in India?[136]

The ruling BJP is trumpeting its achievement in pushing through the Muslim Women (Protection of Rights on Marriage) Bill, which was passed by the Lok Sabha on 28 December 2017. Law minister Ravi Shankar Prasad was seen exchanging sweets with Muslim women and he tweeted on 29 December 2017: 'Sweets offered by these Muslim women on passing of the #TripleTalaqBill gave me immense sense of joy for having done something for the empowerment of women in India.' The triple talaq bill is projected as a signal triumph of Prime Minister Modi.

However, as Vivekananda said, when one points a finger at another, one must remember that three fingers are pointing back at oneself. Does Hindu society not require reform? In Hindu society, divorce is still difficult, and without the possibility of escape, unhappy marriages ruin many lives. Does Hindu society even recognize injustice in its own fold? Or does it even seek to legitimize injustice, such as the torment heaped on widows and girls, or caste abuse? If Hindu society turns a blind eye to the aborting of girl babies or the cruel discarding of the elderly, then can political Hindus really disingenuously claim to fight only for Muslim women victims and publicize their crusade against unjust Muslim personal laws?

A 1974 government survey found that polygamy was 5.6 per cent among Muslims and 5.8 per cent among upper-caste Hindus.[137] National Crime Records Bureau figures show that 8233 women were killed in dowry-related crimes in 2012. A 2011 Lancet study showed that in India, when the first child is a girl, there is a steep decline in the ratio of girls to boys, a decline noticeably higher in educated and richer households than in poorer illiterate ones.[138] The question must be asked, is Hindu society quite free from crimes against women?

Hindutva nationalists and traditionalists busy celebrating the passage of the triple talaq law and the victory over Muslim men should turn their gaze inwards. Were their celebrations held to mark a victory of equality before the law or a victory of the majority community over the minority?

Yet, as Gauri Lankesh had written, Shayara Bano at least got justice, where thirty years earlier Shah Bano did not. In 1985 (as we have noted in Chapter 2 and Chapter 3), in an illiberal blow to women's rights, the Rajiv Gandhi government overturned a Supreme Court ruling that gave alimony to sixty-two-year-old Muslim divorcee Shah Bano in an attempt to win over the maulanas and orthodox Muslim opinion. 'Thirty years ago,' wrote Gauri Lankesh, 'another woman named Shah Bano appealed to the Supreme Court seeking alimony . . . but to appease the Muslim community, Rajiv Gandhi overruled the Supreme Court verdict thereby denying justice to Muslim women . . . drawing back to the present time we have Narendra Modi at the helm of affairs. Dreaming that justice will be meted out to Shayara Bano is nothing but a false hope.'[139]

As we have been arguing, the manner in which the Congress dispensations have bowed before orthodox Muslim clergy in their day, the way they have prevaricated and back-pedalled in the face of maulvis and maulanas, has been an overthrow of liberal principles and a refusal to place gender justice over imagined vote banks. It is this temptation to play footsie with maulanas and maulvis outside the spirit of a constitutional democracy which has, in many ways, paved the way for sadhus and pujaris to enter the political space in the first place. Once the maulanas had been appeased in the Shah Bano case, it was only a matter of time before moves had to be made to appease the sadhus as well and for the Ram Mandir at Ayodhya to gain prominence. Those who opposed the latter sought to co-opt the former.[140]

Today, with the banning of triple talaq, Shayara Bano has been vindicated. To quote her: 'Our religious leaders and maulvis are misusing their powers by keeping us in the dark while they encourage injustice.'[141]

Shayara Bano has got justice but are the Hindutva nationalists using the triple talaq law only to engage in muscle-flexing? Is banning triple talaq on the one hand but keeping up the campaign against 'love jihad' or against Hindu–Muslim couples on the other, simply about putting Muslims on notice, socially and legally? Former vice president, M. Hamid Ansari, while accepting that triple talaq is a terrible injustice and quite 'Unislamic' has said, however, that the law criminalizing triple talaq is an unimplementable administrative edict from the top, which could become a means to needlessly persecute the Muslim man.[142] It was impossible to miss a certain triumphalism on the part of the ruling party when the law was passed. 'I congratulate PM Shri Narendra Modi and the entire government for successfully passing the Triple Talaq Bill - The Muslim Women (Protection of Rights on Marriage) Bill 2017, in Lok Sabha and bringing the practice of Triple Talaq within the ambit of criminal offence,' tweeted the BJP president Amit Shah on 28 December 2017.

Can a commitment to gender justice for Muslim women exist in a vacuum of civil rights for Muslims in general? Is this selective commitment then not simply playing politics? If every time a Muslim falls in love with and marries a Hindu, a violent mob appears on the street, intent on wrecking their relationship, the personal freedoms of Muslims are snatched away. The personal freedom of Hindus are lost as well, if the ban on triple talaq is revealed as little to do with equality and only a moment for Hindutva nationalists to wrap themselves in machismo over minorities of both religion and gender.[143]

There is a self-deluding hypocrisy in banning triple talaq on the one hand and, on the other, effectively criminalizing marital choices between educated adults and even accusing a Union minister of 'Muslim appeasement' if she facilitates the passports of a Hindu–Muslim couple. In 2018, Tanvi Seth and Anas Siddiqui complained to external affairs minister Sushma Swaraj on Twitter that they had been harassed by a passport officer who had asked Tanvi needlessly personal questions, such as why she had not changed her name. The officer was transferred and the couple were issued passports. As a result, Swaraj was relentlessly attacked on social media for helping a

Hindu–Muslim couple.[144] So the 'nationalists' want Muslim women
to be freed of the injustice of triple talaq but Muslims as a whole
must keep battling injustice because of their religious identity!
The ban on triple talaq is hardly worth celebrating if Hindutva
vigilantes continue to vent their wrath against so-called 'love jihad'
or attempt to police Hindu–Muslim marriages and romances or
keep attempting to police women's clothing choices as well as the
roles they must play in families. In this scenario, championship of
the rights of Muslim women sounds pretty meaningless.

Yes, many Muslim leaders may have failed the Muslim woman,
and there's a crying need for Muslim leaders who steer a courageous
course away from orthodox ulemas bent on imposing cultural or
religious norms. The power of traditionalists stems from their ability
to dictate norms and use that power to speak for the community
as a whole, as a monolithic entity. To them, any means to silence
dissent becomes acceptable in order to assert and sustain the claim
that only they represent the community as the 'sole spokesman'.
Political leaders tend to use these orthodox elements to keep the
flock together. Over time, political leaders internalize the orthodox
mindset and adopt the same means to mobilize communities.

Yet progressive, gender-justice-oriented Muslims in India will
only become strong in a political and social environment where the
Muslim feels a sense of equal citizenship with the Hindu. If the
Muslim's patriotism is questioned every time a terror attack takes
place in Kashmir or Pakistan-based zealot Hafiz Saeed makes an
anti-India speech, Muslim orthodox firebrands will gain at the cost
of the moderates.

You can't have gender justice for Muslim women in a silo
while the surround sound remains stridently majoritarian. Justice
for the Muslim woman is a goal every liberal must strive for, but
at the same time the liberal charter is to strive for justice and equal
opportunities for all minorities, including Muslims, both men and
women. How can you say you are ending discrimination against
Muslim women if Muslims as a whole are still discriminated

against? You cannot end discrimination against Muslim women without ending discrimination against all women. Justice for women is inextricably linked with greater doses of democratization for society as a whole. After the Tanvi Seth–Anas Siddiqui fracas, another couple Mohammad Sohail and Monika were harassed and manhandled in Bijnore.[145] Can justice for the Muslim woman be effectively delivered when individual freedoms to love and marry are open to assault and when religious identities remain grounds for attacks? In times of 'love jihad' what does a ban on triple talaq really mean?

The Political Woman

India's women politicians are often cited as examples of the country's openness to women leaders. But there are innumerable instances of prejudice and stereotyping in politics. For example, in February 2018 when Congress MP Renuka Chowdhury burst out laughing in Parliament during one of the prime minister's speeches, her laughter was likened to a demoness' cackle by mostly BJP male politicians and by none other than the prime minister who said 'I have not heard such laughter since the "Ramayana" serial.' In politics the worst stereotypes about women still hold.[146] The adjectives 'mercurial', 'volatile' and 'unpredictable' (words that are only a few shades away from 'witch' and 'dayan') are routinely used to describe India's women politicians.[147]

The Women's Reservation Bill (or the Constitution 108th Amendment Bill) 2008 proposed to reserve 33 per cent of all seats in the Lok Sabha and all state Vidhan Sabhas, for women. It was passed by the Rajya Sabha in 2010, the Lok Sabha never voted on it and the Bill has now lapsed.[148]

Reserving seats for women without making politics more welcoming for them would only heighten the backlash and stereotyping. It has been suggested that a far better quota system—if we are to have quotas at all—is perhaps to have reservations in how many tickets (not seats) parties must give. But women don't fare well in getting tickets either. According to data from the Association for Democratic Reforms (ADR), in the 2014 elections, major parties gave only 8 per cent of tickets to women. Parties headed by women, like the AIADMK, BSP and TMC, gave only 10 per cent, 5.5 per cent and 17 per cent tickets to women, respectively. Any kind of quotas or reservations for women in a polity like ours, dominated as it is by powerful clans and kinship networks, in which women are simply not seen as 'winnable' candidates, may fall prey to misuse.

There's a complex matrix of discrimination against women who wield political power in India. Dynasticism runs deep and daughters and sons rise because of the dynastic principle. In the absence of a male political heir, a female is equally acceptable. Many high achieving sons and daughters who may have distinguished themselves in other professions, when it comes to politics, seem quite at ease in claiming the family's political legacy and slipping smoothly into feudal roles.

Politics remains such a closed bastion of male networks and so old-fashioned in consigning women to the bahu-beti trap that women can rarely rise in politics through a normal route. No wonder women politicians are invariably called by family titles, like 'amma' and 'didi' and 'behenji' as if to underline their relationships with men. In this family soap opera, unpredictability is their weapon. They must embrace a certain public madness and deploy a designer insanity as a tactical ploy. They must seek recourse to their inner Kali and slip suddenly into Kali-hood to keep enemies at bay. By keeping people guessing, they make cadres and opponents stay in line. To be volatile is to be feared and to be feared is to rule. For women politicians, irrationality makes for perfect rationality, their irrationality a mark of the brutal environment in which they operate. Powerful women leaders sometimes appoint women as tokens too, such as when Sonia Gandhi, once the most powerful woman leader in India, handpicked an undistinguished Pratibha Patil as the twelfth President of India.

Powerful women are judged in terribly harsh terms and often face hateful verbal abuse. Mamata Banerjee battled the Left for decades, suffering near-fatal blows to the head and gaining the image of a 'streetfighter'. So-called educated 'bhadralok' Left leaders called her a range of foul names, from 'maid', to 'jomero aruchi' (even the Devil will not touch her) and '420'.[149] In 1995, Mayawati faced threats to her life from SP rivals when the VIP guest house she was staying in in Lucknow was surrounded and besieged by violent SP cadres because she had withdrawn support from the Mulayam Singh Yadav government. Jayalalithaa had her sari torn and hair pulled and was reduced to tears in the Tamil Nadu Assembly in 1989. A swaggering fifty-six-inch-chest-flaunting male politician is admired, but a similarly powerful female leader is invariably dubbed a tyrannical despot and even attacked in public.

Across the subcontinent, women who have managed to succeed in politics have mostly done it through the syndrome Oxford professor Ali Mazrui described as 'female accession to male martyrdom',[150] like Sonia Gandhi, Benazir Bhutto, Sirimavo Bandaranaike, Sheikh Hasina and Khaleda Zia, or women who take on the martyrdom of a dead male relative and rule as his proxy. In the case of Rajiv Gandhi, he acceded to the female martyrdom of his assassinated mother.

Yet whether women they have the luxury of belonging to powerful families or whether they fought their way up, they cannot afford to be 'normal'. The occasional rampaging Kali avatar is the strategy they must adopt. After all, Sita can be ordered not to cross the Lakshman rekha, but nobody dares to tell Kali what to do. Indira Gandhi fought hard against Congress party bosses to establish her authority; in the process, she had to emerge as a populist virago-like authoritarian figure, like Margaret Thatcher, outmanning the men around her, and getting the reputation of an Iron Lady.[151] Unless politics and the nature of political participation changes, women will be perpetually trapped in their Kali avatars. The inherently violent

Big State, which legitimizes violent ways of imposing authority, creates a political culture inimical to women, and makes women imitators of violent men.

That's why liberals in India have constantly called for political reforms to make politics more 'normal'. C. Rajagopalachari spoke constantly about reforming the election system in India so that the talented and honest would join, irrespective of gender. 'What is to be deplored most . . . is the terrible rise in election expenditure . . . money running so alarmingly ahead of education leads one to ask what hope or way out is there for democracy . . . we cannot save democracy for India unless we make elections less expensive than they are today.'[152]

With the rise of money power has also come the criminalization of politics and the rise of goondaism. When politics is about disbursing patronage by securing access to the public exchequer, elections will necessarily become astronomically expensive and spiral into criminalization. For liberals, the real answer lies in reforming politics by restraining and limiting the power of the Big State so that politics does not appeal to those who only want to capture the state apparatus through the election system. When winning elections at any cost is the established norm, money and muscle power will call the shots and in this ferocious political culture where values and ideas don't matter, women will inevitably be marginalized and jaw-droppingly prejudiced views about women will be openly voiced by normless power-displaying forces.

Thus, 'normal' women leaders will not be able to emerge, let alone succeed, and educated progressive women will either be kept out or be forced into regressive and theatrical stances to make their presence felt.[153]

The ascent of women leaders in India, like women sportspersons, thus has little to do with the system genuinely making way for women. Instead, it has everything to do with herculean, life-altering effort and the dewomanizing roles that political women have to play if they want to win in public life.

This is probably the reason women politicians cannot afford to be seen as gender-sensitive or woman-friendly, or accommodative and consensual. How can they when the very acceptance of womanhood is an admission of weakness? The lives of India's women leaders reveal the patriarchy and feudalism of our society rather than its progressive forward movement. Whether it is Mehbooba Mufti in Jammu and Kashmir or Mamata Banerjee in Bengal or the late Jayalalithaa in Tamil Nadu, glass ceilings have hardly been broken in politics, because when women succeed they do so despite the system, not because of it. Sadly, perhaps because these women attribute their success to the prevailing system, they don't feel the need to change it.

The Battle for a Free, Progressive Woman Is the Battle for a Free, Progressive India

The battle for the free woman is a battle for a free-thinking India. There is a need for every liberal to recall how hard our founders fought for freedom for women and how moved they were by the humiliations women had to bear. Listen to the views of Periyar on women:

> The low position given permanently to widows may prove to be the reason for the utter ruin of the Hindu religion and the Hindu society.

Conception proves to be the wicked enemy of women's freedom . . . conception stands in the way of women becoming ascetics, religious leaders . . . while men are free to become any of these. That's why we advocate contraception.

If women and men suffer dissatisfaction and pain . . . telling themselves that simply because they are married they must patiently put up with everything . . . I would say they betray absence of the essential human qualities and also want of self respect.[154]

Upholding liberal, progressive values today means a battle
with militant traditionalist social conservatives and religious outfits
of various hues. In this battle, the liberal woman must make sure
she is not trapped into a privileged feminist, metropolitan English-
speaking corner talking a language that has no connection with
the grassroots. Just as the 1970s feminists made common cause
with anti-alcohol and anti-price-rise agitations (although these
movements did not adequately enough challenge the expansionist
state) today's liberal feminists too must make sure they make
common cause with Dalits, Muslims and other groups seeking
justice, on liberal terms. Gender justice is a mainstream democratic
issue and justice for women is part of the ever-widening movement
for social democracy that Ambedkar dreamt of.

It's all too easy to attack liberal 'modern' women on culture and
class. Militant traditionalism, cutting across religions and cultures,
is now the calling card of thuggish youth driven by cultural and
class hatred. The campaigns by the Karni Sena against Deepika
Padukone and the social media diatribes by Hindutva nationalists
against Priyanka Chopra for wearing a short skirt to meet the prime
minister are not only misogynistic attacks but also attacks against
perceived privilege, success and wealth.

In Karnataka, the Sri Ram Sene, Maharashtra Navnirman Sena,
Karnataka Rakshana Vedike and other myriad 'religious' or 'cultural'
groups have been known to target 'secular' plays, fashion shows, the
information technology and biotechnology sectors. Every aspect of
public life that is characterized by freedom, relative affluence and
upward mobility is under threat and a potential target of violence.
Nor is it a coincidence that these groups also target women whom
they perceive to be liberal or deviant.

Which is why we must learn from the liberals of the 1940s
and 1950s who remained rooted in the Indian ethos even as they
championed liberal values. They were not only liberal but also
embodied an excellence that was both modern and in tune with
Indian traditions. C. Rajagopalachari was considered a scholar in

three languages: Sanskrit, Tamil and English. The first woman to be nominated to the Rajya Sabha, dancer and choreographer Rukmini Devi Arundale, may have been deeply influenced by the theosophical movement but dedicated her life to reviving Indian dance forms and musical traditions by founding the Kalakshetra academy. The veteran freedom fighter and poet Sarojini Naidu's favourite poet was P.B. Shelley but she took pride in the fact that she could speak Urdu, Telugu and Bengali. However Westernized, India's liberal founders could not be accused of living in a cocoon of extravagant privilege. Gandhi, patron saint of Indian liberals, chose the austere life of a fakir. Which is why liberals must reach out to grassroots movements across India, build wide social coalitions—particularly among women—and seek to create deep social alliances and locate the liberal cause in Indian realities as Sharad Joshi did with his campaigns for the Indian kisan.

The 1950s liberals didn't oppose ancient tradition, because they were confident enough to engage with that tradition and interpret the past in the light of the present. They could venture to dig deep into ancient wisdom and boldly assess it in a modern context. The works of philosophers like S. Radhakrishnan, especially his masterly interpretations of the Bhagavad Gita in the contemporary context, the connections he explored between eternal values and a modern India seeking Independence illustrate the liberal desire and capacity to try and resolve the false dichotomy between the 'glorious' past and the 'untraditional' present. That's why the founders of the Indian Republic of 1947 were essentially and incorrigibly liberal. To quote the Mahatma: 'Why do not women enjoy the same freedom as men do? Why should they not be able to walk out and have fresh air? Chastity is not a hot-house growth . . . it cannot be protected by the surrounding wall of the purdah . . . it must be as defiant as Sita's . . . Ram would be nowhere without Sita, free and independent as he was himself . . . for robust independence Draupadi is a better example . . . Draupadi was a giant oak.'[155] Liberals too must emulate that giant oak, deeply rooted in the earth yet reaching for the highest realms in terms of values.

Citizens of India, women across society are yearning for freedom and for greater access to opportunities and for justice. We need to ask, is our aggressive and militant romance with some imagined tradition making us turn our back on the liberal, progressive ideals on which our modern nation is founded? This romance with tradition is actually a pretence; it is a way for militant traditionalists to hide their own ignorance about the real significance of those traditions and values.

Is the cry of the BHU girls going to be met by echoes of the vice chancellor's arcane comments on morality? Is the token woman defence minister or speaker going to blind us to the fact that more and more women are choosing not to work? Are government campaigns going to lull us into ignoring the terrifying statistics of India's missing women, when the 2011 census showed that for 624 million males there were only 587 million females?[156]

Even more frighteningly, a government report showed in 2005 that female foeticide was increasing in affluent, educated areas; in high-income south Delhi, the sex ratio was 762 females per 1000 males.[157] The moral policemen are striking back. Liberal women and men will have to fight for their values, remain actively engaged and keep trying to persuade, listen and argue. When the liberal struggles for a society where there is individual freedom and the rule of law, the liberal by definition struggles for the free woman.

Fighting for the rights of women is about fighting for justice for all of Indian society. Do we want more instances of sati and jauhar? Do we want to place restrictions on whether women can wear what they want? Whether they can drink a glass of beer if they want? Will women not be allowed to make the most of their talents and skills? Do we want more P.V. Sindhus and Avani Chaturvedis? Or do we want to be known as a country where women must sacrifice their freedoms and talents at the altar of so-called 'cultural identity'?

Conclusion

Through this argumentative and reportorial essay, we have seen the manner in which, throughout India's post-Independence history, the Big State or Big Government has constantly sought to increase and centralize its powers at the expense of citizens' individual freedoms. Jawaharlal Nehru, even though he was an idealistic constitutional democrat, created the policy and intellectual space for the Big State because of his belief in a socialistic centrally planned economy. Indira Gandhi used agencies of state power, such as ministries and parliamentary institutions to push her 'Indira revolution'. The Narendra Modi–led BJP has taken state power to new maximalist heights to create a government that pushes its own socioeconomic ideological priorities, through many government agencies. The administrative prowess of the Big State inevitably tends to weaken due to gross government overreach.

As Mahatma Gandhi warned, the danger with the expansion of the powers of the state is that it comes with the expansion of the government's capacity to use coercion. Coercion takes various forms such as denial of various permissions and harassment of citizens by officials. The government is the only entity in a democracy that is legally empowered to use force and carry weapons. Thus, when the power of this legally armed entity increases exponentially, citizens have reasons to worry. Those of us enamoured of the 'danda' to rule India only need to wait until the blow of the danda falls on our own heads to really understand what it feels like. The Big State's capacity for violence needs to be powerfully checked by the rule of law and solid constitutional safeguards on the limits of power. If it is not, then violence tends to become normalized, even legitimized, with the continuous expansion of the state because the state or government begins to coerce citizens to impose its own priorities. Also, once it has expanded, since the state still can't satisfy everybody, some groups are inevitably left out, leading to disaffection—as we have seen in the Jat, Patidar and Maratha protests. This sense of injustice and frustration begins to grow when some groups get state benefits and some don't.

The Big State is invariably in the grip of the ruling party, and when the government or state becomes too powerful, politicians who control this Big State gain enormous powers over citizens' lives. As Gandhi believed, the more power is centralized in the government, the more is the government's potential for unleashing violence and coercion on its own citizens.

Government powers can be used to arrest cartoonists, imprison dissenters, harass citizens through government agencies, deny the cause of justice when ruling party politicians are involved in illegalities (as we have seen in riot cases), give government agencies the power to stage armed 'encounter' killings or killings outside the judicial process, deny passports, cancel FCRA licences for NGOs, slap sedition charges on students, writers and intellectuals and come up with policies that take a severe toll on citizens' well-being. Censorship can be imposed, hate-speak can be deployed from the bully pulpit and public places can be summarily shut down. Amartya Sen has called the demonetization drive of the Modi government a 'despotic act . . . an act that undermines notes, undermines bank accounts, undermines the entire economy of trust.'[1]

If the concept of justice itself is interpreted by political bosses as dependent on the 'will of the people' or the 'majority', then the rule of law is overthrown. And as John Locke said, 'Wherever law ends, tyranny begins.'[2] When obedience or agreement with the government of the day is made the sign of nationalism, then anyone who doesn't constantly obey or fall in line is dubbed 'anti-national'.

The Big State tends to be an ideologically driven state whose high grandees are given to making blistering statements regularly designating ideological enemies. As we have seen, Prime Minister Narendra Modi has made fun of 'secular' people, vowed equal treatment for 'shamshaan' and 'kabristan', and as Gujarat chief minister in 2002 even spoke of Muslims as 'hum paanch hamaare pachees'.[3] Union minister Arun Jaitley has referred to 'half-Maoists' in his tweets. Referring to the rights activists who were arrested in June 2018 under the draconian Unlawful Activities Prevention Act, Maharashtra chief minister Devendra Fadnavis has referred to how the police conducted raids against 'urban Naxals' and unearthed documents to show there is a conspiracy against Modi and a plot to create unrest in the country.'[4] Union minister Ravi Shankar Prasad has referred to how 'anti-national' groups are using the Internet.[5] Ruling party MPs have used language like 'Haramzadon'. When those at the top wield a sharp, abrasive tongue and are seen to be pursuing a fierce ideological agenda, the mob of 'non-state actors', for example, 'gau rakshaks', can get uniquely empowered. Gau rakshaks and lynch mobs act in the way they do because they believe they enjoy immunity from the law. In a way, the gau rakshaks in the twenty-first century are a far more ferocious avatar of Sanjay Gandhi's goon squads in the 1970s, who also operated as violent streetfighters against their own particular 'ideological enemy'—in their case shop-owners who did not display Indira Gandhi's 20 Point Programme on their shop windows, or businessmen who were seen to be avoiding taxes or 'smugglers' or anyone in any way opposing the 'Indira revolution'.

One of the images that must haunt the Indian liberal and give cause for grave introspection, is of the IIT and Harvard educated Union minister for civil aviation Jayant Sinha seen felicitating, garlanding and offering sweets to convicts out on bail in the heinous act of lynching suspected cattle trader Alimuddin Ansari.[6] Is the educated potentially liberal politician today a misfit, bound to bow to different lumpenized group identities? Is the educated politician powerless against the hate-filled mob?

Brutally divisive group identities in India create fundamental obstacles for liberals. The individual and her freedoms and non-violent means of politics mean nothing when frenzied, potentially violent group identities take centre stage. The Big State has heightened these group identities over the years by patronizing them through quotas, sops, schemes and legislations of various kinds. The non-violent liberal upholding the cause of individual freedom finds herself powerless when politics is dominated by identity groups who push their cause through violence. The fear of alienating vote banks, as we have seen, caused most politicians to stay silent during the ravages of the Rajput Karni Sena.

Why are group identities growing stronger? The Oxfam report on inequality in India in 2017 showed that India's richest 1 per cent cornered 73 per cent of the country's total wealth in 2017. It showed that 67 crore Indians saw their wealth rise by just 1 per cent.[7] When economic inequalities rise so sharply, will group identities not inevitably become stronger as Patidar youth roar collectively against the lack of economic opportunities or Jats and Marathas demand reservations?[8]

In conditions of rising inequality, anger and frustration, the ground is ripe for the rise of what Harvard University historian Yascha Mounk calls the 'elected autocrat' or the Mr Fixit, or the strongman–saviour, or those who practice 'democratic authoritarianism'. These are leaders who have gained power through democracy but who are increasingly democracy's greatest adversaries because they delegitimize anyone who disagrees with them and stay in power by mobilizing a fervent base.[9]

The rise of single-party rule, that is, a party constantly in power albeit through elections, is a danger to democracy. In the 2018 Kerala floods, we saw formidable rescue efforts by local organizations. Local governance is strong in Kerala because of balanced political competition, that is, alternating spells in power by either the Left-backed Left Democratic Front (LDF) or the Congress-led United Democratic Front (UDF), has created space for social and civic participation by citizens at large.

By contrast, in Bengal, the dominance of a single party, first CPI(M), then TMC, has resulted in all tiers of local government becoming yoked to a centralized structure and a single-party ideology, thus taking away from the autonomous spirit of local government.

Democracy, as we have been emphasizing, provides a platform for the peaceful negotiation of differing views. Only when negotiations based on genuine differences in views are truly meaningful will diversity flourish—diversity in society, in the economy and in politics. Without the nurturing of diversity there can be no freedom. For example, when former president Pranab Mukherjee visited[10] the headquarters of the RSS to deliver a lecture, this became an occasion for peaceful democratic dialogue. The liberal citizen wished that the former president had said more, that he had said, 'Although I strongly disagree with your views, I would never call you "anti-national" as I believe nobody has the right to call anyone an anti-national, just as nobody has the right to call me an anti-national simply because I hold differing views from you.' Yet, Mukherjee's attempt to engage with his ideological detractors was one that liberals must follow. Liberals must engage with citizens who hold diverse views as equals, not dismiss those they disagree with, as Hillary Clinton once did, as simply a 'basket of deplorables'. In order to do this, liberals must shun the ivory tower and communicate their message to as many who are willing to engage in dialogue and boldly take their message to the streets.

Democracy is not intended to steamroll over all dissent on the strength of merely a large mandate because democracy does not mean majority rule, although that is how it is interpreted in the one-man-one-vote system. Only populists interpret democracy as majority rule, or the rule of the greatest numbers. Democracy is about following the rules and norms of the democratic system, and respecting the role of an aware, active and enlightened citizenry.

What are the duties of liberal citizens of India in today's times of growing fanaticism, violence and rampaging state and political power? From my point of view, here are ten suggestions to become the enlightened citizens Gandhi wanted us to be:

1. Form associations and groups. Book clubs, colony clubs, groups of liberal citizens are very important for dialogue and debate.

2. Don't give politicians too much power over your life beyond what they already have and resist the centralization of power or one party rule. Centralization of political power and concentration of corporate power should equally worry the liberal.

3. Get involved in local government and municipalities, in making your living area a better place and undertake cooperative action to improve it. Devolution of power is an important liberal goal.

4. Don't run away from arguments, be prepared to argue and debate your cause. Always steadfastly and vociferously condemn violence.

5. Reject all forms of religious fanaticism or religious feeling based on hatred for any other religion.

6. If you're wealthy, set up institutions of public value and try to do so without political or government patronage. Remember Rajaji's words on 'trusteeship of the rich'.

7. The most important war worth fighting is the war within: the war between one's best and worst self. Fight the inner war to become a good moral democratic citizen.

8. Speak out fearlessly against a government which does not abide by constitutional values.

9. Do not hero-worship politicians; they are only building their own cults. Believe in your own individual dignity.

10. Acquaint yourself with India's Constitution and its ideals.

Political shenanigans by the ruling party today are dubbed 'Chanakya niti' by an adoring media. But is there place for Chanakya niti in twenty-first-century India? No democratically elected leader today can play by the politics of 'Chanakya niti'[11] or the so-called normless politics of 'saam, daam, dand, bhed' because no leader in a modern democracy can be a despotic ruler as Chandragupta Maurya was. If democrats begin to see themselves as absolute monarchs from the first century BC, then clearly for them democracy is only a facade and elections are only a way to grab power any which way, to then adopt the ruling powers of an unquestioned kind. Gandhi repeatedly enjoins the Indian liberal to place means above ends—the means must be good, moral and decent if the ends are worth achieving.

As we have seen through this polemical book, at the core of the liberal's crusade must be the idea of restoring a sense of justice, just rulers, fair law enforcement and politicians who stay true to their word; citizens should be able to rely on and trust other citizens because they are united in their belief in justice.

We have seen that there are many shades of liberal opinion in India. There are social liberals who believe in civic and social freedoms but do not mind state intervention in key sectors of the economy, pointing to the welfare state of Scandinavian countries. (These kinds of liberals are found in the Congress party.) There are economic liberals who believe in an entirely market-driven economy but who in civic life often endorse the Singapore or China model, where there are widespread restrictions on civic and individual freedom. (Some of these market liberals are sympathetic to the BJP.)

But can liberalism be segregated in this way? Shouldn't the liberal carefully explore the pragmatic middle ground between zealously anti-government libertarianism and Big Government control? Doesn't social liberalism necessarily include economic liberalism and vice versa? Free markets without civic freedoms have caused the rise of strongmen in Russia and China (Vladimir Putin and Xi Jinping); civic freedoms which allow state intervention in the economy and the creation of welfare states have not stopped the rise of populist leaders in Scandinavia, populism also being a reaction to immigrants. In the Scandinavian countries, although higher taxes enable a greater role of the welfare state, government control is minimal and they are considered some of the most free economies in the world. They also have high levels of civil and political freedoms. However, the rise in support for populist ideas even in these countries shows that sections of the population may be alienated even within a welfare state.[12]

The welfare state works well in Scandinavia because those countries have open economies, a tolerant social outlook and relatively homogenous populations. The state, by and large, is not intrusive and enjoys a high level of legitimacy and credibility. In a generally poor, diverse country like India, Scandinavian conditions hardly apply. Here, the need is for more devolved, localized government for effective welfare delivery.

Why does a big government tend to cause alienation? This is because a Big Government creates a feeling of loss of individual agency and that one is being controlled by vested interests, elites, power brokers, et al. Citizens feel powerless. Citizens also experience a growing sense of frustration that even though theoretically in a democracy they are told they are the masters of the government, yet in reality, they are not able to get the government to deliver for them or meet their expectations or make politicians fulfil their promises. This leads to even greater support for populist leaders to rise, on the plank of the disaffection created by the Big Government, which in the end only benefits those in power. Populists seize on the inability of the state to deliver, but when they come to power they put in place their own set of controls. The end result is that the scope and arbitrariness of state power or government power only keeps expanding.[13]

What's the answer? What's the right combination in the role of the government? The liberal, like the thinkers in Hindu traditions, believes it is the quest for answers which is more important than the answer itself. When we seek answers, we don't deny that knowledge is not possible but that it is contextual, so even if we hold strongly to our beliefs, we cannot become blind or dogmatic; we should be willing to test our ideas, respect the right to dissent and not forcibly impose ideas. This is why liberals, as a first principle, seek a limited government, not a Big Government which curtails individual freedoms in personal, social, economic and political choices. Often, absolute certainty among central planners or despots inevitably leads to disruption of individual freedom and economic markets. Choice becomes redundant and citizens are deemed nothing more than sheep to be guided and deployed for whatever reason the planner or supreme leader thinks appropriate.

The answer is not in Big Government or statist solutions or in asking for government protection but in ourselves and the power of what we can do together. This means realizing the importance of liberal, democratic citizenship versus a culture of goons and mobs. It means resisting the calls of the violent 'culture' warriors by recognizing how profoundly anti-Indian they in fact are, because they reject the very foundations of our progressive democratic republic. The idea of India as we have seen is neither nationalist nor political, instead it is civilizational. It's an idea that harks to the pluralist ancient genius of a subcontinent where freedom, iconoclasm and rebellion have always been celebrated, an idea that tries to be a beacon in the world. The subcontinent's long tryst with individual liberty and autonomy was a tradition that Gandhi and our liberal ancestors reignited for the modern era.

Brilliant minds down the years—scientists, doctors, engineers, social scientists—have often believed they had the ultimate answers and should refashion society according to their ideas. A belief in certainty led to many ways of ordering society—along communist or fascist lines. Yet, in subcontinental Hindu, Bhakti and Sufi thought, it has always been the search that was primary, the quest for knowledge; the humility that we do not have knowledge and must constantly seek it was the core belief. Hinduism doesn't provide answers, it provides only ways to seek answers; the quest for answers prevents us from being trapped in blind certainty. Similarly, liberal democracy is a way of dialogue and argument and counter-argument to create possible answers.

The argument here has been that the expansion of the Big State triggers authoritarian impulses among people and a political player soon turns up, willing to ride that authoritarian horse and gallop to power. In many ways, Congress-led dispensations have been 'soft' Big States that failed to adequately devolve power. These 'soft' Big States laid the ground for the rise of an even greater statist force like the Modi-led BJP or the Hindutva-led 'hard' Big State.

Coalition governments by contrast as we have noted, are institutional checks on the power of the Big State. Hemmed in by alliance partners, a ruling party cannot use the organs of government to impose its will. We have noted in Chapter 4 that periods of high growth have tended to coincide with coalition governments.

As we search for answers, the late Vaclav Havel, writer, dissident against the Soviet Union and former president of the Czech Republic, provides some interesting thoughts:

> . . . the issue is the rehabilitation of values like trust, openness, responsibility, solidarity, love . . . structures should naturally arise from below as a consequence of authentic social self-organization; they should derive vital energy from a living dialogue . . . the principles of their internal organization should be very diverse, with a minimum of external regulation.
>
> Do not these small communities, bound together by thousands of shared tribulations, give rise to some of those special humanly meaningful political relationships and ties . . .? Do not these 'post-democratic' relationships of immediate personal trust and the informal rights of individuals based on them come out of the background of all those commonly shared difficulties?
>
> . . . These informed, nonbureaucratic, dynamic, and open communities that comprise the 'parallel polis' a kind of rudimentary prefiguration, a symbolic model of those more meaningful 'post-democratic' political structures that might become the foundation of a better society?[14]

This 'parallel polis' of local citizens' networks, associations, groups, societies and clubs which can create a better society, for Havel, is created from citizens and not by the state, echoing Gandhi's and Rajagopalachari's beliefs in the power of the individual and in her enterprise.

The frail old man in a loin cloth—probably the most successful liberal politician the world has ever seen—the Hindu who believed in the power of the individual atma, the admirer of Jesus and the spirit of self-sacrifice, the Mahatma believed that political renewal can only come from personal renewal. He constantly spoke of morality, social commitment and local self-governance. He saw the pitfalls of Revelation, of the Big State that is convinced of its own omniscience and invincibility, the fallacy of Seeing the Light, of Knowing It All. He was constantly humble, constantly searching, constantly looking and struggling, with humility, for the truth.

Liberals of India, remember, liberal democracy is your responsibility. Without you, without the active, enlightened, aware citizen and her capacity for idealism, humanism, compassion and justice, there can be no democracy. Just as without the striving, searching atma, there is no brahma.

It is the spirit of the search, dear reader, that I seek to communicate to you in this book: let's keep looking for the solutions, let's open the dialogue and search fearlessly, because, as the Upanishads tell us, it is sometimes the search that is the destination, it is the quest which is sometimes the answer, and the pilgrimage itself, which is God.

Acknowledgements

This book was written during 2018 but the ideas contained in it have germinated for decades. My first encounter with the excitement of liberal ideas was when Dileep Padgaonkar, who would become my first boss at the *Times of India*, took me with him to interview the greatest living liberal sage of the time, Sir Isaiah Berlin. Sir Isaiah's words from that interview, held at Oxford University, where I was then a student, echo in my mind to this day. Sir Isaiah spoke of pluralism, of reconciling liberty and equality, the duty to resist with all our might thugs of various hues imposing retribution on the street, that a question may have many different answers. One of his statements still resonates with me: that the human condition is often a peaceful trade-off, even a compromise, between so-called absolutes. It was a wide-ranging and profound interview and made a deep impression on me.

In my journalistic career I was very privileged to have as my first two bosses two deeply and incorrigibly liberal gentlemen, Dileep Padgaonkar, my editor at the *Times of India*, and Vinod Mehta, my editor at *Outlook*. Each impressed on me over the years that if journalists don't stand up at all times for liberal constitutional values, they have no business sitting on judgement over anybody else. Jingoism, fundamentalism, religious hatred and intolerance and toeing any party line or foul language would be unthinkable to these two gallant jousters. My gratitude to them for an early start in treading the liberal path.

This manifesto for the Indian liberal would simply not have been possible without the many conversations I had and the insights I gained from my friend, the radical crusader for individual liberty, head of the Liberty Institute think tank, Barun Mitra. Although I am not as much of an enemy of government as Barun is, I was initiated into realizing the perils of Big Government by him and I benefited immensely from his sharp understanding of how in post-Independence India the expanding role of the government down the decades has systematically undermined the rights of citizens. So many ideas articulated here have emerged from the countless conversations we have had over lunches, on the phone and via email and even WhatsApp! My heartfelt thanks to Barun. I also benefited from email exchanges with the liberal analyst Sanjiv Sabhlok, founder of the Swarna Bharat Party, who is a passionate advocate of liberal politics.

My loving thanks to renowned Bharatanatyam exponent Alarmel Valli for kindly providing me with the beautiful Tamil poem, 'Paripaadal', which I have quoted in Chapter 2. My loving thanks also to Shahida Lateef, close friend of my family, for pressing upon me the importance of the phrase 'garv se kaho hum liberal hain'. My thanks to my journalist colleague Ashish Dikshit for helping me find the powerful lines from Namdeo Dhasal quoted in Chapter 3. My thanks to my patient and meticulous editors at Penguin, Ranjana Sengupta and Premanka Goswami, who believed in the book from the start. My support system at home, Rajdeep, Ishan and Tarini, has my constant gratitude.

Notes

Introduction

1. Dylan Thomas, *In Country Sleep, and other Poems* (New York: New Directions, 1952), p. 34.
2. S. Radhakrishnan, *The Principal Upanishads* (Noida: HarperCollins, 1997), p. 19.
3. David Robertson, *The Penguin Dictionary of Politics* (London: Penguin Books, 1985), p. 187.
4. Daniel H. Cole and Aurelian Craiutu, 'The Many Deaths of Liberalism', Aeon, 28 June 2018, https://aeon.co/essays/reports-of-the-demise-of-liberalism-are-greatly-exaggerated.
5. Ibid.
6. Ibid.
7. Ibid.
8. Nabeelah Jaffer, 'In Extremis', Aeon, 19 July 2018, https://aeon.co/essays/loneliness-is-the-common-ground-of-terror-and-extremism.
9. Ibid.
10. For a list of attacks by moral police senas, particularly virulent in coastal Karnataka, see the list compiled by rights activist Suresh Bhat Bakrabail, quoted in Sagarika Ghose, 'Mangalore's Age-old Harmony Caught in the Cross-hairs of Communal Hate', *Times of India*, 4 May 2018.
11. Minoo Masani in the April 1985 issue of the magazine *Freedom First*, quoting how Thoreau, nineteenth-century American philosopher and campaigner against slavery, was one of Gandhi's inspirations.

12. B.R. Nanda, *Nehru: A Pictorial Biography* (Delhi: Publications Division, Ministry of Information and Broadcasting, 1980), p. 161.

13. Today's government is often defined as one led by 'Hindutva' politicians and the previous government as one led by 'secular' politicians.

14. See section on 'Culture of bans and regulating citizens' in Chapter 3.

15. See section on moral policing on women in Chapter 5.

16. See sections on CBFC and rewriting of text books in Chapter 4.

17. David Robertson, *The Penguin Dictionary of Politics,* p. 307.

18. See Chapter 1 on encounter killings, encounters in Jammu and Kashmir, AFSPA and arrests of activists in Maoist-dominated areas and Chapter 4 on jailing dissenters and murders of rationalists. In 1975, when the Emergency was declared, Indira Gandhi imprisoned 253 journalists and jailed political opponents. Today, for example, the incarceration of Chandrashekhar Azad Ravan, founder of the Bhim Army, since 2017, has been seen by rights campaigners as an attempt by the government to muzzle a popular opponent. Ravan was eventually released in September 2018. Amnesty International, 'Over 100,000 Call for the Release of Chandrashekhar Azad "Ravan" from Administrative Detention', 13 April 2018, https://amnesty.org.in/news-update/100000-call-release-chandrashekar-azad-ravan. The AAP has alleged that the Union BJP-led government is using government agencies to defeat AAP politically. *Financial Express,* 'PM Modi's Obsession with Arvind Kejriwal Is Forcing Centre to Use Agencies against Us', 10 July 2016. The use of laws like the Unlawful Activities (Prevention) Act enacted on 30 December 1967 to arrest activists charged with 'Maoist links' in June 2018 is another example of how the Big State can move to restrict citizens' rights to protest.

19. B.R. Ambedkar, *Annihilation of Caste: The Annotated Critical Edition* (New Delhi: Navayana, 2014), p. 257.

20. CNN, 'Heartless, Cruel, Immoral. Every Major CEO Who Condemned Trump's Zero Tolerance Border Policy', 19 June 2018, https://money.cnn.com/2018/06/19/news/companies/companies-react-families-border/index.html.

21. 'In India if you do too much you destabilise things,' says industrialist Adi Godrej. *Financial Times,* 'India: Narendra Modi Hunts for More Economic "Firepower"', 25 June 2018, https://www.ft.com/content/f0ebfd6c-6a7d-11e8-8cf3-0c230fa67aec.

22. Edward R. Murrow's quote in the 2005 George Clooney–directed film *Good Night and Good Luck.*

23. M.N. Srinivas, *Social Change in Modern India* (Hyderabad: Orient Longman, 1966), p. 77.

24. See Chapters 1 and 2 on Raja Rammohan Roy, Rabindranath Tagore, Mahatma Gandhi, S. Radhakrishnan, Jawaharlal Nehru and B.R. Ambedkar.

25. 'The Collected Works of Mahatma Gandhi', *Young India* 4 (20 October 1927): 352, http://www.gandhiashramsevagram.org/gandhi-literature/collected-works-of-mahatma-gandhi-volume-1-to-98.php.

26. M.K. Gandhi, *Gandhi: An Autobiography, or the Story of My Experiments with Truth* (Gurgaon: Penguin Random House India, 2018), p. 45.

27. Letter to A.S. Suvorin on 1 August 1892. Simon Karlinsky, ed., *Anton Chekhov's Life and Thought: Selected Letters and Commentary* (Illinois:Northwestern University Press, 1997), p. 85.

28. See Chapter 1 on encounter killings and the use of laws such as AFSPA and UAPA.

29. *Hindustan Times,* 'Jat Protests: How Caste Quotas Have Triggered a Race to the Bottom', 22 February 2016, https://www.hindustantimes.com/india/jat-protests-how-caste-quotas-have-triggered-a-race-to-the-bottom/story-wp69TpIRJtQrt1ncX3dq3H.html.

30. Eric Hobsbawm, *Interesting Times* (London: Penguin Books, 2002), p. 17.

31. Jawaharlal Nehru, *The Discovery of India* (New Delhi: Penguin Books India, 2004). Nehru speaks of the appalling poverty and disparities in India. In 1943, the Bengal famine had killed around two to four million and the colonial period had resulted in massive deindustrialization and poverty. See Sumit Sarkar, *Modern India: 1885–1947* (Mumbai: Macmillan, 1983), pp. 30–42. In these conditions of mass poverty, a laissez faire economy was anathema to Nehruvians.

32. From *Modern Review*, a Kolkata-based monthly magazine, reproduced in *Caravan*, 'We Want No Caesars: Nehru's Warning to Himself', 14 November 2016, http://www.caravanmagazine.in/vantage/want-no-caesars-nehrus-warning.

33. See Chapter 3 on bhakti in politics and social democracy being the basis of political democracy.

34. Dhananjay Keer, *Dr Ambedkar: Life and Mission* (Mumbai: Popular Prakashan, 1954), p. 331.

35. Ambedkar's speech in the Constituent Assembly, quoted in Scroll, https://scroll.in/article/802495/why-br-ambedkars-three-warnings-in-his-last-speech-to-the-constituent-assembly-resonate-even-today.

36. Dhananjay Keer, *Dr Ambedkar: Life and Mission*.

37. B.R. Ambedkar, *The Untouchables: A Thesis on the Origin of Untouchability* (New Delhi: Amrit Book Company, 1948), p. 75.

38. Dhananjay Keer, *Dr Ambedkar: Life and Mission*.

39. B.R. Ambedkar, *Annihilation of Caste: The Annotated Critical Edition*, p. 308.

40. M.K. Gandhi, *The Essence of Hinduism*, ed. V.B. Kher (Ahmedabad: Navajivan Trust, 1987), p. 28.

41. 'The Collected Works of Mahatma Gandhi', *Harijan* (18 July 1936): 180, http://www.gandhiashramsevagram.org/gandhi-literature/collected-works-of-mahatma-gandhi-volume-1-to-98.php.

42. Ramachandra Guha, ed., *Makers of Modern India* (New Delhi: Penguin Books India, 2010), p. 202.

43. S. Radhakrishnan, *Eastern Religions and Western Thought* (New Delhi: Oxford, 2007), p. 313.

44. Rajmohan Gandhi, *Mohandas: A True Story of a Man, His People and an Empire* (New Delhi: Penguin Books India, 2006).

45. Rajaji on Nehru's death: 'Eleven years younger than me, eleven times more important to the nation, eleven hundred times more beloved of the nation, Sri Nehru has suddenly departed from our midst and I remain alive to hear the sad news from Delhi—and bear the shock . . .'

46. Ramachandra Guha, ed., *Makers of Modern India*, p. 446.

47. Swatantra Souvenir, Sixth National Convention, http://indianliberals.in.

48.   Zareer Masani, 'Throwing Out Secular Nehru with the Socialist Bathwater', *Open*, 11 August 2017, http://www.openthemagazine. com/article/freedom-issue-2017-essay/throwing-out-secular-nehru-with-the-socialist-bathwater.

49.   Minocher Masani started out as Nehru's confidante and later became a trenchant critic of Nehru's support for socialism and the Soviet Union. A three-time MP in the 1950s and 1960s, Masani began political life in the Congress as a socialist and later broke completely with Nehruvian socialism, becoming an anti-communist and embracing liberalism, founding the Swatantra Party along with Rajagopalachari.

50.   Zareer Masani, 'Throwing Out Secular Nehru with the Socialist Bathwater', *Open*, 11 August 2017.

51.   Sagarika Ghose, 'Dad Faced a Lot of Resistance from within the Congress, Manmohan Singh's Daughter Daman Says', *Times of India*, 5 August 2014.

52.   In the 2006 West Bengal Assembly elections, CPI(M) won 176 out of 294 seats.

53.   Scroll, 'In Addition to *The Satanic Verses*, Here Are Ten Books That India Needs to Unban Now', 1 December 2015.

54.   In May 2018 in Bengal's panchayat elections, TMC cadres were accused of violent attacks on Left and BJP workers. *Times of India*, 'West Bengal Panchayat Election: Violence Toll 25, Repoll Ordered in 573 Booths', 16 May 2018, https://timesofindia. indiatimes.com/india/west-bengal-panchayat-election-violence-toll-25-repoll-ordered-in-573-booths/articleshow/64183006.cms.

55.   Eii Samay, 13 April 2018.

56.   Foreign Policy, 'India's Secularists Have an Authoritarian Problem: Indians Are Increasingly Forced to Choose between Hindu Nationalism and Egalitarian Dictatorships', 10 July 2018, https://foreignpolicy.com/2018/07/10/indias-secularists-have-an-authoritarianism-problem.

57.   Former I&B minister Manish Tewari argued that the I&B ministry should be shut down. See Wire, 'The Time Has Come to Abolish the I&B Ministry Once and for All', 10 April 2018.

58.   See Chapter 3 for more on the attacks on Wendy Doniger, James Laine's book on Shivaji, the ABVP attack after A.K. Ramanujan's

essay, 'Three Hundred Ramayanas', the hounding of painter M.F. Husain, and Chapters 4 and 5 for more on the *Padmaavat* protests.

59. On 15 April 2015, AAP expelled Yogendra Yadav and Prashant Bhushan. In the Delhi polls of February 2015, AAP won a massive victory of sixty-seven out of seventy seats.

60. IndiaSpend, '84 per cent Dead in Cow-related Violence since 2010 are Muslims; 97 per cent Attacks after 2014', 28 June 2017.

61. Quint, 'Jaitley Says "Half-Maoist", Twitter Goes Full Bonkers', 9 June 2018.

62. Livemint, 'Why BJP Can't Afford to Take Its Middle Class Votebank for Granted', 1 March 2018; Christophe Jaffrelot, 'Modi of the Middle Class', *Indian Express*, 24 March 2014.

63. Sample this tweet from the troll handle @Sirjadejaaaa on 18 May 2018: 'Entire libtard and lutyens Presstitute lobby is busy covering Karnataka elections but 13 dead and hundreds injured in #Panchayat elections in West Bengal. No one is calling Mamata banerjee'.

64. *Indian Express*, 'Ram Navami Violence: His Son Dead, Asansol Imam Says if You Retaliate Will Leave Town', 31 March 2018.

65. The letter written in jail by Dr Kafeel Khan quoted in *Economic Times* on 27 April 2018 is titled 'Am I Really Guilty'. On the night of 10 August 2017, Dr Khan went beyond the call of duty to save infant lives in a Gorakhpur hospital when oxygen supplies failed. He was hailed as a hero. However, the doctor was unfairly jailed, perhaps because of his religious background in Yogi Adityanath–ruled UP, until he was finally given bail after several months by the Allahabad High Court, which ruled there was no evidence against him. *Los Angeles Times*, 'When an Indian Hospital Was Running out of Oxygen, These Doctors Tried to Help. So Why Were They Sent to Jail?', 29 June 2018 .

66. In 1988, the Rajiv Gandhi government, hit by the allegations of kickbacks in the Bofors deal, tried to bring in an Anti-Defamation Bill, creating offences like 'criminal imputation' and 'scurrilous writings'. However, a highly successful campaign against this bill led to its withdrawal. Prabhu Chawla, 'Rajiv Gandhi Government Withdraws Infamous Defamation Bill', *India Today*, 15 October 1988, https://www.indiatoday.in/magazine/special-report/story/19881015-rajiv-gandhi-government-withdraws-infamous-defamation-bill-797786-1988-10-15.

67. *The Economist*, 'Emmanuel Macron, the Resolutely Modern Philosopher King', 13 June 2018, https://www.economist.com/books-and-arts/2018/06/13/emmanuel-macron-the-resolutely-modern-philosopher-king.

68. Mario Vargas Llosa, *The Call of the Tribe* (Madrid: Alfaguara, 2018); *The Economist*, 'Mario Vargas Llosa on Freedom, Liberalism, Dictatorship and Ideas', 26 April 2018, https://www.economist.com/open-future/2018/04/26/mario-vargas-llosa-on-freedom-liberalism-dictatorship-and-ideas.

69. Pramod Muthalik, head of the Sri Ram Sene, said on 18 June 2018 that the death of Gauri Lankesh was like the 'death of a dog' and Prime Minister Modi could not be expected to react to it. NDTV, 'Should PM React If Dog Dies?', 18 June 2018.

The Liberal Patriot

1.   The 'Hindu Ekta Manch' in Jammu waved the tricolour and chanted 'Bharat mata ki jai' to demand the release of the accused in the rape and murder of an eight-year-old Muslim girl in Kathua in January 2018. This was widely reported by print and electronic media. Mudasir Ahmad, 'BJP Leader in Front, Hindu Ekta Manch Waves Tricolour in Support of Rape Accused in Jammu', Wire, 17 February 2018, https://thewire.in/politics/hindu-ekta-manch-bjp-protest-support-spo-arrested-rape-jammu; Nazir Masood, '"Horrified" Indian Flag Used to Support Jammu Rapist: Mehbooba Mufti', NDTV, 18 February 2018, https://www.ndtv.com/india-news/horrified-indian-flag-used-to-support-jammu-rapist-mehbooba-mufti-1813598.

2.   Letters to Sardar Patel. Sardarpatel.nvli.in.

3.   Sisir K. Bose and Sugata Bose, eds., *The Indian Struggle 1920–1942: Subhas Chandra Bose* (New Delhi: Oxford University Press, 1997), p. 175.

4.   Ibid, p. 412.

5.   Swatantra Party translates as 'self-rule party', the first party of Indian liberals.

6.   First published in April 1985 in *Freedom First*, which calls itself India's only liberal magazine since 1952.

7.   Ibid.

8. In October 2015, over thirty Sahitya Akademi award-winning writers returned their awards to protest the Akademi's 'indifference' to the murder of awardee M.M. Kalburgi on 30 August 2015.

9. Abhinav Chandrachud, *Republic of Rhetoric* (Gurgaon: Penguin Random House India, 2017), pp. 20–36.

10. In September 2016, the Supreme Court laid down that strong criticism of the government is not sedition, nor is it defamation. Sedition only applies when 'there is incitement to violence or intention or tendency to create public disorder or cause disturbance of public peace'. Utkarsh Anand, 'Sedition Explained: Criticism without Incitement to Violence Isn't Violation of Section 124 A', *Indian Express*, 6 September 2016.

11. Hoot, 'En Masse Sedition in Koodankulam', 26 April 2012.

12. The term 'communalism', which is an Indian contribution to the English language, testifies to this tradition of religion to be mixed up in politics. M.N. Srinivas, *Social Change in Modern India* (Mumbai: Orient Longman, 1972), p. 142.

13. 'RSS Affiliate Says Next CEA Must Believe in Indian Values; Criticises Arvind Subramanian', *Business Today*, 21 June 2018.

14. In an NDTV debate in September 2017, Right-wing analyst Subhrastha repeatedly emphasized her humble social origins in a debate with the author.

15. Ramachandra Guha, *Makers of Modern India* (New Delhi: Penguin Books India, 2010), p. 57.

16. B.R. Nanda, *Gokhale: The Indian Moderates and the British Raj* (Princeton: Princeton University Press, 1977).

17. *Speeches and Writings of Mahatma Gandhi* (Chennai: GA Natesan and Co., 1933), p. 523.

18. *Young India*, 5 May 1920. *The Collected Works of Mahatma Gandhi*, vol. 76 (Ahmedabad: Navajivan Trust), pp. 200–04.

19. Quoted in the *Telegraph*, 14 June 2018.

20. The pre-Independence Congress comprised Right- and Left-wingers, from Patel and Rajendra Prasad on the right to moderates like C. Rajagopalachari to socialists like Achyut Patwardhan and Narendra Dev. Sumit Sarkar, *Modern India: 1885–1947* (Laxmi Publications, 2008), p. 389.

21. In October 2017, Justice D.Y. Chandrachud observed in the Supreme Court that people may not be required to stand up in cinema halls to prove their patriotism.

22. Salil Chaturvedi, a wheelchair-bound writer, was beaten up in Goa for not standing up during the national anthem. 'Disabled Writer Thrashed for Not Standing Up, Says National Anthem Should Not Be Allowed in Theatres', *India Today*, 21 October 2016.

23. Quoted in Jawaharlal Nehru, *The Discovery of India* (New Delhi: Penguin Books India, 2010), p. 628.

24. *Times of India*, 'If BJP Loses in Bihar, Crackers Will Go Off in Pakistan: Amit Shah', 30 October 2015.

25. *Times of India*, 'Those Opposed to Narendra Modi Should Go to Pakistan, BJP Leader Giriraj Singh Says', 20 April 2014.

26. 'There was a meeting at Mani Shankar Aiyar's house between Pakistan's former foreign minister . . . and former Prime Minister Manmohan Singh . . . it's a serious matter . . . it's a sensitive issue . . . while elections are on in Gujarat what was the reason for this type of secret meeting?' *India Today*, 'Mani Shankar Aiyar, Manmohan Singh and Pakistan: PM Narendra Modi Floats "Secret Meeting" Theory at Gujarat Rally', 10 December 2017; *The Hindu Business Line*, 'Why Does Pakistan Want to Make Ahmed Patel Gujarat CM, Asks Modi', 10 December 2017.

27. Koel Sen, 'Arrested Professor Shoma Sen's Daughter Koel Says: My Mother's been Tagged a Maoist after Lifetime of Working with Others', Firstpost, 19 June 2018.

28. 'Lawyer Sudha Bharadwaj Calls Out Republic over False Allegations', Quint, 5 July 2018.

29. Republic World, 'Explosive Letter Exposes Urban Naxal Link To Kashmir Terror', 4 July 2018.

30. *Times of India*, 'SC Says Dissent Is the Safety Valve of Democracy, Orders House Arrest for 5 Human Rights Activists', 29 August 2018.

31. Rediff, 'B. Raman's unpublished 2007 article: Why Yakub Memon must not be hanged', 24 July 2015.

32. These eminent citizens included former Supreme Court judge P.B. Sawant, members of Parliament K.T.S. Tulsi and Ram Jethmalani, actor Naseeruddin Shah and others. 'Full Text of

Petition by Eminent Citizens Pleading Presidential Pardon for Yakub Memon', Huffington Post, 27 July 2015.

33. *Indian Express*, 'Those Mourning Yakub Memon Are Anti-national, Should Go to Pakistan, Says Sakshi Maharaj', 1 August 2015.

34. Liberal Position Paper 15, 'The Essence of Democracy Is Not Majority Rule.' Minoo Masani in liberalsindia.org. Also see 'Justice Ranjan Gogoi Delivers Third Ramnath Goenka Lecture', *Indian Express*, 14 July 2018. 'India needs not only independent judges and noisy journalists but noisy judges and independent journalists.'

35. Muslims were the target of 51 per cent of violence centred on bovine issues over nearly eight years (2010–17) and comprised 86 per cent of twenty-eight Indians killed in sixty-three incidents, according to an IndiaSpend report dated 28 June 2017.

36. Such as in the national anthem judgement, the Afzal Guru judgement and even in the judgement on Dara Singh, accused in the Graham Staines murder case.

37. In January 2011, the Supreme Court had observed: 'In the case on hand, though Graham Staines and his two minor sons were burnt to death . . . at Manoharpur, the intention was to teach a lesson to Graham Staines about his religious activities, namely converting poor tribals to Christianity.' This judgement was criticized. See Alok Tiwari, 'Puzzling verdict in Graham Staines case', *Times of India*, 23 January 2011. See also the open letter published in *The Hindu* in January 2011 by Anand Patwardhan, Praful Bidwai, Ram Puniyani, Shahid Siddiqi and others, saying, 'We take strong exception to the gratuitous observation in the Supreme Court judgement . . . as patently unconstitutional as it goes against the guarantees of freedom of faith.' After criticism of this judgement by civil society in a rare suo moto act, the bench replaced these lines with: 'However, more than 12 years have elapsed since the act was committed, we are of the opinion that the life sentence awarded by the HC need not be enhanced in view of the factual position discussed in the earlier paras.' *Hindustan Times*, 'SC Takes Back Conversion Remark in Staines Case', 25 January 2011; *The Hindu*, 'Court Expunges Its Own to "Teach a Lesson to Staines" Remark', 26 January 2011.

38. The Indian Police Foundation was set up in 2015 to implement police reforms in the *Prakash Singh* vs *Union of India* case. The Supreme Court issued directions that states should implement police reforms but these reforms have hardly happened. See N.K. Singh, 'Awaiting Police Reforms', *The Hindu,* 4 October 2017.
39. Shah Bano case 1985, see Chapter 4 of this book.
40. The national anthem judgement and the death sentence for Afzal Guru could be cited as instances where even the higher judiciary appears to have been affected by the majority sentiment. The 2011 judgement of the Supreme Court in the Dara Singh case, criticized in several quarters, can also be cited here. While dismissing the plea to enhance the life sentence on Dara Singh, accused in the Australian missionary Graham Staines murder case of 1999, the court read out what was interpreted by activists as a cautionary statement against conversions by missionaries: 'It is undisputed that there is no justification for interfering in someone's belief by way of use of force, provocation, conversion, incitement or upon a flawed premise that one religion is better than the other.' The judges also added that Singh's act was actually to 'teach Staines a lesson about his religious activities, namely converting poor tribals to Christianity.' *The Hindu,* Court Expunges Its Own "to Teach a Lesson to Staines" Remark', 21 January 2011.
41. Masani, Ibid.
42. Preface in Amartya Sen, *The Argumentative Indian* (London: Penguin Books, 2005).
43. Rabindranath Tagore, *Nationalism* (New Delhi: Penguin Books India, 2009), pp. 15–45.
44. C.P. Bhishikar, *Sangh Vriksh Ke Beej: Dr Keshav Rao Hedgewar*, tr. Ram Puniyani (New Delhi: Suruchi Prakashan, 1994), p. 20.
45. 'Anti-National RSS: Documentary Evidences From RSS Archives', Countercurrents, https://countercurrents.org/2017/01/17/anti-national-rss-documentary-evidences-from-rss-archives.
46. 'Letter: Sardar Vallabhbhai Patel to RSS Chief Guru Golwalkar—1948', Kracktivist, http://www.kractivist.org/letter-sardar-vallabhai-patel-to-rss-chief-guru-golwalkar-1948-godse-mustread.

47.   Ramachandra Guha, *Makers of Modern India*, p. 444.

48.   *Dawn,* 'Why Liberals Are Losing', 9 July 2016.

49.   *Times of India*, "Wahabi Hinduism" Has Hit Pluralism: Amit Chaudhuri', 1 December 2015.

50.   Reuters, 'India Revises Kashmir Death Toll to 47,000', 21 November 2008.

51.   According to the Indian home ministry, 13,000 civilians and 22,000 militants have died between 1989 and 2017. Greaterkashmir, '13,000 Civilians, 22,000 Militants Killed in Kashmir Since 1989', 29 April 2017.

52.   The killers were later revealed to be from wealthy elite Dhaka families, one of them the son of a prominent businessman.

53.   *Al Jazeera*, 'Living in Fear under Pakistan's Blasphemy Law', 17 May 2014.

54.   See Chapter 5 on glorification of Sati and 'jauhar' as tradition.

55.   Supreme Court judge Justice Ranjan Gogoi called for an independent judiciary, for a 'constitutional moment' for the judiciary which 'has been long overdue'. *Indian Express*, 'Full Text: Justice Ranjan Gogoi Delivers the Third Ramnath Goenka Memorial Lecture—the Vision of Justice', 14 July 2018.

56.   GreaterKashmir, 'After 15,000 Injuries, Government to Train Forces in Pellet Guns', 27 January 2017.

57.   'Perhaps the worst manifestation of a breakdown in law and order is the active encouragement to extra-judicial killings in the name of national security or fighting crime, or for that matter, protecting cows.' Manoj Joshi, 'India, China, Saudi Arabia: "Encounter" Killings Conform Neither to Rule of Law nor Rule by Law, They Just Poison Justice', *Times of India*, 31 March 2018.

58.   Ishrat Jahan was killed on 15 June 2004 in Ahmedabad, Sohrabuddin Sheikh was killed on 26 November 2005 in Gujarat, Tulsiram Prajapati was killed on 28 December 2006 by Gujarat police. Eight SIMI were activists killed on the outskirts of Bhopal in an 'encounter' on 31 October 2016.

59.   Thatcher, the Iron Lady, let Bobby Sands die during a hunger strike in prison in 1981 but the Birmingham Six who were sentenced to life imprisonment in 1975 were let off in 1991 and given compensation of 8,40,000 to 1.2 million pounds.

60. Kuldeep Khoda, 'A Cult of Militancy Being Born in Kashmir', *Times of India*, 4 June 2018.

61. Swatantra Souvenir 1973, available on indianliberals.in

62. A former member of the BJP IT cell, Vinit Goenka, accused the author of 'demeaning' the army in a tweet on 20 June 2018.

63. PUCL, PUDR, Kamini Jaiswal, Gautam Navlakha and human rights groups condemned the hanging. *Times of India*, 'Activists Condemn Afzal Guru's Hanging', 10 February 2013. See also, Arundhati Roy, 'The Hanging of Afzal Guru Is a Stain on India's Democracy', *Guardian*, 10 February 2013, https://www.theguardian.com/commentisfree/2013/feb/10/hanging-afzal-guru-india-democracy.

64. Author interview with Ghalib Guru in *Times of India*, 12 January 2016.

65. Manmohan Singh held talks with the All Parties Hurriyat Conference and mutually agreed to end violence. *Times of India*, PM Hold Talks with Hurriyat', 6 September 2005, https://timesofindia.indiatimes.com/india/PM-hold-talks-with-Hurriyat/articleshow/1221380.cms.

66. Sagarika Ghose, 'Like South Africa, Kashmir Needs a Truth and Reconciliation Commission', *Sunday Times of India*, 18 February 2018.

67. According to the Indian home ministry, 13,000 civilians and 22,000 militants have died between 1989 and 2017. 13000 civilians, 22,000 militants killed in Kashmir since 1989.' Greaterkashmir.com, April 29, 2017. See also, Athar Parvaiz, 'Kashmir Ceasefire Comes After 50% Rise In Armed Encounters, Killings During 2015-2017 Over 2012-2014', IndiaSpend, 18 May 2018, http://www.indiaspend.com/cover-story/kashmir-ceasefire-comes-after-50-rise-in-armed-encounters-killings-during-2015-2017-over-2012-2014.

68. Assam chief minister Sarbananda Sonowal hailed Gogoi as the 'pride of Assam'. *Times of India*, 'Sarbananda Sonowal All Praise for Major Leetul Gogoi', 25 May 2017. *Hindustan Times*, 'Kashmir "Human Shield" Row: Attorney General Mukul Rohatgi Says I Salute Major Gogoi', 25 May 2017.

69. *Hindustan Times*, '"Tie Arundhati Roy to Army Jeep": Paresh Rawal Kicks Up a Storm on Twitter', 26 May 2017.

70. Use of human shields is forbidden by Protocol 1 of Geneva Convention or Humanitarian Laws of Armed Conflict.

71. The Armed Forces (Special Powers) Act, giving the army legal immunity and allowing it to suspend civil liberties, has been in force in Jammu and Kashmir since 1990.

72. The Justice Jeevan Reddy Committee, probing AFSPA in the north-east, said AFSPA is a symbol of oppression and must go. *The Hindu*, 'Repeal Armed Forces Act: Official Panel', 8 October 2006; Press Trust of India, 'Mehbooba Asked for Rolling Back of AFSPA in 2016', 16 March 2017; *Indian Express*, 'Jammu and Kashmir: Withdraw AFSPA from Some Areas, Says Mehbooba Mufti', 16 March 2017. *Indian Express*, 'Mehbooba Mufti Says Time Not Ripe to Revoke AFSPA, Defends Army's Counter FIR in Shopian Incident', 2 February 2018.

73. Two Kashmiri students were beaten up in Mahendragarh in Haryana in 2018. In 2014, the Swami Vivekanand Subharti University in Meerut expelled ten Kashmiri students and suspended fifty-seven for allegedly cheering Pakistan during an India–Pakistan cricket match.

74. *The Hindu*, '14% of Pellet Gun Victims in Kashmir Are Below 15', 22 October 2016.

75. On 11 July 2016, after the protests over Burhan Wani's killing, Insha opened a window of her home in Sedow village and was hit by pellets.

76. Rafiq had been detained under UAPA (Unlawful Activities Prevention Act) and allegedly brutally tortured by the Special Task Forces, forced to drink urine; his trousers were filled with rats and suck the genitals of other prisoners. Huffington Post, 'Rats in Pants, Made to Drink Urine, Called a Terrorist', 20 February 2017. He was released on 16 February 2017.

77. Local Congress politician Khem Lata Wakhloo to the BBC on the 1987 polls: 'The losing candidates were declared winners. It shook the ordinary people's faith in the elections and the democratic process.' BBC, 'Kashmir's Flawed Elections', 12 September 2002.

78. There are variations in the numbers of Pandits who fled the Valley. Some reports say 1,00,000, some 1,50,000 to 1,90,000. By some accounts, by the end of 1990, an estimated 3,50,000 Kashmiri

Pandits escaped from the Valley. Rahul Pandita, *Our Moon Has Blood Clots* (New Delhi: Penguin Books India, 2013).

79. Official statement that CM will acquire land and provide townships for Kashmiri Pandits. In 2017, 3000 jobs were offered to Pandits as part of the PM's special package but 500 of those given jobs refused to return. 'The ongoing proxy war in Kashmir is against India and nationalist forces, so why are you forcing us to go back,' R.K. Bhat, president, Youth All India Kashmiri Samaj. NDTV, 'Why Kashmiri Pandits are refusing to return to their jobs in Valley', 9 August 2017.

80. The Musharraf formula was: (1) Demilitarization and phased withdrawal of troops, (2) No change in borders but free movement across LoC, (3) Self-government without independence, (4) Joint supervision mechanism in J&K involving India, Pakistan and Kashmir. News18, 'When Vajpayee and Musharraf "Almost Resolved" the Kashmir Dispute', 13 February 2018.

81. A.G. Noorani, 'How to Settle the Kashmir Issue', Greaterkashmir. com. 9 October 2015.

82. Instrument of Accession between Maharajah Hari Singh and the government of India on 26 October 1947. See A.G. Noorani, *The Kashmir Dispute 1947–2012* (New Delhi: Oxford University Press, 2014); Victoria Schofield, *Kashmir in Conflict* (United Kingdom: IB Tauris, 2003); Alastair Lamb, *Kashmir: A Disputed Legacy* (Oxford: Oxford University Press, 1991).

83. 'Centre Should Respect Cooperative Federalism: Chandrababu Naidu', *The Hindu*, 7 May 2018.

84. In January 2018, an eight-year-old Bakherwal girl was abducted, raped and murdered in the outskirts of Jammu. In Jammu, lawyers and activists organized under the banner of the Hindu Ekta Manch took out a march in support of the Hindu accused and shouted slogans of 'Bharat mata ki jai'. Lawyers even tried to prevent the crime branch of the Jammu and Kashmir police from filing the charge sheet at the Kathua chief judicial magistrate's court. The Supreme Court shifted the Kathua rape and murder case out of Kathua to Pathankot on 7 May and the trial of the eight accused began on 31 May.

85. C. Rajagopalachari, *A Collection of Articles: 1956–1961*, vol. 1 (Chennai: Bharathan Publications, 1961), pp. 70–76.

86. Candles have been lit at the Wagah checkpost on the India–
     Pakistan border since the late 1990s on the Independence Days of
     both countries. Liberals such as Kuldip Nayar, Sayeeda Hameed
     and Justice Rajinder Sachar participated. Rediff, 'Candle light
     Ceremony for Lasting Indo-Pak Friendship', August 2002.

87. Hoot, 'Simi Live', 2 December 2008, http://asu.thehoot.org/
     media-watch-briefs/simi-live-3484.

88. BJP and allies won a remarkable victory in 2017 in the Uttar Pradesh
     Assembly polls, winning the largest number of seats in Uttar Pradesh
     by any party or coalition since the Janata Party in 1977.

89. Manoj Joshi points out that surgical strikes have emphatically not
     deterred Pakistan and there have been a series of attacks after the
     strikes, notably on the army camp in Nagrota, on a CRPF camp in
     Pampore, and in February 2018 on the Sunjuwan military station
     near Jammu city. 'The Surgical Strikes Videos Are Proof That
     Politics Is Fully in Command, Wire, 29 June 2018.

90. Sagarika Ghose, 'Not The Whole Picture', *Outlook*, 26 July 1999.

91. '"Sangh will prepare military personnel within 3 days which will
     take the Army 6-7 months": Mohan Bhagwat', *Times of India*, 12
     February 2018.

92. *Times of India*, 'Let's Not Romanticise Maoists or Demonise
     Security Forces', 28 May 2013.

93. On 29 March 2010, Arundhati Roy wrote an essay titled 'Walking
     with the Comrades' in *Outlook* magazine for which she was
     accused of romanticising Maoist violence.

94. Speech to DGPs and IGPs in New Delhi, 15 September 2011.

95. Sen was charged under UAPA in 2007, SC granted him bail in
     2011. Sen had allegedly delivered letters from a jailed Maoist
     leader Narayan Sanyal to a local businessman.

96. *Times of India*, 'Ignoring Hunger Is Nothing Short of Genocide:
     Binayak', 2 January 2011.

97. *The Hindu*, 'FIR Lodged against DU Academic for Murder,
     but Granted Relief by SC', 16 November 2016. In 2014, DU
     professor G.N. Saibaba was arrested by Maharashtra Police and
     charged with sedition for alleged links with Maoists. Saibaba is
     90 per cent disabled and was finally granted bail by Supreme
     Court on 4 April 2016. Live Law, 'SC Grants Bail to DU Professor
     GN Saibaba in Sedition Case', 4 April 2016.

98.   Author interview with Badranna for CNN-IBN in February 2014.

99.   Ibid.

100. Sori was once a schoolteacher in Dantewada. She was arrested in 2011, acquitted in 2013 and allegedly tortured. She contested as an AAP candidate in the 2014 polls. BBC News, 'Soni Sori: India's Fearless Tribal Activist', 22 March 2016.

101. Wire, 'There Is an Emergency-like Situation in Bastar, says Shalini Gera', 5 January 2017.

102. After the release of the National Register of Citizens for Assam BJP president Amit Shah referred to Bangladeshi infiltrators as 'ghuspethiye'. *Indian Express*, 'Amit Shah Raises NRC Again: Infiltrators Must be Deported', 5 August 2018.

103. During the Ram Janmabhoomi movement in the 1990s, the slogan was raised: 'Babur ki aulad jao qabristan ya Pakistan.' TwoCircles, 'Are All Indians Sons of Ram?', 9 December 2014.

104. *Times of India*, 'The Student Rohith Was Not a Dalit: Sushma Swaraj', 31 January 2016.

105. *The Hindu*, 'The JNU Incident Has the Support of LeT Chief Hafiz Saeed: Rajnath Singh', 17 February 2016.

106. Wire, 'TV News in India Is Missing the Wisdom That Comes With Age', 4 August 2018.

The Liberal Hindu

1.   The mobilizing cry for the Hindutva nationalist movement is 'Jai Shri Ram' and there is a political campaign for a Ram Mandir to be built at Ayodhya. Thus, Lord Ram is posited as the main deity.

2.   C. Rajagopalachari, *Speeches and Writings* (Swatantra Party Souvenir, Sixth National Convention, 14–15 April 1973).

3.   Swami Vivekananda, *The Nationalistic and Religious Lectures of Swami Vivekananda* (Chennai: Sri Ramakrishna Math, 1985), pp. 7, 77, 79.

4.   Brihadaranyaka Upanishad, III, v.

5.   M. Hiriyanna, *The Essentials of Indian Philosophy* (London: George Allen and Unwin, 1978), p. 179.

6.   C.F. Andrews, ed., *Letters to a Friend* (London: George Allen and Unwin, 1928), pp. 128–37.

7. 'The Collected Works of Mahatma Gandhi', *Harijan* 84 (July 1946): 388–99.

8. Rajmohan Gandhi, *Mohandas: A True Story of a Man, His People and an Empire* (New Delhi: Penguin Books India, 2006), p. 617.

9. *The Collected Works of Mahatma Gandhi, Vol. 15* (Ahmedabad: Navajivan Trust, 1975), pp. 201–03.

10. Swami Vivekananda, *The Nationalistic and Religious Lectures of Swami Vivekananda,* p. 133.

11. Ramachandra Guha, *Makers of Modern India* (New Delhi: Penguin Books India, 2010), p. 500.

12. M.N. Srinivas, *Social Change in Modern India* (New Delhi: Orient Longman, 1966), p. 76.

13. C. Rajagopalachari, *Speeches and Writings*.

14. Ibid. Rajaji's references to the Big State are to the socialistic bureaucratic government of the Nehru years.

15. *Indian Express*, 'Abul Kalam Azad, the Lodestar', 28 March 2018.

16. See 'Burqa Ban, Headscarves and Veils: a Timeline of Legislation in the West', *Guardian*, 31 May 2018. In 2014, the European Court of Human Rights upheld France's burka ban, saying the preservation of a certain idea of 'living together' is the 'legitimate aim' of the French authorities. In the Indian context, however, from a liberal standpoint, banning the burqa would mean similarly banning the wearing of all religious symbols which could throw open a universe of legislative contestation.

17. *The Hindu*, 'Cracker Ban on Diwali against Hindu Tradition', 28 October 2015. In 2014, the BJP-led government established 25 December as Good Governance Day, which was protested by Christians. See 'War on Christmas: Hindutva Groups Are Targeting Indian Christians and Their Biggest Festival', Scroll, 17 December 2017.

18. Hindutva activists filed cases against the paintings of M.F. Husain between 1995 and 2005 saying they hurt Hindu sentiments; the ABVP protested against the essay 'Three Hundred Ramayanas' by A.K. Ramanujan in *Many Ramayanas*, a volume edited by Paula Richman, in 2008, leading to Delhi University dropping the book from its curriculum.

19. Lok Sabha Debates 4.2, 22 April–7 May (columns 7954–68), parliamentofindia.nic.in.

20. Modi: 'We all read about Karna in the Mahabharata. If we think a little more we realize that the Mahabharata says Karna was not born from his mother's womb. This means that genetic science was present at the time.' Also: 'We worship Lord Ganesha. There must have been a plastic surgeon at that time who got an elephant's head fixed on the body of a human being and began the practice of plastic surgery.' *Guardian*, 'Indian Prime Minister Claims Genetic Science Existed in Ancient Times', 28 October 2014.

21. 'Khap panchayats consist of experienced members of society and they make sensible decisions and keep a check on social evils.' *India Today*, 'Manohar Lal Khattar Defends Khap Panchayats in Haryana', 6 December 2014.

22. 'Bhagavad Gita has answers to everybody's problems and that's why I said in parliament that Shrimad Bhagavad Gita should be declared as a national holy book.' *The Hindu*, 'Sushma Pushes for Declaring Bhagavad Gita as National Scripture', 7 December 2014.

23. S. Radhakrishnan, *The Bhagavadgita* (Noida: HarperCollins India, 2003), p. 19.

24. 'By Re-writing History, Hindu Nationalists Aim to Assert Their Dominance over India', Reuters, 6 March 2018.

25. ASER–Pratham Centre Report. ASER 2017 showed that most fourteen-to-eighteen-year-olds can use cellphones but cannot read basic texts. Only 47 per cent boys and 39.5 per cent girls could do simple division. *Indian Express*, 'ASER Report 2017: More Rural Teens Staying Back in School but Struggle with Reading, Math; Girls Worse Off', 17 January 2018.

26. *Times of India*, 'Smriti Irani Defends Sanskrit Replacing German as Third Language in Kendriya Vidyalayas', 14 November 2014.

27. Letter to Lord Amherst on 11 December 1823.

28. 'Aapko tay karna hai ki Dilli mein sarka Ramzadon (those born of Ram) ki banegi ya haramzadon ki (illegitimately born).' *Indian Express*, 'Ramzada vs Haramzada: Outrage over Union Minister Sadhvi's Remark', 2 December 2014.

29. Brihadaranyaka Upanishad, sixth brahmana, Chapter 111. In S. Radhakrishnan, *The Principal Upanishads* (Noida: HarperCollins India, 2005), p. 223.

30. In 1959, Pope John XXIII announced the creation of the Second Vatican Council, known as Vatican II, to address relations between the catholic church and the modern world.

31. See *The Economist*, 'Grounded', 9 January 2018. 'Four years on (after Modi came to power), only one in over 200 state owned enterprises has been sold—to another state owned enterprise. Even those nationalised firms with outside minority shareholders are treated as government departments.'

32. Aryabhata (fifth to sixth century AD), ancient Indian mathematician and astronomer.

33. Republic TV, 'BJP Launches Scathing Attack on Anti-Hindu Comment by Congress', 25 June 2018.

34. 'We won't remain silent if somebody tried to kill our mother. We are ready to kill and get killed,' said Sakshi Maharaj. News18, 'BJP MP Says Ready to Kill and Get Killed for Our Mother, Calls SP's Azam Khan a Pakistani', 6 October 2015.

35. 'Those who eat beef and kill our mother cow should face consequences similar to the ones faced by the victim (Akhlaq)'. *Navbharat Times*, 'Sadhvi Prachi Justifies Dadri Murder, Says Beef Eaters Deserve Such Actions', 4 October 2015.

36. Tweet by Right-wing handle @SharanyaShetty: 'Prashant poojary being hackd to death is nt newsworthy and threat to secularism, rmmbr recent vido incident coverage/ outrage? Shame @ KiranKs', 10 October 2015. Tweet by Subramanian Swamy, 'All the fake news, Commie disinformation and anti-Hindu news is due to cronyism of BARC-like freelancers with foreigners like STAR TV and stooges like NDTV and Uday Shankar etc whereby revenue flow is controlled. Thus the stranglehold on our media. Media needs to be freed.', 19 April 2018. Swamy is implying here that 'Commies' or Leftists or the anti-Hindutva press has a stranglehold on media channels when this is far from the truth.

37. *Hindu Post*, 'The Enemy Within and the 10 Narratives They Push', 27 June 2018. Liberals described as a 'dangerous mix of

traitors, self-servers and fools . . .' who do not condemn Islamic fundamentalism.

38. Another tweet by another Right-wing handle @RituRathaur: 'The shameless silence of liberals and Media in the Theni violence where Muslims destroyed 50 houses of Dalit Hindus exposes their hypocrisy and bias. Their fight for Dalits is fake and Big Fraud. They only use them to keep Hindus divided. Justice and truth has no meaning for this fringe', 8 May 2018. In March 2018, a list was circulated entitled 'Vampanth ke Afwah Tantra', with rumour-mongers of the Left naming a 'Hit List' of journalists. 'Till now a lot is damaged in Kashmir and rest of India by following intellectuals, activists and a strong watch should be taken in times to come', the list was subtitled. Also see Reuters, 'Cyber-Hindus, India's New Breed of Political Activists' 2 December 2013; Swati Chaturvedi, *I Am a Troll* (New Delhi: Juggernaut, 2017); BBC Hindi, 'Why Are Indian Women Being Attacked on Social Media', 8 May 2013.

39. *Times of India*, 'RSS Worker Hacked to Death in Kerala's Guruvayur', 12 November 2017 .

40. The 2016 Kaliachak riots were allegedly sparked by derogatory remarks made by Hindu Mahasabha leader Kamlesh Tiwari. *Times of India*, 'Cops Hurt in Mob Violence in Kaliachak', 4 January 2016.

41. *Times of India*, 'Mob Drags Delhi Dentist Out of Home, Kills Him in Front of Son', 26 March 2016.

42. Manoramaonline, '5 CPM Men Get Life for Killing BJP Activist', 25 June 2018.

43. *Ananda Bazar Patrika*, 'A Town Silenced by Violence', 3 January 2016; *Ei Samay*, 'Flood of Anarchy Unleashed by Hoodlums in Kaliachak', 4 January 2016.

44. During the rise of the 1991–92 Ayodhya movement, regional-language newspapers and media channels began their swing towards an overtly Hindutva agenda. Examples are *Dainik Jagran*, Zee News, India TV and Nai Duniya. *Dainik Bhaskar* and *Amar Ujala* have generally taken a centrist line. In Gujarat, with the exception of *Gujarat Samachar*, which attacks the BJP, most Gujarati newspapers are seen as pro-BJP. In Bengal, *Ananda Bazar*

Patrika takes a centrist line. In Kerala, *Malayala Manorama* is an anti-BJP outlet while *Mathrubhumi* has been seen as a paper of the Left. For more on this see Wire, 'Who Paid for Dainik Jagran's Pro-BJP Exit Poll', 15 February 2017; News Minute, 'All You Wanted to Know about Who Owns the South Indian News Channels You Watch', 25 February 2015.

45.   On 5 February 2015, it was pointed out out that there had been attacks on five churches but the police had registered cases against unnamed persons. See Sagarika Ghose, 'Mangalore Age Old Harmony Caught in Crosshairs of Communal Hate', *Times of India*, 5 May 2018. The article reports how the nuns of the Poor Clare convent named the Bajrang Dal responsible for an attack on them on 14 September 2008.

46.   DCP Delhi Monika Bhardwaj tweeted: '4 juveniles among 9 arrested for murder of Vikaspuri doctor. No religious angle at all as rumoured by some. We appeal u to maintain peace', 25 March 2016. She also tweeted: 'Out of 9 accused person 5 r Hindu. At the moment of 1st scuffle out of 2 I was Hindu. The Muslim accused are residents of UP, not Bangladeshi', 25 March 2016.

47.   *The Hindu*, 'SIT Says Suspect Linked to Sanatan Dharma Sanstha', 1 June 2018; *Indian Express*, 'Two More with Links to Hindutva Outfits Held in Gauri Lankesh Murder Case', 24 July 2018; NDTV, 'Treat Sanatan Sanstha As Terror Outfit if Guilty: Gauri Lankesh's Sister', 4 September 2018.

48.   Scroll, '"We Will Break Your Phones and Bones", Journalists and JNU Students Attacked in Court', 15 February 2016.

49.   See Sagarika Ghose, 'Indian Writers Guilty of Double Standards When It Comes to Dissent', 17 October 2015.

50.   See Sagarika Ghose, 'Netaji & Betaji: Tale of Two Dynasts', *Times of India*, 4 January 2017.

51.   Swaminathan Aiyar, 'A Beef Eating Brahmin Demands His Rights', *Times of India*, 4 October 2015.

52.   DailyO, 'Hapur Lynching Shows Indifference Has Normalized Hate Crimes among Indians', 22 June 2018.

53.   In March–April 2018, the Supreme Court heard a series of petitions asking for a probe into the mysterious death of CBI

special judge B.H. Loya. In April 2018, it dismissed all such pleas and ruled that Loya's death was from natural causes.

54. See Scroll, 'It's All about Market Share: Arnab Goswami's Funder BJP MP Rajeev Chandrasekhar on Republic TV and More', 11 August 2017.

55. In the past, editors such as Vinod Mehta (*Outlook*) and B.G. Verghese (*Hindustan Times*) were seen as Left-of-centre, as were dominant columnists of the 1990s such as Praful Bidwai. Shirin Dalvi, former editor of Urdu daily *Awadhnama* was sacked in 2015 and the daily was closed after she reproduced the cover of *Charlie Hebdo* on the front page.

56. Damayanti Sen was transferred in 2012 when she cracked the Park Street rape case the same year.

57. Quint, 'My Only Religion Was My Uniform', 16 April 2018.

58. *Times of India*, 'Business Sentiment Weakest in India Since 2018: Grant Thornton', 8 May 2018.

59. Sagarika Ghose, 'Bigots and Charlatans Are Controlling Culture and Education, Says Pranab Bardhan', *Times of India*, 21 January 2016.

60. *Hindustan Times*, 'BHU Tops List of Caste Bias Cases, Gujarat University a Close Second', 7 February 2017.

61. *Down To Earth*, 'Poor Social Indicators Must Make Gujarat Rethink Its Growth Model', 18 December 2017.

62. *Indian Express*, 'Government Staff Banned from Wearing Jeans and T-shirts at Work, 24 March 2017; Quint, 'UP Bans Jeans, Tees for Teachers, Tells Them to Dress "Modestly"', 6 April 2017; 'Director of higher education: Teachers are role models for students. If they are dressed decorously students will follow suit.' Colours were also suggested for teachers' clothes such as navy-blue trousers and white or sky-blue shirts for male teachers. *Hindustan Times*, 'UP's Anti-Romeo Squads Strike Terror', 27 March 2017. The Uttar Pradesh police set up 'anti-Romeo' squads to fulfil Yogi Adityanath's poll pledge of making the state safe for women.

63. In the ten-year period between 1992–1993 and 2001–2003, the average growth rate was 6 per cent and poverty declined significantly. Montek Singh Ahluwalia, 'Economic Reforms Since 1991: Has Gradualism Worked?', *Journal of Economic* 16.3 *Perspectives* (Summer 2002).

64. Firstpost, 'Cattle Trade Ban Affected a 15 crore Industry and 25 lakh People', 30 March 2017; *Hindustan Times*, 'Adityanath Orders Closure of Illegal Slaughterhouses, Ban on Cow Smuggling', 30 April 2017.

65. Pehlu Khan was attacked in Alwar in 2017. Shambhu Lal Regar axed to death a Muslim labourer, Afrazul, and filmed it in Rajsamand in December 2017.

66. In March 2017, gau rakshaks attacked the Hyatt Rabari restaurant in Jaipur.

67. *Economic Times*, 'India's Domestic Passenger Market Becomes 100 Million Strong', 23 January 2018. In those early days of liberalization of aviation, when Left politicians were heatedly opposing privatization of the aviation sector, the author was amused to see CPIM chief Prakash Karat once standing in line at the Jet Airways counter in Delhi airport, and he did look a little sheepish!

68. 'All Indians Hindus: Bhagwat.' *Telegraph*, 'Every Indian Is a Hindu, or a Son and Daughter of Bharat Mata: Bhagwat', 29 October 2017.

69. On 1 August 2014, in an interview to IANS, Dina Nath Batra said, 'We need Indianisation of the education system. Whatever is there in NCERT textbooks is not good.' On NDTV in February 2014, Batra said, 'Wendy Doniger clearly says she only wants to write about sex in Hinduism and the content of her books is offensive.'

70. *Indian Express*, 'The Government Would Have Loved It If I Had Quietly Slunk Away but That I Was Not Willing to Do: Amartya Sen', 8 July 2015.

71. Hamid Dalwai, 'The Last Modernist', in *Makers of Modern India*, Ramachandra Guha, ed.

72. Sen UNESCO lecture, 'An Assessment of the Millennium', delivered on 20 August 1998. Full text on Rediff.

73. S. Radhakrishnan, *The Bhagavadgita*, p. 157.

74. Ibid, p. 65, on the quest for jnana being a part of Bhakti.

75. Brihadaranyaka Upanishad (12), Yajnavalkya Kanda, Chapter 111 (v), second dialogue between Yajnavalkya and Gargi: 'What pervades the Sutra?', 'What pervades Akasa?' Swami Krishnananda, *The Divine Life Society* (1985), p. 179.

76. S. Radhakrishnan, *Eastern Religion and Western Thought* (New York, 1959), p. 313.

77. *Samagra Savarkar Vangmaya*, vol. 3, p. 341, Savarkar.org. These views are available in the section entitled 'Cow Protection and Cow Worship'.

78. Ibid.

79. Swatantryaveer Savarkar, Hindu Mahasabha Parva, 1938, p. 173. These views are available in the section entitled 'Cow Protection and Cow Worship' in Savarkar.org.

80. Ibid.

81. In December 2015, then HRD minister Smriti Irani called the AAP attack on finance minister Arun Jaitley as 'blasphemous'. *Indian Express*, 'Charges against Arun Jaitley "Blasphemous, Preposterous": Smriti Irani', 17 December 2015.

82. Mail Online, 'We Will Free India of Muslims and Christians by 2021: Hindutva Outfit Leader', 19 December 2014. See also murder of missionary Graham Staines in 1999 in Odisha by Bajrang Dal activists.

83. The June 2018 Hapur lynching is the latest lynching case. See list of lynchings in the name of the cow on author's Facebook page: https://www.facebook.com/sagarikaghose.

84. Hymn 10.9 in the Rig Veda, 'The Cosmic Being', in G.S. Ghurye, *Caste and Class in India*, pp. 70–71.

85. 'The Collected Works of Mahatma Gandhi', *Harijan* (3 October 1936): 265.

86. Ibid.

87. A criminal complaint was filed against Dhoni for hurting Hindu religious sentiment in 2013, as well as against the magazine. The Section 295A charges were quashed by the Supreme Court in 2017.

88. S. Radhakrishnan, *The Bhagavadgita*, p. 67.

89. Pandurang Shastri Athavale founded the socially reformist Swadhyaya Parivar in 1954.

90. Jonardon Ganeri, 'What Would Krishna Do? Or Shiva? Or Vishnu?', *New York Times*, 3 August 2014.

91. Batra made a list of words—Urdu words like 'mushkil' and English words like 'frock'—that should be taken out of NCERT texts.

'Use of Urdu Persian and English words has created a challenge for students, instead of enjoying texts, they have lost interest.' *Times of India*, 'English, Urdu Words in NCERT Textbooks Irk RSS's Batra', 28 July 2014.

92. Linda Hess and Shukdeo Singh, tr., *The Bijak of Kabir* (San Francisco: North Point Press, 1993), p. 45.

93. Jyotirao Phule founded the reformist Satyashodhak Samaj or Society of Truth Seekers in 1873.

94. Mundaka Upanishad, first Kanda. Sacred-texts.com.

95. Christopher Hill, *Reformation to Industrial Revolution* (London: Pelican, 1967).

96. John Keay, *India* (London: Harper Press, 2000), p. 209. 'Mahmud targeted Somnath in 1025, unleashed 'dreadful slaughter', leaving behind dead exceeding fifty thousand.'

97. Bush in 2005 summit meeting with Prime Minister Manmohan Singh.

98. BBC News, 'Are Most Victims of Terrorism Muslim?', 20 January 2015, https://www.bbc.com/news/magazine-30883058.

99. Social, Economic and Educational Status of the Muslim Community of India: A Report, November 2006, http://www.minorityaffairs.gov.in/sites/default/files/sachar_comm.pdf.

100. Five Hindu godmen or babas including 'Computer Baba' were given MoS status by the BJP government in Madhya Pradesh. NDTV, '5 Minister Babas Spark Political Row in Madhya Pradesh', 4 April 2018.

101. Milli Gazette, 'Haj Subsidy Must Go: Syed Shahabuddin', 15 September 2002.

102. Javed Akhtar received death threats from Islamic extremists for calling a cleric 'insane' in a TV debate. *Times of India*, 'Javed Akhtar Gets Death Threat over Fatwa Statement', 15 May 2010.

103. *Times of India*, 'Why Only Haj? End Subsidies for All Pilgrims', 21 January 2018.

104. Ibid.

105. IndiaSpend, Indian Population Growth Less Dependent on Religion, More on Development, 10 August 2016, http://www.indiaspend.com/cover-story/indian-population-growth-less-dependent-on-religion-more-on-development-80125.

106. IndiaSpend, 'Crimes against Women Up by 83 per cent, Conviction Rate Hits a Decadal Low', 12 December 2017.

107. 'I am a nationalist. I am patriotic. I am born Hindu. So I'm a Hindu nationalist because I am born Hindu': Modi to Reuters in 2013, quoted in PTI, 'Gujarat CM Describes Himself As a Hindu Nationalist', 12 July 2013.

108. *Times of India*, 'Christmas Carol Singers Detained over Allegations of Religious Conversions in MP', 16 December 2017.

109. See author's Facebook list of lynchings, https://www.facebook.com/sagarikaghose/?ref=bookmarks.

110. Slogans: 'Garv se kaho hum Hindu hain', 'Jis Hindu ka khoon na khaule, jo Ram ke kaam na aye'.

111. The Ram Janmabhoomi Babri Masjid dispute is to be decided by the Supreme Court. The apex court has said it will be heard as a land dispute. *Times of India*, 'Ayodhya Case to be Heard as a Land Dispute, Says SC', 9 February 2018.

112. Many Hindu Brahmins such as Kashmiris and Bengalis are non-vegetarian and eat meat even during festivals.

113. June 2017: farmers led by the Punjab Progressive Dairy Farmers Association PDFA claimed cattle slaughter rules were tyrannical. *DNA*, 'New Rules to Hit Cow Breeding Biz in Punjab: Dairy Farmers', 5 June 2017.

114. See Harish Damodaran, 'How Gau Rakshaks Can Derail India's White Revolution', *Indian Express*, 10 April 2017.

115. 'Muslims must stay out of politics as it only helps Modi to polarize society: J.S. Bandukwala, Gujarat Muslim activist.' Scroll, 'Interview: Muslims Must Stay Out of Politics as it Helps Modi Polarize Society', 26 November 2017.

116. The Arya Samaj at first overshadowed the Brahmos in the contest for the loyalties of reform-minded young men, went in for purification of lower castes, in 1893, split between meat-eating vs vegetarianism, anglicized vs Sanskrit-based education. Some sections started drifting to a 'Hindu' mentality. Sumit Sarkar, *Modern India 1885–1947* (New Delhi: Macmillan, 1983), pp. 74–75.

117. *Samagra Savarkar Vangmaya*, vols. 2 and 3. These views are available in the section 'Cow Protection and Cow worship' on savarkar.org.

118. The Bharatiya Jana Sangh won three seats in the 1951 polls, four in 1957, fourteen in 1962, thirty-five in 1967 and twenty-two in 1971. After the Janata coalition collapse in 1980, most Jana Sangh members left to form the BJP. See Craig Baxter, *The Jana Sangh: A Biography of an Indian Political Party* (New Delhi: Oxford University Press, 1971).

119. 'Those who go outside the country eat beef. Even Hindus eat beef. Poor people eat meat to beat their hunger. There is no difference between beef and goat meat.' Lalu Yadav at an election rally in Begusarai. *Indian Express*, 'Hindus Also Eat Beef: Lalu', 4 October 2015.

120. Ram idols had been installed in the Babri Masjid in 1949. Since then a priest had offered prayers there once a year but the temple was kept locked. In 1986, Rajiv Gandhi allowed the temple locks to be opened and the public to enter the temple. In 1989, he also allowed the shilanyas ceremony or laying of the foundation stone of the temple.

121. Nayantara Sahgal, *Indira Gandhi: Tryst With Power*, p. 346. During her first thirty-eight days in office, Indira Gandhi visited twelve shrines from Jammu to Tamil Nadu.

122. David Gilmartin and Bruce B. Lawrence, eds., *Beyond Turk and Hindu: Rethinking Religious Identities in Islamicate South Asia* (New Delhi: India Research Press, 2002).

123. Sagarika Ghose, 'Governments Have a Controlling Mindset. Ease of Doing Business Hasn't Improved: Narayana Murthy', *Times of India*, 16 February 2016.

124. In the 1983 Assam polls, Indira Gandhi used the religious card; in the Muslim Women Act 1986, the Congress failed to uphold gender justice; the ban on Salman Rushdie's *The Satanic Verses* once again was a retreat from liberal principles.

125. 'Our secular friends will create a toofan that what does Modi think of himself? He has taken the Gita with him that means he has made this one also communal.' *Times of India*, 'Modi Gifts Gita to Japanese Emperor, Takes a Dig at "Secular friends"', 3 September 2014.

126. Quoted by election commission of India: https://eci.nic.in/eci_main1/current/Judgement_ceo_24012017.pdf.

127. *Business Standard*, 'Don't Split Your Vote, Mayawati Tells Muslims', 3 January 2017. 'Muslims should be very careful. They should not divide their votes: Mayawati'.

128. *Hindustan Times*, 'The Fatwa Man of Bengal Who Is Offering Rs 25 lakh for Blackening PM Modi's Face', 12 January 2017. 'I have issued the fatwa against Modi because of notebandi . . . Mamata Banerjee should be PM,' said Noor-ur-Rehman Barkati.

129. Yogendra Yadav, 'The Fuss over Friday Prayers: What Secularism Should Really Mean', *Tribune*, 9 May 2018.

130. The high court struck down TMC government's decision to give monthly honorariums to imams. *Times of India*, 'Setback for Mamata as HC Rejects Dole for Imams and Muezzins', 3 September 2013.

131. *Indian Express*, 'BJP Vote Share Rises in Bengal', 12 April 2018.

132. 'Manifesto of Swatantra Party', *Swatantra Souvenir*, 1973.

133. *Indian Express*, 'Stop Harassment of Muslims or Face Consequences: Azam Khan', 1 May 2017.

134. 'Hindus have united after Modi's visit to Assam, it's time for minorities to unite. We, the minorities must stand united and fight against it or else we will lose our existence in Assam.' *Economic Times*, 'Modi Has United Hindus in Assam, It Is Time for Minorities to Unite', 23 January 2016.

135. 'Mr Narendra Modi, this country is not your father's property. This country belongs to me as much as to you.' A police complaint was filed against this speech. News Minute, 'Hate Speech Complaint against Akbaruddin Owaisi for "offensive language" against PM Modi', 7 July 2017.

136. However, the Sarvajan Samaj experiment proved short-lived and Mayawati soon abandoned it. She lost in the 2012 assembly polls and the BSP scored zero in the 2014 Lok Sabha elections.

137. *Indian Express*, 'Abul Kalam Azad, the Lodestar', 28 March 2018.

138. Sagarika Ghose, 'Qaum or Country?', *Outlook*, 9 October 1996.

139. *Frontline*, 'Choosing a President', 5 July 2002.

140. Sixteenth-century Urdu verses, one of which is an invocation to Saraswati.

141. Sagarika Ghose, 'Qaum or Country?', *Outlook*, 9 October 1996.

142. A Muslim MP has been added—Tabassum Hasan won from the Kairana bypoll in May 2018, the first Muslim MP from Uttar Pradesh.

143. Pehlu Khan was attacked by cow vigilantes on 1 April 2017 in Alwar and died two days later. *Indian Express*, 'All Held in Pehlu Khan Lynching Case Out on Bail', 29 September 2017. On 8 July 2018, minister of state for civil aviation and Hazaribagh MP Jayant Sinha garlanded eight men who were convicted—and released on bail—for the lynching of cattle-trader Alimuddin Ansari in June 2017. *Times of India*, 'Union Minister Jayant Sinha Garlands 8 Lynching Convicts, Faces Opposition Flak', 8 July 2018.

144. Dozens of Muslim youth were wrongfully imprisoned for the Mecca Masjid blast case of 2007, and later acquitted and awarded compensation. News Minute, 'The Torture I Endured Still Haunts Me', 16 April 2018.

145. Recent instances of discrimination have widened the divide. An Indian chef at a Dubai restaurant was sacked in June 2018 for anti-Muslim tweets. An Ola Cabs driver was also sacked in June 2018 for refusing to take a passenger to a 'Muslim' area.

146. When Rushdie was stopped from coming to the Jaipur Literature Festival in 2012, a group of authors like Amitava Kumar, Hari Kunzru, Jeet Thayil and Ruchir Joshi read out sections of Rushdie's banned book *The Satanic Verses*.

147. S. Radhakrishnan, *The Bhagavadgita*, p. 341.

The Liberal Thinker

1. Dilip Chitre, trans. and ed., *Namdeo Dhasal: Poet of the Underworld: Poems 1972–2006* (New Delhi: Navayana, 2007).

2. Sagarika Ghose, 'Govts Have a Controlling Mindset. Ease of Doing Business Hasn't Improved', *Times of India*, 16 February 2016. Also see, *Economic Times*, 'India Is Still Very Bureaucratic & Unnecessarily So: Nicolas Berggruen', 25 November 2015. 'Government should be a service organization as opposed to a power organization. It should help people, protect people, give opportunities; it should be an enabler. There is so much vibrancy

in India, but I feel the bureaucratic environment—which the government controls—is really not an enabler. It needs to change for India to achieve its potential.'

3. 'Silicon Valley' is the region in the southern San Francisco Bay Area of northern California, home to many start-up and technology companies such as Google, Facebook, Netflix and Apple. Known as America's technology capital, it is also the home of Airbnb, Uber and Tesla.

4. *Rajaji Reader: Selections from the Writings of C. Rajagopalachari* (Chennai: Vyasa Publications, 1980), pp. 130–32.

5. Minoo Masani, *Freedom First*, April 1985. *Freedom First* was a liberal magazine founded by Minoo Masani which published a monthly edition from 1952 to 2015. The print edition stopped in 2015 and the magazine went online. It was edited for many years by the late S.V. Raju. There are also online collections of articles by liberals such as www.liberalsindia.org and Indianliberals.in, an archive of Indian liberal writings run by the Centre for Civil Society.

6. On 9 July 2018, the Supreme Court upheld the death sentence for the Nirbhaya gangrape-murder convicts.

7. Refer to earlier section on rising crimes against women and the Unnao rape case and the Kathua rape and murder cases.

8. Masani, *Freedom First*, April 1985.

9. C. Rajagopalachari, 'Swatantra Souvenir', 1973. Available on www.indianliberals.in

10. Masani, *Freedom First*, April 1985.

11. Pranab Bardhan, *Society, Conflicts and Cooperation: Essays in the Political and Institutional Economics of Development* (Cambridge, Massachusetts: MIT Press, 2005), p. 3.

12. Author's italics. 'The Collected Works of Mahatma Gandhi', *Harijan* 67 (18 January 1942).

13. Author's italics. Ibid.

14. As quoted by Sibnarayan Ray, ed. *Gandhi, India and the World: An International Symposium* (Philadelphia: Temple University Press, 1970), p. 240; N.K. Bose, *Studies in Gandhism* (Calcutta, 1962), pp. 202–04.

15. 'The Collected Works of Mahatma Gandhi', *Harijan* 65 (18 January 1948).

16. Robert J. Burrowes, *The Strategy of Nonviolent Defense: A Gandhian Approach* (Albany: State University of New York Press, 1996), p. 4.

17. 'Hind Swaraj', in *The Collected Works of Mahatma Gandhi*, vol. 65 (Ahmedabad: Navajivan Trust, 1975).

18. D.G. Tendulkar, *Mahatma: Life of Mohandas Karamchand Gandhi*, vol. 2 (New Delhi: Publications Division, Government of India, 1969), p. 24.

19. Five activists—a professor, a lawyer, a human rights activists and two other activists, Shoma Sen, Surendra Gadling, Sudhir Dhawale, Rona Wilson and Mahesh Raut—were arrested on 6 June 2018 under the Unlawful Activities (Prevention) Act and taken into police custody. These arbitrary arrests have been protested by a range of citizens groups.

20. Jawahar Raja, 'Why the UAPA Must Go', *India Today*, 7 September 2018.

21. Masani, *Freedom First*, April 1985.

22. As pointed out, Modi is a believer in Big Government schemes like Swachh Bharat, Start-Up India, Make In India, Skill India, Digital India, rather like Indira Gandhi's 20-Point Programme or Sanjay Gandhi's 5-Point Programme.

23. C. Rajagopalachari, *Speeches and Writings* (Swatantra Party Souvenir, Sixth National Convention), 14–15 April 1973.

24. Founded in 1959 by C. Rajagopalachari, its members included architect and politician Piloo Mody, veteran farm leader from Andhra Pradesh N.C. Ranga and others.

25. See section on Aadhaar in this chapter.

26. *The Hindu*, 'What is an Electoral Bond and How to Get One', 4 January 2018.

27. *Times of India*, 'CPM Moves SC against Electoral Bonds', 1 February 2018.

28. Rediff, 'PMO Refuses to Reply to RTI on Modi's Foreign Trips', 8 May 2015.

29. Wire, 'Mute Modi: Why Is the Prime Minister Terrified of Holding Even a Single Press Conference?', 4 January 2018.

30. Swaminathan Aiyar, 'NaMo's New Protectionism Looks More Like Nehru, Less Like China', *Times of India*, 18 February 2018.

31.   T.N. Ninan, 'How the Failures and Wrong Doing of Private Sector Have Stymied Reforms', *Business Standard*, 29 June 2018.

32.   In an address to the nation telecast on Doordarshan, Modi appeared at 8 p.m. on 8 November 2016 to announce: 'From midnight, November 8, 2016, today, Rs 500 notes and Rs 1000 notes are no longer legal tender.'

33.   'Demonetization is a "shuddhi yajna". India has undertaken a historic cleansing drive against black money. People have borne pain to vanquish the evil of corruption.' *India Today*, 'In Address to the Nation on New Year's Eve, PM Modi Calls Demonetization Drive "Shuddhi Yajna"', 1 January 2017.

34.   Over 100 deaths allegedly resulted from demonetization. Congress cited over 100 deaths in Rajya Sabha, Mamata Banerjee said Modi is responsible for 120 deaths. IANS, 'PM Modi Responsible for 120 Note Ban Deaths: Mamata', 10 January 2017. Catch News, 'Demonetisation Death Toll, 90 People and Counting As Note Ban Takes Tragic Turn', 9 December 2016.

35.   Arun Kumar, 'Demonetization: Now a Proven Failure?' *The Hindu*, 8 September 2017.

36.   *The Hindu*, 'RBI Refuses to Answer RTI on Whether CEA or Finance Minister Were Consulted before Demonetisation', 1 January 2017.

37.   Yascha Mounk, 'How Populist Uprisings Could Bring Down Liberal Democracy', *Guardian*, 4 March 2018. Also, his new book, *The People vs Democracy: Why Our Freedom Is in Danger and How to Save It* (Cambridge, MA: Harvard University Press, 2018).

38.   Demonetization led to 1.5 million jobs lost and a fall in GDP growth to 7.1 per cent in 2016–17 as compared to 8 per cent in the previous year. Quartz, 'India Lost 1.5 Million Jobs in the Aftermath of Demonetization', 17 July 2017. *Times of India*, 'About 100 Died Standing in Queue: Opposition Statement in December 2016 in Rajya Sabha', 18 November 2016. Congress's Ghulam Nabi Azad said that there had been more deaths due to demonetization than after the Uri attack by Pakistani militants in September 2016. Then I&B minister Venkaiah Naidu called this remark 'anti-national'.

39. Tweet from senior Union minister Arun Jaitley on 8 June 2018: 'The half-Maoist is a serious threat to Indian democracy. Willingly or otherwise, they become the overground face of the underground. Unfortunately, some political parties see the maoist as their instruments in the anti-NDA cause. Its high time people recognised this malaise.'

40. Louis XIV strengthened absolute power for the monarchy, forcing peasants to pay high taxes and eventually leading to the French revolution. Hitler created the Holocaust or the gassing of three million Jews. Indira Gandhi declared the Emergency, jailed opponents and journalists and about 37 lakh people were forcibly sterilized just in the first months of the infamous enforced sterilization drive. Stalin sent 20 million to forced labour camps, or Gulags, forced collectivization, executions and famine. Mao's 'Great Leap Forward' was called by *Washington Post* on 3 April 2016 as the 'biggest mass murder in the history of the world', causing the deaths of around 45 million.

41. BJP allegedly tries to paint sections of people as 'anti-India'. Defence Minister Nirmala Sitharaman said Rahul Gandhi met JNU students notorious for their 'Bharat tere tukde tukde' attitude. Firstpost, 'Nirmala Sitharaman Slams Congress for Playing "Religion Card", Says Rahul Gandhi Engaging in Communal Politics', 13 July 2018.

42. Modi in first Independence Day speech: 'I am an outsider in Delhi . . . far removed from elite class', NDTV, 15 August 2014. Modi won because he was an outsider, argues Meghnad Desai in *Politic Shock: Trump, Modi and Brexit and the Prospect for Liberal Democracy* (New Delhi: Rupa, 2017).

43. BJP leaders have a set of pre-determined enemies. PTI, 'Some People with Left, Socialist and Anti-BJP Approach Are Not in a Mood to Accept Modi as Prime Minister: Nitin Gadkari, Road Transport and Highway Minister', 23 February 2016.

44. Yascha Mounk, 'How Populist Uprisings Could Bring Down Liberal Democracy', *Guardian*, 4 March 2018.

45. According to the CSDS Mood of the Nation Poll 2018, support for the Modi-led BJP was the highest in the 18–25 age group.

46. In the assembly elections of 2017, Congress emerged as the single largest party in Goa and Manipur, but the BJP formed governments in both states through sharp alliance building.

47. In 1980, Indira Gandhi sacked the Akali government in Punjab when she returned to power, and in 1983 topped the Farooq Abdullah government.

48. Turkey is now an elected dictatorship. Yascha Mounk, 'Turkey's Warning: Why Erdogan's Consolidation of Power Should be Cause for Concern in Every Liberal Democracy', Slate, 24 June 2018.

49. Pewglobal.org, 'The State of Indian Democracy', 15 November 2017.

50. Guardian, 'James Harding's Hugh Cudlipp Lecture in Full', 22 March 2018.

51. Yascha Mounk, 'How Populist Uprisings Could Bring Down Liberal Democracy', Guardian, 4 March 2018.

52. The CSDS Mood of the Nation Poll showed a sharp drop in Modi's popularity. The Hindu, 'Positive Perceptions of the Modi Government Has Taken a Dip, Finds CSDS Poll, 15 February 2018.

53. See The Economist, 'Grounded', 9 June 2018.

54. Observers have pointed to trade protectionism and the Modicare health scheme as examples of 'saffron socialism'.

55. Sagarika Ghose, 'No More Singur Moment for Bengal's Intellectuals', Times of India, 16 April 2016.

56. Scroll, 'Mamata Suppressing All Dissent, Says Professor Arrested for Circulating Cartoons', 12 March 2015.

57. DailyO, '13 Die in Bengal Panchayat Polls', 14 May 2018; Wire, 'SC Expresses Shock at Thousands of Uncontested Seats in Bengal Panchayat Polls', 5 June 2018.

58. Yascha Mounk, 'How Populist Uprisings Could Bring Down Liberal Democracy', Guardian, 4 March 2018.

59. NDTV, 'Yes, I Am a Chamcha of Narendra Modi, I Am Proud to Be a Modi Chamcha: Censor Board Chief Pahlaj Nihalani', 8 June 2016.

60. Business Standard, 'Modi Is a Gift to the Nation from God: Venkaiah Naidu', 21 May 2016.

61. Yascha Mounk, 'How Populist Uprisings Could Bring Down Liberal Democracy', *Guardian*, 4 March 2018.
62. NDTV, 'In BJP, Nobody Asks Who Your Father Is: Himanta Biswa Sarma', 22 September 2017.
63. Yadav and Prashant Bhushan were expelled from AAP in April 2015.
64. Ambedkar's speech in the Constituent Assembly on 25 November 1949. Dhananjay Keer, *Dr Ambedkar: Life and Mission* (Mumbai: Popular Prakashan, 1990), p. 330.
65. In April 2016, when film director Ram Gopal Varma criticized Rajinikanth's looks on Twitter, there was such a furious backlash from Rajini fans that Varma had to do a U-turn and praise the Tamil superhero as an 'earthly star'.
66. Modi is the most followed leader on Facebook with 42.7 million followers. Such tweets are common on social media: @nareshvijayvar4: Modiji is a lion; @namokaraj: I am a proud Indian and Modi fan.
67. AAP leader Sanjay Singh has filed a case in the Delhi High Court to get Prime Minister Modi's Parliament attendance details. PTI, 'AAP MP Sanjay Singh Moves HC against PM Modi's Absenteeism', 11 June 2018. TMC MP Derek O'Brien stated in May 2015, 'Please grant a visa to the Prime Minister of India to come to the Rajya Sabha. Second leg of the Budget Session of Parliament was the worst performing parliament in a decade as it hardly functioned.' *Times of India*, 'Budget Session: Lok Sabha Spent Only 1 per cent of Allotted Time on Work, Rajya Sabha 6%', 7 April 2018.
68. Rediff, '36 Fighter Jet Rafale Aircraft Purchased from France in April 2015', 10 October 2017. In a reply to *Business Standard*, the PMO clarified that the prime minister's personal staff strength was sixty-five, while that of the three former prime ministers Manmohan Singh, Vajpayee and H.D. Deve Gowda was fourteen, twelve and two, respectively. *Business Standard* said 356 worked as staff, to which the PMO gave a rejoinder saying the PMO staff strength was in the range of 407–411 in 2011–2014 while it had declined to 385 now. News Minute, 'The PMO Office has 385 Staff Members, Number Has Declined from Past Years', 12 January 2015.

69. *The Economist*, 9 June 2018.

70. *The Hindu*, 'Banning Strikes in Public Utility Services', 2 December 2015.

71. The government cancelled Greenpeace's registration under the FCRA Act in 2015 for allegedly working against the economic interests of India.

72. Ford Foundation in 2015 was placed on a watchlist because it was said to be funding groups acting against the national interest. *Times of India*, 'Govt Puts Ford Foundation Under Watch List', 24 April 2015. Ford was removed from the watchlist in 2016.

73. At Karnataka chief minister H.D. Kumaraswamy's swearing-in in Bengaluru on 23 May 2018, leaders of the so-called federal front, from Mamata Banerjee to Mayawati, Arvind Kejriwal and Chandrababu Naidu lined up in a show of strength.

74. 'The highest growth in India was between 1990–2014 during coalition governments. So in a way, it is consensus-based . . . in Indian situation a coalition produces better results than a strong government.' Former RBI governor Y.V. Reddy at Hudson Institute speech in Washington DC. *Economic Times*, 'Better Growth in Coalition Governments: Former RBI Governor YV Reddy', 29 September 2017.

75. Manmohan Singh had been the RBI governor and before that the head of the Planning Commission during 1985–87.

76. Jean Drèze and Amartya Sen, *An Uncertain Glory: India and Its Contradictions* (New York: Penguin, 2013), p. 281.

77. Sanjaya Baru, 'The Economist as Saviour', *The Hindu,* 2 July 2012. Also see Amit Bhaduri and Deepak Nayyar, *The Intelligent Person's Guide to Liberalization* (New Delhi: Penguin Books, 2000).

78. In January 2015, Greenpeace campaigner Priya Pillai was prevented from travelling to London. The travel ban was later revoked.

79. On 3 March 2015, the I&B ministry directed all news channels not to telecast the BBC documentary *India's Daughter*, based on the Nirbhaya case.

80. The language of 'traitors' is common in the ruling party. BJP MLA Sangeet Som has said that the Taj Mahal was built by 'traitors'. NDTV, 'Taj Mahal Built by Traitors, Says BJP's

Sangeet Som, Hate Speech Giver', 16 October 2017. BJP leader
Subramanian Swamy questioned the patriotic credentials of
then RBI governor Raghuram Rajan, saying he was 'mentally
not fully Indian'. He said this may be the reason the 'RBI
governor is wilfully and deliberately wrecking the Indian
economy'. *Times of India*, 'Raghuram Rajan "Mentally Not
Fully Indian, Sack Him, Subramanian Swamy Writes to PM
Modi', 17 May 2016. Before he left, there were social media
attacks on Rajan in January 2016, saying he was a 'traitor' and
should be 'tried for treason'.

81. Prime Minister led the nation in celebrating the fourth
    International Yoga Day in Dehradun on 21 June 2018 at a massive
    gathering.

82. *Times of India*, 'Surat Couple Praised by Modi in Mann Ki Baat
    Broadcast', 27 November 2016.

83. The rule says 'young' and 'unfit' animals cannot be sold. *Hindustan
    Times*, 'Centre Bans Sale of Cows for Slaughter at Animal Markets,
    Restricts Cattle Trade', 23 May 2017.

84. The beef and leather industry is a multimillion dollar one,
    employing millions and generating more than $16 billion in
    annual sales. Reuters, 'India's Supreme Court Suspends Ban on
    Sale of Cows for Slaughter', 11 July 2017.

85. *Hindustan Times*, 'Centre's Notification Banning Cow Sale for
    Slaughter a Fascist Move: Kerala', 22 May 2017.

86. *New York Times*, 'India's SC Suspends Ban on Sale of Cows for
    Slaughter', July 2017. 'The livelihoods of people should not be
    affected,' said the Court, also stating that the ban should not apply
    to buffaloes.

87. Pawan Pandit, head, Cow Protection Group, quoted in Reuters,
    'India's Supreme Court Suspends Ban on Sale of Cows for
    Slaughter', 11 July 2017.

88. *New Indian Express*, 'Centre's Target Is to Double Farm Incomes
    in Five Years Says PM Modi', 3 November 2017.

89. IndiaSpend, '2017 Deadliest Year for Cow-related Crimes', 8
    December 2017.

90. 'Some 70–80 per cent of gau rakshaks are anti-social elements.
    They don the robes of gau rakshaks to prevent themselves from

being punished.' *Times of India*, 'Self Proclaimed Gau Rakshaks Make Me Angry, PM Modi Says', 7 August 2016. He also said, 'I appeal to real gau rakshaks to expose the fake gau rakshaks.' However, Hindutva outfits even threatened to send legal notices protesting against the 70–80 per cent figure given by Modi and Modi soon backtracked, saying 'only a handful' of gau rakshaks were anti-social and only 'few are opportunists'. News Minute, 'Shoot Me, Not Dalits Says Modi, as RSS Calls for Exposing "Anti-social" Gau Rakshaks', 18 August 2016.

91. *Financial Express*, 'Govt Does Well to Withdraw Restrictions on Cattle Trade', 11 April 2018.

92. *The Hindu*, 'RSS Seeks National Ban on Cow Killing', 9 April 2017.

93. *Hindustan Times*, 'Anyone Found Killing Cows in Chhattisgarh Will be Hanged: Raman Singh', 7 April 2017.

94. *The Hindu*, 'IIT Madras Scholar Beaten Up for Eating Beef During Protest', 30, May 2017.

95. Modi's speech on 2 April 2014 in Bihar: 'We've heard of the Green Revolution, we've heard of the White Revolution but today's Delhi sarkar has taken up cudgels for a Pink Revolution . . . when you slaughter an animal the colour of its meat is pink . . . across the countryside our animals are getting slaughtered . . . our livestock is getting stolen . . . [they are giving] subsidies to people who slaughter cows.' *The Hindu*, Modi Fears a Pink Revolution', 3 April 2014.

96. Huffington Post, 'Haryana Becomes Fifth BJP State to Ban Meat for Jain Festival', 12 September 2015.

97. In May 2015, food safety regulators from Barabanki, Uttar Pradesh reported that Maggi noodles contained seventeen times the permissible amounts of lead. In June India's Food Safety and Standards Authority of India (FSSAI) banned Maggi noodles, available in the market since 1983 and holding 80 per cent of the instant noodles market. Many state governments banned Maggi until tests showed that there were no dangerous amounts of lead in Maggi. On 13 August 2015, the Bombay High Court struck down the nationwide ban on Maggi, calling the FSSAI orders 'arbitrary, unjust and violative of Article 14 of the Constitution'.

98. Louis Dumont, *Homo Hierarchicus: The Caste System and Its Implications* (University of Chicago Press, 1980).

99. 'Beef is not considered commonly eaten food in Kashmir. It's a poor man's food, helps keep people warm in winter,' HC advocate Zaffar Shah told ET magazine, 'Kashmiris always ate mutton, beef is a political statement.' *Economic Times*, 11 October 2015.

100. *Indian Express*, 'J&K HC Directs Police to Strictly Enforce Beef Ban', 11 September 2015.

101. Article 48. Arvind Datar, SC advocate: 'The Constitution does not envisage a complete ban on slaughter of cows but only seeks to prevent or prohibit the slaughter of a particular class of cattle. To completely eliminate the consumption of beef would be unconstitutional as it would deprive sizeable sections of society of the right to consume the meat of their choice.' Arvind Datar, 'What the Constitution Says on the Curious Case of the Holy Cow', Quint, 31 May 2017.

102. Taittiriya Upanishad in S. Radhakrishnan, *The Principal Upanishads* (Noida: HarperCollins, 2004), p. 543.

103. The RSS was founded by K.B. Hedgewar, a Deshastha Brahmin, in 1925. The second sarsanghchalak of the RSS was M.S. Golwalkar, who was a Karhade Brahmin.

104. In fact, after winning seats in beef-eating Nagaland, minister of state for home Kiren Rijiju said beef was not an issue for the BJP. *Hindustan Times*, 'Beef Is Not an Issue for Us, Focus Is on Development', 4 March 2018.

105. Sagarika Ghose, 'Ministry from Hell', *Indian Express*, 4 August 2004.

106. In April 2018, I&B minister Smriti Irani, now shifted from the ministry, sent out a press release saying the government would set up a committee to determine 'fake news' by accredited journalists and if journalists were found guilty, they would lose their accreditation. After widespread protests by journalists, the government was forced to withdraw this order.

107. Manish Tewari, 'The Time Has Come to Abolish the I&B Ministry Once and for All', 10 April 2018.

108. *Financial Times*, 'Foreign Media Groups Stymied by Indian Regulations', 3 December 2015.

109. Abhinav Chandrachud, *Republic of Rhetoric: Free Speech and the Constitution of India* (Gurgaon: Penguin Random House India, 2017), p. 18.

110. In October 2016, Bollywood movie director Karan Johar issued a public statement that he would not cast any Pakistani actors in his films after the Raj Thackeray–led Maharashtra Navnirman Sena threatened to attack movie theatres in which Johar's film starring Pakistani actor Fawad Khan were shown.

111. In February 2017, Ramjas College in Delhi University organized a seminar in which JNU students Umar Khalid and Shehla Rashid were invited to speak. Their presence was objected to by the ABVP and there were violent clashes between student groups causing the seminar to get cancelled. Livemint, 'Ramjas College Protest: ABVP, AISA Activists Clash over Khalid's Invite to DU Seminar', 22 February 2017.

112. NDTV, 'RSS Reviews Modi Government Performance, PM Likely to Attend Meeting', 2 September 2015.

113. *Guardian*, 'India Blocks More than 800 Sites as Part of Government Web Crackdown', 3 August 2015.

114. *Indian Express*, 'India Third Most Porn Watching Country in the World', 3 June 2018, quoting Pornhub's 2017 Year in Review report.

115. In 2015, the documentary was to be shown on NDTV but was banned at the last minute by the government. Ruling party members said the film was 'a conspiracy to defame India'. *New York Times*, 'Broadcast of India Gang Rape Documentary is Banned by Court', 6 March 2015.

116. In 2012, the TMC government banned certain newspapers from state-aided libraries. *Times of India*, 'Mamata Government Bans Mass Circulating Dailies at State Libraries', 28 March 2012.

117. *Times of India*, 'Controversial List of Cuss Words Withdrawn by CBFC', 4 April 2015.

118. The sting revealed how Cambridge Analytica had got unauthorized access to users' Facebook data, which it was attempting to use to influence election outcomes across the world.

119. PTI, 'India Witnessed Highest Number of Internet Shutdowns in 2017–2018: UNESCO', 13 May 2018.

120. *The Economist*, 'The Surveillance State: Perfected in China, a Threat in the West', 2 June 2018.

121. Chidambaram, Speech at IIT, December 2017.

122. Jean Drèze, 'Dissent and Aadhaar', *Indian Express*, 8 May 2017.

123. Live Law, 'Aadhaar: Read the Summary of the Majority (4:1) Judgement', 26 September 2018; *Indian Express*, 'Full Text: Supreme Court Aadhaar Judgement', 26 September 2018; Live Law, 'Aadhaar Project Wholly Unconstitutional. Landmark Dissent by Justice Chandrachud: Full Text', 26 September 2018.

124. *Times of India*, 'Don't Create Panic on Aadhaar Linking: SC to Banks, Telcos', 4 November 2017.

125. An eleven-year-old girl died begging for food as she had no Aadhaar card. NDTV, 'No Aadhaar, No Food? Girl, 11, Died "Begging for Rice", Says Jharkhand Family', 17 October 2017.

126. In January 2018, a Rae Bareilly woman delivered at the gate of a UP medical centre as she was turned away because she did not have an Aadhaar card. *Outlook*, 'Turned Away for Not Having Aadhaar, Woman Delivers at Gate of UP Medical Centre', 30 January 2018.

127. On 21 January 2018, Snowden tweeted while quoting former R&AW chief K.C. Verma's article on the misuse of Aadhaar data by banks and telecom companies, saying it must be criminalized.

128. On 4 January 2018 *Tribune* reporter Rachna Khaira showed how for just Rs 500 anyone could get details of a billion Aadhaar details. The UIDAI registered an FIR against the reporter for the story, which was protested against strongly by journalist bodies.

129. *Times of India*, 'GST, Note Ban, Broke the Back of Small Businesses: Manmohan Singh', 7 November 2017.

130. In October 2017, teenager Zakir Ali Tyagi spent over forty days in jail after a Facebook post on the Yogi Adityanath government.

131. Rashtriya Swayamsevak Sangh, *RSS Resolves: Full Text of Resolutions from 1950–1983* (Karnataka: Prakashan Vibhag RSS, 1983), pp. 15-16.

132. Actor Salman Khan is known to do a regular Ganpati puja in his home; the Lalbaug Ganesha Puja in Mumbai is among the most famous in the city.

The Liberal Dissenter

1.   Raghuram G. Rajan, *Fault Lines. How Hidden Fractures Still Threaten the World Economy* (New Delhi: Collins Business, 2010), p. 239.

2.   *The Republic of Reason, Words They Could Not Kill: Selected Writings of Dabholkar, Pansare, Kalburgi and Lankesh* (New Delhi: SAHMAT with the Raza Foundation, 2018), p. 50.

3.   Govind Pansare, *Who was Shivaji?* (Mumbai: Lokvangmay Griha, 2011).

4.   Ibid.

5.   Sagarika Ghose, 'Politicians Remember Basavanna Only at Election Time, Says the Family of Slain Scholar MM Kalburgi', *Times of India*, 3 May 2018.

6.   According to the police charge sheet, the accused, K.T. Naveen, confessed to plotting Gauri's killing with other accomplices who had also planned to target Mysore-based rationalist K.S. Bhagwan as well as actor Prakash Raj for his 'anti-BJP' statements. Another suspect in the Gauri Lankesh murder, Parashuram Waghmore has told police, 'I killed Gauri to save my religion'. *Times of India*, 'I Killed Gauri to Save My Religion: Waghmore to SIT', 16 June 2018.

7.   The Special Investigation Team of the Karnataka police arrested two men with links to Hindutva group Sri Ram Sene in the Gauri Lankesh murder case. *Indian Express*, 'Two More with Links to Hindutva Outfits Held in Gauri Lankesh Murder Case', 24 July 2018.

8.   *Hindustan Times*, 'Ram Navmi Tableau Celebrates Shambhu Lal Regar', 27 March 2018.

9.   Swati Chaturvedi, *I Am a Troll: Inside the Secret World of the BJP's Digital Army* (New Delhi: Juggernaut, 2016).

10. Tweet by @riot11: Arundhati Roy is a 'maoist anti-national and a rabid Pakistani', 21 May 2017; @SandipGhose: 'Fail to understand why with allies like #ArundhatiRoy, pakistan wastes money on funding the Hurriyat etc [sic]', 22 May 2017; @ParashRm: 'leftist communist/traitors and other antinational and anti Hindu hypocrites have embedded into influential positions in education, politics and media—Prannoy Roy, Sagarika Ghose, Burkha,[sic] Sardesai, Arundhati etc. these scum will sell their mothers for a

few dinars', 1 July 2016; @giniromet: 'I consider likes of Barkha Dutt, Sagarika Ghosh etc more anti-national than Hafiz Sayeed kyonki ghar ka bhedi lanka dhaye', 19 February 2016.

11. NDTV, 'Journalist Shujaat Bukhari's Killers Identified, One Is a Pakistani: Sources', 27 June 2018. Also see Sagarika Ghose, 'Where the Gun Rules: From Shujaat Bukhari to Gauri Lankesh, the Middle Ground Is Under Attack', *Times of India*, 20 June 2018.

12. Abhinav Chandrachud, *Republic of Rhetoric: Free Speech and the Constitution of India* (Gurgaon: Penguin Random House India, 2017), pp. 73–97.

13. Ibid, p. 91. Mukherjee argued: 'partition of Bharat was a tragic folly . . . we believe in the goal of a reunited bharat . . . p. 82. Mukherjee believed arguments for and against partition should be openly made and the public allowed to make up its own mind. Nehru however said, 'No State in the name of freedom, can submit to actions which may result in wholesale war and destruction.' (Chandrachud, p. 83.)

14. On 25 April 2016, Kanhaiya Kumar alleged that a co-passenger on board a Jet Airways flight tried to strangle him. *Times of India*, 'Co-flyer Tried to Strangle Me', 25 April 2016.

15. After Gauri's death, Facebook hit-lists appeared calling for the assassination of the author along with activists Kavita Krishnan and Shehla Rashid, and Arundhati Roy and Shobhaa De. *Hindustan Times*, 'Man Threatening Women Activists, Author, Journo for Being "Anti-national" Booked', 8 September 2017. Also, rape threats against Congress spokesperson's Priyanka Chaturvedi's daughter led to the arrest of the person making the threats. NDTV, 'Man Arrested for Twitter Threats to Congress's Priyanka Chaturvedi', 6 June 2018. External affairs minister Sushma Swaraj faced attack on social media for being sympathetic to a Hindu–Muslim couple, *India Today*, 'Sushma Swaraj Trolled again on Twitter', 30 January 2018.

16. Rawal tweeted on 21 May 2017 that author Arundhati Roy should be tied to a jeep just as Kashmiri civilian Farooq Dar was on 9 April 2017 by Indian army officer Leetul Gogoi: 'Instead of tying stone pelter to army jeep, tie Arundhati Roy'. Major Leetul Gogoi of 53 Rashtriya Rifles received the army chief's 'commendation

card' for sustained efforts during counter-insurgency operations in Jammu and Kashmir.

17. Nikhil Dadhich is followed by Prime Minister Modi; Ashish Mishra's profile declares, 'I am Hindu and Team Modi' and he is followed by Union minister Ravi Shankar Prasad.

18. DailyO, 'PM Modi Called Journalists "News Traders" in 2015', 6 June 2017.

19. In February 2016, Delhi lawyers attacked female reporters while JNUSU president Kanhaiya Kumar's sedition case was being heard in case, shouting 'we will break your phones and bones'. Scroll, 'Journalists and JNU Students Attacked in Court', 15 February 2016.

20. Between 2012 and 2016, eighteen journalists were killed in India. This is according to the World Trends in Freedom of Expression and Media development Global Report 2017–2018 published in *Hindustan Times* on 2 May 2018. According to World Press Freedom Index Report 2018 by Reporters Without Borders (quoted in Firstpost, 25 April 2018), the report mentions 'hate speech' and targeting of journalists by 'troll armies' of Prime Minister Modi.

21. In July 2017, a Madras High Court judge ordered that Vande Mataram should be played and sung in all schools, colleges, universities and educational institutions at least once a week. *India Today*, 'Vande Mataram Now Mandatory in Tamil Nadu Schools and Offices: Madras HC Passes Order', 25 July 2017.

22. 'If a kabristan can be constructed, a shamshaan too should be built. If electricity is given uninterrupted during Ramzan, then it should be given in Diwali without a break': Modi at an election rally in Fatehpur, UP. *Hindustan Times*, 'If a Kabristan Can be Constructed, a Shamshaan Too Should be Built: PM Modi', 20 February 2017.

23. *India Today*, 'Controversy over Vande Mataram in Maharashtra Yet Again', 27 July 2017, https://www.indiatoday.in/india/story/controversy-vandemataram-maharashtra-1026724-2017-07-27.

24. *The Hindu*, 'MLA Won't Chant "Bharat Mata Ki Jai", Suspended', 16 March 2016, https://www.thehindu.com/news/national/mim-mla-suspendedfrom-maharashtra-assembly/article8361194.ece.

25. *The Hindu*, 'Won't Say Bharat Mata Ki Jai: Owaisi', 14 March 2016, https://www.thehindu.com/news/Won%E2%80%99t-say-Bharat-Mata-ki-Jai-Owaisi/article14155038.ece.

26. In 1985, the Anti-Defection Law was brought in by the Rajiv Gandhi government. This was the Fifty-second Constitution Amendment Bill 1985, which read, 'The evil of political defections has been a matter of concern, if not combated it is likely to undermine the foundations of our democracy.' The Anti-Defection law silences party members in the House and stops them from exercising a conscience vote in the face of a party whip. If they disagree with their party, they can be expelled.

27. Madhav Khosla, *The Indian Constitution* (New Delhi: Oxford University Press, 2012), p. 11.

28. Aakar Patel, 'Anti-Defection Law Makes the False Assumption That the Party Is Right, Curbs Legislators' Freedom of Choice', Firstpost, 19 May 2018.

29. For full text of this letter see Wire, 'Retired Bureaucrats Warn of Growing Authoritarianism and Majoritarianism in India', 12 June 2017.

30. The IT Act was passed in 2000. In 2008, Section 66A was inserted under which arrests were made, notably of two young women who were arrested in 2012 for Facebook posts on the funeral of Bal Thackeray. 66A was struck down by the Supreme Court in 2015 as 'vague' and 'unconstitutional'. (NDTV, 24 March 2015.)

31. Khilji laid a long siege to the fort of Chittor in the early fourteenth century, encountered passionate resistance from the Rajputs, 'the women inspiring posterity by hurling themselves into the flames while the men rode out in a still brighter blaze of glory to kill until they were killed'. John Keay, *India, a History* (London: Harper Press, 2000), p. 257.

32. The CBFC suggested a name-change for the film, as well as modifications to the song and dance sequence 'Ghoomar' to make the film more 'befitting' of the character it was portraying and not suggest any possible 'romance' between Alauddin Khilji and Padmavati. Film-maker Bhansali had already clarified that there was no dream sequence or objectionable scene between the characters of Padmavati and Khilji. Also see Chapter 5.

33. *Hindustan Times*, 'Protesting Cadres Attacked a School Bus in Gurugram', 27 January 2018.

34. After the murder of Sahitya Akademi awardee M.M. Kalburgi, it took the Akademi a couple of long months to break its silence to condemn the murder. It finally issued a statement in October 2015.

35. The Lalit Kala Akademi was created in 1954, the Sangeet Natak Akademi in 1952 and the Sahitya Akademi in 1954, which have all inevitably become patronage distribution systems by governments.

36. Firstpost, 'After Protests by Students, JNU Cancels Talk by Baba Ramdev', 28 December 2015.

37. *Indian Express*, 'Full Text of Dalit Student Rohith's Suicide Letter', 19 January 2016.

38. From Ambedkar's speech in the Constituent Assembly, *Constituent Assembly Debates*, vol. 11 (New Delhi: Lok Sabha Secretariat, 2014), pp. 972–81.

39. Report, *India Today*, 'Reality Check: Modi Government Fails to Keep Its Promises of 13 More AIIMS', 26 June 2018.

40. Kancha Ilaiah, *Why I Am Not a Hindu: A Sudra Critique of Hindutva Philosophy, Culture and Political Economy* (Kolkata: Samya, 1996).

41. The hymn from the Rig Veda on the 'Cosmic Being' that assigns upper castes different places in the divine body but leaves out the perpetually polluted 'achhut'.

42. Kancha Ilaiah, *Post-Hindu India: A Discourse in Dalit-Bahujan, Socio-Spiritual and Scientific Revolution* (New Delhi: Sage, 2009).

43. *Mainstream Weekly*, 'Concomitants', 15 March 2014.

44. On 1 January 2018, Dalits gathered at a village near Pune to mark the 200th anniversary of the battle of Bhima-Koregaon. The Battle of Koregaon was fought on 1 January 1818 between the Peshwas and the British, with Dalits fighting on the British side. The rally took a violent turn and five people were arrested in June 2018 and charged with having 'Naxal' links. At the time of the rally, Jignesh was at the Elgaar Parishad, a seminar held at Pune's Shaniwar Wada Fort on 31 December. See Chapter 3.

45. Wire, 'After 25 Years of Broken Promises, India Is Counting its Manual Scavengers Again', 4 June 2018.

46. BBC News, 'An English Goddess for India's Downtrodden', 11 February 2011.

47. Gail Omvedt, *Dalits and the Democratic Revolution* (New Delhi: Sage, 1994), p. 12.

48. National Crime Record Bureau (NCRB) records a six- to eightfold increase in crimes against Dalits over 2013–18 as compared to the last five years and there were 1,93,000 attacks on Dalits over this time period. Wire, 'What Lies Beneath the Alarming Rise in Violence against Dalits', 15 June 2018. Also see, IndiaSpend, 'Crimes against Dalits Up by 25 per cent in the Decade Ending in 2016', April 2018.

49. *Times of India*, 'In Gujarat Dalit Youth's Moustache Forcibly Shaved Off', 27 February 2018.

50. NDTV, 'Police Say Dalit Man Killed in Gujarat for Riding a Horse', 21 March 2018.

51. *Indian Express*, 'Tamil Author Perumal Murugan Announces His Own Death on Facebook', 5 January 2015.

52. *Hindustan Times*, 'Haryana: Postgraduates among the 15,000 Vying for 8 Posts of Peon in Jind Court', 8 January 2018.

53. Sagarika Ghose, 'B. Coms and B. Eds Selling Tea, Paan and Working As Masons', *Times of India*, 7 December 2017.

54. *The Hindu*, '23 Lakh Apply for 368 Peon Posts in Uttar Pradesh', 17 September 2015.

55. Livemint, 'Indian Farmers Call for Free Markets', 21 March 2018.

56. Interview to Manuwant Choudhary, Scroll, 21 December.

57. Barun Mitra, 'Our Socialist Agenda: the Time to Oust It Has Come', 16 January 2008.

58. The Representation of People Act requires that all political parties in order to be registered swear allegiance to socialism. Representation of the People Act (1951) amendment in 1988 Section 29 A states that the application of registration as a political party 'shall be accompanied by a copy of the memorandum or rules and regulations of the association . . . shall bear allegiance to the Constitution of India . . . to the principles of socialism, secularism and democracy . . . and uphold the sovereignty, unity and integrity of India. Liberal parties have argued that they are effectively barred from contesting elections because of the requirement of the socialism pledge.

59. *Business Standard*, 'Mandi Act Needs a New Recipe', 4 January 2014; 'We have convinced 17 states to reform their APMC Acts, says agriculture minister Radha Mohan Singh, see *Indian Express*, 'Radha Mohan Singh Interview: Doubling Farm Incomes Our Priority', 26 May 2016.

60. On 21 June 2018, in a video interaction with farmers, PM Modi promised to double farm incomes by 2022. *Economic Times*, 'PM Modi: Centre Aiming to Double Farmers' Income by 2022', 21 June 2018.

61. Farmer suicides were 12,602 in 2015, 11, 370 in 2016, with not all states included in the latter figure. NCRB figures quoted in *Business Standard*, 'Big Rise in Farmer Suicides in Four States during 2016, Says NCRB Data', 23 March 2018.

62. In a sense, the dignified farmers march on Mumbai was an antithesis of Sharad Joshi's goals. The organizers demanded protection, subsidies and loan waivers rather than freedom.

63. In July 2018, the Modi government raised the Minimum Support Price of fourteen summer (kharif) crops, but farmers say the hikes are not enough and will be implemented only in paddy and wheat and not other crops not covered under MSP. *Indiatimes*, 'If Eating Our Feces and Drinking Urine Opens Modi Govt's Eyes, We Will Do That, Say TN Farmers', 8 July 2017.

64. Swaminathan Aiyar, 'MSP Hike Is a Big Blunder: Farmers Are Producers, Not Objects of Charity', *Sunday Times of India*, 8 July 2018.

65. Liberal group policy paper, Liberal Round Table, Deolali, 24–26 June.

66. C. Rajagopalachari in Swatantra Party Manifesto 1959, indianliberals.com.

67. Arundhati Roy was charged with sedition for speaking at a seminar on Jammu and Kashmir called 'Azaadi: The Only Way' in 2010. Ashis Nandy was charged with sedition for an article in the *Times of India* published on 8 January 2008.

68. *Times of India*, 'I Was Ousted from Nalanda University: Sen', 7 July 2015.

69. Amartya Sen, 'India: The Stormy Revival of an International University', *New York Review of Books*, 13 August 2015.

70. Sagarika Ghose, 'Nobel Laureate Amartya Sen Says Modi Government Wants Control of Academic Bodies', *Times of India*, 7 July 2015.

71. Ibid.

72. S. Radhakrishnan, *The Principal Upanishads*, p. 19.

73. *Times of India*, 'Minister Responsible for Higher Education Rejects Darwin's Theory Again', 1 July 2018 .

74. On 1 March 2017, Modi said in a speech that 'hard work is more powerful than Harvard'. The remark was seen as a riposte to Sen, now professor at Harvard, who had criticized demonetization as 'despotic' as it had 'undermined the entire economy of trust'.

75. Eric Hobsbawm, *Interesting Times* (London: Abacus, 2002), p. 25.

76. Ambedkar in Dhananjay Keer, *Dr Ambedkar: Life and Mission* (Mumbai: Popular Prakashan, 1971), p. 273.

77. Chairman Mao Tse Tung started the 'Cultural Revolution' in China in 1966 to bolster his own personality cult and eliminate his enemies. All schools were closed and young people were encouraged to become part of terroristic 'Red Guard' gangs to rid China of what Mao called the Four Os—Old Customs, Old Habits, Old Culture and Old Beliefs—and 'purge' China of 'impure' people who held 'capitalistic' or 'counter-revolutionary' beliefs. Squads of youths hounded, harassed, humiliated, imprisoned and even murdered their own teachers, professors, intellectuals, sometimes even their own parents. It ended in 1976 but by this time China had lost some of its finest intellectuals and minds.

78. In Cambodia, the dictator Pol Pot ordered the killing of educated people; sometimes even people wearing spectacles, suggestive of literacy, were killed.

79. 'The government we have in Delhi is the most anti-intellectual we have ever had and this is manifested in appointments.' Guha at Bangalore Literature Festival, quoted in *PTI*, 'Modi Government Most Anti-intellectual: Ramachandra Guha', 5 December 2015.

80. *New Yorker*, 'The Ghosts of Mrs Gandhi', 17 July 1995.

81. Interview to BBC News by Arundhati Roy, 'The Violence in India during the Modi Government Is Terrifying', 6 June 2018.

82. Sedition or Section 124A has been slapped on Binayak Sen for meeting a Maoist, on Arundhati Roy for speaking at a seminar on Kashmir entitled 'Azaadi: The Only Way', and on Ashis Nandy by the Gujarat government in 2008 for an article in a newspaper. The then finance minister called the writers protest a 'manufactured protest' and a 'paper rebellion'. *Times of India*, 'Writers Have Manufactured a Controversy & Protest: Jaitley', 15 October 2015.

83. Indira Gandhi patronized intellectuals in her day, and although Raj and Romesh Thapar broke with her on the Emergency issue, they were once part of her 'kitchen cabinet'. Editors have often taken posts of media advisers to governments, and intellectuals have accepted berths in the Rajya Sabha. The Big State has also exercised patronage by bringing its nominees into sports bodies like the Board of Control for Cricket in India.

84. Arun Shourie in *Eminent Historians: Their Techniques, Their Line, Their Fraud* criticizes how Marxist historians have controlled and misused institutions like ICHR and NCERT.

85. Sumit Sarkar on how the Hindu Mahasabha and RSS did not participate in the Quit India movement of 1942, but Sarkar points out that the Communists in 1942 were equally unpatriotic. Sumit Sarkar, *Modern India 1885–1947* (New Delhi: Macmillan, 1989), p. 412.

86. Reuters, 'By Re-writing History, Hindu Nationalists Aim to Assert Their Dominance over India', 6 March 2018.

87. *Times of India*, 'Bigots and Charlatans Are Controlling Culture', 21 January 2016.

88. Activist Dhruv Rathee's interview with BJP IT cell insider on YouTube, 10 March 2018.

89. *New York Times*, 'Freedom of the Press in India', 15 June 2017, https://www.nytimes.com/2017/06/15/opinion/freedom-of-the-press-in-india.html.

90. See Reuters, 'Indian Journalists Say They Are Intimidated, Ostracised If They Criticise Modi', 26 April 2018; *Washington Post*, 'In Modi's India Journalists Face Bullying, Criminal Cases and Worse', 15 February 2018.

91. *Hindustan Times* editor Aparasim 'Bobby' Ghosh was sacked in September 2017; the editor-in-chief of the *Tribune* Harish Khare resigned in 2018. In 2014, the author resigned from CNN-IBN.

92. *Mail Online*, 'Nitish Kumar Accused of Using Government Advertising to Silence His Enemies and Reward Political Allies', 16 February 2013.

93. In April 2018, the information and broadcasting ministry issued a circular saying if a committee set up by it found news to be 'fake', journalists could lose their accreditation. After widespread uproar from media bodies, the circular was withdrawn by the government.

94. Wire, 'As Number of Murdered RTI Activists Rises to 67, It Is Modi Government That Needs to Act Rightly', 12 March 2018.

95. Mobs have routinely attacked journalists. In 1991, Shiv Sena cadres assaulted the offices of *Mahanagar*, then edited by Nikhil Wagle. In 2009, the Sena attacked the offices of TV channel IBN Lokmat. In 2008, Marathi daily *Loksatta*'s editor Kumar Ketkar's home was attacked by activists professing loyalty to Maharashtra icon Shivaji.

96. Eight alleged SIMI activists were gunned down in Bhopal in 2016 in an 'encounter'.

97. Terrorists struck Mumbai between 26 and 29 November 2008.

98. Bee Rowlatt, 'Why Does Everyone Hate Journalists? By Attacking Them We Undermine Our Own Freedoms', *Times of* India, 28 September 2017.

99. Judgement after the *Washington Post* published the Pentagon Papers in 1971.

100. NDTV, 'Chilling Murder in Rajasthan's Rajsamand on Video', 7 December 2017.

101. *Hindustan Times*,' Muslim Boy Stabbed to Death on a Train after Argument Turns into Religious Slurs', 27 June 2017.

102. *Indian Express*, 'Activist Zafar Khan Lynched to Death in Rajasthan's Pratapgarh for Objecting Photography of Women Defecating in Open', 17 June 2017.

103. IANS, 'Right wing Hindu Group Attacks Carol Singers in MP's Satna', 15 December 2017.

104. Wire, 'Anatomy of a Communal Riot', 7 February 2018.

105. Gandhi's salt satyagraha began with the Dandi March in March 1930. It was a completely non-violent movement against the tax on salt.

106. B.R. Ambedkar, *Annihilation of Caste* (New Delhi: Navayana, 2014), p. 243.

107. *The Collected Works of Mahatma Gandhi*, vol. 63 (Ahmedabad: Navajivan Trust, 1975), pp. 134–54.

108. E.J. Dionne Jr, 'Where Are the Conservatives We Need?', *Washington Post*, 23 April 2018.

109. Corruption scandals that hit the UPA government between 2009 and 2014.

110. Mukul Kesavan, 'Market Intellectuals', *Telegraph*, 1 July 2018.

The Liberal Woman

1. *Times of India*, 'Boycott Films by 3 Khans: Sadhvi Prachi', 2 March 2015, https://timesofindia.indiatimes.com/india/Boycott-films-of-3-Khans-BJP-leader-Sadhvi-Prachi/articleshow/46432130.cms.

2. *Indian Express*, 'Priyanka Chopra Trolled on Social Media for Wearing a Short Skirt to Meet PM', 2 June 2017; Zoom, 'Priyanka Trolled Again for Wearing a Mini Skirt', 4 May 2018. TV actor Hina Khan was asked to 'dress respectfully' by orthodox Muslims during Ramzan. *Times of India*, 'Fanatics Asking Hina Khan to Dress Respectfully during Ramzan Should be Condemned', 29 May 2018.

3. The Modi government launched the Beti Bachao, Beti Padhao scheme on 22 January 2015.

4. *Hindustan Times*, 'Padmaavat Row: Rajput Women in Chittorgarh Demand Permission to End Life', 21 January 2018, https://www.hindustantimes.com/jaipur/padmaavat-row-rajput-women-in-chittorgarh-demand-permission-to-end-life/story-eh9REyXLyPXLJmNxkPeSHK.html.

5. Protests against the film by the Rajput Karni Sena began during the shooting itself when there were rumours that it showed the Rajput queen Padmavati in 'a bad light'. The sets were set ablaze. In the days leading up to the release, there were violent protests across India, with a schoolbus even being attacked in Gurugram. On the suggestion of the CBFC, the film was renamed *Padmaavat* to make it clear that it was a work based on a fictional poem. Five other modifications were suggested, including changes to a song sequence entitled 'Ghoomar'. Several disclaimers proclaimed that the film was a work of fiction.

6. See Narendra Dabholkar in *The Republic of Reason, Words They Could Not Kill: Selected Writings of Dabholkar, Pansare, Kalburgi and Lankesh* (New Delhi: SAHMAT with the Raza Foundation, 2018), p. 49.

7. *Hindustan Times*, 'I've Begun to Fear as Even Girls Have Started Drinking Beer: Goa Chief Minister Manohar Parrikar', 10 February 2018, https://www.hindustantimes.com/india-news/fear-the-fact-that-even-girls-have-started-drinking-beer-now-goa-cm-manohar-parrikar/story-QpZ9TnYa7CZSav4TnU6WTM.html; *Citizen*, 'And Now Haryana's New CM Khattar Wants Girls to Dress Decently', 22 October 2014, http://www.thecitizen.in/index.php/en/newsdetail/index/7/1027/and-now-haryanas-new-cm-khattar-wants-girls-to-dress-decently.

8. *Times of India*, Girls in a Mangalore Pub Attacked, Dragged Out by the Hair by Sri Ram Sene', 26 January 2009, https://timesofindia.indiatimes.com/city/mangaluru/Girls-assaulted-at-Mangalore-pub/articleshow/4029791.cms.

9. Jats and Marathas (2016) and Patidars (2015) all staged protests to demand reservations and Backward Class status to gain affirmative action from the state.

10. Then Haryana BJP media coordinator in Haryana Suraj Pal Amu offered Rs 10 crore for beheading actor Deepika Padukone and director Bhansali. 'We will reward the ones beheading them with 10 crore and also take care of their family's needs.' *Hindustan Times*, 'Padmavati: Haryana BJP Leader Offers Rs 10 cr for Beheading Padukone, Bhansali', 20 November 2017, https://www.hindustantimes.com/india-news/padmavati-row-haryana-bjp-leader-announces-rs-10-crore-reward-for-beheading-deepika-padukone-bhansali/story-SNu3xwOyMQmJU3fNzbSVyL.html.

11. The slogan was raised during the #IamGauri protests in Bengaluru on 13 September 2017.

12. Doctors in Tamil Nadu protested the film *Mersal* which they said showed them in bad light. *Times of India*, 'TN Doctors Boycott Vijay-starrer *Mersal*, Prescribe Piracy', 20 October 2017. Brahmins protested against the film *A Woman in Brahmanism* in Hyderabad. *Times of India*, 'City Brahmins Stage Protest against

Film', 15 January 2017. Muslim leaders called for a boycott of the film *Lipstick Under My Burkha*. *Hindustan Times*, 'Muslim Leaders Call for Boycott of *Lipstick Under My Burkha*, Plan Legal Action', 16 February 2017. Congress activists protested against the film *Indu Sarkar* in 2017. *The Hindu*, 'Indu Sarkar Promo Called off Again after Congress Protests', 16 July 2017.

13. *New York Times*, 'Meryl Streep Slams Donald Trump in Golden Globes Speech', 8 January 2017.

14. The film *Fanaa* was embargoed in Gujarat in 2006, apparently because of lead actor Aamir Khan's statements against the Narmada dam. Another 2006 film, *Rang de Basanti*, directed by Rakeysh Om Prakash Mehra and starring Aamir Khan, was pulled out of some theatres in Gujarat after they were attacked by units of the ABVP. The BJP Yuva Morcha head said multiplexes and cinema halls had announced that no film starring Aamir would be screened in halls across the state. Gujarat also banned the 2007 film *Parzania*, directed by Rahul Dholakia, after the Bajrang Dal apparently 'instructed' theatres not to screen the movie. *Times of India*, '*Parzania* Not Screened in Gujarat', 26 January 2007, https://timesofindia. indiatimes.com/india/Parzania-not-screened-in-Gujarat/ articleshow/1465049.cms; *Times of India*, 'Aamir's *Fanaa* Not to be Screened in Gujarat', 24 May 2006, https://timesofindia. indiatimes.com/india/Aamirs-Fanaa-not-to-be-screened-in-Gujarat/articleshow.1549850.cms; *Rang De Basanti* pulled out of Gujarat theatres: *Frontline*, 'Height of Intolerance', 16 June 2006, https://www.frontline.in/static/html/fl2311/ stories/20060616003110800.htm; *Hindustan Times*, Mallika Sarabhai comes to Aamir Khan's rescue', 29 May 2006, https:// www. hindustantimes.com/india/mallika-sarabhai-comes-to-aamirkhan-s-rescue/story-C2QOWMzDLgSIRPvk7DeQgP. html.

15. The CBFC demanded a list of cuts be made in the film *Udta Punjab*. *Indian Express*, 'Udta Punjab Ban: Here Is What the CBFC Does Not Want to Show the World', 13 June 2016. See Chapter 3 on the list of banned swear words and the blurring of alcohol bottle labels.

16. See Nandini Sardesai, 'Udta Punjab: CBFC's Mandate Is Only to Certify Films, Not to Censor or Chop Them Up', *Times of India*, 9 June 2016. https://blogs.timesofindia.indiatimes.com/author/nandinisardesai/

17. See Sagarika Ghose, 'The National Commission for Women Has Failed Indian Women and Should be Scrapped', Firstpost, 12 July 2018: 'The existence of the NCW is now becoming a disservice for women seeking justice, compensation and a fair hearing from the government . . . the NCW is a collection of politicians bent on trivialising women's issues.' Simply an instrument of the Big State to co-opt and cage women's issues in the so called 'zenana dabba' or 'ladies compartment'.

18. Ramachandra Guha, ed., *Makers of Modern India* (New Delhi: Penguin Books India, 2010).

19. *The Collected Works of Mahatma Gandhi*, vol. 42 (Ahmedabad: Navajivan Trust, 1975), pp. 4–6.

20. Ramachandra Guha, ed., *Makers of Modern India*, p. 267.

21. S. Radhakrishnan, *The Bhagavadgita* (Noida: HarperCollins, 2003), p. 43.

22. *Citizen*, 'And Now Haryana's New CM Khattar Wants Girls to Dress Decently', 22 October 2014, http://www.thecitizen.in/index.php/en/newsdetail/index/7/1027/and-now-haryanas-new-cm-khattar-wants-girls-to-dress-decently.

23. NDTV, 'Rs 21,000 Fine for Girls Using Mobile Phones', 3 May 2017; News 18, 'Jeans, Mobile Phones Banned for Girls in Haryana Village, 17 April 2018, https://www.news18.com/news/india/jeans-mobile-phones-banned-for-girls-in-this-haryana-village-1721421.html.

24. The killing of Manoj and Babli, who married against their parents' wishes, was ordered by a khap panchayat in Haryana in June 2007. The five accused were given the death sentence, although these were commuted to life imprisonment in 2011. Nonetheless, the judgement was seen as a crucial landmark in the curtailing of the often-violent diktats of khap panchayats. *India Today*, 'Honour Killers Must be Hanged: SC', 10 May 2011, https://www.indiatoday.in/india/north/story/honour-killings-sc-for-death-sentence-133412-2011-05-10.

25. *Indian Express*, 'On Yogi's Website: Women Power Does Not Require Freedom but Protection',18 April 2007.

26. 'For their own safety, women foreign tourists should not wear short dresses or skirts . . . Indian culture is different from western culture . . . (they should) refrain from going out alone at night.' *Indian Express*, 'Union Minister Mahesh Sharma Advises Tourists Not to Wear Skirts', 29 August 2016.

27. 'Rapes happen because men and women interact freely . . . it's like an open market with open options: Mamata Banerjee'. Firstpost, 'Rapes Happen because Men and Women Interact Freely', 15 October 2012.

28. Congress politician and industrialist Naveen Jindal has been reported as speaking in support of khaps and writing khaps a letter saying, panchayats show a 'new direction' to society. *The Hindu*, 'Navin Jindal Supports Khap Panchayats', 10 May 2010, https://www.thehindu.com/todays-paper/tp-national/Navin-Jindal-supports-khap-panchayats/article16033150.ece.

29. In the Kathua case, an eight-year-old Bakherwal girl was raped and murdered in 2018. In Unnao, a seventeen-year-old was allegedly raped by BJP MLA Kuldeep Singh Sengar in 2017.

30. *The Hindu*, 'Produce 4 Kids to Protect Hinduism: Sakshi Maharaj', 7 January 2015.

31. See Chapter 2 for more on the falling representation of Muslims in politics.

32. National Sample Survey Organisation data quoted in BBC News, 'Why Are Millions of Indian Women Dropping Out of Work?', 18 May 2017. Twenty million women quit work between 2004–05 and 2011–12. The labour force participation rate for women of working age dropped from 42 per cent in 1993–94 to 31 per cent in 2011–12.

33. On 21 September 2017, a woman student was molested in Banaras Hindi University. Women students staged public protests and were lathi charged. They did not get a sympathetic hearing from university authorities, notably the vice chancellor. See *Indian Express*, 'BHU Agitation: a Timeline', 26 September 2017.

34. During the protests women students said they were discriminated against in hostel. *Hindustan Times*, 'How Sexist Rules Stifling Life for Girls in BHU Campus', 25 September 2017.

35. *Times of India*, 'BHU VC's Duty and Modesty Lesson to Hostel Girls Goes Viral', 28 September 2017.

36. The nineteenth-century queen of Jhansi, known as a fierce horsewoman and warrior in battle.

37. The only female ruler of the Delhi Sultanate who ruled in the thirteenth century.

38. A Dalit woman soldier in the 1857 rebellion.

39. Sita raised her sons Luv and Kush in Valmiki's ashram.

40. The twentieth-century Indian freedom fighter, posthumously awarded the Bharat Ratna in 1997.

41. The twentieth-century revolutionary, follower of Netaji S.C. Bose and officer in the Indian National Army.

42. The twentieth-century freedom fighter and Gandhian, India's first health minister.

43. The twentieth-century independence activist and poet.

44. The nineteenth- to twentieth-century Congress activist working for the suffragette movement.

45. The twentieth-century independence activist and revolutionary who participated in the armed Chittagong Armoury Raid in 1930.

46. The twentieth-century freedom fighter, social reformer and socialist, noted for her contribution to India's arts and crafts revival.

47. The twentieth-century independence activist and revolutionary who joined the revolutionary group led by Surya Sen in the 1930s.

48. See Sagarika Ghose, 'Indian Feminism: Coming of Age', *Outlook*, 20 December 1995; Radha Kumar, *A History of Doing: An Illustrated Account of Movements for Women's Rights and Feminism in India, 1800–1990* (New Delhi: Zubaan, 1997).

49. Bhanvari Devi of Bhateri village in Rajasthan was a healthcare worker who was gangraped by upper-caste men in 1992.

50. Ahilyabai Holkar was the eighteenth-century ruler of the Maratha kingdom of Malwa.

51. Ramachandra Guha, ed., *Makers of Modern India*, p. 138.

52. Polly Toynbee, 'False Paeans to the Pope', *Guardian*, 16 October 2003.

53. Ibid.

54. 'Women should come forward and take part in the programmes for the welfare of the society. They should start from their homes to create a mini-India and work for the society without getting distracted by anybody.' *DNA*, 'Women Should Come Out to Work for Nation Building: Bhagwat', 15 November 2016.

55. 'Women's fashion, lifestyle and conduct should be in accordance with Indian culture . . . women should not wear clothes which provoke others (to misbehave with them).' *Times of India*, 'Women's Safety Depends on What They Wear: MP Minister Says', 21 July 2012.

56. On 10 September 2005, a fatwa was issued against tennis player Sania Mirza.

57. On 5 July 2018, NDTV reported that a man who threatened Congress spokesperson Priyanka Chaturvedi's daughter with rape was arrested. See *Times of India*, 'Online Abuse of Women Increasing in India', 6 May 2013.

58. See *Times of India*, 'Twitter War between Barkha Dutt and Raveena Tandon on Dutt's Comment on Karva Chauth As "Regressive"', 1 November 2015.

59. This was the OP Jindal University rape case. The high court noted that the victim being part of 'casual relationships' was a 'compelling' reason. Live Law, 'JGLS Rape Case: SC Stays HC Order Shaming "Promiscuous" Victim and Suspending Convicts Sentence', 6 November 2017, https://www.livelaw.in/jgls-rape-case-sc-stays-hc-order-shaming-promiscuous-victim-suspending-convicts-sentence.

60. Farooqi, co-director of the film *Peepli Live*, was convicted of rape in 2016.

61. *Guardian*, 'A Feeble No May Mean Yes, the Judgement Noted', 26 September 2017.

62. In 2008, doctors Rajesh and Nupur Talwar were accused of murdering their daughter, Aarushi, and domestic help, Hem Raj. They were acquitted by the Allahabad High Court on 12 October 2017. The acquittal has been challenged by the CBI in the Supreme Court.

63. Quoted in Avirook Sen, *Aarushi* (New Delhi: Penguin Books India, 2015), p. 79.

64. *Hindustan Times*, 'Nupur Talwar Working on a Book, Says Jail Official', 9 May 2012.

65. The judgement delivered by a CBI court in Ghaziabad. NDTV, 'Nupur Talwar Asks Supreme Court for Bail after Rejection in Ghaziabad Court', 3 May 2012, https://www.ndtv.com/india-news/nupur-talwar-asks-supreme-court-for-bail-after-rejection-in-ghaziabad-court-480162.

66. The CBI court on 26 November 2013: 'Talwars [were] freaks who became killers of their own progeny . . . in breach of the commandment, thou shalt not kill.' The court also quoted the Koran: 'Take not life which God has made sacred.' NDTV, 'Nupur Talwar asks Supreme Court for bail after rejection in Ghaziabad Court.' NDTV, 'Aarushi Talwar Case: Freaks in the History of Mankind, Says Judge', 26 November 2013, https://www.ndtv.com/india-news/aarushi-talwar-case-freaks-in-the-history-of-mankind-says-judge-542347; Sagarika Ghose, 'Why the Aarushi Talwar Case Is a Rape of Justice', News 18, 26 November 2013.

67. 'What a girlfriend: have you ever seen a 50-crore-rupee girlfriend?' *Times of India,* 'Modi Calls Shashi Tharoor's Wife "50 crore rupee Girlfriend', 29 October 2012.

68. *The Hindu*, 'Full Text of Justice Verma's Report', 24 January 2013.

69. *Indian Express*, 'Death Poor Deterrent: Three per cent Convictions, 94% Accused Know Victims in Child Rape Cases', 23 April 2018, https://indianexpress.com/article/india/death-poor-deterrent-three-per-cent-convictions-94-accused-know-victims-in-child-rape-cases-5146888.

70. 'What is the harm in legalising betting? Above all, do we have enforcement agencies . . . it is very easy to say . . . if you can't enforce it, it is like saying if you can't prevent rape, enjoy it. It is better to legalise it and earn some revenue rather than throwing your hands up and letting things happen as it were.' *Hindustan Times*, 'If You Can't Stop Rape, Enjoy It, Says CBI Director Ranjit Sinha: Remark Sparks Outrage', 25 December 2013.

71. BBC News, 'When I Used to Walk Out of That Ring, It Used to be Actually Like a Raped Woman Walking Out', 21 June 2016.

72. *Indian Express*, 'Rape Accused Should Not be Hanged; Boys Make Mistakes', 11 April 2014.

73. Former President Pranab Mukherjee's son, Congress MP Abhijit Mukherjee, referring to Nirbhaya protestors, 'Those who claim to be students—I can see many beautiful women among them—highly dented-painted'. NDTV, 'Delhi Protests Are by Dented Painted Women: President Pranab's Son', 27 December 2012.

74. IndiaSpend, 'Crime against Women Up 83%, Conviction Rate Hits Decadal Low', 12 December 2017, http://www.indiaspend. com/cover-story/crime-against-women-up-83-conviction-rate-hits-decadal-low-18239.

75. *Times of India*, 'BJP MLA Kuldeep Singh Sengar Arrested', 13 April 2018, https://timesofindia.indiatimes.com/india/cbi-confirms-rape-charge-against-unnao-mla-kuldeep-singh-sengar/articleshow/64116434.cms.

76. NDTV, '"Can Be Raped, Killed": Lawyer For Kathua Child's Family Alleges Threat', 18 April 2018, https://www.ndtv.com/india-news/i-can-be-raped-killed-lawyer-for-kathua-childs-family-deepika-s-rajawat-alleges-threat-1838052.

77. The Right-wing handle @trueindology tweeted on 11 April 2018: 'In Assam since march, at least 6 rapes took place. All perpetrators in these rapes were Muslims and all victims were Hindu girls. But Rape had no religion then. Suddenly since the alleged incident, rape has got a religion. Cows and Lord Ram have also been brought in [sic].' Kerala cartoonist Swathi Vadlamudi, who made a cartoon on the Kathua case and linked it to Lord Ram, was booked by police under Section 295 A for hurting religious sentiments after a complaint filed by the president of the Hindutva outfit Hindu Sangathan in Hyderabad. *Hindustan Times*, 'Hyderabad Journalist Booked for Facebook Cartoon', 17 April 2018.

78. See *Economic Times*, 'Father of Unnao Victim Died in Jail in Judicial Custody While Officials and Doctors Exchanged Letters for Five Days', 12 April 2018.

79. NDTV, '8 Lawyers Charged for Obstructing Cops While Filing a Chargesheet in the Kathua Rape Trial', 18 April 2018.

80. Live Law, 'Supreme Court Issues New Guidelines to Prevent Misuse of 498 A', 27 July 2017.

81. The report titled 'What the Elevator Saw' in *Outlook* on 7 April 2014 suggests that there are inconsistencies in the victim's story.

82. The journalist conducting the CNN–News 18 interview with Sunny Leone on 15 January 2016 was accused of asking questions in a demeaning manner. This led to sharp outrage. See *Times of India*, 'Shanta Gokhale: Letter to Sunny Leone', 27 January 2016.

83. Rediff, 'Apply Anti-terror Laws against Mangalore Attackers: Ananthamurthy', 29 January 2009.

84. Suresh Bhat Bakrabail, noted rights activist in Mangalore has compiled a list of rising incidents of moral policing in coastal Karnataka. Sagarika Ghose, 'Mangalore's Age Old Harmony Caught in Cross-hairs of Communal Hate', *Times of India*, 5 May

85. *Times of India*, 'Woman Stabbed to Death by FB Stalker over "Lifestyle"', 15 September 2018.

86. Interview on 14 January 2016.

87. CBS, 'India Vows Action after BBC Airs Banned Film about Gangrape', 4 March 2015; Udwin's interview with author on 14 January 2016.

88. Interview in 2006.

89. In its judgement delivered on 24 July 2018, the Supreme Court held that the ban on the entry of women into Sabarimala would have to be tested on constitutional grounds. 'After 1950 [when the Constitution came into being] everything should conform to constitutional principles and ethos,' said the court. NDTV, 'Sabarimala Women Ban Will Be Tested Constitutionally: Supreme Court', 24 July 2018, https://www.ndtv.com/india-news/sabarimala-women-ban-will-be-tested-on-constitutional-ethos-supreme-court-1889028; Live Law, 'Devotion Cannot be Subjected to Gender Discrimination, SC Allows Women Entry in Sabarimala by 4:1 Majority; Lone Woman in the Bench Dissents: Full Text of Judgement', 28 September 2018.

90. On 28 October 2012, an Indian-born dentist, Savita Halappanavar, died after being denied abortion in Ireland. In 2018, the move to remove the ban on abortion in Ireland was passed, with 66.4 per cent voting 'yes' in the referendum on 26 May.

91. Brihadaranyaka Upanishad, sixth brahmana, 111.6.1, in S. Radhakrishnan, *The Principal Upanishads* (Noida: HarperCollins India, 1997), p. 223.

92. Mata Amritanandamayi, Radhe Maa, Anandmurti Guruma. See *Times of India*, 'A Few God Women', 22 May 2016.
93. Tulsidas was a sixteenth-century reformer and poet. There are different interpretations of this phrase. Some believe it's a prayer for detachment as Radhakrishnan writes. But the clubbing of animals, lower castes and women can also be misused as a patriarchal, upper-caste mantra.
94. *The Hindu*, 'Shani Shingnapur Temple Lifts Ban on Women's Entry', 8 April 2016.
95. Al Jazeera, Haji Ali Dargah Lifts Ban on Women', 24 October 2016.
96. Wire, 'SC Should Defend Women's Privacy, Autonomy, not Perpetuate "Love Jihad" Myth: Kavita Krishnan', 20 August 2017.
97. See *Indian Express*, 'Hadiya Case: a Timeline', 8 March 2018.
98. Mukul Kesavan, 'Exorcising Hadiya', *Telegraph*, 3 December 2017.
99. The Kerala police had submitted an affidavit saying Shafin was a member of Muslim organizations like the Social Democratic Party of India, which is not, however, banned. Quint, 'Hadiya Case: SC Says NIA Probe Can't Affect Validity of Marriage', 23 August 2017.
100. *Indian Express*, 'Hadiya Case: A Timeline', 8 March 2018.
101. Quint, 'Right to Marry Person of One's Choice Is Integral: Supreme Court', 10 April 2018, https://www.thequint.com/news/india/hadiya-marriage-right-to-marry-person-of-choice-integral-supreme-court.
102. *India Today*, 'Hadiya Has Absolute Autonomy over Her Person, Said the Supreme Court', 9 April 2018.
103. Firstpost, 'Watch: BJP's Yogi Adityanath Tells Hindus to Marry 100 Muslim Women', 27 August 2014, https://www.firstpost.com/india/watch-bjps-yogi-adityanath-tells-hindus-to-marry-a-100-muslim-women-1684103.html.
104. The National Crime Records Bureau (NCRB) 2013 quoted in the Reuters report of 21 August 2015 showed that the majority of rapes were committed by those known to the victim.
105. *The Hindu*, 'For Meerut's Love Jihad Couple, 3 Year Courtship Ends in Nikah', 3 December 2015. The report quotes Kaleem as saying: 'Love jihad doesn't exist. It was created by people to polarise and for political gain.'

106. In 2016, the radio station Radio Mirchi launched a second station called Mirchi Love, launched in several cities, including Ahmedabad, Lucknow, Jodhpur and Pune. The tagline of the station is 'Just pyaar kiye ja'. At the station launch, CEO Prashant Pandey said the market research indicated a huge need gap in the sector of love. Afaqs, 'Radio Mirchi Launches New Radio Station, Mirchi Love', 8 September 2016.

107. *The Collected Works of Mahatma Gandhi*, vol. 75 (Ahmedabad: Navajivan Trust, 1975), pp. 75–76.

108. Gandhi's love for Sarladevi in Rajmohan Gandhi, *Mohandas: A True Story of a Man, His People and an Empire* (New Delhi: Penguin Books India, 2006).

109. See Robert Bly and Jane Hirshfield, *Mirabai: Ecstatic Poems* (New Delhi: Aleph, 2017).

110. Harsha, *The Lady of the Jewel Necklace and the Lady Who Shows Her Love*, trans. Wendy Doniger (New York: New York University Press and JJC Foundation).

111. See Prince Ilango, *Adigal Shilappadikaram: The Ankle Bracelet*, tr. Alain Danielou (New Delhi: Aleph Book Company, 2016).

112. *The Hindu*, 'Andhra Couple Arrested for Killing Techie Daughter', 4 March 2014.

113. *Times of India*, 'Honour Killing in Kolkata, Man Beheads Sister in Public View, Takes Severed Head to Police Station', 8 December 2012.

114. *Times of India*, 'In November 2007, the CBI Summoned Ashok Todi, Priyanka's Father, for Questioning', 19 November 2007.

115. Atlantic, 'The War on Valentine's Day in India', 14 February 2018.

116. *Times of India*, 'Shiv Sena Conducts Lathi Puja, Says Will Use Sticks against Lovers on Valentine's Day', 13 February 2018; *The Hindu*, 'Shiv Sena Terrorises Couples', 15 February 2009.

117. PTI, 'Observe Valentine's Day As Black Day: Shiv Sena Activists', 14 February 2016.

118. B.R. Ambedkar, *The Annihilation of Caste: The Annotated Critical Edition* (New Delhi: Navayana, 2014), p. 287.

119. Live Law, 'Section 377 IPC: Summary of Four Separate Judgements', 6 September 2018.

120. *Hindustan Times*, 'Homosexuality Is Unnatural, Can't Support: Rajnath', 15 December 2013.

121. *Hindustan Times*, 'RSS Leader Says Homosexuality a Psychological Problem', 18 March 2016.

122. *Times of India*, 'SC Must Review Sec 377 Ruling, Allow Gay Relationships: Jaitley, Chidambaram', 29 November 2015.

123. *The Economist*, 'India Is Failing Its Women', 7 July 2018.

124. News18, 'An ASSOCHAM Survey Found in 2012 48 per cent Women in Bengaluru Feel Unsafe on the Nightshift', 8 May 2012.

125. On 5 December 2017, Indian female hockey players protested at being denied facilities by Indian officials in Australia. *Times of India*, 'SAI Orders Investigation Over Mistreatment of Indian Girl's Hockey Team in Australia', 5 December 2017. Also: see open letter to Prime Minister from woman tennis player Nirupama Sanjeev to improve basic facilities in India. *Hindustan Times*, 'Improve Basic Facilities for Sport: India's First Woman Pro Tennis Player', 25 August 2016.

126. We have noted Mamata Banerjee's comments on rape. Jayalalithaa started a cradle baby scheme in 1991 which was criticized as one leading to the abandonment of the girl child. On 26 November 2016, the Madras High Court called the cradle baby scheme 'heartless' and asked, 'How long will the cradle baby scheme continue?' *The Hindu*, 30 November 2016.

127. India Today, 'Modi's Women Ministers Mum on Kathua, Unnao Rapes', 13 April 2018.

128. *Times of India*, 'Bollywood Stars Who Have Spoken on Wage Disparity: Alia Bhatt, Kangana Ranaut', 4 July 2018.

129. Manu Sharma was acquitted in February 2006 by the trial court. After a public outcry and media activism, the case was readmitted in the Delhi High Court in March 2006. In December 2006, Manu Sharma was found guilty by the high court and sentenced to life imprisonment. A 2011 film was made on the case: *No One Killed Jessica*.

130. *Economic Times*, 'The First Woman to Fly a Fighter Jet', 22 February 2018.

131. Wire, 'Online Trolling of Women Is an Extension of the Daily Harassment They Face', 8 July 2018; BBC Hindi, 'Why Are Indian Women Being Attacked on Social Media?', 8 May 2013.

132. Haryana chief minister M.L. Khattar: 'Women must dress decently. If a girl dresses decently a boy will not look at her in the wrong way'. *Indian Express*, 'On Rape, "Outraged" Politicians Have Been Outrageous in the Past', 6 March 2016; *The Hindu*, 'Hindu Women Must Produce 4 Children: Sakshi Maharaj', 7 January 2015. 'All by herself at 3 am at night in a city where people believe . . . you know you should not be so adventurous,' said former Delhi chief minister Sheila Dikshit in 2008. Nirbhaya convict Mukesh told film-maker Leslee Udwin, 'A decent girl won't roam around at 9 o'clock at night. Housework and housekeeping is for girls, not roaming in discos and bars, doing wrong things, wearing wrong clothes.' Mukesh also said he was quoting what he had heard from politicians. Quoted in CBS, 4 March 2015.

133. *Times of India*, 'Sex Ratio Dips, Jains, Sikhs Buck Trend', 31 December 2015.

134. See *Times of India*, 'The Women Who Fought Triple Talaq', 22 August 2017.

135. Ramachandra Guha, ed., *Makers of Modern India*, p. 270. Kamaladevi's words were in response to reforms begun on Hindu personal law in the mid-50s.

136. See Malavika Rajkotia, 'The Case against Abolitionists', *Indian Express*, 2 June 2017: 'To interfere in the rights of a minority community may make the Muslim woman even more vulnerable because all religions are still in the realm of oppressive patriarchies and it should not seem as if Muslim women have been isolated as pawns in a deeper agenda coloured by political interests based on communalism.'

137. Scroll, 'Muslim Women and the Surprising Facts about Polygamy in India', 8 July 2014.

138. Lancet Study led by the Centre for Global Health research, University of Toronto quoted in *Telegraph*, 'Millions of Female Fetuses Aborted in India', 25 May 2011.

139. *The Republic of Reason, Words They Could Not Kill: Selected Writings of Dabholkar, Pansare, Kalburgi and Lankesh*, p. 121.

140. In 1986, the Congress government of Rajiv Gandhi enacted the Muslim Women (Protection of Rights on Divorce Act) 1986 to placate orthodox Muslims. Days later, Rajiv Gandhi opened the locks of the Babri Masjid and subsequently allowed the stone-laying ceremony or shilanyas to placate orthodox Hindus. 'The announcement to reverse the SC judgement [Shah Bano case] and the removal of the locks happened within a span of two weeks. This appeared as a balancing act,' veteran Congress politician Arif Mohammed Khan to Indian Express in an interview. *Indian Express*, 'Unlocking of Babri Masjid Was a Balancing Act by the Then Government', 28 March 2017. Khan had quit the Congress after the overturning of the Shah Bano judgement.

141. *The Republic of Reason, Words They Could Not Kill: Selected Writings of Dabholkar, Pansare, Kalburgi and Lankesh*, p. 122.

142. *Times of India*, 'Hamid Ansari: If you can have Victoria Memorial, why not Jinnah's portrait?', 12 July 2018.

143. In December 2017, BJP Ghaziabad chief Ajay Sharma led a mob against a wedding they called a 'love jihad'. BJP later removed Sharma from his post. Scroll, 'BJP Sacks Ghaziabad Chief Who Created a Ruckus at a Hindu–Muslim Wedding', 28 December 2017.

144. Prashant Patel Umrao tweeted on July 3 2018: 'S. Swaraj launched 'Passport Seva' app on 27 June showing date June 5 by changing rules to save Sadia Anas Siddiqui and to hide her mistake. Fake data produced showing its downloaded 10 lakh times but actually it was crashed.' This tweet was retweeted 2700 times. Apart from this, Swaraj was accused of 'appeasing Muslims' and even of having 'an Islamic kidney'. Right-wing handle @surendrapal45 tweeted on 6 July 2018: 'Her husband should beat her, she is living on one kidney, she got kidney from Nawaz Sharif.' Another Right-wing handle @voiceoftruth tweeted on 3 July on Swaraj: 'side effects of having an Islamic kidney'. See Sagarika Ghose, 'In the Republic of Abuse Even Sushma Swaraj Is Powerless', *Sunday Times of India*, 8 July 2018.

145. *Indian Express*, 'Inter-faith Couple Assaulted in Bijnore', 7 July 2018.

146. 'I have not heard such laughter since the Ramayana serial,' PM Modi said after Chowdhury was heard laughing, even as male MPs, mostly from the BJP, guffawed and minister Kiren Rijiju even uploaded a video of a cackling Surpanakha on his social media page. *Times of India*, 'Have Not Heard Such Laughter Since Ramayana Serial, PM's Dig at Renuka Chowdhury', 8 February 2018.

147. Firstpost, 'Narendra Modi vs 'the Rest': Mercurial Mamata Key to Uniting Disparate Opposition against the BJP', 24 May 2018; *Hindustan Times*, 'Mehbooba's Mercurial Persona', 24 March 2018; Huffington Post, 'Jayalalithaa, One-woman Regime Opaque, Unpredictable', 13 December 2016; Sagarika Ghose, 'Amma, Didi, Behenji, Baji and the Method in Their Moodiness', 17 January 2016.

148. Sagarika Ghose, 'Reservations about the Bill', *Outlook*, 20 July 1998.

149. Senior communist leader Anil Basu in 2011 referred to a red-light area when speaking about Banerjee. Another communist leader, Sushanta Ghosh, referred to Banerjee as someone who 'had not had the opportunity to apply vermilion on her forehead and therefore has a problem with the colour red. News18, 'EC Says It Has Video of Ghosh Abusing Mamata', 11 May 2011. BJP leader Surendra Singh has called Banerjee 'surpanakha', quoted in *Times of India*, 'UP BJP MLA Calls Mamata Surpanakha', 25 April 2018; *Telegraph*, 'Letters to the Editor', 29 April 2011.

150. Ali Mazrui, 'Why Africa Has So Few Heroines', *Daily Nation*, 5 March 2000.

151. Indira Gandhi always strongly denied being a feminist and in her early years she was brought up more like a boy than a girl, signing her letters to her father as 'Indu-boy'. Sagarika Ghose, *Indira: India's Most Powerful Prime Minister* (New Delhi: Juggernaut, 2017).

152. Ramachandra Guha, ed., *Makers of Modern India*.

153. Andhra Pradesh held a first ever three-day National Women's Parliament in February 2017 in Amaravati.

154. Ramachandra Guha, ed., *Makers of Modern India*.

155. Ibid, p. 185.

156. *Business Standard*, 'Census 2011: Population Growth Rate Declines to 17%', 11 February 2013.

157. *Times of India*, 'Delhiites Opt for Sex-selection', 25 March 2005.

Conclusion

1. NDTV, 'PM Narendra Modi's Notes Ban Neither Intelligent Nor Humane: Amartya Sen', 30 November 2016. https://www.ndtv.com/india-news/notes-ban-is-minimal-achievement-maximal-suffering-amartya-sen-to-ndtv-1632057

2. John Locke, *The Two Treatises of Civil Government*, ed. Thomas Hollis, section 202, chapter 18, 1764, http://oll.libertyfund.org/pages/john-locke-two-treatises-1689.

3. This speech was made by then Gujarat chief minister on 9 September 2002. The full text from an NDTV audio recording is available here: https://www.outlookindia.com/website/story/should-we-run-relief-camps-open-child-producing-centres/217398.

4. *Indian Express*, 'Strong Evidence against Those Arrested for Naxal Links, Says CM Devendra Fadnavis', 11 July 2018. Also see Chapter 4 for Jaitley's tweets.

5. 'Anti-national groups/elements also make use of social media networking sites on the internet to post propaganda and anti-national information and for mentoring Indian youths to join such activities.' *Economic Times*, 'Anti-national Groups Using Social Media for Propaganda: Ravi Shankar Prasad', 25 February 2015.

6. Asgar Ansari was brutally killed on 29 June 2017 on the suspicion that he was carrying beef in his van. Wire, 'In a First Jharkhand Court Convicts 11 Gau Rakshaks of Murder in a Lynching Case', 16 March 2018.

7. Economists Lucas Chancel and Thomas Piketty, in a paper entitled 'Indian Income Inequality, 1922–2014: From British Raj to Billionaire Raj', showed Indian inequality was at its highest since 1922 in 2014. This paper's findings went into the World Inequality Report that showed 10 per cent Indians garnered 56

per cent of national income in 2014. The Oxfam report was titled 'Reward Work, Not Wealth'. Quoted in Wire, 22 January 2018.

8. Hardik Patel led the Patidar protests in Gujarat in 2015. *Indian Express*, 'Patidars Battling Falling Agricultural Incomes and Socio-economic Squeeze', 25 August 2015. Jats were seeking inclusion in the OBC category to make them eligible for economic benefits. The Maratha silent protests of July 2016 were triggered by the rape and murder of a schoolgirl; they also demanded reservations due to rising unemployment.

9. Yascha Mounk, 'Turkey's Warning: Why Erdogan's Consolidation of Power Should be a Cause for Concern in Every Liberal Democracy', Slate, 24 June 2018, https://slate.com/news-and-politics/2018/06/turkeys-election-should-be-a-warning-to-every-democratic-country.html.

10. *Indian Express*, 'Full Text: Pranab Mukherjee's Address at RSS Headquarters in Nagpur', 8 June 2018, https://indianexpress.com/article/india/full-text-pranab-mukherjees-address-at-rss-headquarters-in-nagpur-5209081.

11. News channels have referred to BJP president Amit Shah's shrewd politics as 'Chanakya niti' or politics played according to Chanakya's famous prescription 'saam, daam, dand, bhed', referring to the monarch using fair means or foul to get his ends. Chanakya was the fourth century BC adviser to the Gupta emperor Chandragupta Maurya.

12. *The Economist*, 'Moving in, Moving Right', 25 August 2018. The article reports how the Sweden Democrats party, an anti-immigrant party with Neo-Nazi roots is gaining popularity.

13. It is generally believed that Right-wing politics comes to the fore when economics follows a new liberal path. The Scandinavian countries are welfare states. See this explainer: Andreas Moller Mulvad and Rune Moller Stahl, 'What Makes Scandinavia Different?' *Jacobin*, April 2015, https://www.jacobinmag.com/2015/08/national-review-williamson-bernie-sanders-sweden.

14. Vaclav Havel et al., 'The Power of the Powerless: Citizens against the State in Central and Eastern Europe', ed. John Keane (London: Hutchinson, 1985).

Bibliography

Ambedkar, B.R. *Annihilation of Caste: The Annotated Critical Edition.* Introduction by Arundhati Roy. New Delhi: Navayana, 2014.

Andersen, Walter K. and Shridhar D. Damle. *The Brotherhood in Saffron: The Rashtriya Swayamsevak Sangh and Hindu Revivalism.* New Delhi: Vistaar Publications, 1987.

Baxter, Craig. *The Jana Sangh: A Biography of an Indian Political Party.* Oxford: Oxford University Press, 1971.

Bly, Robert and Jane Hirshfield. *Mirabai: Ecstatic Poems.* New Delhi: Aleph, 2017.

Chandrachud, Abhinav. *Republic of Rhetoric: Free Speech and the Constitution of India.* Gurgaon: Penguin Random House India, 2017.

Dabholkar, Narendra, Govind Pansare, M.M. Kalburgi and Gauri Lankesh. *The Republic of Reason: Words They Could Not Kill.* New Delhi: SAHMAT with the Raza Foundation, 2018.

Desai, Meghnad. *Politic Shock: Trump, Modi, Brexit and the Prospect for Liberal Democracy.* New Delhi: Rupa, 2017.

Desai, Narayan. *My Life Is My Message,* vols. 1–4. Translated from the Gujarati by Tridip Suhrud. Hyderabad: Orient BlackSwan, 2009.

Drèze, Jean and Amartya Sen. *An Uncertain Glory: India and Its Contradictions.* London: Allen Lane, 2013.

Dumont, Louis. *Homo Hierarchicus: The Caste System and Its Implications.* New Delhi: Oxford University Press, 1980.

Gandhi, Mohandas Karamchand. *An Autobiography, or, The Story of My Experiments with Truth.* Translated from the Gujarati by Mahadev Desai. Gurgaon: Penguin Random House India, 2018.

Gandhi, Mohandas Karamchand. *The Essence of Hinduism*. Compiled and edited by V.B. Kher. Ahmedabad: Navajivan Trust, 1987.

Gandhi, Rajmohan. *Mohandas: A True Story of a Man, His People and an Empire*. New Delhi: Penguin Books India, 2006.

Ghurye, G.S. *Indian Sadhus*. Mumbai: Popular Prakashan, 1953.

Guha, Ramachandra, ed. *Makers of Modern India*. New Delhi: Penguin Books, 2010.

Guha, Ramachandra. *India after Gandhi: The History of the World's Largest Democracy*. London: Macmillan, 2007.

Hess, Linda. *The Bijak of Kabir*. San Francisco: North Point Press, 1983.

Hill, Christopher. *Reformation to Industrial Revolution*. London: Penguin Books, 1967.

Hiriyanna, M. *Essentials of Indian Philosophy*. London: George Allen & Unwin, 1978.

Ilaiah, Kancha. *Buffalo Nationalism: A Critique of Spiritual Fascism.* Kolkata: Samya, 2004.

Ilaiah, Kancha. *Why I Am Not a Hindu: A Sudra Critique of Hindutva Philosophy, Culture and Political Economy*. Kolkata: Samya, 1996.

Jenkins, Ron. *Subversive Laughter: The Liberating Power of Comedy*. London: Free Press, 1994.

Kautilya. *The Arthashastra*. Edited, rearranged, translated and introduced by L.N. Rangarajan. New Delhi: Penguin Books India, 1992.

Keay, John. *India, a History: From the earliest Civilisations to the Boom of the 21st Century*. London: Harper Press, 2000.

Keer, Dhananjay. *Dr Ambedkar: Life and Mission*. Mumbai: Popular Prakashan, 1954.

Khosla, Madhav. *The Indian Constitution*. New Delhi: Oxford University Press, 2012.

Krishnananda, Swami. *The Brhadaranyaka Upanishad*. Rishikesh: Divine Life Society, 1983.

Moon, Vasant, ed. *Dr Babasaheb Ambedkar: Writings and Speeches*, vols. 1–9. Mumbai: Government of Maharashtra, 1979–91.

O'Hanlon, Rosalind. *Caste Conflict and Ideology: Mahatma Jotirao Phule and Low Caste Protest in Nineteenth Century Western India*. Cambridge: Cambridge University Press, 1985.

Omvedt, Gail. *Dalits and the Democratic Revolution: Dr Ambedkar and the Dalit Movement in Colonial India*. New Delhi: Sage, 1994.

Pandita, Rahul. *Our Moon Has Blood Clots*. New Delhi: Penguin Books India.

Radhakrishnan, S. *The Bhagavadgita*. Noida: HarperCollins, 2003.

Radhakrishnan, S. *The Principal Upanishads*. Noida: HarperCollins, 1997.

Rajan, Raghuram. G. *Fault Lines: How Hidden Fractures Still Threaten the World Economy*. Noida: HarperCollins, 2010.

Richman, Paula, ed. *Many Ramayanas: The Diversity of a Narrative Tradition in South Asia*. Oxford: Oxford University Press, 1991.

Robertson, David. *The Penguin Dictionary of Politics*. London: Penguin Books, 1986.

RSS Resolves: Full Text of Resolutions from 1950 to 1983. Bangalore: Prakashan Vibhag, Rashtriya Swayamsevak Sangh, 1983.

Sarkar, Sumit. *Modern India, 1885–1947*. New Delhi: Macmillan, 1983.

Sen, Amartya. *The Argumentative Indian: Writings on Indian History, Culture and Identity*. London: Penguin Books, 2005.

Sen, Avirook. *Aarushi*. New Delhi: Penguin Books India, 2015.

Sivananda, Swami. *The Bhagavad Gita*. Shivanandnagar: Divine Life Society, 2003.

Srinivas, M.N, ed. *Caste: Its Twentieth Century Avatar*. New Delhi: Penguin Books India, 1996.

Srinivas, M.N. *Social Change in Modern India*. Hyderabad: Orient Longman, 1966.

Sundar, Nandini. *The Burning Forest: India's War in Bastar*. New Delhi: Juggernaut, 2016.

Tapasyananda, Swami. *The Nationalistic and Religious Lectures of Swami Vivekananda*. Madras: Sri Ramakrishna Math Printing Press, 1985.

Thapar, Romila. *A History of India: Volume One*. New Delhi: Penguin Books India, 1966.

Tusa, John. *Conversations with the World*. London: BBC Books, 1990.